Harvey,

Hope this book may help you through your teenage years.

Love you,

Gran. x

SEEDS OF THE KINGDOM

SEEDS OF THE KINGDOM

A Year of Devotional Readings
Collected from Seeds of the Kingdom,
the daily devotionals written by team members of
Ellel Ministries International

COMPILED BY
LIZ GRIFFIN

FOREWORD BY
PETER HORROBIN

Sovereign World

Published by Sovereign World Ltd
PO Box 784
Ellel
Lancaster
LA1 9DA
United Kingdom

www.sovereignworld.com

ISBN: 978 1 85240 621 9

Cover design by Oliver Schwartz
Typeset by The Book Design Company
Printed in the United Kingdom

Foreword

Daily devotionals have always had an important and valuable influence on my life. One of the oldest and most used is a compilation of morning and evening Scripture readings which was compiled by the whole of Samuel Bagster's family, and was first published in the early part of the nineteenth century. Only a few months before Eunice Bagster, Samuel's wife, died she was honoured by a personal visit from Queen Victoria, who knelt at Mrs Bagster's bedside to receive the blessing of her *'revered and venerable servant'*. The copy of *Daily Light* given to me by my parents has always been a much valued and much loved volume.

Another devotional book which is precious to me, is my father's copy of *Morning and Evening Daily Readings* from the writings of Charles Haddon Spurgeon, the Baptist minister whose preaching in the latter part of the nineteenth century, at London's Metropolitan Tabernacle, attracted many thousands Sunday by Sunday. He became known as the 'Prince of Preachers' and his printed sermons are universally recognised as containing some of the best Christian teaching available anywhere in the world. Dad wouldn't go to sleep each night until he had read *'his Spurgeon'*. I can see him now, even in his old age, propped up on his pillow reading the well-worn volume before going to sleep. He valued the daily input from a man who not only knew his God, but understood how to communicate truth that would impact the lives of men and women.

A third book of devotional readings which I, and thousands of others, have found to be a precious contribution to their Christian walk is *My Utmost for*

His Highest. This remarkable volume was compiled from the preaching of Oswald Chambers by his wife, in the years following his premature death in Egypt during the First World War. Oswald Chambers was converted through the preaching of Spurgeon, but tragically died aged only forty-three on 15 November 1917, as the result of a ruptured appendix, while serving as an army chaplain. He suffered the extreme pain of appendicitis for three days before seeking medical attention for himself, refusing to take a hospital bed needed by wounded soldiers.

Today there are many other devotional volumes, which have followed in the tradition of these great classics of Christian literature.

The original vision for *Seeds of the Kingdom* was birthed out of a desire to provide daily encouragement and teaching for those whom God has touched through the work of Ellel Ministries. A new website was launched and ever since, a daily devotional, contributed to by different members of the Ellel Ministries team, has been posted at www.seedsofthekingdom.com. Additionally, many thousands of people receive the devotional as a daily email.

The popularity of *Seeds of the Kingdom* has grown steadily, providing, as it does, daily insight on aspects of the Christian journey, especially as it impacts our need for Christian healing and discipleship. But it has only ever been available to those who have daily computer access. There are still many people who are not wired to today's technology and there are many others also who would still value having a book in their hand, as they read and spend time with the Lord on a daily basis.

So, after three years of our producing an online daily devotional, Liz Griffin has compiled this first devotional volume of Scriptures and Readings from the daily devotionals published on the Seeds of the Kingdom website. While this volume can never compete with or replace the great Christian classics referred to above, I believe it will nevertheless play a strategic part in helping many people to move on in their Christian pilgrimage – especially as they wrestle with their own personal issues of discipleship and healing. I pray it will be a great blessing to many people.

Peter Horrobin
International Director of Ellel Ministries
July 2011

Ellel Ministries main website www.ellelministries.org
Ellel 365 – online training school www.em365.org
Seeds of the Kingdom website www.seedsofthekingdom.com

Contributors

Goran Andersson, together with his wife Roswitha, worked as a missionary in Japan from 1967 to 1985 and then pastored a church. He has worked with Ellel Ministries since 2004 and is now Director of Ellel Ministries in Sweden.

John Berry is Team Pastor and part of the leadership team at Ellel Glyndley Manor, with his wife Jennie, having previously been in Baptist church ministry for over thirty years.

Otto and Sharon Bixler were pastoring in a Vineyard church before joining the full-time Ellel team in 1990 and beginning the work of Ellel East (covering Eastern Europe and Russia) in 1992. They were Regional Directors of Ellel East until retiring in 2011 and still enjoy teaching worldwide for Ellel.

Patrick Chambron, with his wife Valerie, leads the work of Ellel Ministries in France where they have also been pastoring a church for many years.

Ian Coates served with Ellel Ministries from the beginning until 2010. He was part of the Executive Leadership team and Centre Director at Ellel Grange.

David and Denise Cross joined the Ellel Ministries team in 1993. David is now the Western Europe Director of Ellel Ministries. Over the last few years he has written books called *Soul-Ties*, *God's Covering*, *Trapped by Control* and *The Dangers of Alternative Ways to Healing*. Denise is the Centre Director of Glyndley Manor and has recently written *Rescue from Rejection*.

Richard Fila first came to know Ellel Ministries at Ellel Grange in 2006 and has attended the NETS school at Ellel Pierrepont. He works for the Corporate Support Team which supports the Ellel centres around the world and is based at Ellel Grange.

Linda Fode, along with her husband Allen Fode, serves as Director of Ellel Canada West located in Calgary, Canada. Linda's passions are to foster people's relationship with the Father and release them into their destiny in God.

Liz Griffin, together with her husband Paul, became involved with Ellel Ministries in 1991 and worked on the full-time team at Ellel Grange for fifteen years before retiring in 2011. They still teach and minister to those seeking healing in their lives and together have written two books, *Anger: How Do You Handle It?* and *Hope and Healing for the Abused*.

Lindsey Hanekom has worked at each of the UK centres but is now settled at Ellel Scotland with her husband, Johann, and their young son, Kyle, and soon-to-be child. She is part of the Ellel 365 Team as well as being responsible for the marketing and publicity for Blairmore.

Andreas Hefti leads the work of Ellel Ministries in Germany. In 1998 he attended the nine-week Flagship Programme and then worked at Ellel Grange for eight years. In 2003 he set up the Modular School in Altensteig (South Germany).

Richard and Nicky Hemery. Richard has been part of the Ellel Ministries team at Pierrepont since 2001 working as the bookshop manager. Nicky joined the Ellel Ministries team at Pierrepont in 1995 as Jill Southern-Jones' PA. She now enjoys being a full-time mum.

Peter and Fiona Horrobin. Peter is the Founding and International Director of Ellel Ministries. He has written and is currently developing Ellel 365 – an online training school. This is specifically designed to help people understand and apply the practical truths of God's Word into their lives. Fiona has been a key part of pioneering the work of Ellel Ministries International. From over twenty years' experience of ministering into broken lives, she is passionate to see healing as integral to discipleship and Christian growth.

Martin Knapp, together with his wife Ginny, became involved with Ellel Ministries in 1990 and taught and worked for a number of years at Ellel Pierrepont. Martin became the Centre Director of Ellel Grange in April 2010.

Tamas Kovacs has been a part of the Ellel work in Hungary since the early 1990s. He joined the staff full-time in 1999, and became the Director of the Hungarian centre in 2006.

Patricia Lake is now the secretary to Peter Horrobin, having joined the Ellel team in January 2000. She was also in ministry in her local Pentecostal church before feeling the call of God to serve in the healing and deliverance ministry at Ellel Grange.

Paul and Anne Lawrence are the Assistant Directors at Ellel Grange. They joined the team in July 2010 after studying on the NETS Training Programme at Pierrepont.

Jilly Lyon-Taylor is part of the Leadership Team at Ellel Pierrepont. Her desire to see people healed led her to the NETS Training Programme at Pierrepont, and now she teaches and ministers there.

Grace Marshall is a member of the Corporate Support team, based at Pierrepont, and also works one day a week as a doctor in general practice near Southampton. Previously she was a full-time GP for fifteen years and a member of the Ellel associate ministry team and teaching team.

Pat and Lindsay O'Reilly are both on the associate team at Shere House, South Africa. They attended the Flagship Programme at Ellel Grange in the UK and this revolutionised their lives.

Jim Person and his wife and four children are missionaries to Hungary, and are serving as Assistant Directors for Ellel East Regional Nations, where they travel to Romania, Slovakia, Serbia and other countries teaching in Ellel schools.

Alistair Petrie is an International Adviser to Ellel Ministries. He is a world-renowned speaker who has spent over twenty years studying how individuals and communities can overcome the work of the enemy and enter into their corporate identity and destiny in Christ.

Roger Pook joined the full-time staff of Ellel East in Hungary in January 1996 after a career in language teaching and financial services. He is Regional Director of Ellel for Central and Eastern Europe and together with his wife, Christine, teaches and ministers throughout the former communist world.

Beryl Puffett is the Centre Director of Shere House in Pretoria, South Africa. She is married to Derek who is the Regional Director of Ellel Africa. They have a son Michael who is a pastor in Maidstone, Kent in the UK and a daughter who lives in South Africa.

Herman Redelinghuys is a trained social worker who spent most of his career in the corporate training environment. He joined Ellel Africa's part-time team in 2005 and is mostly involved with prayer co-ordination for the ministry.

Gunvor Rekstad has been the director of Ellel Ministries Norway since 2005. She was involved in teaching, prayer ministry and Christian counselling for many years before becoming involved in Ellel Ministries.

Joan Rono worked in full-time ministry in her church in Kenya before joining the young people's team at Ellel Grange in 2008. She is now working as a Youth Pastor at Ellel Grange.

Alison Scarborough is the Deputy Director, ministry manager, and one of the teachers at Glyndley Manor, near Eastbourne, where she has been on the team since she completed the 'Nine-Week School' in 1996.

David and Margaret Silvester. David was a lecturer of engineering craft skills before being called by God in his early fifties to become a pastor of a Baptist church. Margaret had a career as a teacher. They were involved in establishing a healing ministry in the church before joining the Ellel Grange teaching and ministry team in 2000.

Julie Smith has received deep healing in her own life, primarily through ministry at Ellel Grange and then attending the Modular School at Glyndley Manor; she went on to join the Glyndley associate ministry team. She now works part-time for the International Director's Office and is an associate teacher for the ministry.

Pam Smith has been a friend and helper of Ellel Ministries since 1992 and has been involved with Healing Through Creativity courses. As writer of the Shepherd Love series, she has a passion for the comfort and encouragement that leads people towards enjoying abundant life in Jesus.

Jill Southern-Jones was a successful businesswoman before becoming the Director of Ellel Pierrepont. Jill's book, *Sex: God's Truth*, is an essential guide to the restoration of godly order in sexual relationships.

Margaret Southey has had a career in education. Her passion is to understand the truth of God's Word and to share it with others. She is part of the ministry and teaching team of Ellel Africa.

Jeanne Tate has been a volunteer at Ellel Ministries South Africa since 2005. She is currently devoting three days a week to maintaining the database and assisting the full-time team wherever possible.

Andy and Cath Taylor met and married at Ellel Grange where they were both on the team. They went on to help pioneer the first Ellel centre in Australia and now live in Florida with their three boys and lead the Ellel USA team. Andy is a member of the Executive Leadership of Ellel Ministries.

Paul and Diane Watson were involved in establishing the first Australian Ellel Ministries centre 'Gilbulla' near Sydney but are currently leading the work in Western Australia, based at 'Springhill' near Perth. Paul was an Anglican minister for fifteen years in Sydney, Australia before joining Ellel Ministries full time in 2004 and is now the Regional Director for Australia Pacific and India.

Angela Weir has been associated with Ellel Ministries from the very beginning, first as an associate member of the ministry team and later as an associate teacher. She trained as an actress, and after her marriage and move to Cumbria, taught drama in a girls' school.

Wendy Whitten joined Ellel Ministries in 1993 and served the Lord in the UK centres, as well as spending many years with Ellel Ministries in Eastern Europe, India and the Netherlands.

Cristy Williams has been working for Ellel Ministries Canada since March 2008. She is the centre's administrative assistant and is currently training in prayer ministry and teaching.

Malcolm Wood and his wife Anna joined the Ellel team as House Managers at Ellel Grange in 1990. Since then they have been involved with many aspects of the developing ministry. In 2001 they became Directors of Ellel Scotland, now at Blairmore House.

Acknowledgment and thanks to Karen David who has been collating the 'Seeds' and encouraging the writing of them since the devotional began in 2008.

January 1 | Two Seas

Malcolm Wood

Whoever is thirsty should come to me, and whoever believes in me should drink. As the scripture says, 'Streams of life-giving water will pour out from his side.'

John 7:38, GNB

Those who are familiar with the maps in the back of their Bible or who have had the privilege of visiting Israel will be aware of the fact that in that country there are two large areas of water. But these two 'seas', as they are known, are so very different.

In the north one gives pleasure to all who view it, sit beside it, sail on it or swim in it. Its shores are surrounded by green fertile land where sheep safely graze. Trees and crops produce their harvests. Children play happily at the water's edge and shoals of fish swim in its depths. It's certainly a place of natural beauty, portraying life, vitality and productivity.

On the other hand the 'sea' in the south couldn't be more different. Surrounded by a harsh barren landscape where there's no grass, trees, crops or sheep, the salt-laden water can't support life. There are no fish. The whole area presents a picture of total desolation. This sea is so rightly named 'the Dead Sea'. The other is of course 'the Sea of Galilee'.

Two seas – so different, and yet they have one thing in common. The River Jordan flows into both of them. Why then are they so different? I'm told the answer is that, with the Galilee, the river flows in and out of it and so fresh water is continually flowing through it. But, with the Dead Sea, there is no way out. The water either evaporates in the heat of the region or is absorbed by the salt-laden ground.

This is such a challenging picture for the believer. We all have the potential of receiving the continual flow of the blessings of God into our lives – but what do we do with them? We can either hold on to them for ourselves, thinking that by so doing we are absorbing all that God has for us. Or we can allow these blessings to be used to bless others (the outflow) and produce fruit in our lives.

Our lives can either become dry, barren and fruitless or be a source of blessing to others. It depends on whether we allow the Lord by His Spirit to flow through us to others. The choice is ours!

PRAYER: *Dear Lord, help me to become so full of You that I just can't help but overflow with Your love and blessing to others, in Jesus' name, Amen.*

JANUARY 2 | STRENGTH FOR THE WEARY

LIZ GRIFFIN

> *He strengthens those who are weak and tired ... young people can fall exhausted. But those who trust in the LORD for help will find their strength renewed. They will rise on wings like eagles; they will run and not get weary; they will walk and not grow weak.*
>
> Isaiah 40:29–31, GNB

Do you ever feel weary? I don't mean tired. I mean weary of everything – the spiritual battle against forces of evil, the disappointment of relationships being difficult, the lack of progress in goals you want to reach. It's tempting to give up.

Elijah was a tower of strength, combating the false prophets of Baal on Mount Carmel and challenging the people of Israel about choosing God's ways. Then the next day he lost all hope in the face of Queen Jezebel's death threats and ran for his life. *'Elijah walked a whole day into the wilderness. He stopped and sat down in the shade of a tree and wished he would die. "It's too much, LORD," he prayed. "Take away my life; I might as well be dead!"'* (1 Kings 19:4, GNB). Yet despite his feelings he was still in a close relationship with God, and God heard his cry and sent an angel to supply his needs. Later he told God how lonely it was to be the only one in the land serving the Lord. God gave him the names of three people who were to help him and revealed the fact that 7,000 people were still true worshippers.

The prophet Isaiah once spoke to the people of Israel saying, *'Israel, why then do you complain that the LORD doesn't know your troubles or care if you suffer injustice?'* (Isaiah 40:27, GNB). Like Elijah, the people needed to know more about the nature of their God and His almighty power. Isaiah said God calls each star by name and created the entire universe. He cares about the weak and the tired and strengthens them. As they trust Him He renews their strength so they can rise up as if they have strong powerful wings, like an eagle. Then they can move forward in God's purposes, running and walking. '*But those who trust in the LORD for help will find their strength renewed. They will rise on wings like eagles; they will run and not get weary; they will walk and not grow weak*' (Isaiah 40:31, GNB).

PRAYER: *Dear Heavenly Father, when I feel weak and weary help me to remember that I can renew my strength in You. Help me to rise in my spirit like the eagle, in Jesus' name, Amen.*

JANUARY 3 | PROFESSIONAL CHRISTIANITY!

ANDY TAYLOR

> *But Amos replied, 'I'm not one of your professional prophets. I certainly never trained to be one. I'm just a shepherd, and I take care of fig trees.'*
>
> Amos 7:14, NLT

When walking down the Biblical Prophets' Hall of Fame you will be sure to find Amos! He was one of the minor prophets who dealt some pretty weighty blows as he pronounced God's judgement upon Israel for its complacency, idolatry and oppression of the poor. Yet when he was told by Amaziah to leave Bethel and to stop bothering them with his prophecies he makes a very interesting statement.

He declares that he's neither a prophet nor the son of a prophet. In the NLT version of the Bible it says, 'I'm not one of your professional prophets.' What Amos is basically saying is that he had no special heritage, training or experience to do what he was doing. He was a simple shepherd who took care of fig trees, yet God called him away from his flock and told him to go and prophesy to the people of Israel.

On an increasing level we're being told that we need professionals in the church – whether it be professional teachers, apostles, intercessors or even healers. The fact is that God doesn't need professionals to do His work. He needs people who are willing to follow Him in obedience, no matter what. There's a reason why God says in 1 Corinthians 1:27 that He will choose things the world classes as foolish to confound the wise – Amos is a case in point!

Are you held back from serving God because you don't think you're enough of a professional in that area? Look again at the Scriptures – if God is interested in calling shepherds who look after fig trees to do His work, He's also interested in calling you to do His work.

PRAYER: *Thank You, Lord, for the giftings You have given. I offer them into Your hands for You to use – I want to be obedient to You and do whatever You ask me to do, in Jesus' name, Amen.*

JANUARY 4 | ABUNDANT LIFE

ALISON SCARBOROUGH

> *The thief does not come except to steal, and to kill, and to destroy. I have come that they may have life, and that they may have it more abundantly.*
>
> John 10:10, NKJV

Looking out of my window today it is grey, gloomy, the rain has been falling for hours and everything looks somewhat dismal. I spent a great deal more time travelling over the Christmas holiday than I had planned, due to the coldest December in the UK since records began, and along with many others I seem to have had some nasty bug or other! When I see a cluster of things like that I find it is easy to become low in spirit and I pick up on the first part of the scripture that says the thief comes *'to steal ... kill, and ... destroy'* (John 10:10, NKJV).

But hold on a minute, what is said next by Jesus is amazing! Jesus declares His intention to recover and restore to us what was His Father's plan for us all along and to break and block the thief's plans to stop us receiving it. He has given us the opportunity to not only have life, but to have it more abundantly. In Genesis God made everything, declared it good, and then gave it all to Adam. At the fall the thief came in, but Jesus is doing what He said and gives us the possibility to receive more life and to share this life with others.

How is it possible to receive more of the fullness of life and have abundant life, especially when things seem really hard? Well, abundant life doesn't mean an absence of adversity, but more about how we grow in the midst of difficulties. It's about letting our character be grown towards Christ-likeness.

What does that mean in real life? Well, thankfulness helps us see what Jesus has done for us already. We need the rain to top up the water table, and our immune systems have done a good job in seeing off the several thousand other viruses that have come our way. Little random acts of kindness help us give life to others, a smile on a long and tiresome journey, a kind word, and help with a suitcase. We receive life by giving out. Looking for the beautiful, the delightful, the amazing, and the good in all our everyday, 'ordinary' things of life is how we will start to see and appropriate life more abundantly.

PRAYER: *Father God, thank You that Jesus has come so that I might have life abundantly. Help me to start to see and to take hold of all that this means for me. Thank You for all the ordinary things of my life; help me to see Your extraordinary hand each day that I might know the fullness of life You have for me and give all the glory and honour back to You. Amen.*

JANUARY 5 | WALKING AND LEAPING!

PETER HORROBIN

> *They recognised him as the same man who used to sit begging at the temple gate called Beautiful, and they were filled with wonder and amazement at what had happened to him.*
>
> Acts 3:10

Everyone knew the crippled man. He was a permanent fixture at the gate Beautiful. No doubt he had his regular donors who always gave him money as they entered the temple. It was a good spot to beg for money. But on the day he asked Peter and John for money they declined to give him any, but gave him what they had! In the name of Jesus they healed him and people were filled with wonder and amazement.

When I was very young a missionary friend of my parents was invalided home from missionary service in Nigeria. She was suffering from cancer and the tumour was growing progressively larger as her last days approached. The doctors gave her about three weeks to live. She had left behind a thriving mission work amongst leper children and the greatest agony of her heart was not that she was soon going to meet her Lord, but that the children back in Nigeria needed her.

All the mission supporters were praying for her – including my mum and dad, but not even they were ready for the news when it came. News, not of her passing into the presence of her Lord, but that the tumour had miraculously and completely disappeared overnight. Instead of preparing for her last days on earth she got up and wrote letters to all her prayer supporters telling them what God had done. Her wish had been fulfilled: the hearts of the children crying for their adopted 'mum' had touched the heart of the Father. He had stretched out His hand and touched her dying body. She was totally healed and lived many more years to serve the Lord. Everyone was totally amazed.

I understand just what the people must have thought when they saw the crippled man, no longer begging, but dancing with joy! When Peter and John were hauled before the high priests to give an account for what had happened they were able to testify to the fact that it was through the name of Jesus that the crippled man had been healed, but that there was an even greater miracle available to all from the hand of the same Lord Jesus – the gift of salvation.

The physical miracle gave them the opportunity to tell of how this same Jesus wants to heal our broken hearts and restore us into relationship with the Father and enjoy Him forever, in time and eternity. All healing is a witness to the salvation that Jesus won for each one of us on the cross. The One who heals is also the One who saves!

PRAYER: *Thank You, Jesus, for the miracle of healing – and that the even greater miracle of salvation is available now to everyone who chooses to believe and receive You as Saviour for themselves, in Jesus' name, Amen.*

JANUARY 6 | EVERY KNEE WILL BOW

LIZ GRIFFIN

> *Turn to me and be saved, all you ends of the earth; for I am God, and there is no other … Before me every knee will bow; by me every tongue will swear.*
>
> Isaiah 45:22–23

I read a report in the newspaper that an eminent scientist has written a book in which he concludes that the universe created itself because scientific laws such as gravity were in place. The newspaper said that he once appeared on television and said that you could call these laws 'God' if you liked but you couldn't communicate with that 'God'.

What a contrast to what I had just read in Isaiah chapter 45 that morning! *'It is I who made the earth and created mankind upon it. My own hands stretched out the heavens; I marshalled their starry hosts'* (Isaiah 45:12). And in verse 18 I read, *'For this is what the LORD says – he who created the heavens, he is God; he who fashioned and made the earth, he founded it; he did not create it to be empty, but formed it to be inhabited – he says: "I am the LORD, and there is no other."'*

God was imparting His living Word to Isaiah in the same way as He did with Moses (who then wrote the book of Genesis). Each prophet who revealed more of God to His people would have a full knowledge of what God had said on all the previous occasions when He spoke to human beings. They knew He was a God who communicates and whom they could relate to. He is a personal God, who is 'love' and who cares passionately about relationships. In fact the Godhead is like a family or a community – Father, Son and Holy Spirit.

He is a personal God, who is 'love' and who cares…

Jesus came to make it completely clear about who God is and what He is like. And so the apostle Paul was able to expand even more on what Isaiah had been told about every knee bowing and every tongue swearing before God. The full and wonderful truth is now *'that at the name of Jesus every knee should bow, in heaven and on earth and under the earth, and every tongue confess that Jesus Christ is Lord, to the glory of God the Father'* (Philippians 2:10–11).

How sad that one religion declares that God can't have a son and that a scientist should declare that we can't have a relationship with an impersonal scientific law (which he says is responsible for our very existence). The logical conclusion from his belief is that we shouldn't experience any kind of emotions or suffering in this life, because where could they have come from – a scientific law such as gravity?

PRAYER: *Dear Heavenly Father, I thank You for the life-giving truth in Your Word and the way You show Yourself to be a loving Father to us. Thank You that Jesus came to help us to know You and that the Holy Spirit remains with us now. Please unveil the eyes of those who think they have discovered a universe without Your love, in Jesus' name, Amen.*

JANUARY 7 | TALKING TO ONESELF!

PETER HORROBIN

Praise the LORD, O my soul; all my inmost being, praise his holy name. Praise the LORD, O my soul, and forget not all his benefits.

Psalm 103:1–2

Talking to oneself is sometimes seen as a sign of senility – the sort of thing that people do when they are beginning to lose control of their senses! Not so in the Bible. There are many places when it seems as though the psalmist, for example, is talking to himself, but in reality he is a very long way from losing his senses. He is doing the most sensible thing he could possibly do!

Let me explain. God has given us a spirit, a soul and a body. It's with our spirit that we are most able to commune with God, and are most sensitive to him. All of us, however, have trouble with that soulish part of our being which always seems to want to go beyond or outside of God's best for our lives. Even the apostle Paul was struggling with this when he said that he knew what was right but often found himself wanting to do what was wrong! So it is with you and me. Our spirit and our soul seem to be at war with each other. The only way forward is for the spirit to take charge and tell the soul what to do.

That's exactly what David is doing in our reading. He's telling his whole inner being – everything that's within him – to praise the Lord. For he knows that, when we're doing that, we can't be going wrong. Then he says to his inner being: don't forget all the benefits which come from God. It's as if David's inner being must be objecting to doing what his spirit is saying. So his spirit has to remind his soul of all the blessings which have come from God, through obedience to Him!

Let me encourage you to 'do a David' and remind yourself of all the blessings God has brought into your life. What a wonderful way to ensure that your whole being keeps on track with God and continues to love and serve Him all your days.

PRAYER: *Help me, Lord, to remind my inner being of Your wonderful goodness, so that everything I am will want to both love and serve You, in Jesus' name, Amen.*

January 8 | David Cross

The Divine Cheque Book

For it is He [Jesus] who is the 'Yes' to all of God's promises. This is why through Jesus Christ our 'Amen' is said to the glory of God.

2 Corinthians 1:20, GNB

I was recently in Northern Ireland and talking to my friend Jim. He and his wife Irene now manage the Ellel Ministries Centre at Ballyclare. Jim was explaining to me how he saw God's promises of wholeness and freedom as being like a cheque book which Jesus has given to each one of us. This divine cheque book contains countless promises, all fully signed by Jesus. However, as with many business cheques, *two* signatures are required in order to be able to cash these particular divine cheques and so receive the precious payments. Each cheque needs the addition of our own signature, to complete the process, but many Christians fail to put their own name to all the amazing promises of restoration from God.

Here are some of the promises that were spoken out through the prophet Isaiah (Isaiah 61) and which later became a resounding 'Yes' through Jesus:

1. God has made an everlasting covenant with you.
2. God has defeated the enemy who is against you.
3. God has released you from those things that have a hold on you.
4. God has provided His comfort for you when you are in sorrow.
5. God has healed your broken heart.
6. God has ended your shame and disgrace.
7. God has given you a joy that will last forever.
8. God has saved you from all that would harm you.

Have you and I signed our names on each of these cheques? Does each one have our agreement or 'Amen'? There is an endless supply of promises but each requires our clear response in order for us to personally receive the full value of the payment that Jesus has made through the cross.

Prayer: *Father God, Your promises to mankind were all endorsed, affirmed and distributed at the cross. Please show me how to put my name to each of Your divine cheques, so that I may appropriate every promise You have made for my wholeness and freedom, through Jesus Christ, Amen.*

January 9 | Walking in Darkness

Lindsey Hanekom

Let your light shine before men, that they may see your good deeds and praise your Father in heaven.

Matthew 5:16

One of the things about living in Scotland we have had to get used to is the short days of the winter time. Waking in the dark, going to work in the dark and the darkness settling in well before leaving work can leave you feeling down and wanting to hide away in the warmth, familiarity and light of your own home.

You only need to read a newspaper or watch a news bulletin on TV to know that the days of this world are darkening as the evil one gains momentum in his efforts to keep the human race away from God. What is our response to this? Is it to sit in the comfort and warmth of a safe life – church, ministry, family – and never venture into the darkness in the world around us?

In this verse Jesus is telling us to let our light shine before men; before those who live in darkness. For that we have to move out of our comfortable, familiar and safe environments. We need to be willing to walk in the darkness of the world, displaying the Light that is Jesus Christ.

Jesus is telling us to let our light shine before men; before those who live in darkness.

So let's not hide this eternal light in our churches, in our ministries or in our family units. Let us, with confidence, take our light into the place where it's needed – the world of sinners, the world of strife, hatred and persecution; the world that Jesus came from heaven to and the world He died for.

Prayer: *Father God, I'm sorry I've hidden Your light away from those who need to see it the most. I pray You will help me let my light shine as I walk in the world I live in and that those who see it will turn their praises to You. For Your name and Your glory, Amen.*

JANUARY 10 | ABOUND IN HOPE

PAM SMITH

Now may the God of hope fill you with all joy and peace in believing that you may abound in hope by the power of the Holy Spirit.

Romans 15:13, NKJV

The apostle Paul wrote to the Christian believers in Rome and said he was praying that they would abound in hope and bring this hope to others: *'Now may the God of hope fill you with all joy and peace in believing that you may abound in hope by the power of the Holy Spirit'* (Romans 15:13, NKJV).

When we know Jesus in our life we discover the mystery of the gospel, which is *'Christ in you, the hope of glory'* (Colossians 1:27). We begin to see His glory and all that He is and receive the joy and hope in believing. One of the saddest things in the world is to have no hope. I hear people described as 'no hopers', but I believe that there's hope for everyone, whatever place they're in. It's those very 'ones' that Jesus wants to redeem and restore, although many would pass them by.

Sometimes a kind word, a few moments of time to listen, a caring touch, a small gift or a prayer for them as we go by may be part of a chain of events that lead that person to Jesus. When they know that someone really cares, it gives them a reason to hope.

When Jesus touches someone with His love you can see the light of hope that comes into their eyes, as their spirit responds to His love. There's great comfort in God's hope, whatever troubles we face. In Hosea we read that the Lord turns the Valley of Trouble into *'a door of hope'* (Hosea 2:15, NKJV).

We can only 'abound in hope' by the power of the Holy Spirit. His power within us causes us to know things for certain, and we have a hope that is eternal, for, as Christians, we don't only have a hope in this earthly life.

'This hope we have as an anchor of the soul, both sure and steadfast, and which enters the Presence behind the veil' (Hebrews 6:19, NKJV).

When darkness seems to hide His face,
I rest on His unchanging grace.
In every high and stormy gale,
My anchor holds within the veil.

On Christ the solid Rock I stand,
All other ground is sinking sand.
All other ground is sinking sand.
(Edward Mote, 1836)

PRAYER: *Lord, we pray that we may spread Your light and love to give a glimmer of hope to those You long to touch. May we not pass them by, in Jesus' name, Amen.*

JANUARY 11 | THE WISE AND FOOLISH BUILDERS

JOAN RONO

Therefore everyone who hears these words of mine and puts them into practice is like a wise man who built his house on the rock.
Matthew 7:24

I always love to read the words of Jesus as He taught people. He sometimes spoke plainly and sometimes in parables. He taught with such wisdom and authority that it demanded that the listeners pay attention. At the end of the parable in Matthew 7:24–27 the people were amazed at the teachings of Jesus because of the authority He spoke with.

In this parable there are two men who built houses. One built a house on rock so that when the storms came the house didn't fall, but the other man built a house on sand, and when the storms came that house fell, and with a great crash, Jesus adds.

The parable was a symbol of two people who both heard the words of Jesus. One put what he heard into practice, but the other didn't. The similarity between these people is that they both had to experience the storms that came.

I believe that this message is as much for believers as it is for unbelievers. We live in a time where there's a great exposure of the Word of God from the media, the churches and thousands of outreaches. I would say the world is full of hearers of God's Word, but only a few people are committed and willing to do as the Word of God says, either because of ignorance or unbelief.

The painful truth is that we're always exposed to the storms of life that are all over the world: inflation, wars and conflict, global warming, insecurity, drugs, terrorism, to name but a few.

How do you deal with all this as an individual? I believe that the answer is in God's Word, reading or hearing it and doing as it says. Then when the storm comes, your foundations are strong and nothing can shake them.

There are questions in our time that we can ask about issues we face, that Jesus answered in His teachings. He taught about money and material things, divorce, hostility, forgiveness, lust, insecurity, and persecution, amongst many other things. Jesus has all the answers about what's affecting us in this day and age. The answers for us are contained within His teachings if we will hear what He's saying and then go and do what He says.

PRAYER: *Father God, I thank You for Your Word and the opportunities You have given me to hear or read Your Word. Forgive me for my ignorance and unbelief. Lord, lead me deeper into understanding Your Word and give me the strength and grace to put Your Word into practice. Amen.*

JANUARY 12 | A NEW BEGINNING

PAM SMITH

> *And the LORD God formed man of the dust of the ground, and breathed into his nostrils the breath of life; and man became a living being.*
>
> Genesis 2:7, NKJV

In the Bible we read of how the very first human being came into being: *'And the LORD God formed man of the dust of the ground, and breathed into his nostrils the breath of life; and man became a living being'* (Genesis 2:7, NKJV). And I remember as a student nurse, one of the most unbelievable and impacting things that I ever experienced was seeing, for the first time, the birth of a baby. First I saw the head, then the little body, then I heard that first baby cry, and suddenly it was there, from a tiny space into a big world – a brand new little person. To me it was a complete miracle. I was full of awe for quite a few days.

There's also something beautiful and exciting about seeing someone born of the Spirit. That's the ultimate new beginning. This is when God breathes the breath of His Holy Spirit into our spirit and new life comes to us through faith in Jesus Christ. As Jesus said to Nicodemus, *'Most assuredly, I say to you, unless one is born of water and the Spirit, he cannot enter the kingdom of God. That which is born of the flesh is flesh, and that which is born of the Spirit is spirit. Do not marvel that I said to you, "You must be born again." The wind blows where it wishes, and you hear the sound of it, but cannot tell where it comes from and where it goes. So is everyone who is born of the Spirit'* (John 3:5–8, NKJV).

You can't see what's going on inside people when they're born again, but you can see the change and the fruit in their lives. If you would really like to begin your life all over again, and leave the old life behind, turn around and ask the risen Saviour to breathe His life into you, and begin to see the world with a completely new perspective, with a clean heart, a new hope, knowing that He holds your future firmly in His hand.

And if you're a believer and need a new, fresh touch from the Lord, ask Him to fill you again with His love. His mercies are new every morning. He can make today a new beginning for you just like a new bud in spring responding to the warmth of the sun.

PRAYER: *Dear Lord, thank You for Your mercies this very morning. Breathe on me, breath of God, fill me with life anew, that I may really know You and love You, in Jesus' name, Amen.*

JANUARY 13 |
ROGER POOK

WHY DO THEY HATE ME SO MUCH?

Happy are you when people hate you, reject you, insult you, and say that you are evil, all because of the Son of Man!

Luke 6:22, GNB

Do you ever look at the 'readers' comments' sections of online newspapers? Be careful – it can be quite disturbing!

Whenever there is an article or editorial to do with Christianity (or any other faith), it is followed by a rash of comments mostly with this theme: *'Religion is based on a set of myths and lies, and these myths and lies have brought untold misery to humanity throughout history. We need to throw out the myths, expose the lies and duplicity of those who propagate them, and bring freedom to the millions who are fooled by religion.'* This is what many people genuinely believe nowadays.

Only a few decades ago, religious faith was generally seen as 'a good thing' even by those who did not have any faith themselves. (At the same time, people could describe themselves as 'Christian' when all it meant was a belief in doing good, with a casual nod to traditional religious observance.) But nowadays, a declaration of personal faith can expose us to ridicule or outright hostility.

Is this surprising? Not at all! Should we be worried? No! Should we be prepared? Yes!

If you feel that you just don't seem to fit in with the world around you, it's because you don't! But this is no excuse to withdraw from the world entirely. Instead, we are to be in the world but not of the world (John 15:19). We are to be salt and light (Matthew 5:13–14). Salt preserves and adds flavour, but it also stings and people try to keep it away from the corrupt places. Light exposes evil, therefore evil prefers the dark and hates the light.

So, let's be salt and light! *'Happy are you when people hate you, reject you, insult you, and say that you are evil, all because of the Son of Man!'*

PRAYER: *Lord God, whenever I am discouraged by the lies of the enemy, please bring Your truth into my heart so that I can stand up to whatever comes against me. I choose to be salt and light. I choose to believe Your truth and to live by it, whatever the world says. Amen.*

JANUARY 14 | RADICAL DISCIPLESHIP

PETER HORROBIN

> *A number who had practised sorcery brought their scrolls together and burned them publicly. When they calculated the value of the scrolls, the total came to fifty thousand drachmas [pieces of silver]. In this way the word of the Lord spread widely and grew in power.*
>
> Acts 19:19–20

Becoming a Christian is not just a case of looking forward to heaven when we die. It's also choosing to separate ourselves from former things in our lives here on earth which were ungodly. If we try and live for God without separating ourselves from the things of the enemy, then they will become a curse on our lives which may even drag us back into the ungodliness of our former lives.

The converts to the faith in Acts 19 owned some very valuable things – the books which gave them the knowledge to practise sorcery. It was these which gave them the ability to earn money through what they did. Knowledge is power and can be converted into wealth, when others want what we've got! These books were valuable, but they were also evil. So they made no attempt to sell them, not even to give the money to the poor, for whoever got hold of and used these books would be trapped into the enemy's control. Radical action was needed – a good bonfire!

It's vital that we are just as radical with ungodly things in our own home. Leave them there and they're a source of spiritual danger. But if we choose to follow the same path as these new Christians in Ephesus, and destroy any of the works of the evil one which might still be in our possession, then we will not only be freed from their power, but we will also know God's blessing on our lives.

In Ephesus it was this action that witnessed so powerfully to the surrounding people – and as a result the Word of the Lord spread through the region. Many times I have watched as people destroyed such things and then entered into the joy of the Lord as a result. God always honours those who honour Him by being obedient to His Word.

PRAYER: *Help me, Lord, to identify anything in my home which should have been got rid of. I do not want to give houseroom to any of the works of the enemy. I choose to cleanse my home of all the works of darkness, in Jesus' name, Amen.*

JANUARY 15 | FROM DOUBT TO FAITH

DAVID SILVESTER

Thomas said to him, 'My Lord and my God!'

John 20:28

I've always known Thomas, the disciple of Jesus, as 'Doubting Thomas'. This description of him is based upon the account after the resurrection of Jesus, where he said, *'Unless I see the nail marks in his hands and put my finger where the nails were, and put my hand into his side, I will not believe it'* (John 20:25). From that one incident he has usually been identified as the doubting disciple. Yet Thomas was one of the twelve Jesus sent out with authority to drive out evil spirits and to heal every disease and sickness. Afterwards, *'The apostles gathered round Jesus and reported to him all they had done and taught'* (Mark 6:30).

Those twelve men had been with Jesus, listening to His teaching and watching Him perform many miracles. Then Jesus had sent them out to teach as He taught and do as He had done, and they had gone in response to His instruction. Thomas was among that group of disciples. He must have fulfilled what Jesus had commissioned them to do as they went 'in His name'.

When Jesus died the bottom was knocked out of Thomas's world. Like the other disciples he was devastated. None of them had really grasped what Jesus had said to them only a few days earlier – that He would rise from the dead on the third day. Thomas missed the first visit of Jesus to the disciples after the resurrection, and when the others told him they had 'seen the Lord', it was more than he could take in. His last glimpse of Jesus was of Him being taken and crucified. He'd witnessed the horrors of what Jesus had to endure, and was bereft of His leadership now. He said, *'Unless I see the nail marks in his hands and put my finger where the nails were, and put my hand into his side, I will not believe it.'* Wouldn't we have reacted in the same way, if we had been in his shoes?

We all have experiences that test our faith, but even in those times I believe the Lord comes to us and says, 'Reach out your hand ... Stop doubting and believe.'

A week later, when Thomas was in the house with the other disciples, Jesus came to them again saying, *'Peace be with you!'* Then Jesus spoke to Thomas: *'Put your finger here; see my hands. Reach out your hand and put it into my side. Stop doubting and believe'* (John 20:26–27). This was all Thomas needed. He responded immediately by worshipping Jesus and exclaiming, *'My Lord and my God!'* We all have experiences that test our faith, but even in those times I believe the Lord comes to us and says, *'Reach out your hand ... Stop doubting and believe.'* Coming through those experiences we're also able to declare with confidence, 'My Lord and my God.'

PRAYER: *O Lord Jesus Christ, I am sorry for those times when I have struggled in unbelief and doubt, and I thank You for who and what You are, the risen and exalted Saviour, my Lord and my God. As I reach out my hand to You, please take it and hold it, and lead me into deeper experiences of Your loving presence. Amen.*

January 16 | Lost Glasses

Fiona Horrobin

What is the price of two sparrows – one copper coin? But not a single sparrow can fall to the ground without your Father knowing it.

Matthew 10:29, NLT

On holiday I took off my glasses in order to wash my hair. When the time came to put them back on again, I could not see where they were! I was in a different place and couldn't locate them without my glasses on! After a while I became frustrated – they must be somewhere. Finally, in my frustration, I asked the Lord to help me find them. As quickly as I had asked for His help, the thought came to my mind that the Creator of heaven and earth, a majestic and awesome God, could not possibly be aware or bothered where my glasses were! How silly of me!

My thoughts went to our recent holiday to Iceland and Greenland: the glaciers, icebergs, 5,000-feet high majestic mountains, the massive waterfalls and much more that we had been overwhelmed by. Here I was in the Outer Hebrides and just last night we had returned from watching a brilliantly red sun setting over the ocean. The crashing waves had reminded me how God had set everything within His order and, because of this, the evening's full moon would keep the ocean within its boundary and prevent it from flowing over us.

I continued looking for my glasses with these memories occupying my thoughts, when into my mind came the wonderful passage of Scripture which tells us that not even a sparrow falls to the ground without our Father in heaven noticing. I was deeply impacted and overwhelmed with the love of God for His creation.

How could I doubt that the Maker of heaven and earth, the sky, the sea, the majestic mountains, the tiniest of shells, fish or flowers, would know where my glasses were! At that moment I saw how ridiculous it was of me to think that the Creator of the universe was not capable of ordering my life and helping me if I asked Him. A God who is capable of creating this remarkable earth with its perfect balance, order and beauty who is not also interested in every detail of my life does not make any sense whatsoever.

I cannot thank God enough that He gave His Son, Jesus, to open up the way for me to have relationship with Him and that Jesus left His Holy Spirit to lead, guide and comfort me. To think that He plans for my good, desires to help me with the smallest details of my life and to invite me to be in relationship with Him is a wonder beyond words for me today. Yes, He does want to be involved in all that concerns us, He does wait to be invited and He is a Father who longs to help us and longs for us to trust Him to provide and care for us.

My glasses, hidden from my eyes through the patterns on the bedspread, were instantly located as these thoughts filled my mind. Far more consequential was the deeper experience I received through asking the Lord to help me. In return He showed me the enormity of His love and care – wider than the widest ocean, deeper than the deepest sea and higher than the highest mountain. Why would I not turn to Him for every detail in my life and trust Him in every circumstance.

PRAYER: *Dear Lord Jesus, I am so grateful for Your intimate knowledge of me and for Your tender care. I place my life afresh in your hands today, knowing that You are not distant or unaware of everything concerning me. I ask You, Lord Jesus, to help me order my life according to Your principles and Your ways because, as Creator, You know the best way and I need Your help. Amen.*

JANUARY 17 | OBEDIENT FAITH

MARGARET SILVESTER

> *It was by faith that Abraham obeyed when God called him to leave home and go to another land that God would give him as his inheritance. He went without knowing where he was going.*
>
> Hebrews 11:8, NLT

Abraham stands out as someone who truly knew and obeyed God. There were three major meeting points in his life that proved to be turning points in his walk with God and the growth of his faith.

Firstly, Abraham believed that God would guide him. In faith he obeyed God's command. He set out on a journey without knowing where he was going. God said, *'Go,'* and Abraham went. Because he obeyed God's command he received God's promise, *'I will make you into a great nation and I will bless you'* (Genesis 12:2). Not many of us are called to take such great leaps of faith, but we're all called to take steps of faith as we journey through life, trusting God and obeying Him in ordinary things.

Secondly, Abraham believed that God keeps His promises. When he was an old man, and it was humanly impossible for Sarah his wife to bear a child, God worked a miracle for them and Isaac was born. The miracle came about because Abraham believed the promise. God doesn't grant us our every wish, but sometimes He does give us a conviction deep down in our heart that He will do something that's humanly impossible. He's the God of the supernatural.

Thirdly, Abraham proved that God was first in his life. When his faith was tested to the ultimate, when it seemed that God was even going back on His word, Abraham obeyed. He offered his only son, Isaac, as a sacrifice (Hebrews 11:17). In the most extreme of circumstances he still continued to believe the promise that his descendants would be born through Isaac. Abraham's faith was unlimited, because he believed that God's power was unlimited.

Abraham is called '*the spiritual father of those who have faith*' (Romans 4:11, NLT). We may think that men and women of faith who obey God with uncalculated obedience are extraordinary. They are in fact ordinary people; people just like us, with unshakeable faith in an extraordinary God. They are examples for us to follow. Obedient faith is not blind faith. It's simple trust in the God who calls ordinary people into His eternal purposes.

Is there a step of obedience that you should take today, trusting the Lord?

PRAYER: *Heavenly Father, thank You that You are true to all Your promises and that You are One who speaks to Your children. Help me to listen to what You have to say. Please increase my faith. Teach me to live my life in obedience to Your Word without counting the cost. I bring my prayer through the name of Jesus, Amen.*

JANUARY 18 | GUIDANCE – PART 1

DAVID SILVESTER

I will guide thee with mine eye.

Psalm 32:8, KJV

From infancy the KJV was the only translation of the Bible used in our home and church, and so many Bible phrases still come to mind in that form today. It is therefore not surprising that scriptures in this form come to mind in everyday experiences.

Hence, the above verse came to mind whilst awaiting a return flight from Innsbruck. Looking out from the airport terminal building, the view of the airport's location was quite amazing. It soon became evident that our inbound flight the previous week was between two mountains with not a great distance between them. Now an experienced pilot would have no difficulty negotiating that approach on a clear day, but our inbound flight was in thick low cloud!

So how does a pilot manage to negotiate such a descent in those conditions? It is because the pilot is guided by instructions from the Air Traffic Control Officer, and that officer is using the 'eyes' of radar. This reminded me of the words of Psalm 32:8.

Similarly, as we face difficult situations of life, it is such a comfort to know that we have a Heavenly Father who is constantly caring for our welfare, watching over us, and ready to guide us when we are 'tuned in' to hear and listen to His guiding instructions.

In the same way that the airline pilot is tuned in to Air Traffic Control, and they are using radar to guide and direct him in those difficult situations where eyesight is insufficient, so those who trust in the Lord are able to look to Him to direct the path of their life. This is where the words of Proverbs 3:5–6 become so meaningful: '*Trust in the LORD with all your heart and lean not on your own understanding; in all your ways acknowledge him, and he will make your paths straight.*' Acknowledging here means inviting God to come into the situation, and letting Him direct the way ahead.

There has to be trust in, and a deliberate act of submission to God's way and will for our life.

There has to be trust on the part of the pilot in the person at the other end of his radio link, in just the same way that there has to be trust in, and a deliberate act of submission to God's way and will for our life. This, in the long term, is by far the safest and most fruitful course for us to take.

PRAYER: *Thank You, Heavenly Father, for Your loving care, and for the way You are constantly watching over me as I travel through life. Thank You too that You respond and are ready to provide the guidance I need to take me safely through the uncertain paths of life. Amen.*

January 19 | Guidance – Part 2

David Silvester

I will guide thee with mine eye.

Psalm 32:8, KJV

I live on a bend in the road, with a bush obstructing the view, which can make things difficult when I try to reverse a car out of the drive. So it seems to make more sense to reverse the car into the drive when there is no traffic about. This manoeuvre is, of itself, not too difficult, but the real difficulty comes when I try to get the car backwards into the garage, especially as there is not much clearance between the vehicle's side mirrors and the door frame.

This difficulty has been overcome in a very simple manner. Initially, I line up a single marker on the rear window of the car with the centre rib of the garage door, then with a number of suspended markers I have strategically placed inside the garage. Keeping the suspended markers lined up with the mark on the window whilst reversing makes the manoeuvre relatively simple.

Just as it is important for me to keep my eyes on those markers, making sure that everything is 'in line' to guide me, so it is with the Christian's daily walk with the Lord. This is where we need to keep things 'in line' with what we know from God's Word, and let the 'markers' of His Word be our guide. Endeavouring to live with everything 'in line', honouring God in this way, in the knowledge that He is also continually watching over us in order to guide and direct us, leads us further into fulfilling His will. This is how we learn to live a fulfilled life as we serve Him. But the danger comes when our eyes are distracted and diverted into things that are not 'in line' with what God has planned for us.

The writer of Hebrews 12:2 says, *'Let us fix our eyes on Jesus, the author and perfecter of our faith'*, so that we, by keeping 'in line' with Him, will always do those things that honour Him and bring added blessing into our lives.

Prayer: *Father God, I thank You that You teach me godly principles from everyday situations. Please help me to keep my eyes fixed on those 'markers' that bring me increasingly 'in line' with Your will for my life. Thank You for constantly watching over me and guiding me into the line of Your will. Amen.*

January 20 | At Your Word, Lord

Alistair Petrie

Master, we've worked hard all night and haven't caught anything. But because you say so, I will let down the nets.

Luke 5:6

Life can be so frustrating at times. We work hard, but often seem to see very little return from our labour. In fact, we often get into a cycle of life that goes like this ... we go to work, to earn the money, to buy the bread, to get the strength, to go to work ... and so on! Life has to have more meaning than that!

Suddenly Jesus interrupts the cycle of life for Peter who is a professional in his line of work. He knows the seasons – the tides – the ways of the fish. He knows the ebb and flow of the real world – or so he thinks! In Luke 5, Jesus literally requests something that goes completely against a fisherman's common sense. Why should he cast nets in broad daylight? 'Besides, there are no fish in there, Lord! We've worked hard all night – and we have nothing to show for our labour!' But something happens!

For Peter, it was not his knowledge, his experience, or even his skills that counted, but rather an encounter with the Lord Himself – and the word that Jesus gave Peter that day became binding in his entire being, even if he did not understand it from human experience. Peter's reply was significant for his own being – and for us. 'Because You say so (at Your Word) I will be obedient.' Suddenly, the net burst with the fruit of obedience – even to the point that others had to come and help with this extraordinary catch – a sign of the authority Jesus had over the land, the sea, and the heavens. Extraordinary! Incredible!

No matter what giants may face us and no matter how futile it may appear to go against the tides of life, it is then in our weakness that God's strength is made perfect. In the midst of impossibility, Jesus loves to intervene, and show the urgency and magnificence in believing and responding to His Word – especially when things look hopeless and we just want to give up. Simply put, if we dare to believe in the midst of impossibility and uncertainty, and express obedience to His will, then His call to us will unveil the miraculous, but only after we are obedient to His Word. It is when we dare to uphold and obey the commandments of God, and not be intimidated by the signs of the times, that Jesus will prove His might! It was true for Peter – and it will be true for you and me, no matter what we are going through at this very moment.

PRAYER: *Father, I acknowledge that there are times when I wonder if You will ever show up! Forgive me when I depend more on my human logic than on Your Word! You know what I am going through at this very moment. You are the God of the impossible and today I choose once again to trust You with all my heart and to lean into Your understanding of what I am going through. At Your Word, Lord, I am ready to try once again and 'to let down the nets' and wait for the catch. In Jesus' name, Amen.*

JANUARY 21 | WORSHIP

JILL SOUTHERN-JONES

> *Yet a time is coming and has now come when the true worshippers will worship the Father in spirit and truth, for they are the kind of worshippers the Father seeks.*
>
> John 4:23

This verse makes me wonder how we get to be true worshippers. I believe that as we hunger for more intimacy with God, His Spirit beckons us to come closer and then we can really start worshipping Him. We need to remove ourselves from centre stage and put God in His rightful place. We must focus on giving Him the honour that He deserves.

I sometimes picture believers, in every time zone around the world, who are praising our eternal God. I think the Kingdom of God must need more people who are first worshippers, rather than workers. If workers don't focus on Jesus as their reason for working and don't find their reward in Him, they will become disgruntled. They won't feel that their contribution is sufficiently appreciated. But those who have worshipping hearts become sacrificial servants in their work.

Psalm 103 tells us not to forget all God's benefits. We can think of past answers to prayers, our present provision and joys, and all there is of God that we have yet to experience. But in the light of *who* He is, our worship can never be big *enough* and our passion can never be intense *enough*.

Charles Spurgeon said: '*The Lord always deserves to be praised for who He is Himself, for His works of creation and providence, for His goodness towards His creatures and especially for the tremendous act of redemption and all the marvellous blessings flowing therefrom.'* He says, *'Learn to practise the eternal Hallelujah.'*

God is here *with* us – He is here *for* us. When we still our hearts before Him He will sing over us, because worship is relationship: *'The LORD your God is with you, he is mighty to save. He will take great delight in you, he will quiet you with his love, he will rejoice over you with singing'* (Zephaniah 3:17). Our love relationship with God flows both ways, from us to God and from God to us. But we can never praise God enough. Even when we get to heaven and it will be our whole focus for eternity, how can we *ever* praise Him enough?

PRAYER: *Father, I want to worship You. You are 'the Living God'. Teach me to become the kind of worshipper that You seek – one who worships You in spirit and in truth. In Jesus' name I pray, Amen.*

JANUARY 22 | DIFFERENT VESSELS FOR DIFFERENT USES

PETER HORROBIN

> *Yet, O LORD, you are our Father. We are the clay, you are the potter; we are all the work of your hand.*
>
> Isaiah 64:8

This week I walked through a huge store, absolutely filled with different specimens of pottery. Every single design was unique. And every item had a specific use. As I looked at this overwhelming display of man's creative ability, I began to think of how it illustrates the creativity of God in the vast breadth of design and function on display.

Many will have sung Christian worship songs which express this theme, with words such as 'You are the potter, we are the clay' – recognising that God is the Master Potter and we are His creation. But many of the people who have sung these songs may still be wishing they are like someone else. Some walk through our doors looking for help on Healing Retreats. They see someone else's looks or gifting and then see themselves negatively as a result. They feel inferior, and before very long depression and even despair can follow.

It's easy to forget that God did not make us to be like anyone else. He made us to be the person we are. Each one of us is a much loved, special creation. The world idolises certain people, and the rest of humanity seems to want to copy the 'stars'. But God doesn't want us to be like anyone else – He rejoices when we are content with who we are and seek to fulfill the destiny that the Master Potter has for each one of us.

It's as we follow in the footsteps of Jesus that an extraordinary miracle takes place – in our character we become more like Him – and in our humanity we become more like the person God intended us to be in the first place.

PRAYER: *Thank You, Father God, that, as the Master Potter, the works of Your hand are always perfect. Help me, Lord, to so walk in Your ways that I both reflect Your true character to the people around me and grow into the person You intended me to be, in Jesus' name. Amen.*

JANUARY 23 | SOME OF THE SECRETS OF UNANSWERED PRAYERS

IAN COATES

> *For the eyes of the Lord are on the righteous and his ears are attentive to their prayer, but the face of the Lord is against those who do evil.*
>
> 1 Peter 3:12

How often do we feel that our prayers have not been answered or perhaps even heard? We seem to have no response and there seems to be no solution to our problem and we start to lose our faith.

This is a situation I have come across many times in ministering to others. People know that what they are being tempted to believe about God is not true, but they are left with trying to reconcile an impossible problem. Many believers have gone away from God because they have believed lies about Him, instead of clinging to the truth and facing the reality of their condition.

In John 8:31–32 Jesus says that if we hold to His teaching, we really are His disciples, and then we will know the truth and the truth will set us free. But what is the truth and how will it set us free? Jesus is the Truth but we also need to see the *truth* about ourselves, and it's only at that point that our lives begin to change. It's only when we see ourselves as sinners and repent and turn from our sin that the truth of who Jesus is can bring about the changes in our lives that lead to salvation for eternity.

It's the same with the other issues in life when our prayers don't seem to be answered! Let me show you some of the secrets to unanswered prayers!

In Isaiah 59:2 it says that *'your sins have hidden his face from you so that he will not hear'*. But in Proverbs 15:29 it says, *'He hears the prayer of the righteous.'* Are there sins that are hidden from us? *'If I had cherished sin in my heart, the LORD would not have listened'* (Psalm 66:18). So we see that sin and iniquity will be a barrier to us hearing God.

Do we do the things that please Him? 1 John 3:22: *'[We] receive from him anything we ask, because we obey his commands and do what pleases him'*, and what about the idol in our hearts of Ezekiel 14:3? God says, *'Should I let them enquire of me at all?'* We can soon begin to see that God wants to speak to us but it's our issues that can so often get in the way.

I often ask the question of audiences: 'How many of you worry or tend to get anxious?' Nearly all respond that they do. If we look at Scripture in Matthew 6 and Philippians 4 we see that this will separate us from God. And what about our selfishness? In Proverbs 21:13 we read that if we ignore the poor we will cry out and not be answered!

It's important that we don't have an unforgiving spirit if we are to hear from God – read Mark 11:25! Unforgiveness is a definite blockage to the Holy Spirit and we can relay many stories of transformed lives as forgiveness has been expressed.

Finally, what about our motives for speaking to God? In James 4:3 we see that it's possible for us not to receive because we ask with wrong motives as pleasure seekers!

PRAYER: *Search me, O God, and know my heart; test me and know my anxious thoughts. See if there is any offensive way in me, and lead me in the way everlasting, in Jesus' name, Amen.*

JANUARY 24 | OBEDIENCE AND GOD'S FAITHFULNESS

HERMAN REDELINGHUYS

But after I have been raised, I will go before you to Galilee.
Mark 14:28, NKJV

Have you ever made an appointment with someone knowing that there's only the slightest possibility that the person or yourself will be able to honour the appointment?

In the Word of God we find a few such appointments. God made an appointment with Abraham, saying to him, I will meet your descendants in this very place 400 years from now. Joseph, knowing he was part of this promise, made arrangements for his bones to be buried in 'the Promised Land'. Moses, despite his fears, left his sheep in the desert because of this appointment. In the Word we witness how even the fluctuations of trust and obedience over the generations still worked together with the faithfulness of God to bring into being 'the Promised Land'.

In the Scriptures Jesus made the same kind of seemingly impossible promise to the disciples. He promised He would die – and He was found to be faithful. Then He promised He would be raised from the dead – and He was found to be faithful. Finally He promised to meet His disciples somewhere in Galilee – and, yet again, He was found to be faithful.

God makes His promises to us with the full knowledge that we have a free will and that we might not receive His promises. Our character and response will only be known when it is tested. The testing and risk God takes is all part of the promise. If we respond with obedience it brings us in line to receive from His faithfulness. Even when we get it wrong, like the Israelites and Jesus' disciples, God in His mercy wants to restore us and bring us into obedience and steer us back into His faithfulness. It's wonderful to know that God wants to grow our character as He leads us into His promises.

PRAYER: *Thank You for Your love and promises in my life, Lord. Where I have missed Your promises because of my reaction or disobedience I ask for Your mercy and grace to restore me, so that I can follow You in obedience. Thank You that it's Your unfailing love and faithfulness that draws me towards You. Amen.*

JANUARY 25 | THE FATHER HEART OF GOD

MARGARET SILVESTER

Show me your glory.

Exodus 33:18

Before Moses resumed his journey to the Promised Land, he was yearning for a special revelation of God – a spiritual perception of who God was and what He would do for His people. He was told to hide in the cleft of a rock and his prayer would be answered.

The Lord came down in a cloud and passed before Moses, revealing His name and character to him – '*The LORD, the compassionate and gracious God, slow to anger, abounding in love and faithfulness, maintaining love to thousands, and forgiving wickedness, rebellion and sin*' (Exodus 34:6–7). This is how God is. It's how He has revealed Himself to be. This description of His character is given several times throughout the Old Testament, sometimes in full and sometimes in part. He's not just 'loving' – He's 'abounding in love'. The way God's love is most often described in the Bible is 'unfailing.' It's covenant love, which will endure forever. God can never break His covenant.

What we think of God is the most important thing of all. It will affect every aspect of life – how we think and behave, how we relate to God and other people, and how we love. Many Christians know and believe what the Bible says, but their heart cry is for their head knowledge of God to become heart experience. Their view of what God's really like has been distorted. For many the truth of Scripture doesn't seem to be in keeping with their own experiences of life. Their image of God is, in many respects, the opposite of what He's really like.

Like Moses, we all need a revelation of God. But it's in Jesus that we can see the full revelation of God's heart. Jesus is 'one with the Father'. Jesus came to show us the Father, and to reveal the depth of His love. '*This is how God showed his love among us: He sent his one and only Son into the world that we might live through him*' (1 John 4:9).

The difference between Christianity and other world religions is that in Christianity God can be known personally. A Christian is a person who knows God as 'Father'. In the Old Testament the word 'Father' is used about God very few times. But in the New Testament it's used well over a hundred times. 'Father' is the name by which Jesus addressed God and it's the name He taught us to use.

Many people have an image of 'Father God' which is rooted in their experience, or lack of experience, of their earthly father. They have dressed God in another person's clothes. Whatever our experience of an earthly father – good or angry, protecting or absent, affirming or distant, caring or abusive, accepting or rejecting – the One who Jesus came to reveal is the perfect Father.

Question: Do you know God's Father love deep in your heart, or do you find it difficult to see Him as the Bible describes Him?

PRAYER: *Heavenly Father, thank You that Your Word is true. Please reveal to me Your Father heart, because I desire to come closer to You. Amen.*

January 26 | You Fit!

Cath Taylor

You do not belong to yourself, for God bought you with a high price.

1 Corinthians 6:19–20, NLT

It is a human need to know we 'fit in'. To know we have a place. To know we belong. To know someone cares.

Not all of us feel or know this deep in our hearts, where it counts. Circumstances, our upbringing, and life itself have perhaps been used by the enemy to create a sense deep in our hearts that we are alone and different.

The wonderful truth is that no matter what we may feel, no matter what the enemy may tell us and no matter what has been spoken by others in our lives, we all have a wonderful place of absolute, concrete, belonging. A place we can take ownership of and enjoy once we have come to the Lord through His cross.

Just like a piece of a jigsaw puzzle, all of us (whether we know it or not) are a piece of God's puzzle. There is a place set aside within the Lord's heart that waits for us to come and rest, to enjoy being simply a part of His picture. There's a place in His heart and His plans that is perfectly designed and shaped for you and for me. It's a unique place where we fit and belong and are 100% accepted, not because of anything we can do, say or earn – but just because it's the place He bought for us as His children. It's when we come to this place that we find comfort for our loneliness, and peace for our striving. It's the place that assures us we belong, we fit, we have a place – we're not forgotten or overlooked. We have a purpose, a significance, and a worth that is entwined into the very heart of our Father God.

Prayer: *Lord Jesus, thank You that I belong to You. Thank You that You have given me an eternal place where I fit, that I don't need to be worried about where I may fit in terms of the world and the people around me, because I can rest in the amazing place of Your ownership, paid for by You. Lord, I ask that You will reveal more of who I am in You, as I draw close to You, in Jesus' name, Amen.*

January 27 | Our City is Now Strong

Liz Griffin

In that day, everyone in the land of Judah will sing this song: Our city is now strong! We are surrounded by the walls of God's salvation. Open the gates to all who are righteous; allow the faithful to enter.

Isaiah 26:1–2, NLT

What a picture of protection and security! A city with high walls which are the Lord's walls, His salvation. There is a way into this city through the gate. But if we are safe inside, we long for others to be able to come in too. We cry out from our hearts: '*Open the gates to all who are righteous; allow the faithful to enter*' (Isaiah 26:2, NLT). Jesus later on said He was the gate. He is the way people can come into God's presence and be saved.

But just before this verse, in Isaiah chapter 25, we read about some high and fortified walls which were built of pride and God destroyed them. It is when God brings down those hateful walls (that mighty stronghold of the enemy) that everyone in Judah will sing for joy. They will rejoice in the salvation of the true and Living God.

Isaiah goes on to speak directly to the Lord: '*You will keep in perfect peace all who trust in you, whose thoughts are fixed on you!*' (Isaiah 26:3, NLT). I first became aware of these words when I learnt them as a 'scripture in song'. Isn't it amazing how some songs get into your spirit and never leave you? I was recently praying healing for an elderly lady and I mentioned I had been reading these words that morning in the Bible. She became quite excited and said, 'My grandmother had those words in a picture frame in her house. I can see it now; it was black with gold words.' It seemed to be a vivid memory the Lord was giving her. I wondered how many have had the privilege of having such a blessing as a young child.

Isaiah tells us why we can put our trust in God. It's because He's so strong and dependable and will never let us down. I know that Isaiah had a life-transforming experience of the presence of the Lord when he was in the temple. We read about it in Isaiah chapter 6. Isaiah spent the rest of his life fulfilling the Lord's call upon him to bring prophetic words. He was able to confidently exhort us all to: '*Trust in the LORD always, for the LORD GOD is the eternal Rock*' (Isaiah 26:4, NLT).

Prayer: *How blessed we are to know the way to security and peace through You, Lord Jesus. Help us to focus our thoughts on You rather than a million other things which would pull us into anxiety. Thank You that You are the eternal Rock for us and we can shelter in Your shadow of protection, in Jesus' name, Amen.*

January 28 | Larger than Life

Lindsey Hanekom

> *Let us run with patient endurance and steady and active persistence the appointed course of the race that is set before us.*
>
> Hebrews 12:1b, AMP

We recently undertook a long car journey from Scotland to England, which ordinarily is not a problem. However, this journey was different as the UK was, as the TV would report it, in the grip of 'the Big Freeze'.

Before our journey we had been led to believe that the roads were treacherous and that all travel would be dangerous. Yet the truth was the roads weren't that bad, although certain sections needed careful navigation and driving through them was hard work. As we approached the more difficult sections of roads we found ourselves asking, 'What are we doing? We should have stayed at home.' Yet only a short time later we were back to the clear roads that allowed us to travel safely at reasonable speeds.

We often refer to our Christian lives as a journey, which it is. It's a journey that many would advise us not to embark upon, citing all the reasons why it could be difficult. I firmly believe one of the enemy's most successful strategies is to make himself seem bigger than he really is and to make things seem harder than they are.

Yes, there will be difficult times in our lives. Yes, we will have to slow our journey down incredibly to navigate a safe course through it. Yet if we want to get to the end of our journey we'll have to keep moving. The enemy would love to concern us with the dangers ahead and try to put us off moving on. Even along the way it may feel as though we'll never see a clear road again and we may ask the question, 'What am I doing?' But there's a clear road ahead and patient perseverance is what's needed to push through.

It's true that some people get genuinely stuck on their life journeys – just as many in the UK got stuck on snowy and icy roads. They need to seek God and ask for His timing and perspective – maybe even wait for Him to clear the road ahead of them so that they can keep going. If we'd believed the media hype we'd still be at home, missing Christmas with our families. Equally, if we believe the exaggeration of the enemy about the difficulties on our life journeys then we'll never move into the destiny God has for each one of us.

When we consider the hindrances to our life journey let's not allow the enemy to become larger than life, and let's ask God for His perspective on our situation. Then, as today's scripture says, *'Let us run with patient endurance and steady and active persistence the appointed course of the race that is set before us.'*

PRAYER: *Father God, I recognise that You alone can see my life's pathway and I pray that You'll encourage me on my journey with You. I pray You'll clear the paths ahead of me and that I won't be discouraged by the whispers of the enemy. Amen.*

JANUARY 29 | GIVE THANKS

JILLY LYON-TAYLOR

He who sacrifices thank-offerings honours me, and he prepares the way so that I may show him the salvation of God.

Psalm 50:23

I wonder how many of us began today by giving thanks to God. The problem is that we don't always feel like giving thanks, but the Bible doesn't say anything about giving thanks when we feel like it! If we always waited for our feelings to come in line with what is right, we might not get up in the morning, or give away our money, or do the things that God is prompting us to do. We would certainly not enter into praise and worship as often if we always waited until we felt like it! There are times when we have to command our soul (our will, our mind and our emotions) to do what God wants and not what our carnal nature desires. David did this in Psalm 103:1–2 when he tells his soul to: *'Praise the LORD, O my soul; all my inmost being, praise his holy name. Praise the LORD, O my soul, and forget not all his benefits.'*

As we begin to make a choice to praise the Lord and to remember all the benefits of our inheritance, we will connect with God in our spirits and be able to bring Him the kind of worship, in spirit and in truth, that He seeks from us (John 4:24). Also, as we turn our focus onto God and all that He has done for us, we become less focused on ourselves and our needs.

Thanksgiving has the same effect. We are told in 1 Thessalonians 5:18 to *'give thanks in all circumstances'* – which means that in the midst of whatever storms we may be going through, we should still give thanks to God for who He is and what He has done for us.

Today's verse from Psalm 50 tells us that our thanksgiving honours God, particularly when it is a sacrifice for us. The rest of the verse goes on to say that as we sacrifice thank-offerings, it prepares the way for God to show us His salvation. Salvation for the believer involves much more than just the moment we are born again and are saved from sin and death (vital though that is) – it is also about the ongoing work of healing and sanctification that Jesus wants to do in our lives once we have believed. As we offer thanks to God He is able to show us more of the inheritance that He has for us.

Why not start to thank Him now!

PRAYER: *Lord, forgive me for the times I have been so self-centred that I have forgotten to thank You. I want to thank You now for who You are and for all You have done for me. Amen.*

JANUARY 30 | FRIENDSHIPS

BERYL PUFFETT

There is a friend who sticks closer than a brother.

Proverbs 18:24b

While we were having a coffee and talking about friendships my friend and I made some interesting observations. Before we were saved we had mutual friends who enjoyed having parties and social events. Some became friends after we met them at school events, and their children were friends of our children. Some were work colleagues who became our friends. There were dear friends of the family and friends of friends. Many had worldly values and having fun together was what it was all about.

Once we met Jesus – so much changed. My friend said she actually lost all her worldly friends and felt quite alone and isolated, until the Lord started adding very valuable friends to her life – friends who were prepared to walk the difficult road of tragedy with her – friends who loved her when she was not the nicest person around – friends who helped her to grow in Christ (one who became a treasured prayer partner on a weekly basis) – older women who shared their wisdom with her and encouraged her during the difficult times with her children. And then she mentioned our spouses that were given to us to be friends forever.

It makes me think of Jesus! He had very special friends too! *'And Jesus, walking by the Sea of Galilee, saw two brothers, Simon called Peter, and Andrew his brother, casting a net into the sea, for they were fishermen. Then He said to them, "Follow Me and I will make you fishers of men"'* (Matthew 4:18, NKJV). And they became His close friends. It makes me wonder how much we treasure the friendships that we have. Did they happen by coincidence? Or were they God-ordained?

We have a special and unusual friendship in our family. My mum's mother had a best friend. They were there for each other through two world wars. Both of them had daughters – my mum and her daughter, who became best friends and lived together while their husbands went to war. They also had daughters – my friend and me. Then we had a daughters too, who are close friends today. Four generations of close friendships. God puts people across our path during our lives on earth and He creates friendships that will encourage and nurture us.

PRAYER: *Lord Jesus, thank You for being my friend and for teaching me about precious friendships in my life. Help me, Lord, not to take them for granted, but to nurture them and appreciate them as much as You do. Thank You for blessing me with wonderful friends who have had such a great impact in my life. Help me, Lord, to be a good friend in all circumstances, in Jesus' name, Amen.*

JANUARY 31 | DEALING WITH THE BROCCOLI!

CATH TAYLOR

> *Therefore I, a prisoner for serving the Lord, beg you to lead a life worthy of your calling, for you have been called by God. Always be humble and gentle. Be patient with each other, making allowances for each other's faults because of your love.*
>
> Ephesians 4:1–2, NLT

My little Isaac is five years old. For a child with two older brothers he's remarkably easy-going, but poor Isaac has one recurring problem that faces him each day at around 6pm, which causes him enormous distress. You're probably thinking homework, early bedtime, bath time … but no, none of those quite reasonable five-year-old hurdles are his real problem.

Isaac's real obstacle comes in the green, yellow or orange pile of nutrition on his dinner plate. His problem? Vegetables.

Vegetables are the bane of Isaac's life. What is normally a great day of fun at school or with friends can be transformed into a moment of sheer torture and anguish by the glimpse of a pan of boiling water on the stove. I think if you asked him, Isaac would declare all vegetables disgusting and to be avoided at all costs, but high (if not highest) on this list of untouchables would be the vilest offender – broccoli!

With this in mind, imagine my surprise a few weeks back when halfway through our evening family meal, I realised that we were no longer enduring the same pleas for negotiations or mercy. Not only were there no protests but there were also no longer any bright green little 'trees' on Isaac's plate. When I very calmly asked Isaac where the broccoli had gone, he simply showed me how he'd discovered a secret way to disguise the 'horrible taste'. The answer for my little guy came in the huge pile of tomato ketchup that sat on his plate. He'd quite merrily covered his broccoli in ketchup to such an extent that when he put it in his mouth all he could taste was yummy, salty, tomatoes!

As adults we may be able to rationalise how and why we have to eat our vegetables. But I wonder what you do in this sort of situation: you have to cope with a person who creates a reaction in you similar to that which Isaac has with broccoli. I'd be surprised if we don't all have people in our lives that we struggle with, for one reason or another. They've hurt us by rejecting us or offending us in some way. Perhaps they remind us of someone who caused us pain in the past. Maybe they just press buttons in our hearts and we struggle to stay in godly, healthy relationship with them. Whether they're wrong in the way they've treated us, or we struggle to cope with their particular personality – the reality is, as human beings, relationships can be tough sometimes.

We try to cope. We try to figure out ways around the problem. It's like pushing the person around our plates. We struggle with our emotions and assign blame to others or ourselves. All this seems justified, but it just prolongs the agony. But how about choosing a higher way instead of trying to fix it in our own strength? We could make a choice to forgive them, if that's appropriate. We could quit looking at their faults and weaknesses and choose to view them through God's eyes. Our Heavenly Father loves them as much as He loves us. We could ask Him to pour into our hearts His acceptance, His love and His abundant grace!

PRAYER: *Lord Jesus, Thank You for Your amazing grace in my life. Your never-ending love and acceptance of me goes far beyond anything that I deserve. Lord, will You give me Your heart for all the people in my life. Will You help me to see them through Your eyes, and will You give me the love and grace I lack in my own strength. In Jesus' name I pray, Amen.*

FEBRUARY 1 | HUMILITY

JOAN RONO

> *In the same way, you who are younger, submit yourselves to your elders. All of you, clothe yourselves with humility toward one another, because God opposes the proud but shows favour to the humble.*
>
> 1 Peter 5:5

The first thing I would ask myself is: what is humility? Jesus gives us a good example Himself, the Lord of lords and the King of kings coming into the world as a little baby. He was born in a stable, lived as a carpenter and most of all He desired no recognition even when His ministry was filled with miracles, signs and wonders. All He wanted was to reveal the Father to us. He lived to die!

What a great example He gave when He stooped down in front of His disciples and started washing their feet, when He went into the houses of tax collectors and sinners, and when He healed the lepers and touched them. He didn't condemn a sinful adulteress. His life was filled with humility and He taught humility. He took the place of a servant, even though He was a king!

We live in a world where morality has drained away and disappeared from this generation. People are seeking fame and recognition. The Church has lost some of the most valuable treasures, called humility and integrity!

Recently, I was watching clips of a political satire from my country and was shocked to see that the Church was being ridiculed because of mismanagement of funds and they were showing a preacher bragging about his very expensive car in front of a crowd in a gospel crusade! But it's not just in one country. It's a worldwide situation that requires us, as the Church, to search ourselves. Are we imitating Christ's humility? Or are we conforming to the standards of the world? Are we seeking recognition, or are we serving Christ and seeking His glory?

This scripture instructs us to be clothed in humility. Why? Because God opposes the proud and gives strength to the humble. *'Let this mind be in you which was also in Christ Jesus, who, being in the form of God, did not consider it robbery to be equal with God, but made Himself of no reputation, taking the form of a bondservant, and coming in the likeness of men. And being found in appearance as a man, He humbled Himself and became obedient to the point of death, even the death of the cross'* (Philippians 2:5, NKJV).

PRAYER: *Father, please forgive us if we have conformed to the standards of the world and not Your standards. I pray that we can have humility and integrity as we follow the example of our Lord Jesus Christ. Amen.*

FEBRUARY 2 | STEP BY STEP

ANNE LAWRENCE

Your word is a lamp to my feet and a light for my path.

Psalm 119:105

Over the past few months I have been training for a half marathon with my husband and some of our colleagues. The other night when we ran back up the drive it was very dark. Without lights it was a struggle to see. As I looked ahead, I couldn't see anything. After a while, I looked down and noticed that in fact there was a bit of light and I could see the ground in front a bit clearer, making it easier to run. When I lifted my head again, once more I couldn't see a thing.

That made me think of my life and walk with the Lord. I have a tendency to always look ahead and to the future and I don't always focus on 'now'. However, the future is often not clear because the Lord has not revealed our path to us yet. What He wants us to focus on is today and the things He has prepared for us today. When we focus on the future, the path may seem unclear or hazy but when we look at today, He gives us light to take the next step.

This walk takes faith, perseverance and trust in Him. He encourages us to hide under His wings (Psalm 91) and to take His yoke which is easy and His burden which is light. He promises to guide and direct our path, but He doesn't promise to tell us the whole plan at the beginning.

Why doesn't He do that? We'd often love Him to and can sometimes feel impatient. He doesn't tell us the whole plan because He wants relationship with us; He wants us to grow in our love for Him; to discover more of who He is and to discover more of who we are. The goal is important – Paul encourages us to run the race with perseverance to win the prize – but the journey is also important because the Lord is wooing us and drawing us closer to Himself.

So today, let's focus on what the Lord has prepared for us for this day. Let's keep our eyes fixed on Him and allow His light to illuminate the way step by step. As we take each step with Him, we'll be able to stop now and again and look back and see how far we have come.

PRAYER: *Thank You, Lord, that You love us so much that You want relationship with us. You want us to know you intimately as You know us intimately. Help me to focus on what You have put in front of me today and to take each step with You as You light the path ahead. I choose to trust You and to patiently walk with You, in Jesus' name, Amen.*

FEBRUARY 3 | EARPLUGS OF THE SPIRIT!

PETER HORROBIN

> *The LORD our God said to us at Horeb, 'You have stayed long enough at this mountain. Break camp and advance ...'*
>
> Deuteronomy 1:6

There are times and seasons in life. Sometimes it's right to patiently wait on God and serve Him faithfully in one place. But even when that happens it's vital that we are constantly listening to His voice and not sinking into the deafness of complacency. If we are staying put somewhere it should only be because we know that's the place God still wants us to be.

A time without major change is not a time when we should stop listening to God for new directions. It should be a time when we constantly know God's encouragement to stay where we are. We need to keep the spiritual telephone line open, so that when the moment is right to move on, we clearly hear God's voice and are ready to obey.

From time to time I have met people who stayed in one place in their spiritual life for much longer than God intended. Complacency, laziness and being at ease became earplugs of the spirit. Their attentiveness to the voice of God diminished and they didn't hear or recognise God's voice when it came.

Our scripture for today, in which God was giving instruction to all of Israel to break camp and get up and go, is an encouragement for us all to review our lives and make sure we are still in the right place. It may be that the time has come to break camp and advance, and begin to conquer new territory for the Kingdom of God. Sometimes it's fear of the future which makes people switch off from God. But, if He truly is the one who knows what is best for each one of our lives, what have we got to lose from trusting Him, and at least asking for His affirmation that we're still in the right place? It could be that there are some exciting times ahead for you!

PRAYER: *Lord, I only want to be in the place in my life that is in harmony with Your plans and purposes. I choose to remove the earplugs from my spirit – please show me any changes that I need to make, in Jesus' name, Amen.*

February 4 | The Authentic Word of the Lord

Paul Watson

It is the man of God who defied the word of the LORD.

1 Kings 13:26b

We are not given his name – only a description. He was *'the man of God'*. His part in the drama of salvation history is fleeting, but we can learn a lot from his story.

I want to raise an important point. If God calls us to do something, we need to complete it and not allow ourselves to be waylaid by something that sounds good, but may not be from the Lord.

I will try to summarize 1 Kings chapter 13. Jeroboam was king of Israel – at that time the ten northern tribes, as distinct from the southern kingdom of Judah. Jeroboam had departed from the Lord's ways and had established altars to worship false gods. He had led God's people astray. God raised up a prophet – *'the man of God'* – to bring a strong warning to the king, specifically against the profane altars. He came to Bethel, and in the course of the presentation of the message, God's power was manifestly experienced. God had specifically warned the man of God not to eat bread or drink water or to return by the way he came, so when the king invited him home for lunch, he refused and headed home by another route. However there was a local man, described as *'an old prophet'* (1 Kings 13:11) who, for some undisclosed reason, upon hearing of the miraculous signs performed by the man, followed after him, and invited him to return and eat with him. He lied, saying that an angel had given him this word. So the man of God returned and ate – and then suffered the consequences of disobeying God. It's quite a sobering story.

It made me think. I've spoken with a good number of Christians who have known a call of God to a course of action, a ministry to fulfil, a destiny to live – and yet have then been confused or even waylaid by someone bringing them a 'word from the Lord' which has actually not been what the Lord has said at all. Sometimes then the person is not only confused, or caught in fear of disobeying the new 'word', but sadly is now in disobedience to the original command of the Lord.

I believe that if God has a word for us He tells us – in one way or another – directly. We know in our spirit that He has spoken. I also believe that He can use other believers to affirm or confirm that word, as they bring a prophetic utterance. I believe this is the right order. God speaks to us first, and prophecy from others will confirm the word He has spoken. We are then to follow through to completion all that He has asked of us.

Hence I am really cautious to test every word that a person brings, to assess if it resonates with what the Holy Spirit is saying to my spirit.

Sadly, it appears that the *'man of God'* in this passage, who had been doing so well, failed to check whether or not God had changed His orders, and acted according to a false word of prophecy, to his great loss.

Men and women of God, please be cautious to obey only the authentic word of the Lord.

PRAYER: *Dear Heavenly Dad, please help me to know Your will and Your voice so that I may not be led astray by false words. Amen.*

FEBRUARY 5 | PRACTICES THAT BECOME IDOLS

JILLY LYON-TAYLOR

> *The LORD said to Moses, 'Make a snake and put it up on a pole; anyone who is bitten can look at it and live.' So Moses made a bronze snake and put it up on a pole. Then when anyone was bitten by a snake and looked at the bronze snake, he lived.*
>
> Numbers 21:8–9

On one occasion when the people of Israel were in the desert and they grumbled against God and against Moses, the Lord sent venomous snakes amongst them. Many of the people were bitten by the snakes and died. However, God once again showed His mercy, and when Moses interceded for the people He provided a way out for them. Moses was to make a bronze snake on a pole, and when anyone was bitten he could look at it and live.

This was God's solution for that particular time, and it was also pointing the way to Jesus on the cross being the way to eternal life (John 3:14). However, the Israelites allowed those instructions from God to become a formula for them, which then became an idol and was passed down the generations as a tradition. We read in 2 Kings 18:4 that they still had the bronze snake many hundreds of years later. They had given it a name (Nehushtan) and had been burning incense to it. It had to be destroyed by King Hezekiah along with other idols and objects of false worship.

The bronze snake was something given by God at a particular time, but the people had taken their eyes off Him and had looked to the object and to the practice instead. The instructions were intended for one occasion and not as a blueprint to be followed for all time. Are there things in our lives that we are continuing to do just because God showed us on one occasion it was the right thing to do then? Have we become religious in that practice and has it become an idol in our lives? Are we relying on the practice, rather than on Jesus Himself? Are there traditions that have been passed down through our families or churches that we are continuing, rather than looking to Jesus? Let's get rid of any idols in our lives today and look to Jesus and to Him alone.

PRAYER: *Lord, forgive me for making an idol of anything, or repeating practices passed down the generations, rather than looking to You for life and healing. Thank You that if I look to Jesus I have everything I need. Amen.*

FEBRUARY 6 | THAT'S EASY

SHARON BIXLER

Come to Me, all who are weary and heavy-laden, and I will give you rest ... For My yoke is easy and my burden is light.

Matthew 11:28, 30, NASB

On a recent trip to visit the grandkids in the USA, we came upon an advertising campaign for a large office supply chain called Staples. They had adopted the slogan of 'That's Easy' to sell their customer service. It had taken root very well in American society and they were even selling a buzzer-type button that audibly spoke 'That's Easy' when pressed.

One of these buzzer buttons made its way into our son's home one evening through the church home group that was having their weekly meeting there. Our four-year-old grandson, Jacob, was greatly taken with this button and the noise it produced when pressed. As bedtime came, he insisted on taking the button upstairs to his bed with him. As our son, Brett, finally settled him into bed and came down to rejoin the home group, we were all in prayer for our needs. As the person praying finished, in perfect timing came the response from above: 'That's Easy.' It brought a good laugh to us and a 'Thank You, Jesus' for His quick reply. As the next people prayed in succession, we were amazed again and again that at the end of each prayer came the auditory response from above of 'That's Easy'. We all knew the real operator of the button was Jacob, but marvelled at the truth that although our burdens seem heavy, as we transfer them to Jesus … well, for Him, 'That's Easy', and we find our loads considerably lightened. It left the impression with me to go quickly with my burdens to Jesus, because at His desk I will find the 'That's Easy' button. There I can find rest instead of anxiety and burden. God is waiting to receive your burdens, and His response of 'That's Easy' is just a second away.

PRAYER: *Jesus, I come to You today with my burden of ________. Forgive me for not coming sooner. Thank You that I can cast my cares on You, for You care for me. Help me remember to come to You quickly in the future, for Your yoke is light. Amen.*

FEBRUARY 7 | TRAINING FOR BATTLE

CRISTY WILLIAMS

> *These are the nations the LORD left … They were left to test the Israelites to see whether they would obey the LORD's commands, which he had given their forefathers through Moses.*
>
> Judges 3:1, 4

I've been learning how to throw a pot on a potter's wheel at a local community centre. After six hours of practice I can successful centre my clay on the wheel. How easy it looked, but with my inexperienced hands I found the clay constantly going off centre. It wasn't until I concentrated all my strength on steadying my hand, and leaning into the clay, that I could centre it. It required both mental determination and physical strength. Throwing a pot is a skill that must be learned and with it 'new muscles' are built.

The Israelites weren't in any shape to put their hands to battle. God needed to know that His people could stand against their opponents and not shrink back in fear. So He hand-picked Israel's opponents to train them for war and test them, to see if their hearts would remain obedient when the heat was on.

We see these testing times in our own lives, but aren't too excited when they come. It can be frightening if we don't know the intention of God's heart for us. It's not to see us squirm, or even to remind us that He's more powerful than us. It's to equip us with the tools we need to succeed!

He allows us to go through trials and shaky times to produce His strength in us. Jesus completed His life-purpose on earth by going through many trials and each time passing the test. We're to follow His lead and walk into and through the fires of our lives, believing that He's producing new muscles in us. God's a Master Potter who moulds the clay into His exact design.

PRAYER: *Lord, I thank You for continually moulding me into Your masterful design for my life. Show my heart that Your tests are not to crush me, but to train me to endure in this world. I give You permission to train my hands for the spiritual battles I must go through and I rely on Your strength to bring about the victory. I choose to trust in Your faithfulness, in Jesus' name, Amen.*

FEBRUARY 8 | GRASSHOPPERS AND GIANTS

MARGARET SILVESTER

> *We even saw giants there … We felt like grasshoppers next to them, and that's what we looked to them!*
>
> Numbers 13:33, NLT

The Israelites had seen God work miracles since leaving Egypt. They had seen God's power displayed for them at the Red Sea. Necessary food had been supernaturally supplied on a daily basis. They were now camped in the southernmost region of the Promised Land, having reached the goal of their journey and the fulfilment of God's promise.

When the spies were sent out to view the land, God again reminded them of His promise: '*Send some men to explore the land of Canaan, which I am giving to the Israelites*' (Numbers 13:2). It took forty days for the exploration of the land and then the report was given. Sadly, ten of the twelve spies seemed to have lost sight of the promise and nature of God so their view of reality was distorted. In consequence, the obstacles seemed too great and they were overwhelmed with fear.

Firstly, they saw fortified cities, powerful people and giants. Secondly, they saw themselves as grasshoppers and were convinced that the people of Canaan also saw them in that way. A battle between giants and grasshoppers would be a losing battle. They hadn't learned to see themselves through God's eyes. They were His people, dearly loved and chosen out of the nations as His special possession to fulfil His special purpose. Faith in Him would bring victory. They could go and take the land, but they were crippled with fear and ended up the grasshoppers they feared they were, wandering in the desert for forty years.

Caleb had a different spirit (Numbers 14:24) and he spoke words of truth to the fearful Israelites. *'We should go up and take possession of the land, for we can certainly do it'* (Numbers 13:30). To him the giants appeared as grasshoppers because he saw them through God's eyes. He wasn't crippled with fear because his trust was in the unfailing promises of the unfailing God. Grasshopper or giant – how do you see yourself?

PRAYER: *Heavenly Father, I'm Your child, dearly loved and chosen. I bring my fears to You today and I put my trust in Your unfailing love. In my own strength I can do nothing, but in Your strength I can do everything you ask me to. Thank you that Your strength is made perfect in my weakness. Amen.*

FEBRUARY 9 | WHO CAN I TRUST?

DAVID CROSS

> *I, too, am a man placed under the authority of superior officers, and I have soldiers under me. I order this one, 'Go!' and he goes; I order that one, 'Come!' and he comes; and I order my slave, 'Do this!' and he does it.*
>
> Luke 7:8, GNB

Why are some people easier to trust than others?

I travel by aeroplane a lot these days and each time I board the aircraft I unconsciously choose to trust the pilot. I found myself thinking about this recently and wondering why it seemed relatively easy to trust this person who, for a few hours, would carry a significant responsibility for my life. On every trip, in prayer, I put my life into the hands of Jesus, but clearly I also need to put some trust in particular people.

It occurred to me that I was particularly encouraged when I noticed the uniform that the pilot and crew were wearing. I realised that this was not just that they looked smart but it signified something hugely important for me in my ability to entrust the safety of the flight into their hands. The uniform reminded me that they were men and women operating not just in authority but under the authority of the airline company. I realised that I felt safe to allow them to exercise serious life or death decisions, on my behalf, because I believed that they had been delegated rightful authority and also given the ability to do the job successfully. This reflects something of the godly order that we see described in the Bible.

It seems that the Roman officer, in the verse above, recognised this order in the life of Jesus and was thus able to entrust the well-being of his servant into His hands. The officer knew that those that exercise safe and effective authority and power need to be under right authority. Jesus was not wearing a uniform but the complete submission of His life to the Father was clearly evident in the way He presented Himself, not just promoting His own identity, but always seeking to reflect the One who sent Him. In the Body of Christ those who are truly trustworthy will be the people who are seeking to operate in rightful order and under godly authority, increasingly reflecting the character of the One who is the true Head of this Body, Jesus Christ.

PRAYER: *Father God, help me to be a trustworthy member of the Body of Christ. I understand that there is nobody perfect on this earth, but please continue to cleanse me so that others may increasingly discern Your authority and character in my life. Amen.*

FEBRUARY 10 | THE WINTER IS PAST

NICKY HEMERY

> *See! The winter is past; the rains are over and gone. Flowers appear on the earth; the season of singing has come, the cooing of doves is heard in our land.*
>
> Song of Songs 2:11–12

In the winter our garden doesn't look at its best! In fact it tends to look rather messy in places. During the past two winters we've had heavy snowfalls. Then a transformation takes place overnight and our messy, dull, colourless garden is covered in a thick layer of white snow. The divide between lawn and flowerbed disappears. All the sharp edges are rounded and the steps or ledges can't be seen. Everything looks the same – it's all covered up. The reality of what lies under the surface is hidden for a while – until the snow melts.

Several years ago God showed me I had entered into unreality, in my attempt to mask the less attractive, sinful and damaged areas of my life. Just as the snow temporarily covers our messy garden, making it look more attractive to the eye, so I'd covered my sin, pain and wounds with a layer of unreality. I was hoping to mask the truth I didn't like!

But God showed me that the 'snow' needed to melt so that reality could be exposed. The gardener can only tend to the garden once the snow has melted. My Father God needed me to let Him into the reality of my life. He was asking me to allow Him to gently deal with those areas I didn't like – as He wanted to bring truth and healing.

The good news is that an experienced gardener will tidy, prune and dig the soil in the winter to prepare it for sowing seeds in the spring, and then an abundance of colour and beauty can grow once more.

Sometimes there's a sense of 'winter' for a season in our life. It may seem easier to cover up the reality from ourselves and others, but just as snow prevents a gardener from doing his work, so we can prevent God from working in our lives. We need to allow God to tend our life, in order that the precious new growth of spring and the beauty of summer may take place.

PRAYER: *Heavenly Father, thank You that it's Your truth that sets me free, as I'm real with You and myself, and allow You into every corner of my life. Please help me to be real and to allow You to have Your way in my life, that I may receive Your healing and be fruitful. Amen.*

FEBRUARY 11 | SUDDEN STORMS

LINDSEY HANEKOM

> *He alone is my rock and my salvation; he is my fortress, I shall never be shaken.*
>
> Psalm 62:2

Here in Scotland we're famous for many things. One is the amazingly dramatic weather changes we can experience in a short space of time. There have been many times when I've set off from home in T-shirt and sunglasses for a quick shopping trip, only to have the heavens open and rain thunder down on me, soaking me right through. But if I take my waterproof jacket with me, when the weather turns, I'm ready and prepared. Walking in the rain still isn't necessarily pleasant, but it isn't so terrible either.

And that's how life is. Life can throw things at us so suddenly that it shakes us up. It may be a traumatic event, a harsh word, a shocking discovery, an accident or any number of things that you just can't see coming. It shakes your security. It changes the direction of your life in a day (or even a single moment).

Just as I need to have my protective coat with me at all times (even when I think I don't need to), we need to be in the protection of God at all times. We need to know that whatever turmoil may come our way, He *is* there to give us protection, security and peace. As the rain washes over my protective jacket, so can the turmoil that rages around us, when we're steady on our Rock.

This doesn't make us immune to bad things happening to us; just as wearing a coat doesn't make the rain stop falling. It may not be an enjoyable experience, but we can work through the turmoil knowing that God will keep us safe to the end.

So let's set our foot on the Rock of our salvation and enjoy the security and protection of knowing, whatever happens, He will *always* protect us – as long as we allow Him to.

PRAYER: *Father God, You're the Rock of my salvation and my protection in times of trial and trouble. I ask You to help me live my life under Your protection (even when I think I am safe). In Jesus' name I pray, Amen.*

FEBRUARY 12 | IN EVERYTHING GIVE THANKS

PAM SMITH

> *Rejoice always, pray without ceasing, in everything give thanks; for this is the will of God in Christ Jesus for you.*
>
> 1 Thessalonians 5:16–18, NKJV

People often say that they really want to know God's will for their lives. Here's a verse that plainly states what God's will for you is, in Christ Jesus: *'Rejoice always, pray without ceasing, in everything give thanks; for this is the will of God in Christ Jesus for you'* (1 Thessalonians 5:16–18, NKJV).

How do we rejoice always? We're to live 'one day at a time'. We're given enough grace for this day to live for Him. Sometimes I'm rushing around with a 'to do' list as long as my arm, when suddenly I remember, I'm living my life today. I should be rejoicing – living in His deep joy.

I read once that if you want to know how rich you are, make a list of all the wonderful things you have that don't cost any money. I began to think of the great salvation, love and mercy that are mine, the comfort of the Holy Spirit, and what a Friend I have in Jesus. There's the family God's given me, my grandchildren, relationships with friends, and my wonderful Christian brothers and sisters. He's given me gifts of art and music and an appreciation for the beauty of the natural world. The list is endless. I have so much to rejoice in.

How do we pray without ceasing? As we go about our day we can breathe our prayer to God, committing our thoughts to Him as we go. It doesn't even have to be by spoken words. We can pray without ceasing by including the Lord in our thoughts and actions. We can pray with our hands as we make or do something. Billy Graham's wife had a notice over her kitchen sink saying: *'Divine Service performed here three times a day!'* Or it could be even a whisper of 'Lord, please help me.'

How do we pray without ceasing? As we go about our day we can breathe our prayer to God, committing our thoughts to Him as we go. It doesn't even have to be by spoken words.

How do we give thanks in everything? As we go through our day, continuing our living conversation, we can be thanking Him *in* what we go through. Our verse says, 'in everything', not 'for everything'. We can thank Him for being with us in our situations, giving us strength to meet our needs and grace to meet our difficulties. We can give thanks in pain and in joy. This is His will for us in Christ Jesus.

PRAYER: *Lord, please help me to remember to be in a 'living conversation' with You and to go through this day with thanksgiving in my heart, in Jesus' name, Amen.*

February 13 | Spiritual Exercise

Lindsey Hanekom

Not that I have already obtained all this, or have already been made perfect, but I press on to take hold of that for which Christ Jesus took hold of me.

Philippians 3:12

Following knee surgery a few weeks ago I was referred to a physiotherapist for further help. Having had to subject myself to physiotherapy once before, I was dreading my next session. The day came and, having gone through the obligatory 'Tell me when it hurts' stage of the process, I was asked to walk up and down the room. With a professional eye fully focused on my gait, the therapist simply commented, 'Yes. We are going to have to teach you to walk properly again.'

Now this came as quite a shock to me. I thought I walked fine. In fact, I love walking. I walk lots. I have been walking for a long time! But she was adamant: 'You are compensating for your bad knee and your body can't remember how not to.' And so she taught me how to walk again with exaggerated steps to force my body into submission against its memory of the past years.

> Are we actively choosing to push through into uncomfortable positions that are good for us and bring us the full healing?

Alongside this came a list of exercises to do to build up the muscles around the knee that have been depleted due to this compensation. It seems to me that the essence of physiotherapy is to push you just into the uncomfortable zone until it becomes relatively easy and then you change the exercises to push you further. Whilst difficult and uncomfortable at the time, the benefits of these exercises are incredible and bring hope for the future.

Many of us have been blessed by receiving a measure of healing from God, either physical, emotional, spiritual or a mixture of all three. But have we responded to this by sitting and waiting for the next thing that God will do or have we put our will into line and worked through the results of the pain? Have we willingly retrained ourselves and recognised the compensations we made in our own lives to protect ourselves from the pain? Are we actively choosing to push through into uncomfortable positions that are good for us and bring us the full healing? If you are sitting waiting for God to complete a work in you, maybe He is waiting for you to take responsibility for your healing and start doing your spiritual exercise.

Prayer: *Lord, I want to press on toward the goal. I don't want to stay where I am. Please show me how to move forward and to receive all that You have for me. Please continue to bring Your full healing to me as I take up my responsibility in the healing process. Amen.*

February 14 | Following the One who Goes Before You!

Herman Redelinghuys

But go, tell His disciples – and Peter – that He is going before you into Galilee; there you will see Him, as He said to you.

Mark 16:7, NKJV

I believe these words of the angel were to encourage the disciples and also to show them a principle of how the Kingdom is established. *'He is going before you.'*

When you go into unknown, difficult terrain, you need strength and, if you are in the forefront of the expedition, the ability to open up the way. As you establish and prepare the way, the rest of your team can follow, as long as they stay on the route. In a similar way God said to Moses, *'For My Angel will go before you and bring you in'* (Exodus 23:23, NKJV).

So when Jesus spoke these words, *'I will go before you'*, I believe that He may have had three things in mind. Firstly He wanted to encourage them that He is the faithful one – He does what He has said He will do. Secondly I believe that He wanted to meet with them to establish and empower them as His disciples. Lastly I believe He wanted to say to them: *'I go before you. I have prepared the way. All authority and power belongs to me. I walk before you as you go.'*

At times in our walk with Jesus we may feel alone, discouraged and powerless and we may sense the task we've been given is too great and difficult. Today Jesus wants to remind us that He has gone ahead of us to establish a way even within the challenges we are facing now. He asks us to keep our eyes on Him as He walks before us, and He asks us to follow in His powerful footsteps, in humility and obedience.

PRAYER: *Thank You, Lord, that You have gone before me. Thank You that You have prepared the way through the victory on the cross. Today I choose to walk in humility and obedience in the way You have prepared for me. Amen.*

FEBRUARY 15 | COMING HOME

DIANE WATSON

> *Jesus replied, 'If anyone loves me, he will obey my teaching. My Father will love him, and we will come to him and make our home with him.'*
>
> John 14:23

On the plane coming to the UK from Australia, I felt like I was coming home.

I was born in the UK (my parents immigrated to Australia when I was eight years old), but though I was coming back to the UK, it wasn't the country I was thinking of as home; it was the place I was going, where my Christian family were, at an Ellel centre called Pierrepont.

Thirteen years ago I had been the first student on the very first six-month NETS Programme at Pierrepont. At that time, as I felt God had called me to come, I had left my four children and husband back in Australia for the six months. It was exciting but also daunting. It was during those six months that I made many friends and where my life had been transformed. It was going back to that place and to the people there that felt, to me, like going home.

My views of what a home is have changed radically over the years. I used to yearn for my own home, but realised more and more that when we are being obedient to God's will, He gives us the contentment to make wherever we are our home. We may not own an earthly house, but even if we do, that is not necessarily home. The old saying, 'Home is where the heart is', is true. Where our family, either biological or Christian brothers and sisters are, that is our home.

The scripture that speaks about God the Father and Jesus, His Son, making their home in us, is truly amazing. The best place to be in all the world is in the will of God, being obedient to Him. You don't need earthly homes or houses to make you feel content and secure. When we are doing God's will He provides for all our needs more than we could even ask or imagine and He makes His home in us.

PRAYER: *Loving Heavenly Father, help me to be obedient to Your teaching and to love You with all my heart so that You may feel welcomed into my heart and make your home in me, in Jesus' name, Amen.*

FEBRUARY 16 | A NEW KIND OF LIFE

MALCOLM WOOD

> *Therefore, if anyone is in Christ, he is a new creation; the old has gone, the new has come!*
>
> 2 Corinthians 5:17

The natural world of God's creation gives us so much to wonder and marvel at. There are many examples of His power giving life to multitudes of living organisms, plants and creatures. Every living thing gives testimony to its source of life – God Himself. No wonder the psalmist could say, *'Let every creature praise his holy name for ever and ever'* (Psalm 145:21).

2 Corinthians 5:17 tells us that, as born-again believers in Christ, we are a *'new creation'*. We have a new kind of life. Our spirits have come alive with Christ. So what evidence is there that we're spiritually alive?

When Jesus raised the widow of Nain's son to life, the young man *'sat up and began to talk'* (Luke 7:15). This was real evidence that he was alive! What evidence is there from how we talk to others that the Jesus we love and worship really is alive? The apostle Paul encourages us to make use of every opportunity to speak for the Lord (2 Timothy 4:2).

Another lesson from someone who was brought back to life is found in John 11:17–44 where we read of the resurrection of Lazarus. As he rises from his place of burial we're told that he was still bound in his grave clothes and the Lord gave the instruction: *'Take off the grave clothes and let him go!'*

So many of us can be restricted in our spiritual growth because we're still bound to things of the past. Jesus came to bring us life in all its fullness (John 10:10). For us to find the reality of what that means we need to heed the writer of Hebrews and *'throw off everything that hinders'* (Hebrews 12:1). Although we can be alive (as Lazarus was), it may be necessary to be cut off, or be released, from our grave clothes, so that we can move on and be able to really enjoy and demonstrate the fullness of new life.

PRAYER: *Help me, Lord, to see those things in my life which are holding me back from fully enjoying all that You have for me, and then help me to cut myself free with the help of your Spirit, in Jesus' name, Amen.*

FEBRUARY 17 | YOU ALSO OUGHT TO WASH ONE ANOTHER'S FEET

LIZ GRIFFIN

> *If I then, your Lord and Teacher, have washed your feet, you also ought to wash one another's feet. For I have given you an example, that you also should do just as I have done to you.*
>
> John 13:14–15, ESV

Peter certainly didn't understand what Jesus was doing when He started to wash his dirty feet on that evening they were celebrating Passover. Jesus told him he would understand it later. Jesus explained that, even though He was the leader, He could humble Himself and take the place of a servant to them, out of love. How Jesus must have longed for them to get the message! Once before He'd told them, *'But whoever would be great among you must be your servant, and whoever would be first among you must be slave of all'* (Mark 10:43–44, ESV). He wanted them to follow His example in loving and serving one another and said, *'If you know these things, blessed are you if you do them'* (John 13:17, ESV).

After Judas had gone away to betray Jesus to His enemies, Jesus taught them many other things and He started by giving them a great commandment. *'A new commandment I give to you, that you love one another: just as I have loved you, you also are to love one another'* (John 13:34, ESV).

I find this teaching of Jesus is so easy to understand. But it's not so easy for me to put it into practice. I wonder whether I can really believe those words of Jesus, *'It is more blessed to give than to receive'* (Acts 20:35, ESV).

I may not be required to literally wash the dirty feet of my friends and colleagues but the principle of it remains. Can I do acts of service out of a loving heart without grumbling or complaining? Can I make an effort to serve the needs of others and do it to the extent that I find pleasure and satisfaction in it?

PRAYER: *Dear Heavenly Father, I want to be more like Jesus and follow His example. I know it means dying to self and looking for opportunities to bless others. Help me not to be too lazy or indifferent to the needs of others, in Jesus' name, Amen.*

FEBRUARY 18 | FOLLOWING JESUS

JILL SOUTHERN-JONES

> *Peter answered him, 'We have left everything to follow you! What then will there be for us?' Jesus said to them, 'I tell you the truth ...'*
>
> Matthew 19:27–28

Following Jesus is more than just putting your feet down in someone else's pathway. True followers of Jesus face great challenges and have great opportunities.

There is a real cost and a real sacrifice when we choose to become a disciple of Jesus Christ. Jesus told us we would need to take up our cross daily and follow Him. The challenge is, 'Is Jesus worth it? Is Jesus worth your sacrifice?' We all know that the answer to that question is a resounding 'Yes!' But it is not always easy to make the right choice when faced with the temptations of life – many of which can seem very attractive.

We all need to know the fact that God has a dream and vision for each of our lives. And the key to knowing God's unshakeable call on your life is to get to know God better! Do you really know God? Do you spend quality time with Him? Getting to know God takes time – *'Be still, and know that I am God'* (Psalm 46:10). God will test what's in our hearts, but the good news is that God will always use what He's tested.

This 'knowing God' is much more than an intellectual knowledge of Him; it's a deeper understanding than that. In your heart you need to be at peace with yourself, to know 'I'm OK'. You need to know your uniqueness and giftings – those talents God has given you. You need to know yourself and your abilities – even your limitations.

But above all you need to know the heart of God for you. *'For I know the plans I have for you,' declares the LORD, 'plans to prosper you and not to harm you, plans to give you hope and a future'* (Jeremiah 29:11).

Let's pray as we go through today that when we're tested, we'll make the right choices as we follow Him and then come forth as gold.

PRAYER: *Lord, I present myself afresh to You today. Search me and know my heart, for I desire, with Your help, to walk in Your ways and in Your destiny for my life. Help me to hear Your voice and to know You more, in Jesus' name, Amen.*

FEBRUARY 19 | GOD REALLY KNOWS YOU!

LINDSEY HANEKOM

You know what I am going to say even before I say it, LORD.

Psalm 139:4, NLT

On a recent visit from my mum I found myself, on several occasions, telling her exactly what my son, Kyle, was about to do. I just know how he will respond in certain circumstances. For example, I know that if I take down the biscuit tin I will very quickly hear the word, 'Please'. I also know that if I turn the tap on in the bath upstairs he will run up the stairs shouting, 'Bath!' and start trying to strip his clothes off. The list could go on and on. Such knowledge is only available because I am constantly with Kyle. I watch him in every situation, for both my enjoyment and to ensure his safety.

It reminded me of this verse of Scripture. God knows us so well that He knows exactly how we will respond in any given situation. He isn't dictating to us what to say or do but He simply knows us and therefore He knows how we will react to every circumstance of life.

God not only watches us to ensure we're safe; He actually enjoys watching His children as they go through life. Just as I smile with a knowing smile when Kyle behaves in certain ways, God must look at us with a smile as well. He loves knowing us, He loves watching us as we go through our daily lives and He loves us unfailingly, even when He knows we're going to do something wrong.

As much as I know my son, God knows each one of us infinitely more. He knows every move we're about to make and every word we're about to speak. God knows us so thoroughly that it's impossible to hide from Him, as it says in verse 12 of this psalm.

As much as we would like to think we are unpredictable and that we can hide our behaviour from God, we can't. There is such freedom in knowing this truth; knowing that no matter what we think, do or say, God knows us and still loves us unfailingly.

Prayer: *Father God, You know me completely, without exception. Help me to rest and find freedom in knowing that You love me unfailingly even though nothing is hidden from You. Amen.*

February 20 | Red Key, Blue Key

Paul Lawrence

Be self-controlled and alert. Your enemy the devil prowls around like a roaring lion looking for someone to devour.

1 Peter 5:8

I had a bright idea that had surprising consequences the other month. The problem was that I had two door keys on my key ring that looked the same. One for my home and one for the office. I kept putting the wrong key into the wrong door and this got really frustrating. To solve the problem I went out and bought two little plastic covers for them so I could tell them apart. To make it a bit of fun I chose a red cover and a blue cover.

For a joke, or what seemed like a bright idea, I put the red one on the office door as red means danger and trouble (during each day I have to make some tricky decisions) and I put the blue cover on my home door as this had a meaning of peace and quiet for me.

And then it started to go wrong. Even though I had put the red cover on my office door key as a bit of joke for myself and to make it easy to remember, things started to go wobbly. A mindset came over me every time I reached for the red key for my office door that this was a place of danger and trouble. I had more problems in my office life than before, and it puzzled me. It suddenly dawned on me that I had given the enemy rights to my office life that I never wanted to, just by calling my office a place of danger and trouble as a joke. Peter talks about the enemy as a roaring lion looking for someone to devour, and, unwittingly, I had given the enemy an opportunity to attack me. *'Be self-controlled and alert. Your enemy the devil prowls around like a roaring lion looking for someone to devour'* (1 Peter 5:8).

The truth is the Lord has given me this office and this job and even though times might get tough He will guide me through. The burden is His to carry and not my own. I had, in effect, said that wasn't the way I see my job or office, and that I expected to have problems all the time during my working day. After a few days I switched the key colours around and now have blue for my office and red for my home key. I haven't made any statements on what the colours mean, but just see them now as a way of remembering which key fits which door. Things have returned to normal again. Some days are challenging, some relaxing, some have difficult decisions to be made and some are times to share a joke with fellow colleagues, but all are now free from pronouncements.

The goods news is that, if we have put things into our lives and uttered words or pronouncements over them, sometimes, as in my case, as a joke, we can say sorry to the Lord and break the power of the words in the name of Jesus, and declare and live by the truth.

PRAYER: *Thank You, Lord, for everything You have given me. Today, if there is something in my life that has given the enemy a foothold, please would You show me so I can deal with it, in Jesus' name, Amen.*

February 21 | A Plumb Line not a Pendulum

David Cross

> *Justice will be the measuring line for the foundation, and honesty will be its plumb line. Hailstorms will sweep away all the lies you depend on, and floods will destroy your security.*
>
> Isaiah 28:17, GNB

We recently held a weekend teaching course looking at the subject of alternative therapies. There are hundreds of medical treatments being offered these days which claim to bring restoration to body, mind and spirit. Unlike the science-based treatments normally available through the doctor, the results of these alternative therapies are rarely quantifiable or repeatable. They are very often referred to as *'holistic'* treatments, recognising the healing needs in the whole of our being.

Many involve the diagnosis of our spiritual condition, looking at the unseen *'energy flows'* in and around the body. The Bible would call these practices, which sometimes use devices like pendulums, divination. They are based on ancient occult techniques. The diagnosis is followed by a variety of procedures which aim to bring balance to the spiritual disorder within us, in turn bringing healing to our physical disorder.

In one sense these practices are along the right lines. We *do* have a problem with the spiritual condition of our lives. Jesus says, *'Blessed are the poor in spirit, for theirs is the kingdom of heaven'* (Matthew 5:3). The problem is that none of these alternative therapies recognise that the *sin* of mankind is the root of the spiritual disorder. Throughout the Bible, God shows His people that their problems are the result of being out of line with His laws and commands. God uses the picture of a plumb line to illustrate how He views the distortion caused by sin.

Doctors do amazing work in bringing relief to our physical bodies. Praise God for all that medical science has given to us. However, if our *spiritual* condition truly needs restoration, I suggest that there's only one safe person to go to for both diagnosis and treatment. His name is Jesus. Our spiritual condition is best viewed with the plumb line of God's Word, not with the pendulum of the occultist.

PRAYER: *Lord, I ask that You will forgive me for any times when I have not looked to You for the right spiritual answers to problems in my life. I am grateful for the plumb line of Your Word and that I can always trust what You say and do, in Jesus' name, Amen.*

FEBRUARY 22 | INTIMACY WITH THE FATHER

JILLY LYON-TAYLOR

> *Who is he who will devote himself to be close to me? declares the LORD.*
>
> Jeremiah 30:21

If someone were to ask you what you were devoting your life to, I wonder what your answer would be – career or family, the Church, service for God or a particular ministry? Valid though all these things may be, this verse shows that above all God wants us to devote ourselves to being close to Him.

God chose us before the creation of the world for relationship with Him and He predestined us to be adopted into His family (Ephesians 1:4–5). When we receive Jesus as Saviour and believe in His name, the adoption happens and we become children of God (John 1:12). While many human fathers are absent, distant, or do not make time to be with their children, God is the perfect Father who wants to be with His children, loving us, protecting us, providing for us, comforting us, healing us and bringing the discipline we need. He is always there for us, but we don't always choose to come close to Him. We know that sin separates us from God, but sometimes it is our busyness, our preoccupation with self, with our problems, even with our work for Him, that keeps us from intimacy with Him. Relationships need time and effort. Are we going to devote ourselves as a first priority to being close to Him?

To do this, we need to make time for Him – time just to be in His presence with no agenda, to sit at His feet, to listen to Him, to hear His heart. This will bring pleasure to Him as our Father. It will also result in us changing more into His likeness and being more effective for Him. Moses' face was radiant after He had spoken with the Lord (Exodus 34:29). What about us?

PRAYER: *Lord, I am sorry that I have not made it my first priority to be close to You and that I have allowed busyness, distractions, and even my work for You to crowd out my intimacy with You. Please forgive me, and help me to get my priorities right in future. In Jesus' name I pray, Amen.*

FEBRUARY 23 | GOD HOVERS OVER US

DAVID SILVESTER

Like birds hovering overhead, the LORD Almighty will shield Jerusalem.

Isaiah 31:5

From our study window we can look out towards the Bowland Hills, but one morning something that caught my eye was not the beauty of the hills, but a bird of prey. It was hovering, waiting to pounce upon some unsuspecting creature to eat for its breakfast.

Observing this basic incident of nature reminded me of how our loving Heavenly Father is constantly hovering over us. But He's not waiting to 'pounce on us' in judgement. He's waiting for the right moment to lavish His love and blessings upon us.

It's sad to hear some Christians go through a period of difficulty and say, 'I think God is judging me', or 'God has sent this trial to punish me for something', or 'Why is God testing me with this?'

James 1:13–15 says: '*When tempted, no-one should say, "God is tempting me." For God cannot be tempted by evil, nor does he tempt anyone; but each one is tempted when, by his own evil desire, he is dragged away and enticed. Then, after desire has conceived, it gives birth to sin; and sin when it is full-grown, gives birth to death.*'

James is saying that temptation is the test of a person's moral strength to resist sin, and that God's holy nature is such that there is nothing in Him for sin to appeal to. Sin is totally foreign to God's nature.

What we need to recognise is that many of the things in life we might consider as trials have deep roots, and these roots need to be dealt with. God, in His love for us, hovers over us, longing to pour His rich blessings into us, but if there's some sin that hasn't been dealt with at its root we need to face the fact that our sin separates us from God (Isaiah 59:2). It could be preventing us from receiving His blessings.

The words of 1 John 1:9 are so true: *'If we confess our sins, he is faithful and just to forgive us our sins and purify us from all unrighteousness.'*

In ministering to many people, and getting to the root of a problem, we've witnessed amazing healings as they've confessed (spoken out loud and owned up to their sins in the presence of witnesses) and repented of those sins. This is where much healing begins.

PRAYER: *Dear Lord God, holy and awesome God, thank You for the way You watch over me in love. Please forgive me for thinking You're judging me when I experience problems. Please reveal to me any sin that lies at the root of the problem and give me the courage to seek help and have the problem dealt with in the proper manner, in Jesus' name. Amen.*

FEBRUARY 24 | DOING IT OUR WAY

MALCOLM WOOD

> *But Naaman went away angry and said, 'I thought he would surely come out to me and stand and call on the name of the LORD his God, wave his hand over the spot and cure me of my leprosy.'*
>
> 2 Kings 5:11

As a boy, whenever I expressed my surprise that something had happened contrary to my expectation and said,'Well! I thought ...' my father would respond by saying, 'Naaman thought things too – but he was wrong!' We often get it wrong, don't we? We think we know how things are going to happen, and how God will act in response to a particular situation. But the problem is with our perspective. We only see things from our viewpoint – not God's.

Isaiah 55:8–9 tells us quite clearly that God's ways are different from ours: *'For my thoughts are not your thoughts, neither are your ways my ways,' declares the LORD. 'As the heavens are higher than the earth, so are my ways higher than your ways and my thoughts than your thoughts.'* Yet it's a lesson that He has to teach us over and over again.

It's a lesson that Naaman had to learn. He eventually came to acknowledge the sovereignty of the one true God – the God of Israel. If only we could learn to 'enquire of God' as David did (1 Chronicles 14:10, 14). Instead we charge off and fight the battle our way and then wonder why we aren't successful. We need to learn to ask God for direction and join in with His plans. But instead we make our own plans, and then ask God to bless them.

Although Naaman was a successful and highly respected leader he had a problem and sought an answer. In the process he learnt to listen to others, humble himself and submit to what God was asking of him. The result was his complete healing and all the glory went to God.

The same can happen for us whether we're a leader or not. Frank Sinatra's song *'I did it my way'* was extremely popular for many years, but the truth is we must learn to do it *God's* way, not *our* way.

PRAYER: *Lord Jesus, I'm sorry for so often wanting to be in charge and doing things my way. Please help me to learn to ask You to direct my plans and give me the grace to submit to Your way for my life, so that You get all the glory. Amen.*

FEBRUARY 25 | OUR GREAT INHERITANCE

JILLY LYON-TAYLOR

> *In his great mercy he has given us new birth into a living hope through the resurrection of Jesus Christ from the dead, and into an inheritance that can never perish, spoil or fade.*
>
> 1 Peter 1:3–4

My mother died recently, but before she went she told each of us about the things she wanted us to have from her belongings. These things were earmarked for us, and her hope was that we would use them and enjoy the inheritance she had left for us.

These verses in Peter's letter tell us that in a similar way, once we are adopted into His family, God promises each of us an inheritance. Unlike earthly goods, this inheritance can never perish, spoil or fade. It's not vulnerable to fire, theft or fluctuating financial markets! But just as I had to claim and collect the items left to me by my mother, we each need to come to God to receive what He has promised us, and we need to use and enjoy the benefits of each aspect.

Our inheritance in Him includes eternal life, forgiveness of sin, abundant life now, health, healing, provision, security, unconditional love and acceptance, and so much more, but most of us are not living in the benefit of all that has been promised.

Romans 8:17 tells us that as God's children we are *'heirs of God and co-heirs with Christ'*. The fullness of our inheritance may not be manifest until we go to be with the Lord, but as heirs of the King of kings we should be living extraordinary lives now in the knowledge of who our Father is and what He has promised us! Are we? Why not come to Him today and start to live in more of the benefits of your inheritance now?

PRAYER: *Heavenly Father, thank You that as Your child You have promised me an inheritance that can never perish, spoil or fade. Forgive me for ignoring aspects of my inheritance. Please help me to live in the benefit of all that You have promised me. In Jesus' name I pray, Amen.*

FEBRUARY 26 | THE TRUTH ABOUT LIES

JILL SOUTHERN-JONES

> *You belong to your father, the devil, and you want to carry out your father's desire. He was a murderer from the beginning, not holding to the truth, for there is no truth in him. When he lies, he speaks his native language, for he is a liar and the father of lies.*
>
> John 8:44

The truth about Satan's lies is that we very easily assimilate them into our belief system as truth. They can feel very true! I'm thinking of such as: 'God can't use you!', 'God isn't interested in you!', 'God doesn't really love you!', and 'You have completely blown it with God!'

Thinking about this I once asked God to show me any lies that I believed as truth, and this lie came quickly into my mind: 'God could abandon me in the moment of my deepest need!' How awful it was for me to believe this lie, but it felt very true. The purpose of the lies of Satan is to separate us from faith in God.

But I believe that Jesus speaks clearly to us. In John 10:2–5 Jesus uses a figure of speech about a man who is a shepherd. He calls his sheep by name and leads them out. The sheep know his voice and follow him, but they run away from a stranger because they don't recognise a stranger's voice. Then Jesus explains clearly that He is 'the Good Shepherd'. *'My sheep listen to my voice; I know them, and they follow me'* (John 10:27). Jesus also said, *'I am the way and the truth and the life'* (John 14:6). So I asked Jesus to speak truth to me that would disempower this lie. I sensed Him saying, 'I will never ever leave you or forsake you, especially not in the moment of your deepest need!' The lie was cancelled!

How could I have believed such a terrible lie of the enemy? Do you think it is possible that the father of lies has lied to you? Believing lies holds us into fear and rejection and many other things. Sometimes before we can be free we need to ask Jesus, who is the truth, to speak His truth into us personally. Jesus' truth has greater power than Satan's lies.

PRAYER: *We thank You, Jesus, that You taught us that the knowledge of the truth will set us free. Please come and expose to us today any of Satan's lies that we believe are true. Please speak to us by name, that we may walk more deeply in Your truth. Thank You, Jesus. Amen.*

FEBRUARY 27 | THERMOMETERS AND THERMOSTATS

MALCOLM WOOD

> *I know all the things you do, that you are neither hot nor cold. I wish you were one or the other!*
>
> Revelation 3:15, NLT

During the recent cold spell, which we in the UK have been experiencing, no doubt much attention has been given to thermometer readings and thermostat settings.

I once came across a small article about these two devices.

A thermometer is placed in a room, often hanging on the wall, and enables us to see the temperature of the room at a glance. It has no connections to anything else and has no power to make the room hot or cold. It just reflects its environment and adjusts itself to it.

A thermostat can look very much like a thermometer and it also hangs on the wall but, instead of being alone and individual, it has connections –

powerful connections! If the room's hot, it has ways of making it cooler, and if it's cold, it has ways of making it warmer.

Instead of being affected by its environment, the thermostat changes that environment. It does something about its surroundings, whereas the thermometer adjusts itself to them.

Most people can be classified in a similar way. Thermometer personalities are chameleons. They adjust and compromise. They take on the moral and spiritual temperature of the group they are with. They merely reflect their environment. They do nothing to change it.

Thermostat personalities are changers. They lead and transform. They aren't content with the 'status quo'. They aren't complacent. They're concerned and burdened. They care. Things and conditions must improve. So, by using the connections they have, they send messages of prayer to God (the powerhouse above): '*We need help. Things must be different. The moral and spiritual climate must be changed. It's too cold. It's freezing. We desperately need fire and heat to melt and change our world, our nation, our town, our churches, our hearts.*'

The question is: are you a thermometer or a thermostat?

PRAYER: *Dear Lord, forgive me for those times when I've been complacent about those things that are going on around me – the things that make Your heart sad. Fill me afresh with Your Spirit. Give me Your passion for all that's good, honest and true. I want to influence those around me, so that they're directed to You, in Jesus' name, Amen.*

FEBRUARY 28 | YOU LIFT ME UP!

DAVID CROSS

But I am in pain and despair; lift me up, O God, and save me!

Psalm 69:29, GNB

When I was at a Christian seminar in Northern Ireland recently, I was intrigued to hear the speaker say these words: 'With Jesus, I am never down. I am either up or getting up.'

Life's full of ups and downs and sometimes the lows can be very low. It would be unreality to claim that our journey as a follower of Jesus is always on an emotional or spiritual mountaintop. Christians have bad days and sometimes these can extend into bad weeks and more. However, the great news is that we have now become part of One who is far above all rule and authority and power and dominion, and every name that is named, not only in this age but also in the one to come (Ephesians 1:21).

In other words whatever problem is pressing down on us at any moment of our lives, Jesus is above it! What is more, He invites us to be lifted up and to be seated with Him in the heavenly places (Ephesians 2:6). By ourselves it is impossible to truly rise above the troubles of this world, but in Him we have the opportunity to get up and to look down on all that would otherwise overwhelm us.

If you need to get up today, take His hand and find that place with Jesus which has been prepared just for you. Seeing life from His perspective makes all the difference. There is absolutely nothing more powerful than Him and He will be in charge for eternity.

PRAYER: *Father, thank You that no issue is bigger than Jesus. I choose today to get up and sit with Him above every problem. In Jesus' name I pray, Amen.*

FEBRUARY 29 | THE WAY OF LOVE

MARGARET SILVESTER

> *A new command I give you: Love one another. As I have loved you, so you must love one another. By this all men will know that you are my disciples, if you love one another.*
>
> John 13:34–35

We live in a world without absolutes, where pluralism is a common belief. No one religion is thought to be the sole and exclusive source of truth and all religions are held to be different interpretations of revelation from the same God. Like us, the early Christians lived in a pluralistic world and were known as those who belonged to 'The Way'. This title recalls Jesus' description of Himself when He said, '*I am the way*' (John 14:6), the one and only way of salvation and the way to the Father.

For the first believers to claim that Jesus is the only way caused much controversy (Acts 19:23). To exclusively follow Him meant the death sentence (Acts 22:4), being written off as a sect (Acts 24:14) or being tried for one's faith.

In the Roman world, where emperors were worshipped as gods, onlookers were puzzled by the followers of The Way, who worshipped one God. They were different. They were marked out by what they believed and by what they did. Their faith was a living faith and they lived it out in a hostile world.

The Way was, and still is, the way of love. The early Christians won converts, not simply by what they said, but also by their kindness and compassion for one another. Ordinary people looked on and wanted to live the same way they did. Tertullian, a second-century writer, said of them, 'Look how they love one another and how they are ready to die for each other!'

We have the words of Jesus Himself: *'A new command I give you: Love one another. As I have loved you, so you must love one another. By this all men will know that you are my disciples, if you love one another.'* When the world looks on and sees love in action among believers, they too will want what we have. The word used for this kind of love is 'agape' love. The essence of it is self-sacrifice. It's unique and is distinguished by its nature and character. It's a love that is of, and from, God – whose nature is love itself. It's the love outsiders saw in the followers of The Way, and the love that drew them into living faith.

PRAYER: *Heavenly Father, thank You for the uniqueness of Jesus. Thank You that by the power of the Holy Spirit I too can live in the world and be marked out as different. Today, take my lips and let them speak as Jesus spoke. Take my mind and let me think as Jesus thought. Take my heart and let me love as Jesus loved, so that the people in my world will be drawn to Him. Amen.*

MARCH 1 | RIGHTS OR PRIVILEGES?

JULIE SMITH

He shall eat at my table like one of the king's sons.

2 Samuel 9:11, NKJV

I recently went to see the film, *The King's Speech,* which tells the story of King George VI's accession to the throne after his brother's abdication. There is one scene where the abdicating king angrily demands, *'Don't I have any rights?'* to which his brother, who is being forced into a role he wasn't born for, answers, *'You have many privileges.'*

After watching the film, I began to think how, in a society that is fast being overtaken with the issue of 'human rights', even as Christians it can be so easy to be sucked into having this kind of heart attitude. We can have thoughts like, *'I deserve better than this'*, *'What I want is important'*, *'Other people should consider how I feel'* or *'God promises healing – I'm angry that He hasn't healed me yet.'* We don't always voice these thoughts, but deep down we can be fostering the kinds of attitudes that underpin them which are, in reality, rooted in self-interest and rebellion against God.

As Christians we know that we gave up any 'human rights' we ever had at the fall, and every single time we sin. The simple truth is: we don't have any human rights! But we do have many privileges.

I love the story of Mephibosheth, the crippled son of Jonathan (2 Samuel 4:4–6), who also lost all his rights. He lost his rights to the privileged life of royalty when his grandfather, Saul, and his father, Jonathan, were killed and David became king. But remembering the covenant of friendship he had with Jonathan, David later sought out Mephibosheth with a desire to show him *'the kindness of God'* (2 Samuel 9:3, NKJV).

Mephibosheth knew he had lost his rights to royalty and fell on his face, prostrating himself before the king in fear (2 Samuel 9:6). But David, a type of Jesus, said to him, *'Do not fear, for I will surely show you kindness ... and restore ... you'* (2 Samuel 9:7, NKJV) and, true to his word, David gave back to him all the privileges of being one of the king's sons. 2 Samuel 9:13 tells us that *'he [Mephibosheth] ate continually at the king's table'* (NKJV).

We gave up any 'human rights' we ever had at the fall, and every single time we sin. The simple truth is: we don't have any human rights! But we do have many privileges.

What a great story and a valuable reminder to us, who have no rights, that because of Jesus and His ultimate sacrifice, paying the penalty of death for each one of us on the cross, we have been given many totally undeserved privileges. Like Mephibosheth, we are redeemed, restored to sonship and have a place at our Father's table, where we can enjoy intimate relationship with Him and feed on His Word and all His wonderful promises to us.

Prayer: *Father, I'm sorry for the times when I have forgotten that the only righteousness I have comes from the shed blood of Jesus and being clothed in His righteousness. Please help me not to be someone who's seeking for 'my rights' to be met, but one who is motivated by thankfulness for the undeserved privilege of being Your child and the many blessings You have poured into my life. Amen.*

March 2 | Checklist Christianity!

Andy Taylor

Jesus replied, 'You must love the Lord your God with all your heart, all your soul, and all your mind.' This is the first and greatest commandment.

Matthew 22:37–38, NLT

Imagine the scene … Throughout life a man is told that in order to be a 'good husband' he should 'do' certain things for his wife. If he does them, she will know that he loves her and they will have a happy marriage! The list might include things like: have a daily hug, tell her you love her each day and buy flowers every week. To make his 'job' as a husband easier, he might even make this into a checklist – just to make sure he doesn't forget anything.

Let's be clear, everything on the list is great, but what happens if it just becomes a list of jobs to be done? They are now done out of a sense of duty rather than a heart of love. How would the wife feel? That the words are empty? Would she question her husband's love for her?

Has this checklist mentality crept into your relationship with God? Do you have a list of things you 'must do' in order to be a 'good Christian'? This list might include: praying twice a day, reading the Bible every morning and giving to the poor. Again, all of these things are fantastic, but what happens if they are being done out of a sense of duty rather than a heart of love?

The truth is that God just wants relationship with us. He wants the motivation behind our actions to be love for Him rather than duty. The above verses talk about the quality and quantity of love that we should have for God. We are to love Him with ALL our heart, soul and mind. That basically means that we are to love Him with everything we are. The challenge for today is to ask God to rekindle our love for Him so that our life is no longer dominated by a checklist but rather a love that comes from our whole heart, soul and mind.

Prayer: *Forgive me, Lord, for times when my heart and my actions have not been joined – when I have done the right thing, but for the wrong reasons. Help me to be so motivated by love, that to serve You is a joy and not a chore, in Jesus' name, Amen.*

March 3 | One of Those Days!

Malcolm Wood

Though the fig tree may not blossom, nor fruit be on the vines ... Yet I will I rejoice in the LORD, I will joy in the God of my salvation. The LORD God is my strength.

Habakkuk 3:17–19, NKJV

At some time or other we all have what can only be described as one of those days! You know – the sort of day that starts when you wake up and realise that the alarm clock hasn't gone off and you're late! In your panic you fall out of bed, trip over the slippers left at the bottom of the bed, go into the bathroom and discover there's no hot water and the toothpaste tube is empty. Stumbling over the loose piece of carpet on the landing (which you've been meaning to fix for ages) you rush downstairs to find the kitchen sink is blocked and, added to which, you burn the toast. Things don't seem to improve outside the house either, because the car doesn't want to start and you're too late for the bus. So the day continues, until later you eventually collapse back into bed with a sigh of relief saying, 'Thank goodness today's over. It's just been one of those days!'

You may be able to identify to a greater or lesser degree with something like this, but hopefully not too often with the kind of day described by Habakkuk in chapter 3, where we have a picture of a terrible set of circumstances. There's no food, no cattle, no crops, no harvest and no prospect of provision at all. It's a picture of utter deprivation, destitution and hopelessness. If someone was faced with a situation like this, it would be easy to understand that he or she would just give up. That's not the case here!

Having described such dire conditions, Habakkuk, in verse 18, declares, '*Yet I will rejoice*.' How could this be so? The subsequent verses explain it all. He had come to realise that true joy and satisfaction are not dependent upon material possessions. Even amidst adversity and difficulty he recognised that:

1 God was his Saviour (verse 18)
2 God was sovereign (verse 19) and therefore in control of everything
3 God was his source of strength (verse 19) and therefore able to help him in every situation
4 His safety and security were found in God (verse 19)

May the Lord enable us all to trust Him more, especially when the going gets tough.

PRAYER: *Thank You, Lord, that whatever happens You are still the Sovereign Lord – and I can trust You. In the midst of difficult days I pray that You will be my inner strength and my encouragement at all times, in Jesus' name, Amen.*

MARCH 4 | REINFORCED AND ROOTED

JOHN BERRY

> *I pray that out of his glorious riches he may strengthen you with power through his Spirit in your inner being, so that Christ may dwell in your hearts through faith. And I pray that you, being rooted and established in love, may have power …*
>
> Ephesians 3:16–18

The other day I was helping a friend of my daughter to lay some concrete on her front driveway. The road level was several inches above the drive level, and we were making a slope to connect the two. The infill for this slope was probably not the best of materials. It was crushable, loose and had a lot of gravel in it. I was concerned that we might put the concrete on and the infill would give way and the new slope would collapse. Our remedy was to put a sheet of reinforcing steel mesh in the concrete, to provide the necessary strength even if the infill were to shift a bit. Time will tell if we got it right!

The apostle Paul knew that human beings have weak points in them. His prayer for the Ephesian Christians included a plea that the Lord would provide the necessary reinforcing out of his glorious riches to enable these believers to continue their walk with God. He wanted them to be able to grow in their knowledge and experience of God's love. He prayed for the Lord to strengthen them powerfully through the Spirit of Christ, so they would be rooted and established in love. The result would be Christians with an inner spiritual strengthening – solid believers with a reinforced core!

There are times when we may feel that we're on shaky ground. Maybe we're moving into uncertain futures or ministries, or maybe we're living in a hostile environment. There's a danger we could collapse. Let's take Paul's prayer for the Ephesian Christians for ourselves and seek the Lord to strengthen us by His Spirit, so we'll remain rooted and grounded in love, not crushed and broken by our situation.

Prayer: *There are times when the foundations of my life have been inadequate – sometimes because of what I've done and sometimes because of what others have done. Help me to see where reinforcement is needed, so that I will not break under the pressures of life, in Jesus' name, Amen.*

March 5 | In the Pit!

Jill Southern-Jones

But they saw him in the distance, and before he reached them, they plotted to kill him.

Genesis 37:18–19

Well, they would see Joseph in the distance with the sun glittering on his coat of many colours, wouldn't they? Joseph's brothers were still angry at the teenager's behaviour. So they decided to teach him a lesson and stripped off his robe (verse 23) and threw him into a pit. Joseph must have been thankful that there was no water in the pit or he would have quickly drowned!

Have you ever felt you were in a pit? The pit makes us totally dependent on God. Maybe it's a pit of depression, a pit of rejection or even a pit of failure. We need to acknowledge that we can't climb out of such a pit ourselves and, instead, throw ourselves into the arms of our kind and loving God.

What would happen to Joseph's dreams now? What do you think was going on down in the pit? Did Joseph know the presence of the Lord in the pit? Did he really call on the name of the Lord?

The pit can be a very humbling experience and gives time for reflection. God was starting to prepare Joseph for his destiny. When you read the stories of God's saints, you will find that all of them at some time or other experienced being in a pit. God will always test those he uses and use those He tests.

When other people seek to throw you into a pit, can you continue to obey God alone, even when circumstances have turned against you? Are you hearing God's Word in your heart and reading the Word of God, so you can learn to trust in Him and know His voice? Are you developing your relationship with Him?

Joseph was rescued from the pit. God will rescue us from our pits because He's chosen us to belong to Him and we are in an unbreakable, covenantal relationship with Him. We not only know God, but God also knows us, and loves us unconditionally. God doesn't want us to become pit dwellers! Does it feel that you are down a pit? Have you asked God to rescue you from your pit?

Prayer: *Help me, Lord, to trust You in every circumstance of life – even when it feels like I'm in a pit. I know that You will rescue me out of the slimy pit and put my feet upon a rock. Be with me through each step of today, as I choose to trust You with my life, in Jesus' name. Amen.*

March 6 | A Different Message

Ian Coates

See to it that no-one takes you captive through hollow and deceptive philosophy, which depends on human tradition and the basic principles of this world rather than on Christ.

Colossians 2:8

In this letter Paul tells us that Christians are complete in Christ, not lacking anything or having deficiencies as the Gnostics of the day were teaching. We're complete in Christ Jesus and I believe we should no longer consider ourselves sinners but saints (who still have the potential to sin)! This completeness we have in Jesus means putting off the sinful nature, resurrection from spiritual death, forgiveness of sin, and deliverance from legalism and evil spirits (Colossians 2:11–15).

Many Christians are taking on the world's standards, yet seem totally unaware of the fact. The challenge to us as Christians is, *'Can we be identified as different from the rest of the world? Or are we just trying to conform like everyone else?'* But we can be *'men of a different spirit'* (see Numbers 14:24). Shouldn't we stand out from the crowd? Or are our fears and inhibitions holding us back from being the people God created us to be?

God calls us to be a holy people. Are we seeking a life of ease and pleasure, or are we seeking to move into our God-given destiny, work and calling? How many seek position and status rather than a servant heart? God has not called us to success, but faithfulness, fuelled by compassion.

The world is gripped by fear but, as believers, we can know freedom and what it means to be loved by a Father who is a covenant-keeping God. We are loved and accepted. And that means we don't need to live in the fear of being rejected by anyone, because our security is in Him. We're also constantly bombarded in the media with the realms of unreality. Films, TV programmes and soaps all lead away from the truth and reality of our lives. But it's only as we encounter the truth of Jesus that our lives are going to be transformed.

Jesus came to set the captives free, heal the broken-hearted, and take all our pain on the cross. Jesus came that we might have life, and have it more abundantly. We do have a different message to bring to the world, not just a theory or theology, but a life-transforming experience in Jesus. Let's lay hold of all that He's won for us on the cross. He's a covenant-keeping God who has made every provision for us in Christ Jesus.

PRAYER: *Thank You, Jesus, that in You I can be made complete. Help me to come into a deeper and closer relationship with our Father and to experience all the blessing that You have won for me on the cross. I choose to put away old habits of behaviour and choose to face the reality of my life knowing that You can bring about the changes that are going to glorify Your name, in Jesus' name, Amen.*

MARCH 7 | I AM THE WAY

DAVID CROSS

Jesus answered him, 'I am the way, the truth, and the life; no one goes to the Father except by me.'

John 14:6, GNB

The other day I had a phone call from a distressed mum. 'My seven-year-old son is wanting to join in the Judo class at school. Everyone else is doing it and he will be so upset if I stop him. The teachers say that it is just good exercise.'

Oh how hard it is for Christian parents to know where to draw the line in giving godly boundaries to their children. We don't want to spoil their fun but we do want to keep them from harm. The important thing is that parents should be able to make their decisions with sufficient understanding, as well as prayerfully seeking God's direction. I tried to give this mum a little understanding of this particular issue.

I sent her a typical quote describing the basis of Judo as seen by one non-Christian practitioner and commentator: 'In the course of development, there was once a period when Judo was simply an art to fell down the opponent and in another period more importance was attached to physical culture. But the purpose is to be true to the standard of human life and its significance so rich that no simple words can express its implication. In other words, there is a union of body and soul, containing spiritual and physical factors put together.' The word Judo actually means the way of submission. It comes from roots in the martial art of Jujitsu, an ancient Samurai combat technique without weapons. These techniques almost always followed philosophical as well as practical paths of training. If there is a philosophical or spiritual aspect to the foundation of any activity in which we are invited to join, it is important that we take time to consider that it is truly safe.

Jesus knows our spiritual needs and declares Himself to be the best spiritual path to follow. In fact He says that He is the only way both to the Father and to the abundant spiritual life which He desires for each of God's children. In His mercy, God will look for us even on a wrong spiritual path which we have taken, but He will only ever point us to the one true path that is Jesus.

PRAYER: *Oh Father, give us the wisdom to make right choices for ourselves, and for those for whom we are responsible, so that we do not stray too far off the safe path of our spiritual journey with You, in Jesus' name, Amen.*

MARCH 8 | HOW FIRM IS YOUR ANCHOR?

JILLY LYON-TAYLOR

We have this hope as an anchor for the soul, firm and secure.

Hebrews 6:19

Recently my husband and I spent a few days in Devon where we were able to enjoy some wonderful coastal walks. We passed many little bays and river estuaries where yachts and small fishing boats were moored in the water. Each boat was secured to its mooring which in turn was firmly anchored in the sea bed. As the tide turned or the wind changed direction, the boats would turn to face into whatever was coming at them, and they would bob up and down on the surface of the waves, no matter how rough the sea became.

Seeing them made me think of the anchor that we have in Jesus Christ. When our lives are firmly anchored in Him, we can turn to face head-on any storms that come our way, and we can also hold firm against every tide of opinion. No matter how rough the circumstances of our lives become, we will be able to ride waves of difficulty and adversity and not be overcome by them. Hope in Jesus Christ is an anchor that will never fail or disappoint us. He is the same yesterday, today and forever (Hebrews 13:8), and He will never leave us or forsake us (Hebrews 13:5).

However, although Jesus has promised never to leave us, sometimes we stray from Him. We do this when we sin, or when we forget about Him and go our own way. Why not make sure that there is nothing that has caused you to wander away from Jesus today? Then you can be sure that you have an anchor that will hold you firm and secure whatever happens.

PRAYER: *Lord Jesus, thank You that hope in You is like having an anchor, firm and secure. Forgive me for the times I have wandered away from You and have not been anchored in You. Help me to hold firmly to You at all times. Amen.*

MARCH 9 | THE FIRST MIRACULOUS CATCH OF FISH – PART 1

PATRICK CHAMBRON

When they had done so, they caught such a large number of fish that their nets began to break.

Luke 5:6

The story of the apostle Peter is rich in lessons for us: this remarkable man of God, used powerfully in healing and miracles, is an undeniable element in the building of the early Church. He was a really dynamic character, who left everything when Jesus called him.

However, he had his own need of inner healing and his own human weaknesses.

Peter had a call on his life – to be a fisher of men and a fervently evangelistic apostle, but this man, who in some ways was quite sure of himself, had a deep problem with fear. He was gripped by fear three times when, after Jesus' arrest, it was pointed out that he was one of Jesus' disciples.

It's clear that it wasn't always the Lord who inspired Peter's thinking. Jesus shared with Peter that His mission was to suffer and die for the salvation of mankind and Peter's thoughts were carnal, but Jesus then addressed what was in Peter, not Peter himself, attributing it to Satan (which suggests that Peter needed deliverance).

One day Jesus was teaching the crowds from Peter's boat and then told Peter to go out into the deep water and cast his nets for fish. Despite having fished all night without any success, Peter did this and *'they caught such a large number of fish that their nets began to break'* (Luke 5:6). He was gripped by fear because he understood, through this powerful miracle, that Jesus was the Son of God and that he, a sinner, needed a Saviour more than anything else (Luke 5:8–9). We might say, 'Glory to God, what a miraculous catch!' On the other hand, when the net tore, a lot of the fish were lost, falling back into the sea. Even though the boats were full of fish, they would have been fuller still if the net hadn't broken! The torn nets would have to be mended before they could be used again. But the time had come for Peter to give up fishing and to follow Jesus. In future he would be fishing for the souls of men.

PRAYER: *Thank You, Lord, that You provide miraculous answers to prayer, in seemingly impossible situations. Help us to believe and trust in You even more, for Your might and power is greater than our comprehension! In Jesus' name I pray, Amen.*

MARCH 10 | THE SECOND MIRACULOUS CATCH OF FISH – PART 2

PATRICK CHAMBRON

Simon climbed aboard and dragged the net ashore. It was full of large fish, 153, but even with so many the net was not torn.

John 21:11

In the Word of God there is a second fishing story involving Jesus and Peter. It's just after Jesus' death and resurrection but the disciples are finding it hard to believe He is risen. Peter is discouraged. He hasn't recovered from the fact that he denied Jesus. With his companions he's returned to his secular job – fishing; guilt, sadness and failure have overwhelmed him. What's more, they've fished all night without catching a thing! Suddenly a man calls to them from the beach (John 21:4–6). They recognise Jesus and He tells them to cast their nets into the water, which they do, and to their great surprise the net is filled with big fish. The writer of the Gospel of John mentions that although the net was filled with so many fish it didn't break, and I believe the Holy Spirit has shown me something significant here.

It's surprising to see that on this second occasion of a miraculous catch, the net full of 153 large fish did not break, as it did in the first miracle. As I was meditating on this, the Holy Spirit showed me that the net represents the Church of Jesus Christ. This 'net' will be able to catch and hold on to ALL the 'fish' (without breaking and without losing any).

Peter needed inner healing in order to enter fully into his destiny. Jesus is cooking fish over a wood fire which would remind Peter of the time a few days earlier when, at another wood fire, he'd betrayed Jesus (Luke 22:55–56). Jesus prepared everything needed to restore Peter as a person back into ministry: the wood fire, the words of encouragement and the confirmation of his calling.

In the same way Jesus wants His Church to be restored so that it may be fit to receive the new souls who will be coming, burdened with their problems and needing a shepherd to tend them. We must strengthen and mend the 'nets' of the Church so they will be able to hold all the fish without breaking.

PRAYER: *Thank You, Lord, that You provide miraculous answers to prayer, in seemingly impossible situations. Help us to believe and trust in You even more, for Your might and power is greater than our comprehension! In Jesus' name I pray, Amen.*

MARCH 11 | CLEAN HANDS AND A PURE HEART

PETER HORROBIN

> *You cannot fast as you do today and expect your voice to be heard on high.*
>
> Isaiah 58:4

Fasting is a good and valuable discipline. When the heart is rightfully in tune with God it is a precious means of focusing our attention on God, as we curtail our appetites for other things. Fasting sharpens one's intercession and makes one spiritually more aware of the voice of God. Even the Bible can seem to come more alive, as the Spirit of God quickens God's truth to our own spirit.

But fasting, like every other act of religious discipline which is done with a wrong motive, breaks the heart of God, making people, who in reality are far from it, look pious and holy to others. Jesus reserved some of his harshest words for the Pharisees, who made a show of religion but whose hearts were a million miles away from being in a right relationship with God. In Isaiah 1:15 Isaiah had to tell the people that God would not even listen to their prayers because their hearts were so far from Him.

There are times when I have prayed with individuals about the problems they were having in their lives, and often I have been forced to ask myself why their prayers in the past had not already been answered by God. For, surely, God loves His children and would long to hear the cry of their hearts and answer their very reasonable prayers.

But then God has led me to lift a particular stone, covering an area of their lives that was in darkness. And suddenly it all becomes clear, as once again the question of the psalmist comes into sharp focus. He says in Psalm 24:3–4: *'Who may ascend the hill of the LORD? Who may stand in his holy place? He who has clean hands and a pure heart, who does not lift up his soul to an idol or swear by what is false. He will receive blessing from the LORD.'*

If we are looking to God to hear and answer our prayers, let's be sure we have got the basics of godly living in place before we try and impact the throne of God with disciplines such as fasting.

PRAYER: *Lord, I want to have clean hands and a pure heart. Please expose darkness in my life so that I may clean out the dirt and come to You in repentance for forgiveness and cleansing, in Jesus' name, Amen.*

MARCH 12 | PICK 'N' MIX!

CATH TAYLOR

> *Because he holds fast to me in love, I will deliver him; I will protect him, because he knows my name.*
>
> Psalm 91:14, ESV

There are so many great things about America: donuts for breakfast, Starbucks on every corner, movies you can rent from a vending machine for just $1 … but one of my own personal favourites of America is a store called Target. Target is like every woman's dream shop. It sells everything you could ever need under one roof and everything is nice!

My family know that Target is one of my weaknesses. They know that once I'm in this delightful shop I never leave without buying something, but they also know I can't get past one particular aisle in it. The pick 'n' mix candy aisle! It is just wonderful! No longer do I have to suffer the black jelly beans that pollute a pre-packaged bag. Instead, with my children's expert help, we can pick and choose the colours, flavours and types we really want.

I was reminded of this aisle when I was reading Psalm 91 recently, and was struck by verse 14. The ESV verse quotes the Lord saying, *'I will protect him, because he knows my name.'* In my NLT version the verse says, *'I will protect those who trust in my name.'* Know and trust go hand in hand. No matter what we say from our mouths, we are barely going to trust someone we don't know.

This got me thinking. Do I know God's name? Do I trust in His name? Do I embrace all of who God is or do I pick and choose (pick 'n' mix) His character depending on the names I like or feel comfortable with? Maybe we feel safe 'knowing' Him as God Almighty and Creator but do we dare to get to know Him as Jehovah-Rohi (the Lord our Shepherd)? I may say He is my King but do I truly in my heart know Him as Jehovah Jireh (my provider)? Alternatively, maybe we like the idea of Father God and Jehovah Shalom but do we over-focus on that side of His name and forget that the One we call Abba is no 'Sugar Daddy' but is indeed a Holy God?

If we want to really grow in relationship with the Lord and know His hand on our lives and His protection, then we need to grow in our understanding of who He is, and actually get to 'know' this One in whom we are going to trust! It's not enough to just pick our favourite few names and define Him by those limitations. He wants us to know the whole of who He is. It may take us a lifelong journey of truly discovering all the aspects of His name and identity, but what an amazing, rewarding, secure and fulfilling journey that will be!

Prayer: *Lord, what an amazing God You are! There's so much to Your character and name that I need to learn and discover, to continue to grow in my relationship with You. I'm sorry for the times I've limited You and constrained You to my own experience, understanding or desire. Lord, I want to know all of who You are and to worship You, in the truth of who You are, and not who I've made You or want You to be. Please continue to show Yourself to me as I walk in Your paths. In Jesus' name I pray, Amen.*

March 13 | Serving but Distracted

Linda Fode

> *Martha welcomed Him into her house. And she had a sister called Mary, who also sat at Jesus' feet and heard His word. But Martha was distracted with much serving ...*
>
> Luke 10:38–39, NKJV

The story of Martha and Mary is perhaps a familiar one, but it's only in the New King James Version of the Bible that we find the following translation: *'And she had a sister called Mary, who also sat at Jesus' feet and heard His word.'*

It's frequently taught that Mary put her relationship with Jesus first while Martha was the worker, the anxious one, the sister with misplaced priorities; the one that was chastised by Jesus.

But I don't believe that's the issue. The issue is that even though she spent time with Jesus, welcoming Him warmly into her home, she was too distracted to benefit from the event. She was too distracted to be at peace and enjoy the time with Jesus in her home. In other words she was too worried and pulled away by something else. She was too anxious; too occupied or busy.

When she did finally approach Jesus, it was with a complaint, full of resentment and bitterness. Expressing her emotions of bitterness, anger and frustration to Jesus wasn't the problem, however.

I believe that the problem for Martha was that she had never learned to look into the face of Jesus and receive His love as He looked at her – that look of approval or pleasure. She missed His comfort. She lost the joy of the event. Perhaps she was locked into memories of the past or concerns about the future. Whatever it was, she had lost the enjoyment of the present moment.

If we could have known the full story I'm sure we would have seen that when Jesus spoke the words *'Martha, Martha'* He did so with loving eyes. Is there anything today distracting us – pulling us away from the comfort, peace, and direction that come from sitting 'at the feet of Jesus'? Has our serving Jesus got in the way of our being with Jesus?

PRAYER: *Jesus, today I choose to let You look at me and raise my head to look into Your eyes. Today I choose to let go of the distractions and just be with You. Amen.*

MARCH 14 | THE LAW

JOAN RONO

As the rain and the snow come down from heaven, and do not return to it without watering the earth and making it bud and flourish, so that it yields seed for the sower and bread for the eater, so is my word that goes out from my mouth: It will not return to me empty, but will accomplish what I desire and achieve the purpose for which I sent it.

Isaiah 55:10–11

Recently in Kenya we got a new constitution and it was the people who voted on whether to accept it or not. The constitution is very important as it governs the nation. The people had to accept the law of the new constitution before it could become valid. The people of Kenya made the choice, not just the government.

Every nation and kingdom has a system of law. Sometimes the law is good and sometimes it's bad. But all the same the law is meant to govern the nation. The law is made by those in authority and then the people of the land must choose whether or not they will obey it. There are those who choose to break the law and the authorities have to bring them to justice and administer the appropriate penalty.

We're part of what goes on in the world but we're also strangers in the world. We're part of a different kingdom, even though we're in this world.

The kingdom we're in has a king and a law. In other words, though we live in this world and we're under different constitutions, we don't live for this world. We're looking forward to a better place, a Kingdom that's everlasting, with Jesus as Lord and King. The apostle Peter addresses his letter to *'God's elect, strangers in the world'* (1 Peter 1:1). We're looking forward to the day when we will receive a rich welcome into the eternal Kingdom of our Lord and Saviour Jesus Christ.

We should trust in all it says in God's Word, not just the Law, but also the promises in His Word. Our King is faithful to fulfil every word He speaks.

The laws of God's Kingdom are written in His Word (the Bible). Jesus always taught about the Kingdom of heaven, what it's like, who can enter, who can't, and what you should do to be a good citizen of this Kingdom. It's all written in the Word of God.

These are the laws that govern us as the sons and daughters of His Kingdom and we should trust in all it says in God's Word, not just the Law, but also the promises in His Word. Our King is faithful to fulfil every word He speaks.

When the situation you are in seems impossible, look at His Word: what does our King say? *'Nothing is impossible with Me'* (see Luke 1:37). When you're sick, what does our King say? *'By My stripes you are healed'* (see Isaiah 53:5). The Word He has given us is an answer and solution to all our troubles and fears.

Prayer: *Dear Lord, help me to trust in You as my King and to have confidence in Your Word. Thank You for letting me be a son [or daughter] of Your Kingdom. I put my trust in You afresh, and believe Your Word for every situation I'm in at the moment, Amen.*

March 15 | This is a Day of Good News!

David Silvester

We're not doing right. This is a day of good news and we are keeping it to ourselves.

2 Kings 7:9

In 2 Kings 7 we read how Samaria had been under siege for some time; their food had all gone and people were starving. When God caused the besieging armies of Aram to hear noises that made them think the Samaritans had somehow got other armies to come to their rescue, they fled at night leaving everything behind!

The next day, four leprous men discovered the abandoned camp with its wealth and food, and after beginning to enjoy the spoils they felt guilty, and said, '*We're not doing right. This is a day of good news and we are keeping it to ourselves*' (2 Kings 7:9). God had convicted them that the people in the city should also enjoy the spoils.

Sometimes we may be a bit like those people in Samaria when we've experienced God's intervention in our own life, and He's delivered us from the oppression of the devil and saved us. We're also like those lepers because we've discovered God's provision of nourishment and riches for our soul. He's not only saved us from the oppressor, but He's also given us all we need for our spiritual good, our sustenance and our blessing. These are things He wants us to share with the people who we know are struggling to survive.

When we've experienced God working in our life like that, we need to be reminded of the words that Jesus said: '*You are the light of the world … Let your light shine before men*' (Matthew 5:14, 16). So for us to keep to ourselves what God has done for us is not doing right.

After Jesus had healed a man and delivered him of evil spirits, He said, '*Go home to your family and tell them how much the Lord has done for you, and how he has had mercy on you*' (Mark 5:19).

Only you know the kind of bondage you may have been delivered from. When we've known God's saving power in our life we've got such good news to tell others about what He can do for them also, through Jesus. This is the 'good news' of the gospel that's too good to keep to ourselves.

There's a song with the refrain:

It is no secret what God can do,
What He's done for others, He'll do for you.
With arms wide open He'll welcome you!
It is no secret what God can do.
(Carl Stuart Hamblen)

God wants us to go and share the good things He's done for us with others and let them know that Jesus loves them just as much as He loves us, for *this is a day of good news, and it is not good to be keeping it to yourself.*

PRAYER: *O Lord God, thank You for what You've done for me, giving Jesus to save me. Thank You for all the blessings I've received since trusting Jesus as my Saviour. Please give me the sensitivity and courage to tell others of what Jesus means to me and how He longs to bless them also. Amen.*

MARCH 16 | POWER CUTS AND GOD'S FAITHFULNESS

ANDY TAYLOR

> *But watch out! Be careful never to forget what you yourself have seen. Do not let these memories escape from your mind as long as you live! And be sure to pass them on to your children and grandchildren.*
>
> Deuteronomy 4:9, NLT

Power cuts are a fact of life – especially if you live in the country. I remember a time when Cath and I had left our boys in the bath for a couple of minutes while we chatted in the living room. We knew all was OK because there was a huge amount of noise coming from the bathroom, as they merrily emptied the water onto the floor during one of their bath-time adventures! Then, suddenly, the lights went out because of a power cut. It was pitch black. Now the noise from the bathroom was different, as the shock of no longer being able to see their noses caused fear and panic to take over. I remember Cath and I trying to reassure the boys that all was OK as we literally crawled along the floor trying to find a flashlight! Our concern was for the kids – not for us. We knew that the power would soon be restored and the lights would return. How did we know this? Experience! We had been through many power cuts – and had lived to tell the tale!

In the above passage we see Moses strongly urging Joshua to never forget the experiences of seeing God help His people to overwhelm the kingdoms east of the River Jordan. He was not to let these memories escape his mind and he was to pass them on for the benefit of future generations. This experience was something that was to be a source of peace, so that when facing an impossible battle, Joshua could remember God's faithfulness in the past and find courage for the future.

PRAYER: *Help me, Lord, to remember Your faithfulness in my own life and draw encouragement from it. I know that even in the most impossible of situations You're faithful and You don't change. I want to share these experiences with my children and grandchildren so that they too can grow and have the courage to step out in faith and trust You as a loving Heavenly Father, in Jesus' name, Amen.*

MARCH 17 | SHOW ME THE PATH

CATH TAYLOR

> *Show me the path where I should walk, O LORD; point out the right road for me to follow. Lead me by your truth and teach me, for you are the God who saves me. All day long I put my hope in you.*
>
> Psalm 25:4–5, NLT

There's a TV show in the US that Andy and I really enjoy watching. During the show a group of contestants compete in various games to win prizes and privileges for their particular team.

One of the games they play involves a team member being blindfolded and having to navigate an obstacle course to a final destination. The blindfolded person has to rely on just one team member (a navigator), who is given a bird's-eye view of the obstacle course, shouting out instructions. To watch the blindfolded team member struggle to hear their navigator's voice whilst dodging the obstacles is great fun – especially when there are three or four teams all competing at once.

The outcome of the game depends very much on the character of the person who's blindfolded. Sometimes you get blindfolded contestants who are just so desperate to win they don't even try to listen to their navigator. They just steam on ahead, tackling whatever comes their way, and usually end up causing themselves all kinds of harm. Other contestants may spend so much time standing still and trying to listen to the navigator and ensure that they're hearing right, that they never actually move. I think the wisest contestants (who often end up winning!) are the ones who tentatively step forward using their feet and hands to judge what's ahead while straining to hear the instructions of their navigator.

When I look back on my Christian life, there have been times when I've been like these contestants. It's as if I've been blindfolded and can't see the path that's ahead for me. It's a vulnerable and scary time, even though I know I'm on the path that God set for me. How amazing though that my Navigator, the Lord Jesus, sees the whole picture, and His directions are perfect. He guides me along the whole path that lies ahead of me and walks right by my side, holding my hand. David said, '*Yet I still belong to you; you are holding my right hand. You will keep on guiding me with your counsel, leading me to a glorious destiny*' (Psalm 73:23–24, NLT).

When we surrender to the Lord's direction we can be like those wise contestants. We start to walk forward, yes, perhaps tentatively and with caution, but secure in the knowledge He will keep us safe!

PRAYER: *Lord Jesus, I want so much to walk the paths that You have set for my life. Lord, please will You give me courage to walk Your ways. Give me ears to hear Your voice. Give me hope, knowing Your plans are always for my good. And lastly, give me an unshakeable peace in the knowledge that You walk right by my side, holding my hand. Amen.*

MARCH 18 | JOB FORGAVE HIS FRIENDS

MARGARET SILVESTER

My ears had heard of you, but now my eyes have seen you.

Job 42:5

Job set out on a journey that began with the question, 'Why do I suffer?' He ended that journey with a powerful confession of faith: 'Now my eyes have seen you.'

Three friends walked the journey with Job. Sadly, they misrepresented God and His ways to Job. When Job said to God, 'My ears had heard of You', he was referring to all that his friends had said about God. Being convinced that Job was suffering because he had sinned, they judged him harshly. This condemnation caused him great confusion and added to his suffering.

Eventually God said He was angry with Job's friends: *'You have not spoken of me what is right'* (Job 42:7).

God held Job's friends accountable for their misrepresentation of His ways and for their judgmental attitude towards Job. Their penance was to sacrifice a burnt offering for themselves and allow Job to pray for them (Job 42:8). Job is asked to extend mercy and forgiveness to his friends. There is to be no bitterness, no getting even – simply heartfelt forgiveness. It is this, rather than his own repentance, that results in Job's restoration and the latter part of his life being more blessed than anything he had previously known (Job 42:12).

Job had a revelation of God. He then repented and experienced God's forgiveness (Job 42:6). It was then that he was able to truly forgive those who had deeply wounded him, and was able to pray for them.

At the centre of the universe is a loving, faithful Creator. His love is unfailing, enduring and unconditional. He can be trusted – even when we don't understand the events of our life. God the Father revealed Himself in the Person of Jesus and He's abounding in love and forgiveness. His forgiveness to us is a gift of His grace. That grace is offered to us day by day, enabling us to forgive, and even pray for, those who have wronged us. Is there someone in your life today whom you are struggling to forgive?

PRAYER: *Heavenly Father, thank You that You are abounding in love and forgiveness. Please give me the grace to forgive others, as I have been forgiven. Amen.*

MARCH 19 | THERE IS ALWAYS HOPE

DIANE WATSON

See, I am doing a new thing! Now it springs up; do you not perceive it? I am making a way in the desert and streams in the wasteland.

Isaiah 43:19

Where we live in Western Australia we can have up to six months without rain. The ground and landscape is a desert, dry and brown. The sheep on the hillside look the same colour as the land – dirty brown.

However, when the rains start to fall, within days the countryside changes from brown to green. While the land was dry and brown I wondered how anything could possibly survive and grow out of the dusty soil, but as the land is watered the grass seedlings which were there all along spring to life. It gives hope out of what seemed to be dry and barren.

Our God is a God of hope. When our lives seem dry and barren, God can bring life and hope when times seem hopeless. Nothing and no one is forsaken.

Often it is said that the physical reflects the spiritual. We can learn so many lessons from God's creation.

PRAYER: *Lord, Heavenly Father, help me to trust in You, even when my life may feel dry and barren. You are my hope and life; help me to allow those streams of living water to flow through me to bring life into my weary soul, in Jesus' name, Amen.*

MARCH 20 | ARE YOU GETTING WORN OUT?

ROGER POOK

If the axe is dull and its edge unsharpened, more strength is needed but skill will bring success.

Ecclesiastes 10:10

Are you working with a blunt axe? Are you whacking away at the same old problems in the same old way but achieving less each time? Or are you working harder and harder to achieve the same result as before (and getting worn out in the process)?

Maybe you need to make some changes? In the first place, this could mean taking some time off in order to sharpen your axe. Just how you do this is up to you and God, but we know one thing for sure – God doesn't expect your life to be static or totally repetitive. He would love you to try something new or go back to Him for refreshment. As they say, a change is as good as a rest. If what you do now doesn't seem to be working any more, do something different or in a different way. Nobody watches the same film over and over to see if it has a different ending, so why do we try to solve our problems in the old ways that are no longer effective? Spend some time in asking God honest questions – Father, do you really want me to go on like this? Listen to the Father's advice on how to sharpen things up.

Secondly, learn how to use the sharpened axe in a skillful way. A skilled woodsman uses the weight of the axe to do the work, while an amateur sees it as an exercise in lifting and pounding. He soon gets worn out. So, learn to be a professional. Learn how to use the amazing spiritual gifts that God provides for our daily walk. They are the smooth arc of the steady swing, and the weight behind our axe as it cuts into the problems.

Thirdly, learn when to take a rest. The strongest and most skilled woodsman knows when he needs to take some time out so as not to get tired and careless. Many decades ago I was very impressed when a fellow-Christian said, 'I just want to burn out for Jesus.' Now I would reply, 'And when you have burned out, what use will you be to Jesus?'

To paraphrase Ecclesiastes 10:10 – Don't work harder, work smarter.

PRAYER: *Help me, Lord, to reassess the things I do. Please show me where I need to make changes so that my life will be more fruitful. For your Kingdom's sake, Amen.*

MARCH 21 | FLY LIKE AN EAGLE

LINDSEY HANEKOM

> *But those who wait on the LORD shall renew their strength;*
> *They shall mount up with wings like eagles.*
>
> Isaiah 40:31, NKJV

The sight of an eagle flying is an awesome sight indeed. Not purely due to the size of these magnificent birds, but also because of the ease and confidence with which they fly. A master of the sky, the eagle uses the air currents to cover miles of ground with minimal effort. A small movement of its wingtips every now and again is all it takes for the eagle to continue its soaring.

This verse tells us that to 'fly' with this ease we need to wait on the Lord. When I consider the word 'wait', I think of two things. The first is patience; waiting for something to happen. Even if we know it is going to happen we need to wait patiently and trust that it will come to pass at the right time.

The second is serving; similar to a waiter serving at a table. As a waiter you would only bring what the person you were serving ordered, not something else entirely, even if you consider it a better meal.

We can be impatient, or even unhappy, with waiting for God to bring something to pass, leading to us trying to make it happen sooner. The outcome may be the same, but it could eventually take a lot longer or the outcome could even result in failure. God's ways are very different from our ways, but they are always better! We can also work at doing things that God hasn't even asked us to do, whilst ignoring the things that He originally asked of us!

Both of these cause unnecessary work, similar to an eagle flying underneath the strong air currents that could support it enough to allow it to soar. The eagle would have to work hard, wouldn't ever move very far and would tire very quickly. In reality, an eagle living in those conditions wouldn't survive. And we tire very quickly when we are not doing the things God has made us for!

For those of us who want to move forward in rest and peace, we need to listen to God, trust His timing and only do what He asks of us. Let us wait on the Lord and enjoy flying high like an eagle, for that is a place of rest and fulfilment.

PRAYER: *Father God, help me see where I am impatient and which of my 'works' are not what You have asked for. Help me to rise up like an eagle as I trust in You and wait on You with my whole heart, in Jesus' name, Amen.*

MARCH 22 | BE STILL

MARGARET SOUTHEY

> *Be still, and know that I am God; I will be exalted among the nations, I will be exalted in the earth.*
>
> Psalm 46:10

My husband had an aunt whom I loved to visit when she was alive. She was a warm, godly woman who shared her wisdom with me. It was her understanding of raising her two sons that I especially valued as I had a son who was growing up fast. Once she told me that over the years she had learnt the art of 'hanging around' her sons. I was fascinated by this comment as I knew her to be very wise but I also knew that sons, especially adolescent ones, certainly didn't want their mothers to hang around them. Over the years, I did learn something of her art. I learned to leave my son well alone when he was with friends or busy but that when he was alone with not much to do and sitting on the step with a cool drink staring into space, I would per chance be doing much the same thing. It was an art that produced rich rewards; I heard things that my son would not normally have thought to tell me.

At some point in my life, the words, *'It's important to hang around*

God' came to me. This is also an art but of a different kind. God is always available to us. He doesn't have 'on' and 'off' days or times when He wants to be alone or with His friends. The art rather is to learn how to be still and quiet ourselves so that we can hear Him. This doesn't come naturally as the world clamours for our attention. We feel we should be doing something or fulfilling our Christian duty in some way or another. We seldom stop. My experience is that God doesn't speak to me in the two spare minutes that I have between the breakfast table and the car. However, when I take time to sit quietly, do nothing in particular except perhaps sit on the step with a cup of coffee, that's when I hear His voice. He may give me an idea, a thought or even a rebuke about something He wants me to put right. Whatever it is, as with my son, I'm always grateful to have heard Him. The rich experience I have when I am quiet before God encourages me to do it more and more.

PRAYER: *Father, I want to hear Your voice and what it is You want to say to me. When I do hear You, I'm always better equipped to deal with the things of life that come my way. Please help me to be still. Amen.*

MARCH 23 | TRADITIONS OF MEN

LIZ GRIFFIN

You have let go of the commands of God and are holding on to the traditions of men.

Mark 7:8

The Pharisees gathered around to find fault with Jesus and asked Him a question: 'Why don't your disciples live according to the traditions of the elders?' I believe it was really more of an accusation.

Jesus strongly confronted them by calling them play-actors (hypocrites) and gave a quotation from Isaiah 29:13 about those who pretended to worship God but their hearts were far away from Him. He then said, *'You have let go of the commands of God and are holding on to the traditions of men.'*

Today this statement causes me to pause and wonder whether any of us are doing the same. Are our hearts close or far away from God? Do we put traditions ahead of the commands of God? What is our highest value in life? Is it to do the will of God? If so then do we allow ourselves to be controlled by traditions that are not in line with God's will?

Do we do things which others expect us to, although they're not right in

God's eyes? It's not an easy thing to be different from those around us in our job, family, school (or even church). The line of least resistance is to do things to keep others happy, to agree with their ideas, but then afterwards, before God in the secret place, we feel ashamed.

Followers of Jesus are to be salt and light for this world. This might mean that some will disapprove of our values, ideas, opinions and way of life. We might be rejected, ridiculed or sneered at. On the other hand someone might discover God's truth through our influence. What a privilege to make it possible for someone else to enter the Kingdom of God.

PRAYER: *Dear Heavenly Father, may I never deny You or Your Son Jesus by failing to stand up for the truth that I know. Help me to be a witness for You and bring light into the darkness of this world, in Jesus' name, Amen.*

MARCH 24 | LIFE BY THE SPIRIT

JOAN RONO

> *You, however, are controlled not by the sinful nature but by the Spirit, if the Spirit of God lives in you. And if anyone does not have the Spirit of Christ, he does not belong to Christ. But if Christ is in you, your body is dead because of sin, yet your spirit is alive because of righteousness.*
>
> Romans 8:9–10

Jesus' selection of His close disciples could have been disapproved of by everyone living in His day. Pharisees had disciples who followed them and these people were often well acquainted with Scripture, they fasted and gave generous offerings to the temple. Such people were considered to be suitable disciples. Disciples were called by a rabbi and they would follow him, the one who had called them.

But Jesus didn't follow the traditional protocol of the day. Instead, He chose those who were unlikely candidates for discipleship. Among them were fishermen, a tax collector, a doubting man and a betrayer! It's obvious that He wasn't looking at their outward appearance, but at their hearts.

These men didn't even know how to pray, for Luke tells us, '*One day Jesus was praying in a certain place. When he finished, one of his disciples said to him, "Lord, teach us to pray, just as John taught his disciples*"' (Luke 11:1). Nor did they keep to the traditions of the Pharisees. '*So the Pharisees and teachers of the law asked Jesus, "Why don't your disciples live according to the tradition of the elders instead of eating their food with 'unclean' hands?"'* (Mark 7:5). Jesus selected imperfect men, who were unqualified in every way, and taught them how to be His disciples. But He didn't just make them His disciples. He also made them His friends.

One day He taught them that they need 'a helper'. They were to follow this helper, the Holy Spirit, and listen to Him. The Holy Spirit, who was promised, was given to them on the day of Pentecost. Their lives were transformed and they no longer did anything in their own power or strength!

Good works can be done by anybody, but righteous living is beyond good works. It's living to please God, following His will, and obeying Him. You can't do this by strength of mind and flesh, nor good works. It's only by the Holy Spirit.

Paul clearly shows us that our lives should be controlled by the Spirit of God who indwells us. It's the Spirit who enables us to live righteous lives that are pleasing to God. We can let the Holy Spirit control our lives and produce fruit, as the disciples did after Pentecost. They were able to declare the Word of God boldly and to perform miracles.

PRAYER: *Lord, teach me to follow Your Holy Spirit and to live to please You, not just by works, but by total reliance on Your Spirit. Thank You for Your salvation and the gift of 'The Helper', Your Spirit. Amen.*

MARCH 25 | TRUSTING GOD'S PROMISES

HERMAN REDELINGHUYS

But after I have been raised, I will go before you to Galilee.

Mark 14:28, NKJV

In this scripture we see Jesus making a very important appointment with the disciples to meet Him in Galilee after He was raised from the dead. An appointment is a promise to meet a person at a particular place in the future. The nature of an appointment is perhaps also a way to understand the promises of God, as a place where God wants to meet or do something in our lives in the future.

So many of us have experienced disappointment when we have let others down, or others have let us down. Very often a history of such experiences of empty promises by others or ourselves may lead us into a place where we start to protect ourselves from being disappointed. We may miss out on the fullness of life because of our lack of trust. The way we are unable to trust has an effect on how we react to God, His Word and His promises.

We read in the Word how Jesus kept His promise after He was raised from the dead. He surprised His disciples by meeting them on a beach in Galilee and we see how Jesus then took particular care to restore Peter back into a relationship with Himself. In the ministry we often see how God restores people's trust in His faithfulness so that they can pursue all His purposes for them.

Courage to trust again starts with recognising the presence of mistrust in our lives. God may show a situation where we need to forgive someone or even forgive ourselves. As we repent of our sins, forgive and find the courage to trust again, God will restore us.

PRAYER: *Thank You, Lord, that You are a faithful God. Lord, I ask today that You'll help me to start growing in my faith and being able to trust You. Thank You that all Your promises are 'yes' and 'amen' in Christ Jesus, Amen.*

MARCH 26 | PUT MY TEARS IN YOUR BOTTLE

MARGARET SOUTHEY

Put my tears into Your bottle; Are they not in Your book?
Psalm 56:8, NKJV

This is a beautiful picture. There's a sense of the Lord validating and treasuring our tears and our pain. We're created as tender beings. God purposes it that way. He wants our hearts to be soft so that we're open to Him and so that we can relate sensitively to each other.

This means, however, that our hearts are vulnerable to hurtful experiences. They're just as vulnerable to receiving emotional and spiritual blows as our bodies are to receiving physical blows.

We come from a variety of cultures. In some cultures we learn that physical pain is acceptable but that emotional pain isn't. It's alright to walk around with a plaster cast on your leg or arm but your emotional hurt needs to be hidden.

If we constantly receive the message that emotional pain is unacceptable, we might try to reject it and deny it's there. This isn't godly behaviour. Our emotions are God-given. When He heard that Lazarus had died and saw the anguish of his family and friends (John 11), *'Jesus wept'*.

There are some experiences that are very painful and the appropriate thing to do is to cry. Jesus cares deeply about our hurts. He doesn't mock our tears. He treasures them and keeps them safe in a bottle and records them in His book.

However, Jesus can do more than just validate our tears. He can pour His healing balm into the wounded places. When Jesus heals, He heals the centre of the wound. His is not a superficial healing where a scar grows on top but the inside is still sore.

Jesus loves us to bring our requests for healing to Him so that He can touch and restore us.

PRAYER: *Thank You, Lord, that You have given me emotions and that You care when my heart hurts. You don't scorn my tears. I want to tell You today what hurts me. Please come with Your healing balm and bring Your healing and Your peace, in Jesus' name, Amen.*

MARCH 27 | TRUST OR WORRY – YOU CAN CHOOSE!

TAMAS KOVAKS

> *Wherever your treasure is, there the desires of your heart will also be.*
>
> Matthew 6:21, NLT

What kind of relationship do you have with your wallet? Do you look at it as your provider or as an instrument of blessing in the hand of God?

Lately, God has confronted me in this area. I tend to pinch, literally, every penny, looking for ways to save as much money as I can! I was anxious if I thought I didn't have enough for the month.

But God confronted me: *'Do you think that I'm unable to provide? Just let me into your wallet and watch what I will do – even for you!'*

Ultimately God wants our whole, undivided heart. If He finds that money is taking some or all of it He will ask us to lay it down for our own good. Anxiety and fear attaches itself to our heart if we trust in what we have and what we can earn and don't trust in God to provide.

God is calling us to give Him our whole heart – and our money, or the lack of it, cannot be the one thing hindering this. He wants to give us a much better life and it comes by delighting in Him instead of worrying; then we will have a real peace and joy in our hearts.

Prayer: *Dear Heavenly Father, please forgive me for trusting in what I can see and what I can have – instead of You. I give my whole heart to You now. Please be Lord over my wallet and I give my fears and my anxieties to You, in Jesus' name, Amen.*

March 28 | Opened Eyes

Jim Person

But their eyes were restrained, so that they did not know Him.

Luke 24:16, NKJV

A while ago I had my eyes checked and was given a new prescription for lenses. Shortly after I had these new glasses I noticed my sight was blurred and I was having trouble seeing clearly. When I had my eyes rechecked I was told that I was given the wrong prescription. It made me think that just like me with my wrong prescription it's possible to go through life with blurred vision, seeing but not perceiving, seeing with eyes that are restrained or kept from seeing correctly. We live in a fallen world. We can get grit in our eyes from the dirtiness of the world. It's often for that reason we see in part and don't fully see Jesus for who He is. But sometimes God hides things from our sight as He hid Jesus from the disciples on the Emmaus road (Luke 24:13–35). Either way, we don't see as we should and need God to open our eyes and minds. We can walk along life's road not recognising that it's Jesus who's walking besides us and speaking to us along the way, showing us truths if we could but see them.

As with the two disciples journeying along the road to Emmaus, we can receive the Word of God but still not see what's there in front of us. Jesus wants to open our spiritual eyes as He did with them, so that we might fully comprehend the Scriptures and see with new understanding.

Let's ask Jesus to give us a new holy vision so that our spiritual sight might be opened and we can see the Word with a new set of 'opened eyes'.

Prayer: *Dear Lord, help me to see, to really see. Lord, I sometimes see Your Scripture in part, because my vision is restrained from seeing correctly. Would You open my eyes, and clear my vision, so that I can fully see and understand all that You have for me? I want to have the eyes of my heart opened so I can understand and comprehend Your Scriptures and enter into Your truths revealed to me. Thank You, Jesus! Amen.*

March 29 | Disturbing the Peace

Cath Taylor

You will keep in perfect peace all who trust in you, whose thoughts are fixed on you! Trust in the LORD always, for the LORD GOD is the eternal Rock.

Isaiah 26:3, 4, NLT

We have a ten-month-old Golden Retriever puppy called Sadie. Sadie is the sweetest-tempered dog you could ever meet, but for amateur naive dog owners, like Andy and me, she continues to present us with her challenges.

With the help of our trusty *Golden Retrievers for Dummies* book we have weathered most challenges (the chewing of Isaac's limbs, and digging excavations; to name just a few). However! There is one trait that is proving slightly tedious to us and, quite probably, to all neighbours within a few miles' radius of our previously peaceful, countryside community. Sadie's backyard barking!

Whenever Sadie is let loose in our fenced backyard she turns from the pleasant, sweet-tempered pup that we all love, into what sounds like a Rottweiler from hell. The poor goat that lives in our neighbours' garden gets the worst affront of Sadie's barking, but she isn't too picky who or what she barks at – the neighbours' children, squirrels, passing trains, school buses! The only thing that will stop Sadie from barking is when Andy or I walk outside and shout, 'SADIE, STOP BARKING! BE QUIET!' She will stop straight away, look incredibly sheepish and plod about her business of trying to destroy every planted shrub we possess.

Isn't this similar to the peace-disturbing barks we hear from the enemy in our hearts? How often are you simply trying to go about your day, walking with the Lord, and there the enemy is barking some accusation or insecurity into your heart. His barks are so familiar, always full of accusation, negativity and fear. Reminding us of our failings and weaknesses, scaring us with the unknowns, replaying hurtful words and wounds in our lives (that we thought were dealt with). Bark ... Bark ... Bark ... until it is all we can hear, niggling relentlessly around our hearts. Robbing us of the peace and security we have in the One who holds our life securely in His hands.

Whatever tactic he uses, Satan's plan is always to take our eyes off Jesus. When we listen, and entertain his lies, not only do we temporarily lose the peace and safety God has available for us, but we find our eyes so fixed on ourselves that we fail to walk in the paths our Heavenly Father has laid out for us.

So, next time the enemy is barking his accusations, negativity and fear into your heart, I would encourage you to recognise it for what it is, and tell him to STOP! Use Scripture to remind him of the truth of who you are in Christ and just who your Heavenly Father is. Fix your thoughts firmly on Him and put a stop to anything disturbing your precious perfect peace.

PRAYER: *Father God, I am sorry for listening to the sometimes relentless words of doubt and negativity from the enemy. Today, Lord, please help me to remember to tell the enemy to be silent and to instead focus my heart on the words of peace and hope and life that You speak to me. In Jesus' name, Amen.*

MARCH 30 | COURAGE

JILL SOUTHERN-JONES

Be holy, because I am holy.

1 Peter 1:16

I was once challenged by someone asking me these questions: 'Do you believe in Jesus? Do you belong to Jesus? Do you behave like Jesus?' The last question is a huge one for most of us. I would like to ask it this way: 'How do we behave when no one's looking?'

I consider a holy character is the world's most pressing need. Think about it – if all 7 billion inhabitants of this earth had holy characters, there would be no wars, no hunger, no family break-ups, no crime and no poverty. Of course, that can't happen until Jesus Christ returns and this whole earth is made new. If we're hoping for a major move of God, either individually or corporately, then I believe we need to be working on having a holy character.

Our character is not just what we've done but who we are. Love is part of our character. Love is being tender-hearted but sometimes it's being tough. Like Jesus we are to have a radical love for the broken, the hurting and the wounded. A most important chapter in the Bible for us to study is 1 Corinthians 13.

A holy character includes courage. My father, who was in Dunkirk in May 1940, told us of the huge acts of courage done by the allied soldiers who were being evacuated from the beaches of Dunkirk. The first boat my father was on was bombed and caught fire, but he went into the water to save a friend before getting to safety on another boat. He ended up back in Margate, very thankful for his deliverance. As I listened to such stories I can remember thinking, 'When I grow up, I want to be a woman of courage!'

We make choices that show whether we're courageous or cowardly. We can choose to do the right thing or the convenient thing. Do we stick to Biblical principles or cave in for the sake of our carnal nature, our comfort, our greed, or other people's approval of us? These choices come at us every day in rapid succession. Do we go with the flow, or stop, and choose to be courageous when other people are not?

Things like owning up to the truth take courage, and how much courage is required today to stay sexually pure in a sex-crazed culture? What about when your non-Christian family or friends say that you're terribly old-fashioned or even a little bit strange? Even to become a Christian takes courage. We have to own up to our sins before a Holy God.

Today, take time out to consider your willingness to be courageous on a daily basis because courage is part of a holy character.

PRAYER: *I thank You, Jesus, that You had the courage to go through with the cross and set Your face steadfastly towards Jerusalem. Help me to stand with great courage in a difficult or hostile place and to behave like You, especially when no one is looking. Amen.*

MARCH 31 | SOMETHING RARE AND BEAUTIFUL

BERYL PUFFETT

Finally, brothers, whatever is true, whatever is noble, whatever is right, whatever is pure, whatever is lovely, whatever is admirable – if anything is excellent or praiseworthy – think about such things.

Philippians 4:8

In Scotland when you go for a walk in the exquisite countryside you may be privileged to catch a glimpse of the red squirrel. It is there for one moment and then it skips away to surprise another unsuspecting person taking a leisurely stroll.

How often do we miss the rare and beautiful surprises that our Heavenly Father wants us to see and enjoy? A magnificent sunset, a glistening waterfall, a tiny baby with dimples and a toothless smile, the gentle eyes of the elderly and the reassuring touch of a loved one.

Jesus reached many hearts with His gentle touch, His kind eyes and His caring ways. How often do we miss these precious moments in our busy schedules and time-driven lives?

May you stop and smell the new rose on the bush, and encourage a toddler that his crumpled picture is the most gorgeous one you have ever seen! Seize the moment and create some 'suddenlies' in the lives of others.

Our scripture verse encourages us to ponder on the precious things of God: '*Finally, brothers [and sisters], whatever is true, whatever is noble, whatever is right, whatever is pure, whatever is lovely, whatever is admirable – if anything is excellent or praiseworthy – think about such things*' (Philippians 4:8).

PRAYER: *Lord Jesus, help us to appreciate all You have created so wonderfully and show us how to teach others to see the rainbow in every storm.*

April 1 | Preferring One Another

Patricia Lake

Jonathan said to David, 'Go in peace ... May the LORD be between you and me ... forever.'

1 Samuel 20:42, NKJV

Jonathan was the kind of son any parent (and particularly King Saul) would have been proud of. Yet, he held the difficult position of balancing his respect and honour for his father, who was also king, on the one hand, and on the other hand his friendship and loyalty to David who he knew was the Lord's 'anointed', whilst knowing of his father's intention to kill David!

What is commendable about Jonathan was his complete selflessness. He was the king's son and rightful heir to the throne of Israel, and he could have tried to hold on to what was naturally and rightfully his. Instead, having recognised that God was with David, he bowed to God's sovereignty and, in humility, stepped aside in favour of David. A lesser man would have felt usurped and would probably have been jealous, angry or even bitter that someone else – in this case his best friend – was about to acquire his royal inheritance.

There was no sign of greed or avarice in this young man Jonathan. He was not greedy for wealth or gain and he did not pursue the fame, pomp and ceremony that came with the trappings of royalty. In fact there is no sign of a wrong heart attitude at all.

He honoured his father, Saul, and wasn't angry/bitter with his father for getting it wrong, though Saul's disobedience to God cost Jonathan the throne of Israel. Indeed, Jonathan died fighting shoulder to shoulder with Saul, honouring his father until the day of his death.

Although he never became king, Jonathan's integrity and his fear of the Lord and loyalty to God's anointed, secured the inheritance of his own son (Mephibosheth) and that of future generations of his family, through this very same friendship with David.

We often aspire to being like David, men and women 'after God's own heart', but we can also aspire to be like Jonathan, the noble son of King Saul. Today, we can prefer and honour one another, recognising the anointing of God on our brothers and sisters in the Lord, knowing that Christ died and shed His precious blood for each one of them.

PRAYER: *Dear Heavenly Father, help us to prefer and honour one another like Jonathan did, and like our Lord Jesus who gave His precious life for us, in Jesus' name. Amen.*

APRIL 2 | AN UNDIVIDED HEART

MARGARET SILVESTER

Teach me your way, O LORD, and I will walk in your truth; give me an undivided heart, that I may fear your name.

Psalm 86:11

What a prayer! It's a prayer about God's ways, God's truth, and it's about God's desire for my heart and yours. It's a prayer that God will definitely answer, because it's the way He wants me to live.

To learn God's ways and to walk in God's truth is all about lifestyle. It's ongoing transformation – by having my mind renewed. Then my daily decisions can line up with God's will and purposes more and more. It's the way to freedom.

An undivided heart is a heart fully committed to God and to His will. An undivided heart is set on God and is willing to submit to Him in complete surrender. It's a heart like the heart of Jesus, who loved the Father and only did what the Father commanded Him (John 14:31). Jesus is seated on the throne of the undivided heart and He reigns there as Lord. True love, obedience and service can only come from an undivided heart.

We are told: *'Love the LORD your God with all your heart and with all your soul and with all your strength'* (Deuteronomy 6:5). Love for God must be exclusive. It can't be shared with other gods. He alone is worthy of the highest devotion and praise. This kind of love is a response from the heart that has experienced the wonder of God's unconditional love. God doesn't simply love in words – His love has been expressed to the fullest extent in the sacrifice of His Son Jesus.

We are told: *'Obey [the LORD your God] with all your heart and with all your soul'* (Deuteronomy 30:2). In the Bible true obedience is not forced – it's the fruit of love. Real obedience is sometimes costly; it takes risks and leaves the consequences to God. Jesus said, 'If you love me, you will obey what I command' (John 14:15).

We are told: *'Serve the LORD your God with all your heart and with all your soul'* (Deuteronomy 10:12). This is service which is rooted in love for God and obedience to God. Service from an undivided heart has nothing to do with striving, nor does it seek recognition or reward. It springs from a living relationship of love and obedience with the living God.

Do you have an undivided heart, or are there areas in you which need to be recommitted to the Lord?

PRAYER: *Today, Lord, please give to me an undivided heart to love You, obey You and serve You in the way You desire. Amen.*

April 3 | The Tenth Commandment

Joan Rono

> *You shall not covet your neighbour's house. You shall not covet your neighbour's wife, or his manservant or maidservant, his ox or donkey, or anything that belongs to your neighbour.*
>
> Exodus 20:17

I looked up in the Oxford dictionary the word 'covet' and found the meaning to be: 'To want something very much, especially something that belongs to somebody else'.

The pressure in the world's media today, amongst other things, is for the latest model of car, the best house, the newest fashion in designer clothes and the lifestyle of the richest and most famous celebrity. The pictures in newspapers and magazines are used to advertise these things for people to desire and buy.

All these things are not all bad, but the attitudes of our hearts towards these things could be sinful. What goes on in your mind when you see someone with the latest car, a new house, clothes and other things, that you really want to have? What is your attitude towards wanting these things?

The tenth commandment gives us a guideline on what we should not do. We should not covet things that belong to other people. Then what should we do instead? Luke 11:9 says, *'So I say to you: Ask and it will be given to you; seek and you will find; knock and the door will be opened to you.'* God knows your needs and desires and He satisfies the desires of all living things. Look to Him and He will give you all you need. Psalm 37:4 says, *'Delight yourself in the LORD and he will give you the desires of your heart.'*

PRAYER: *Thank You, Father, that You care about me and my needs and desires. Forgive me where I have coveted other people's belongings. Help me to look to You and trust You for my needs. Thank You, Lord. Amen.*

APRIL 4 | COME

DAVID SILVESTER

> *So He said, 'Come.' And when Peter had come down out of the boat, he walked on the water to go to Jesus.*
>
> Matthew 14:29, NKJV

The invitation of Jesus to Peter comes in response to Peter saying, *'Lord, if it is You, command me to come to You on the water'* (Matthew 14:28, NKJV).

We may wonder what those terrified disciples in the boat thought of Peter when he said this. We can imagine some of the thoughts they might have had about him, and the criticisms they may have made. But the difference between the men in the boat and Peter was that Peter had both heard, and listened to the words of Jesus, *'Be of good cheer! It is I; do not be afraid'* (Matthew 14:27, NKJV).

Could it be said of us that there are times when we only hear part of what the Lord might be speaking to us, so that we miss the more challenging parts? We all love to hear the comforting bits, but when it comes to the challenging bits, do we also fail to hear and listen?

In my own experience, it was in responding to the invitation, *'Come'*, that

I was led into the most exciting and fruitful period of my life. Responding meant getting out of the boat of a successful and secure career, to step onto the unknown and untried waters of church leadership.

This step of obedience led into some amazing experiences of ministry of prayer for healing and deliverance. All of this would have been missed by only listening to the comforting words and not responding to the challenging words of God's call.

It is in taking the first steps of faith to carefully listen to God as He speaks, and responding to what He instructs, that we begin to see how He is able to use an ordinary person like you and me to become effective for Him.

PRAYER: *O Lord God, please sharpen my hearing and enable me to carefully listen to Your voice. Then give me the courage to trust and respond to Your words of instruction. Please help me to discern what is from You and to respond in obedience, I pray. In Jesus' name I pray, Amen.*

APRIL 5 | LETTING GO OF THE SAFETY BAR!

CATH TAYLOR

> *Trust in the LORD with all your heart and lean not on your own understanding. In all your ways acknowledge him, and he will direct your paths.*
>
> Proverbs 3:5–6

A few months back I did something really brave that I haven't done for years! I rode a roller-coaster! No, it wasn't one of the kiddy ones at a fairground – this was a full-grown adult, scary version!

A friend of mine (who is a seasoned roller-coaster rider) 'bullied' me to go on it, with a good dose of friendly, harmless, peer pressure. Did I enjoy it? Not a chance! I hated ever second of the four minutes that I sat with my eyes shut tight, hands gripped white to the safety bar, as we twisted and turned, upside down, dropping death-defying heights … to me it was sheer torture! My friend on the other hand sat giggling and laughing all the way through, her hands waving in the air – apparently she found the whole thing marvellously enjoyable! When they eventually let me off, my hands ached from gripping hold of the bar, my legs felt like jelly and for days after, every muscle in my body complained from the four minutes of extreme stress I had put it through!

I'm telling you this because the Lord has challenged me over the last few years, that for some of us this is how we live our lives with the Lord. We say we're happy to let Him be in control and we walk the paths He sets for us, but we don't fully surrender and rest in Him, knowing that He is Lord.

He longs for us to fully surrender to Him our cares, so that we can experience a peace that surpasses all else. A peace that comes from fully knowing He is in control and we don't have to be. We don't need to grip hold of the safety bar of life and prepare ourselves for the 'inevitable crash', because God's path for us (wherever it leads) is secure. It takes practice though! Just like riding roller-coasters, with your hands raised in the air (going against your natural instinct to hang on tight), so we have to practise letting God be in control and learn to rest, secure in Him.

I would encourage you today to fully surrender to your Heavenly Father the cares and concerns in your life. Laying them down at the foot of His cross, hands off the safety bar, resting secure in the knowledge that the life God has for you is the very best and He is faithful.

Prayer: *Father God, I'm sorry for the times that I have said You are Lord of my life – and yet in my heart I have failed to truly trust and surrender to You. Lord, I choose to surrender to You today – to Your plans and your purposes for my life, knowing they are the very best for me. I take my hands off the safety bar and I rest back in You, and give You a chance to prove Yourself faithful once again in my life. In Jesus' name I pray, Amen.*

April 6 | Sensational News!

Peter Horrobin

The reason the Son of God appeared was to destroy the devil's work.

1 John 3:8

I read a book recently which was attempting to describe what the work of the cross was all about without any reference to the devil. It was a bit like trying to describe a game of soccer without mentioning the idea of a goal! Some things are just not possible!

Satan's last temptation of Jesus was to challenge Him to use His powers to flick out those Roman nails and come down off the cross. The devil's last attempt to grasp victory from the jaws of defeat was to try and stop Jesus from laying down His life voluntarily before coming under his authority. For Satan is the god of this world. And if Jesus were to die then there would be nothing that could prevent His resurrection. The curse of death could only fall on those who had come under the influence of sin. And here was Jesus, totally sinless, about to die! Satan, death and hell were about to be defeated.

Satan had failed. What a nightmare for the god of this world. Jesus was about to overcome death, and from that moment onwards anyone who would choose Jesus as their Saviour, and come under the covering authority of the Son of God, would also escape the judgement of death.

In the Church calendar this day is known as Good Friday. I feel like screaming from the housetops that it's not just GOOD Friday. For in reality it's totally stupendous, unbelievably wonderful, out-of-this-world sensational, miraculous, beyond comprehension Friday! As the old hymn says, '*There was no other good enough to pay the price of sin, He only could unlock the gate of heaven and let us in*' (Cecil F. Alexander, 1847).

PRAYER: *Dear Father God, saying thank You seems a totally inadequate response to such incredible grace. We are so very, very grateful that we can remember with joyful thanksgiving the most important act there will ever be in the whole history of the world and the universe, in Jesus' name, Amen.*

APRIL 7 | OUT OF THE BOX

LINDSEY HANEKOM

> *I praise you because I am fearfully and wonderfully made; your works are wonderful, I know that full well.*
>
> Psalm 139:14

As I was tidying away my son's toys I found myself becoming frustrated that they just didn't fit nicely into his toy-box. Various shapes, sizes, colours, textures and materials mingled together to form the basis of his educational, yet irrationally and unevenly shaped collection of toys. Even the books didn't seem to be normal book-shapes! As such, they just wouldn't fit neatly together in a convenient and sensible box. As I tried to wedge in a particularly non-conformist toy, I found myself thinking of how we can be like these toys.

We are all amazingly and uniquely created in the most imaginative way. We all have so many facets to ourselves. There are our personalities, likes, and dislikes, talents, even our physical bodies. Yet we're conditioned by life to fit into stereotypical boxes. It could be the box for the good Christian or the box for the perfect wife, husband or parent. It could be that we should all look a certain way, wearing similar clothes and fitting them perfectly. Or it could be enforced upon you by your job, your community or your family.

It could even be a box you create for yourself in order to feel secure. Such pressures lead us to becoming frustrated as we strive to conform and gain man's acceptance. Yet it's impossible to conform because you just don't fit the box. Ultimately you'll fail in gaining man's full acceptance. Many of us go through life working so hard to fit into the appropriate boxes that we lose sight of who we truly are.

For us to gain God's acceptance we simply have to be ourselves; the true self that God foreknew (Jeremiah 1:5) and created from His heart of love and unlimited imagination. God's acceptance is unconditional and is everlasting. Man's acceptance is fickle, fallible and conditional.

As it is, Kyle's toy-box is simply buried beneath a jumbled collection of bright colours and exciting opportunities for fun and learning. Maybe that's how it should be for us. Rather than trying to conform to a box-like standard, we should just enjoy being an exciting and colourful jumble of all that God made us to be!

PRAYER: *Father God, thank You for making me, me. I'm sorry I've tried to squeeze myself into boxes that constrain my true self and I ask You to help me find more of the real me and enjoy my life as You wanted me to. Amen.*

APRIL 8 | REIGNING IN LIFE

PAUL WATSON

> *For if, by the trespass of the one man, death reigned through that one man, how much more will those who receive God's abundant provision of grace and of the gift of righteousness reign in life through the one man, Jesus Christ.*
>
> Romans 5:17

The apostle Paul is contrasting the difference here between Adam's sin opening the way for death to reign, and the action of Jesus Christ, which brings life.

Those who have put their trust in Jesus have moved from the place where death once reigned, to the place where they now reign in life. In Christ, we reign in life. How does this work out? Even in trials, troubles, failures, sickness, disappointments, sorrows, tragedies, and physical death – we reign because of Jesus Christ!

Perhaps you feel that the circumstances of your life don't give a lot of physical evidence that you're reigning as a king. Or it could be that you aren't, currently, facing major difficulties. Maybe life is ticking along OK. But it still doesn't feel like you're 'reigning'.

The life that Paul is speaking of is more than a span of years, months, weeks and days. It refers to the deeper, spiritual reality of our eternal existence. Through sin, death was allowed to reign – bringing about spiritual death – separation from God for eternity. But through the death and resurrection of Jesus, eternal life is available to all who receive Him. The hidden reality, taken hold of by faith, is that we have a new life in which we do indeed reign. Nothing can take this from us.

Knowing this enables us to live our earthly life with a different perspective. I know a family who are currently living through the very painful reality of a loved one's battle against incurable cancer. This family knows the trials of our earthly existence, but also, in the very face of death, they are reigning in life.

What about you?

Prayer: *Father God, thank You for Your abundant grace and the gift of righteousness! Thank You for Jesus Christ. I choose today to reign in life. Amen.*

April 9 | Removing the Covers!

Cath Taylor

But you desire honesty from the heart, so you can teach me to be wise in my inmost being.

Psalm 51:6, NLT

When we first moved to Florida we were given a rather old-fashioned pair of sofas. As the sofas were excellent quality but just not our style, we decided to disguise them with modern sofa covers. They looked great, but took up lots of time each day rearranging and adjusting them trying to keep them in place. Despite being washed many times, after three years of being sat on by the family and the dog, the covers were officially dead! No cushion, throw or pillow was going to pretend otherwise! So, a few months ago, I pulled off the covers and tossed them in the trash.

This got me thinking. How much do we hide ourselves under cushions, blankets and covers trying to be something that we aren't – trying to fit other people's expectations or 'likes'? Maybe we have produced our own covers because we really dislike what's underneath and we feel ashamed and afraid that the real 'me' isn't good enough.

It's scary, but just too easy to do! Instead of allowing the Lord to reveal the truth of our hearts, we cover it over and pretend it's not there. Whatever's underneath – jealousy, bitterness, pride, a hunger for love and acceptance, greed, a deep search for significance and worth, judgement and criticism (the list goes on) – God wants us to be real. He wants us to come to Him in truth – flaws and all.

What a relief to give up the pretence and the sheer effort of keeping ourselves covered! Jesus sees all the beauty and muck that we've hidden, and He accepts us. Does He want us to change? Absolutely...

What a relief to give up the pretence and the sheer effort of keeping ourselves covered! Jesus sees all the beauty and muck that we've hidden, and He accepts us. Does He want us to change? Absolutely, but we can't do it ourselves in our own strength. Only He can bring the true change to our lives, as we acknowledge our need (or repent of our sinful ways), and allow Him to transform us deep on the inside.

Today, will you ask the Lord to show you any covers you have adopted and dare to trust Him to reach underneath with His love and His truth?

PRAYER: *Lord Jesus, I'm sorry for the times I have tried to re-create myself into someone I deem more acceptable either to You or the people in my life. Thank You that, as the craftsman of my life, You love me as your precious creation. Lord, please help me to be real. Would You show me the covers I have placed over my heart, and would You help me to begin a journey of walking in true relationship with You. In Jesus' name I pray, Amen.*

April 10 | Reminding God

David Cross

If they shall confess their iniquity, and the iniquity of their fathers, with their trespass which they trespassed against me, and that also they have walked contrary unto me ... Then will I remember my covenant with Jacob, and also my covenant with Isaac, and also my covenant with Abraham will I remember; and I will remember the land.

Leviticus 26:40,42, KJV

God does not just want relationship with us; He wants covenant. Unfortunately we are covenant-breakers. We naturally walk in iniquity, which simply means that we are out of line with God and with His commands for our well-being. Actually the iniquity which we carry comes not only from our own sin but also from the inherited iniquity of our forebears. Sin issues run in the family.

Thankfully one person has walked the earth in perfect obedience to the terms of God's covenant. His name is Jesus. If we've chosen to be part of God's family through Jesus, then He acts as our representative in the New Covenant which has been established through the cross. This statement of covenant, a life and death commitment by God towards His people, was first clearly spoken to Abraham, but God promised to continue the same covenant relationship to Abraham's descendants.

Galatians 3:29 tells us that followers of Jesus are all regarded as Abraham's descendants, partakers in this extraordinary covenant with God. How do we enter into the full benefit of this deep place of fellowship and restoration? God prompts us to openly acknowledge and to turn away from iniquity. This iniquity is caused by our own sin and the past sin in our family. Jesus carried all this iniquity for us at the cross but God says that our confession acts as a 'reminder' of His promises to restore us.

God will never forget His commitment to us but every dad loves to hear his children being honest in their response to his challenges. Our Heavenly Father loves to hear us speak the truth to Him about our imperfect lives. Then He can point us to the saving work of His perfect Son Jesus, who died on the cross.

Today's a good day to give God the opportunity to 'remember' His covenant with you.

Prayer: *Thank You, Lord, for Your covenant faithfulness, Your amazing love and for all the promises that were fulfilled in Jesus. Thank You, Lord, that because of Your covenant love and the faithfulness of Jesus my sins were dealt with at the cross. In Jesus' name I pray, Amen.*

April 11 | The Promise of God's Presence

David Silvester

> *Behold, I am with you and will keep you wherever you go, and I will bring you back to this land; for I will not leave you until I have done what I have spoken to you.*
>
> Genesis 28:15, NKJV

These were God's words spoken to Jacob in a dream as he was running away from home after deceiving his father into giving him the blessing of the first-born, the blessing which was really for his older brother, Esau.

I wonder if we are sometimes aware of God making His promise known to us, and yet there comes a time when we feel, like Jacob, we have messed things up, and it's all hopeless. We then wonder when and how we might ever get things back into proper order and onto a right footing.

Jacob had managed to get Esau to sell the birthright of the elder son to him (Esau had set no value on this birthright). Then, following that first act of manipulation, Jacob cheated Esau out of the first-born's blessing from their father. As a result Esau was determined to kill Jacob when the right opportunity arose.

We may not always understand the ways of God, or why He'd chosen Jacob above Esau, but we do know that God's ways are perfect, and that He has plans for us which are designed for our good (Ephesians 2:10).

God had told Isaac regarding these two sons that from them would be formed two peoples, and that *'the older will serve the younger'* (Genesis 25:23, NKJV).

God chooses whoever He wants in order to fulfil His plan and purpose, and in a similar way Jesus has chosen us along with many others to follow Him (John 15:16).

However inadequate and unsuited we might feel regarding our life and service for the Lord, I believe we can take the words God spoke to Jacob and apply them to ourselves: *'Behold, I am with you and will keep you wherever you go, and I will bring you back to this land; for I will not leave you until I have done what I have spoken to you.'* We also can know that God is with us, and He's working out what He's planned. The end result God has in view is that we might bear fruit, whereby He will be glorified.

PRAYER: *Father God, I know that I don't always understand Your plans and Your ways, but I do understand the promise of Jesus to be with me to the end of the age. Please help me to be aware of that, and enable me to be fruitful in all that You lead me into, I pray, in Jesus' name. Amen.*

APRIL 12 | FROM DARKNESS TO LIGHT

LINDSEY HANEKOM

> *This is the verdict: Light has come into the world, but men loved darkness instead of light because their deeds were evil.*
>
> John 3:19

On a recent walk with our dog in a local forest we were surprised to see that the forestry commission had been busy harvesting wood. Having walked in the forest for many years we knew the paths exceptionally well, but we were amazed at how the whole vista had changed with the felling of the trees.

One particular path was dramatically changed, as it was once a dark path, enclosed on both sides by imposing trees. Now there was light and space and you could see beyond the trees into the beauty of the surrounding countryside.

As I walked along this path I started to feel a little nervous about where I was going. The scene had changed so much that I felt disorientated, and questioned whether or not I was actually on the right path.

It made me think of the times when God did a deep work in my life and I felt as though I no longer knew who I was, where I was, or where I was heading. Yet this feeling, however disorientating or scary, was a result of light coming into the places where there was no light. The sense of disorientation was real. It was as though the whole scene of life had changed. It opened up new views and perspectives; it made the walking easier and safer; it meant that I could walk with the security and freedom of knowing that there were good things beyond where I was.

The danger is that the initial sense of unease in the forest could have caused us to turn round and return to where we came from. It's easy to think that the unknown way is too scary to travel along and this fear could prevent us from moving forward. As I walked along the path I looked for familiar landmarks that would mean I was on the right path even if the whole outlook was new to me.

When God brings us through healing we don't change who we are or where we are at, in our time-limited journey. He opens up new possibilities, hope and freedom. We'll still remember the old landmarks but now there's much more to our life. So don't choose the safety of what's familiar, even though it's darkness, but persevere, and walk along the pathway of life in freedom and with hope.

PRAYER: *Father God, thank You for the healing work You do in my life. Help me to move on in You and not fear the openness that You provide for my life. Amen.*

APRIL 13 | FAITH IN ACTION

DAVID SILVESTER

Then he took his staff in his hand, chose five smooth stones from the stream, put them into the pouch of his shepherd's bag and, with his sling in his hand, approached the Philistine.

1 Samuel 17:40

Many of you, like me, will know the story of David and Goliath from childhood. Yet on reading this passage again recently I wondered, 'Why choose five stones when only one was necessary, and why a staff?'

Perhaps we're a little like David in that situation? There are times when we're uncertain about what might be necessary as we move on to serve the Lord. As the saying goes, we equip ourselves with 'belt *and* braces!'

David's faith in God motivated him to go out alone against Goliath. His experiences of God enabling him to overpower a lion and a bear were sufficient for him to trust God in this situation. He knew he could overcome the enemy single-handed.

When we face a difficult situation, are we able to look back and recall those times where God has enabled us to overcome? Can we testify of His powerful intervention? This encourages us to 'step out in faith' believing He will help us.

Our God is such an amazing God. He has promised to 'never leave or forsake us' when we go in obedience to do what He has called us to do (Deuteronomy 31:6). David was so confident that God would enable him to defeat Goliath that he could discard Saul's armour and take the simple things God had given him the skill to use.

As we face the difficult situations of life, let's first recall God's faithfulness and help and thank Him for those experiences. Then, encouraged, let's look to Him to make us an overcomer, through the strength and ability He has equipped us with. Furthermore, as we experience the victory He gives, let's not forget to give Him all the glory, for without His help we would only fail.

PRAYER: *Father God, I thank You for all those past experiences of Your help and enabling, when I have been successful in difficult situations. As I face fresh challenges, I ask You to help me overcome with Your strength, as I offer to You the gifts and abilities You've put within me, in the name of Jesus, Amen.*

April 14 | Be Vigilant

Angela Weir

> *Be vigilant and cautious at all times; for that enemy of yours, the devil, roams around like a lion roaring [in fierce hunger], seeking someone to seize upon and devour.*
>
> 1 Peter 5:8, AMP

It's lambing time and the field behind our house is filled with young lambs. They're now at the age when they gather together and have team races up and down the field, jumping off all four feet at once as they turn. They're a joy to watch. Sadly, a fox has taken eight of them.

Foxes are crafty creatures. They slink up in the dusk when all the sheep are settling for the night, and pounce when they're least expected. That's what the enemy does with us. We may think that all is going smoothly and that we're moving on in the right direction when all of a sudden we find that we've slipped back into old habits of thought or deed. If the enemy roared more loudly we would be more alert to his tactics!

A sure way to be on our guard is to work with Jesus and His Holy Spirit, allowing the truth of His Word to penetrate into our hearts and show up any darkness in our lives.

This means that we have to keep studying the Bible. So many Christians don't bother to read His Word daily and large numbers believe that much of it isn't relevant for today. I was told by an ordained clergyman that the Bible was the inspired Word of God, but it was written by fallible men so we didn't have to believe all of it! Which bits do we leave out? There are plenty that would make us feel more comfortable if they weren't there, but the Bible *'is God-breathed and profitable for instruction, for reproof and conviction of sin, for correction of error and discipline in obedience, for training in righteousness, in holy living, in conformity to God's will in thought, purpose and action'* (2 Timothy 3:16, AMP).

Let's keep close to the Shepherd, read His Word and beware of the 'foxes'!

PRAYER: *Lord Jesus, You say that heaven and earth will perish but that Your words will not perish or pass away. Please give me a passion for Your Word and help me to build my house on You, my Rock, and please show up the weaknesses in my defences where the enemy has access. Amen.*

April 15 | God's Own People

Liz Griffin

> *Sing and rejoice, O daughter of Zion, for behold, I come and I will dwell in your midst, declares the LORD. And many nations shall join themselves to the LORD in that day, and shall be my people. And I will dwell in your midst, and you shall know that the LORD of hosts has sent me to you.*
>
> Zechariah 2:10–11, ESV

It was a time of discouragement for God's people who had returned from Babylonian exile in 536 BC and had laid the foundation of the new temple. Twenty years had gone by and Jerusalem was only partly rebuilt and powerful opposition had blocked their progress on rebuilding the temple.

Zechariah was given a message of hope from God to give to them. After the seventy years of judgement they were to come into a time of mercy, blessing and prosperity. Their enemies would be destroyed, as whoever touched God's own people were touching the 'apple' (or pupil) of His eye. God would *'dwell in their midst'* so they could now *'sing and rejoice'*.

Then comes the staggering announcement that *'many nations shall join themselves to the LORD in that day, and shall be my people'*. The meaning of that statement affects me personally and everyone else who was born a Gentile, not one of the chosen race. God never changed His mind about Israel (or Zion) being chosen as His very own people. He remains true to His covenant relationship with them for ever. *'And the LORD will inherit Judah as his portion in the holy land, and will again choose Jerusalem'* (Zechariah 2:12, ESV).

God also promised, *'And I will be to her a wall of fire all around … and I will be the glory in her midst'* (Zechariah 2:5, ESV).

Because Jesus died on the cross and made atonement for the sins of the world, everyone has a chance to be included in that covenant relationship, to be a part of God's own people and also be *'the apple of His eye'*. The apostle Paul explains how Gentiles are shoots of wild olive trees which can be grafted into the main olive tree, Israel, the people of the covenant. *'But if some of the branches were broken off, and you, although a wild olive shoot, were grafted in among the others and now share in the nourishing root of the olive tree, do not be arrogant towards the branches. If you are, remember it is not you who support the root, but the root that supports you'* (Romans 11:17–18, ESV).

When I read the messages of God to His people throughout the Old Testament I can understand that they were spoken to particular situations, but I am also allowed to apply them to myself as a daughter of Zion through my connection in Jesus, the Messiah. It is just as true for me as for Israel that *'The LORD your God is in your midst, a mighty one who will save; he will rejoice over you with gladness; he will quiet you by his love; he will exult over you with loud singing'* (Zephaniah 3:17, ESV).

PRAYER: *Thank You, Father God, that I am grafted into the olive tree and I belong to You. Thank You that Your Son, Jesus, has joined me to Your own chosen people and that I am in a covenant relationship with You forever. Amen.*

APRIL 16 | CALLED – BUT NOT YET READY!

JILL SOUTHERN-JONES

Listen to this dream I had …

Genesis 37:5–8

Looking at the story of Joseph we see that he had to go through a series of tests before God could bring him fully into his destiny and use all the amazing gifts and abilities God had given him. All of us face similar tests in our Christian walk – how would you cope with Joseph's tests?

Joseph's first test was: The pride test.

Joseph had given a bad report about his brothers to his dad (Genesis

37:2). In other words, he told tales! Joseph was the favourite son and his coat of many colours gave him the opportunity to parade his position as 'Dad's favourite' to his brothers.

Then he had a dream that really was from God, but he made the mistake of bragging about his dreams. Joseph had a pride problem which really upset his brothers. God gave him the dream early in life; he was only seventeen. Perhaps God wanted to surface the pride so he could deal with it sooner rather than later.

When the angel spoke to Mary, the mother of Jesus, we're told that *'she treasured up all these things and pondered them in her heart'* (Luke 2:19). She too was young, but how differently she handled God's destiny in her life!

You don't have to tell people who you are in order to be someone. If you can't handle the dream you definitely can't handle the destiny! Joseph was seventeen years old when he got the dream but he wasn't ready to step into his destiny until he was thirty years old. Joseph was blessed and loved by God – and God loved him enough to help him face the problem of pride. We too are blessed and loved by God and called into His Kingdom purposes. How would we fare if God tested us for pride? There's a little pride in all of us!

PRAYER: *Lord, I don't want pride to be in my life. When You reveal my destiny, or give me dreams and visions, help me to handle them wisely. Please deal with any insecurities in me, which are the root of pride. Help me deal with any pride in my life today, in Jesus' name. Amen.*

APRIL 17 | THE INTEGRITY OF GOD

LINDA FODE

> *I will confess and praise You [O God] with my whole heart; before the gods will I sing praises to You. I will worship toward Your holy temple and praise Your name for Your loving-kindness and for Your truth and faithfulness; for You have exalted above all else Your name and Your word and You have magnified Your word above all Your name!*
>
> Psalm 138:1–2, AMP

In our Western culture we ratify a verbal agreement by 'shaking on it'. The handshake is an important symbol of trust. We 'shake hands' right hand to right hand. Most people are right-handed. In order to shake an enemy's hand you had to put down your weapon or, here in the 'Wild West', holster your gun.

In some Eastern cultures the gestures of trust and agreement are even more intimate. They often involve greetings of kissing both cheeks and reaching out with both hands.

We have an expression that says, 'My word is as good as my name.' You can trust that I will fulfill my word to you based on my good name from the past.

God sets an even higher standard of integrity and faithfulness for Himself. He exalts His name (who He is) and His Word (what He says He will do) above everything else. And of those two, He magnifies His Word even above His good name. This is the foundation of our faith. We can absolutely trust that our God, as revealed in Scripture, is who He says He is and will do what He says He will do. God has complete integrity.

We can put down our weapons and come close. We can enter into agreement (covenant) with Him without fear. His Word is our weapon against the lies of the enemy. It is the basis on which we have forgiveness and assurance of salvation. It gives us hope in perilous times.

Look for the 'fingerprints' of God on your life: where He met you, carried you, supplied your need and healed you.

For some of us it can be a bit of a journey from fear to trust. We hold tight to our weapons of self-protection and self-fulfilment. We stay distant from the Father and approach Him as slaves rather than beloved sons and daughters.

Begin today by remembering those times, those places, where the Word was true for you. Look for the 'fingerprints' of God on your life: where He met you, carried you, supplied your need and healed you. Look for the 'footprints' where He went before you. Find scriptures that match your experience and memorise them. Speak them out when the enemy pursues.

Choose today to see the faithfulness and integrity of your Father. Pick up your weapons and defeat the spirits of slavery and fear. Choose to trust.

PRAYER: *Father, give me eyes to see You as You really are. Enable me to trust. Train me to war against the enemy and his lies. Make me a person of integrity, in Jesus' name, Amen.*

April 18 | Tribulation Worketh Patience

Tamas Kovaks

And not only so, but we glory in tribulations also: knowing that tribulation worketh patience.

Romans 5:3, KJV

I have to admit this is one of the scriptures I don't like. I think it's because it's uncomfortable. God tells us that in order to have one of the fruits of the Spirit we have to go through tribulation. I'm sure you've prayed it as well: 'Oh God, please give me more patience! I need it now.' And the response from heaven is … trouble.

> The encouraging fact is that God promises in His Scripture that He's going to be with us in times of trouble. He never leaves us nor forsakes us … We can always count on Him.'

Farmers say each plant needs a certain kind of soil to flourish. Some need acidic; others might need alkaline. So it is with the fruits of the Spirit. Each fruit grows in a special spiritual environment that God orchestrates, and for patience to grow it needs tribulation. That is trouble with a capital 'T'.

The encouraging fact is that God promises in His Scripture that He's going to be with us in times of trouble. He never leaves us nor forsakes us (Deuteronomy 31:8). We can always count on Him cheering us on: 'You can endure, just hold on, I'm holding your hand.' After we've been through the times of trouble and we look back, the end result is evident: we're more patient with others and more able to endure in difficult situations.

Prayer: *Father, I pray that You'll give me grace to endure. I want You to grow this fruit in my life, so I'll become more like You. Please let me know that You're with me and You're carrying me forward. Thank You that You'll be with me until the end of the age. Amen.*

April 19 | Cath Taylor

The Emperor's New Clothes

This is real love. It is not that we loved God, but that He loved us and sent His Son as a sacrifice to take away our sins.

1 John 4:10, NLT

Have you ever read the story *The Emperor's New Clothes* by Hans Christian Andersen? Since being a little girl it has been one of my favourite stories. In the tale a rather vain self-obsessed emperor unwittingly hires two swindlers to design him a fabulous new outfit. The swindlers produce the most fantastic elegant cloth using their great weaving talent that makes fabric so light and fine that it is 'virtually invisible'. The swindlers tell the Emperor it is only invisible to anyone who is too stupid and incompetent to appreciate its quality!

Not wanting anyone to think him incompetent or stupid, the Emperor parades around the town in his new magnificent (non-existent) outfit and all his subjects pretend they can see it and appreciate its value. Only a little boy at the back of the crowd, who has no reason to care what people think of him, has the sense to shout, 'The Emperor's naked!'

It's a funny story in which we all laugh with disdain at the rather stupid Emperor and his whole town of followers who bought into the lie. No doubt we all like to align ourselves with the young boy, confident that, in the same situation, we would be the ones to cut through the unreality just like he did.

I wonder how true this is though? I wonder as we look at our hearts, how similar in fact we are to the Emperor. How much do we care about what people think of us? How easily do we strive for perfection and success, keen to quench the thirst of our hearts for acceptance, approval, value and worth? Perhaps we take temporary fixes in man's praise or our own achievements, not realising that we have quite merrily bought into the greatest lie of the greatest swindler of all.

But the profound truth in Scripture breaks through this lie in the same way as the young boy called out the truth to the crowd. '*This is real love. It is not that we loved God, but that He loved us and sent His Son as a sacrifice to take away our sins*' (1 John 4:10, NLT). This truth that God loves us breaks through all our striving and straining and calls us to rest. His love for us determines our value. His love secures our identity – a child of God.

So I encourage you to lay down any search in your heart for significance or approval from man. Rest in the knowledge of God's great love. Let Him whisper His truth into your heart – 'It's enough for you to be just as you are, My precious child. Because of who I am, you can be who you are.' I want to pray with the apostle Paul, *'May you experience the love of Christ, though it is so great you will never fully understand it'* (Ephesians 3:19, NLT).

PRAYER: *Lord Jesus, I'm sorry for the times I have allowed the longings of my heart to lead me into a search for man's approval. Father God, I acknowledge that my worth and value is quite simply sealed in You and in Jesus' death on the cross. Please reveal more of who You are and Your amazing love and acceptance of me, as I keep my eyes fixed on You alone. Amen.*

APRIL 20 |
DAVID CROSS

CLAIMING THE GROUND

> *After this the Lord chose another 72 men and sent them out two by two, to go ahead of him to every town and place where he himself was about to go.*
>
> Luke 10:1, GNB

We sometimes hear of those who are 'claiming' their town or city for Jesus. There may be meetings and marches to declare authority against the powers of darkness which rule over the area and promote sinful lifestyles. When Jesus sent out the seventy-two disciples to proclaim the truth and the healing power of God's Kingdom, He warned them that there would be strong spiritual opposition. But He didn't tell them to do battle directly with these unseen hostile powers.

God knows the spiritual condition of every nation, community and household in the world. It's His desire that all will come to a place of receiving Jesus. But there's powerful spiritual opposition from an enemy who has been given rights to rule over places where those occupying that ground have been in rebellion to God. No one can fully confront that opposition unless the hearts of the people living there soften and turn towards the Lordship of Jesus. It's particularly effective when leaders repent and are willing to come under God's authority, as they spiritually represent the people coming under their sphere of influence.

Very often in the stories of families and communities who've come to Christ, we find that a few ordinary believers have been in intercession, agreeing with God about the sinfulness in their own lives and in that of their neighbours. Rather than our 'taking on' the ruling powers of the enemy, God's way of progressing His Kingdom is to look for those who are willing to stand in agreement with Him about sin. This intercession weakens the enemy's hold and creates breakthroughs in the defences of the powers of darkness.

Those who are prayer warriors amongst us in the Body of Christ should seek the Lord about what he wants us to do in our communities so that we can be sent out by Jesus like the seventy-two disciples. He will show us how to stand in agreement with Him, disable the enemy's strongholds and with His authority claim the ground for God's Kingdom use.

PRAYER: *Help me, Lord, to listen more carefully to Your instructions, so that the things I do will also be those things that You have asked me to do, in Jesus' name. Amen.*

APRIL 21 | LEARNING TO SKATE!

CATH TAYLOR

> *That is why we have a great High Priest who has gone to heaven, Jesus the Son of God. Let us cling to him and never stop trusting him. This High Priest of ours understands our weaknesses, for he faced all of the same temptations we do, yet he did not sin. So let us come boldly to the throne of our gracious God. There we will receive his mercy, and we will find grace to help us when we need it.*
>
> Hebrews 4:14–16, NLT

My two oldest children, Jake and Ben, were recently invited to a family roller-skating event. Parents were invited to skate too. Once at the rink, with the roller skates securely fastened to my ankles, I started to wonder if, perhaps, I'd bitten off more than I could chew! I struggled to my feet with images gripping my mind of all the potential bones I could break, and realised very quickly that I was quite seriously out of my depth! I had to decide – was I going to admit defeat and recognise I was not the twelve-year-old roller-dancing-queen that I used to be, or was I going to give it a go and quite possibly fall flat on my face? I chose to give it a go.

In the grand scheme of life and the universe it really didn't matter whether I skated or not (it's certainly not part of my destiny!), but in our Christian walk we are faced with opportunities where our choices really do matter. Are we going to face the very real possibility of failure and embarrassment by doing something we have a feeling God is asking us to do, or do we choose the easy option and sit on the side and watch everyone else? Sometimes it's fear that holds us back from stepping out and trusting God – 'What if I get it wrong?' Sometimes it's pride – 'What will people think of me?' Sometimes it's pure human logic – 'It just doesn't make sense.' And sometimes we've positioned ourselves so comfortably, confident we'll give it a go 'when we've got it perfect', that we've become the experts at never giving God a chance.

Just as Jesus asked Peter to step out of the boat and to walk on the water and trust Him, I believe Jesus will give us similar opportunities. Jesus can prove Himself faithful if we're only willing to step out. As with the skating, we can make a choice. Do we give it a go or do we sit back and watch? It wasn't enough for me to just fasten on the skates and stand up holding onto the safety barrier. You only begin to skate when you step onto the rink, let go of the barrier and give it a go. In a similar way, unless we give the Lord a chance to prove Himself faithful, will we ever really learn to trust Him? If we don't trust Him, will we really grow deeper in our relationship with Him?

PRAYER: *Lord Jesus, I believe You're trustworthy and faithful. I'm sorry for the times I've doubted You, or the times I've walked away from opportunities where You wanted to prove Yourself to me. Open my eyes to see places in my life where I can have an opportunity to step out and trust Your faithfulness, so that I can grow deeper in my love for You and understand more of Your heart for me. In Jesus' name I pray, Amen.*

APRIL 22 | WHAT IS DIFFERENT ABOUT THIS NAME?

GRACE MARSHALL

Therefore God exalted him to the highest place and gave him the name that is above every name, that at the name of Jesus every knee should bow ...

Philippians 2:9–10a

Did you know that there is one word so powerful that no newspaper, magazine or book editor will publish it? Not in the secular Western media, anyway. It's surprising, because they actually publish nearly everything and they certainly don't mind shocking people because if something shocks the reader, often that gains publicity and sales.

But there is something they are afraid to publish and that is the name *Jesus.*

It's not because they are avoiding religion. They will print the name 'God' without a problem. They don't have a problem with the word 'church' or even 'Christ'. But if you look, you will rarely find *Jesus* in a serious article; only if the purpose is to mock or attack. If they need to refer to Jesus in a normal article, then they prefer a word like *Christ*. Now there is no such problem about the name of any other religious figure, such as Moses, Buddha, Mohammed, Krishna or any other you can think of. Why is the name *Jesus* so different?

I don't think it's just anti-Christian prejudice (although that exists). The reason is much simpler. The name *Jesus* has to be avoided as much as possible because it makes the readers feel uncomfortable. No other name has such a powerful impact. Have you ever wondered why?

It is by far the most powerful name in the whole world and people feel the power of it. It is a feeling they don't like, although they can't explain it, which is why the newspapers have to avoid it.

There is a reason for this phenomenon, and it is explained in today's verse: the name of Jesus is the name which is above every other name. It's not just His name which is powerful – Jesus is hugely powerful. God has exalted Him to the highest place. At the name of Jesus every knee will bow. In fact the Bible says that Jesus will be the Judge before whom every one of us will stand at the end of our days (2 Corinthians 5:10).

The main reason why people feel uncomfortable with the name of Jesus is because somewhere deep in their subconscious, in their spirit, they know that one day they will face Jesus in judgement and of course that is frightening.

Praise God, Jesus also has the power and the desire to reconcile us to God. He can do that because He, the Judge, has actually willingly taken the judgement for us in love! As it says in 1 John 4:17–18: '... *we will have confidence on the day of judgment, because in this world we are like him [Jesus]. There is no fear in love. But [his] perfect love drives out fear.*'

So let us be encouraged! The Lord Jesus is unique and the fact that editors are afraid to use His name is just confirmation that His name is above any other name. We have the privilege of being His. We are even called by His name! And we have been given the most extraordinary privilege of using the name of Jesus. He invites us to pray in His name.

Let us use the most powerful name in the world often, and pray to Him and get to know Him who loves us. Amazing! He loves *us*!

PRAYER: *Lord Jesus, I praise You because You are the Lord of all! Thank You so much for loving me and for giving me the privilege of using Your extraordinary name. Amen.*

April 23 | Called to be with Jesus

Jilly Lyon-Taylor

Jesus went up on a mountainside and called to him those he wanted, and they came to him. He appointed twelve ... that they might be with him and that he might send them out to preach and to have authority to drive out demons.

Mark 3:13–14

We are often encouraged to identify our particular calling – to preach, to teach, or to evangelise. But I wonder if you've noticed that in Mark's gospel the first call of the disciples was to be *with* Jesus, and then He sent them out to preach and to cast out demons. For each of us our prime call is to be with Jesus, set apart for Him, spending time with Him. All else will follow from our relationship with Him.

In this account Jesus went up on a mountainside and called those He wanted to come to Him. Presumably in order to respond to Him they had to leave the clamour of the crowds and the demands of the people below and go up higher to be separated and alone with Jesus.

Is Jesus calling you to go up the mountain to a higher level of intimacy with Him? That may mean temporarily separating yourself from the hubbub of life…

Is Jesus calling you to go up the mountain to a higher level of intimacy with Him? That may mean temporarily separating yourself from the hubbub of life, leaving those things that clamour for your attention – even the good and worthwhile concerns that God may have given you in the past – in order to be with Jesus, to listen to Him and to hear His heart. If you do this as a priority, you'll be able to do the things He is calling you to do.

In the story of Martha and Mary, Jesus told Martha that Mary had '*chosen what is better*' as she sat at Jesus' feet and listened to Him (Luke 10:42). Will you choose what is better today, to go up the mountain to be with Jesus?

Prayer: *Lord Jesus, please forgive me for the times I have ignored Your call to be with You. I want to make it a priority to respond to You, to come up the mountain to be with You. Thank You that You want to be with me. Amen.*

April 24 | Integrity

Joan Rono

Then the LORD said to Satan, 'Have you considered my servant Job? There is no-one on earth like him; he is blameless and upright, a man who fears God and shuns evil.'

Job 1:8

Job is one man in the Bible who held his integrity, even in the face of loss and calamity. God commended Job for being upright!

Job's friends visited him and spoke a lot of words to him, some to encourage him and some to rebuke him. But Job remained focused on God. He knew that God had authority to take and to give. He didn't open his mouth to dishonour God. His faith in God was as strong in his loss as it was in his time of plenty. *'In all this, Job did not sin by charging God with wrongdoing'* (Job 1:22).

One thing I learnt about integrity is: it's not what we do when people are looking at us that matters, but what we do when we're alone. God saw who Job was beyond the multitude of his wealth. If Job's integrity came from wealth, fame, friendships and other things that he held dear, then the devil could have prevailed. But his integrity was there because he walked in the fear of God and did what was right in the presence of God.

It's the heart that makes a man rich. He's rich according to what he is, not according to what he has. Job was rich because he had an intimate friendship with God; his virtue was in God. He was upright before his Maker. He explained his relationship with God as an intimate one. He walked with God and did everything in honour (Job 29).

Integrity is upright, honest, reliable, trustworthy. It's not easily influenced into wrongdoing. It also means being complete and undivided. We live in a society where integrity is far from people's hearts and a thing of the past. It's not easy to find a person of integrity.

The truth is that God honours that commitment. Doing what's right when nobody else is watching is NOT an easy thing. God knows it isn't easy. Here's what His Word says about it: *'Better is a poor man who walks in his integrity than a rich man who is perverse in his speech and is a [self-confident] fool'* (Proverbs 19:1, AMP).

Are you a person of integrity? You can be with God's help!

Prayer: *Lord, I need Your help to maintain my personal integrity. I want to be the kind of person that everyone knows keeps her word. I want to be Your example of living a life without compromise. Please help me, Lord. Help me to take my commitments seriously. Help me say what I mean and mean what I say. And mostly, help me to ALWAYS do the right thing, even when nobody else is watching. I ask all things in Jesus' name, Amen!*

April 25 | Carried in Loving Arms

David Silvester

> *Fear not, for I have redeemed you; I have summoned you by name; you are mine. When you pass through the waters, I will be with you; and when you pass through the rivers, they will not sweep over you. When you walk through the fire, you will not be burned; the flames will not set you ablaze. For I am the LORD, your God, the Holy One of Israel, your Saviour.*
>
> Isaiah 43:1b–3a

In situations beyond our control, and when all else seems to be failing and there is little hope of coming through, this is where God's faithfulness to His promises can really become our experience.

After being discharged from hospital following an operation, things began to go seriously wrong. Within a few days, and having been re-admitted to hospital, doctors and nurses were unable to discover the problem causing me to sink so low.

On the day the nurses were expecting me to die, my wife read these words to me and prayed for me. She gave me to the Lord who had the power to heal and the authority to take me to Himself. When she left me, she expected there would be an emergency operation to ascertain what was wrong. That did not happen, but after examining me a few times, the surgeons recognised something was happening which they could not explain. They postponed the operation to the next day. Two and a half hours after my wife had prayed for me, I walked to the telephone to tell my family that 'visiting time is back to normal'.

The following morning, and reading those same verses, I was struck by what follows in verse 4: '*Since you are precious and honoured in my sight, and because I love you …*' The impact of those words brought tears of joy and absolute wonder. God had been there all the time, carrying me through that difficult experience. Hallelujah!

When we go through difficult situations beyond our control, and are unaware of His presence, God IS there to support us and carry us through.

PRAYER: *Thank You, Lord, that in difficult situations I can experience the fulfilment of the promises of Your Word. Please forgive me for the times I worry about situations beyond my control, and help me to rest in peace knowing that You are faithful to Your promises because You love me so much. Amen.*

APRIL 26 | ONE HEART

RICHARD HEMERY

> *May he give you the desire of your heart and make all your plans succeed.*
>
> Psalm 20:4

I was reading Psalm 20 verse 4, when I realised I had misread a word. I had read, 'May he give you the desires of your heart and make all your plans succeed.' But actually it says, *'May he give you the desire of your heart and make all your plans succeed.'* Maybe we are used to saying 'our heart's desires', but the Bible, here and elsewhere, tells us our heart can only have one desire. If we have another desire, it supplants the first desire in our hearts.

Jesus says the same thing in Luke 16:13: *'No servant can serve two masters. Either he will hate the one and love the other, or he will be devoted to the one and despise the other. You cannot serve both God and Money.'* The object of our service, our affection, where our heart really lies, cannot be divided. Jesus uses the example of money, but it can be extended to other things too.

As He says in Matthew 6:21, *'For where your treasure is, there your heart will be also.'* Whatever is foremost in your life, the thing you treasure, this will attract your heart like a magnet.

The other half of verse 4 of Psalm 20 is *'and make all your plans succeed.'* The second part of the next verse is *'May the LORD grant all your requests.'* It is not wrong to have many plans and many requests, but we can only have one desire in our hearts. Let it be the Lord.

PRAYER: *Please, Lord, make my heart serve You only. Give me grace to make You the desire of my heart. Be my treasure, Lord, in Jesus' name, Amen.*

April 27 | Faithful God

Goran Andersson

The LORD is faithful to all his promises and loving towards all he has made.

Psalm 145:13

This is a breathtaking statement! When we consider the many promises given in God's Word to mankind, to Israel, to various nations and groups of people, to the Church, and to individuals, it's staggering to think that not one of them will end up forgotten or ever be revoked.

There are many people who can testify to the truth of this statement. Moses testified to heaven and earth, *'He is the Rock, his works are perfect … A faithful God who does no wrong …'* after 120 years of walking with the Lord in very challenging, changing and gruelling circumstances (Deuteronomy 32:4). And the author of Hebrews says, *'… he who promised is faithful'* (Hebrews 10:23).

The faithlessness of His people, their sins, their falling away and walking astray have never changed His heart. He's as faithful as ever. He was faithful to David when David fled for his life. He was faithful to the three men in the fiery furnace. He was faithful to the frightened disciples in a shaky boat on a stormy sea. And He was faithful to the ten lepers believing His word that they would be healed. And He's faithful to you.

Your situation today is probably unique. No one has ever been in exactly the same circumstances, faced your situation, been tested like you, or had the opportunities you have today. But what you're meeting today doesn't take God by surprise. This day of your life was written in His book long ago. He prepared, ahead of time, the works which you can choose to do today. Whatever you'll come up against today – remember your God is faithful to all His promises. You needn't worry, but you need to learn to trust Him.

How can He be so faithful, in spite of what we are and what we've done? The answer is simple, and staggering: 'The Lord is loving towards all he has made.' He loves you. That's the only reason – and that's enough!

Prayer: *Thank You, Lord, for Your unchanging love, that I can depend on You in all circumstances, and that I can trust Your wonderful promises, in Jesus' name. Amen.*

APRIL 28 | CHARIOTS OF FIRE

PAM SMITH

Then Elisha prayed, and said, 'O LORD, I pray thee, open his eyes that he may see.' So the LORD opened the eyes of the young man, and he saw; and behold the mountain was full of horses and chariots of fire round about Elisha.

2 Kings 6:17, RSV

Sometimes the trials seem to loom very large. Problems can be magnified and very much 'in your face' so that nothing else can be seen but the problem. The enemy commander is not Ben Hadad, as in Elisha's story, but Satan. The spears and darts come in the form of temptations and trials.

At these times, does faith shrink as troubles appear as giants? No! My power and strength is small, yet my God is so great. Jesus comes saying, *'Don't be afraid because I am with you.'* He is the mighty Rock of safety and protection. We can run to Him.

Oh that we could know and see, like Elisha, when troubles are stacked up against us, the Host of heaven's armies is on our side, and the Captain of the Host is Jesus (Joshua 5:14).

As we yield to Him, He can command His chariots to rescue us from the attack, entrapment or deception of the enemy.

The Scriptures tell of the people who trusted God that won battles and overthrew kingdoms. He gives me the skill in war and strength to bend a bow of bronze, *'For though we live in the world we are not carrying on a worldly war, for the weapons of our warfare are not worldly but have divine power to destroy strongholds'* (2 Corinthians 10:4, RSV).

We are not defenceless. May we be able to see the power available to us and understand how to use it. Let us put on the armour God has given us. There is more to our universe than the things we can see with our physical eyes.

We can be overcomers. We can live pure lives. We can be fearless witnesses. We can be a people filled with the love of Jesus.

PRAYER: *Lord, help me to fully yield to You and resist the enemy. Would You open my eyes to see Your power and glory and to know how to stay under Your loving protection, in Jesus' name. Amen.*

April 29 | The Body

Joan Rono

And he is the head of the body, the church: the starting point of all things, the first to come again from the dead; so that in all things he might have the chief place.

Colossians 1:18, BBE

Of all God's creation the thing that amazes me most is God's most unique creation, man. God not only made him a spiritual being but a physical and emotional being with a body, a soul and a spirit.

I have observed this fact about my own body: when I see a part of my body is facing danger, another part of my body tries to protect it. For example if I was walking along and something flew up and over my head, maybe only the leaf of a tree, both my hands would react by covering my head to protect it.

Last year I fell and broke my ankle. Though the place that hurt was my ankle, my whole body went into shock and trembled. The rest of my body also reacted. My mouth called for help (having been instructed by my mind to do so) and my hand rubbed my leg, trying to comfort it. It's just amazing how the whole body responds in harmony together.

Paul's letter to the Colossians says that the Church is a body, and Jesus is the head of this body. And this is what Paul wrote in Romans: *'For, as we have a number of parts in one body, but all the parts have not the same use, so we, though we are a number of persons, are one body in Christ, and are dependent on one another'* (Romans 12:4–5, BBE).

The most interesting thing to me is what Paul says in Colossians chapter 12, and I recommend that you read it. He says that the Body of Christ (the Church) should function as one. What an amazing way of describing the role we have as the Church. It would be ridiculous to think of my mind saying, 'It's just the ankle so I'll ignore it,' or my mouth saying, 'It's just the ankle; what's that to do with me?' God created the body in such a way that all its parts automatically respond to one other.

We as the Church, the Body of Christ, should be able to respond to one another in love. Jesus said, *Love one another and when you do this the world will know that you are mine.* Instead of casting blame and pointing the finger we should protect, strengthen, encourage, uplift and support one another. We should pray in unity with each other for the sake of the gospel, especially in these last days.

Each individual member is a part of the Body, and every part should coordinate and move together. If all of us do our part then God will command a blessing (Psalm 133). Do your part today. Encourage someone, pray for someone, pray for the nations where there is persecution of believers and pray for those whom God has called into the fivefold ministry.

PRAYER: *Father God, I thank You for the price paid on the cross so that I can be part of Your Body. I pray that You will open my eyes to see what part of the body I am. Help me to do what is right for Your Church, Your Body. Give me a passion to love the body of Jesus and see that it grows. Amen.*

APRIL 30 | THE BREATH OF GOD

PETER HORROBIN

But it is the spirit in a man, the breath of the Almighty, that gives him understanding.

Job 32:8

Have you ever wondered how it is that man is so clever? Why is mankind so creative? Why is it that all human beings, the good and the bad, the born again and the atheists, are all capable of such amazing intellectual achievements?

The answer lies in this amazing verse from the book of Job which tells us that the very spirit of man is indeed the breath of the Almighty – and that it is this which gives man his understanding. So all of the human race is benefitting from the creative genius of Almighty God, the Creator of all things. There's nothing creative that man does, drawing on the ability to understand things, which doesn't come from God himself. Every great book, every amazing painting, every intellectual achievement, every technological breakthrough – in every case the source is the genius of God, whether people recognise it or not!

But having said that, isn't it extraordinary that so many people, who have such creative and intellectual ability, are at the same time so stupid! As the Bible says, it's the fool who says in his heart there's no God. Their eyes have been so blinded by the god of this world. In their enthusiasm to deny the existence of the Creator they can't see that without the Creator they couldn't do anything – not even write a book to try and prove that God does not exist!

They also imply that if you believe in God you can't enjoy yourself. What utter nonsense! True joy only finds its source in the Creator – as Nehemiah discovered. The joy of the Lord was his strength. Those who do their own thing and have no fear of God become wise in their own eyes. They lose their sense of spiritual reality and demonstrate the foolishness that is expressed by those who don't recognise the amazing truth in our scripture.

An old hymn says, *'Rise up, O men of God! Have done with lesser things'* (William P. Merrill). Let's rise up as men and women of God and draw on the understanding He gives to His children. Let's move on from the lesser things to become the dynamic, creative and joyful Kingdom people that give such pleasure to their Creator.

PRAYER: *Lord, we pray for all those who are influenced by the arguments of those who deny Your existence. Open their eyes to see the foolishness of denying You and show them the Saviour who loved and died for them so that they can know Father God for themselves, in Jesus' name, Amen.*

MAY 1 | ARE YOU A £5 NOTE OR A 20P?

JILL SOUTHERN-JONES

The greatest among you will be your servant.

Matthew 23:11

One day, a few years ago, I was rushing along as usual in my Volvo, when the engine cut out and the car stopped. It was pouring with rain and I didn't have a coat. I saw a red telephone box some way ahead. There was nothing for it but to grab my handbag, lock the car and run to the phone box.

By the time I arrived, I was absolutely soaked. I looked in my purse for a 20p to make a call and found, to my great dismay, that I only had a £5 note.

What could I do now? As complete frustration overwhelmed me, the Lord spoke. 'You have a £5 note and you need a 20p piece.' 'Yes, Lord, I know that!' And the Lord said, 'Sometimes, I need you to be a 20p piece because there are times when a £5 note is useless. Are you willing to be a 20p piece when I need you to be, or are you always wanting to be a £5 note?'

I wasn't expecting the Lord to speak to me and I was profoundly affected. As I considered this challenge, I started to cry (as if I wasn't wet enough already!) and said, 'O Lord, I humble myself afresh before You and agree. I'm willing to be a 20p piece for You whenever You need me to be one.'

Through my tears, I looked down to get a tissue from my bag and my eyes caught sight of a 20p piece in the returned coin slot. How remarkable of God! I was able to use it to make the call and get the help I needed.

I've never forgotten that moment. He's the Master, I'm the servant. It's so important that I'm willing to serve and learn to be servant-hearted as Jesus Himself was.

PRAYER: *Lord, teach me today to be wholly available to You, to serve in whatever way You choose. I'm willing to be a 20p piece whenever You need me to be one. Help me to learn to be servant-hearted, in Jesus' name, Amen.*

MAY 2 | SYMPHONY OF AGREEMENT

JILLY LYON-TAYLOR

> *I tell you that if two of you on earth agree about anything you ask for, it will be done for you by my Father in heaven.*
>
> Matthew 18:19

At first reading, this verse (Matthew 18:19) makes praying with others appear very easy – as if all we need to do is decide what we're going to ask for and it'll be done! However, the word *'agree'* means much more than reaching a consensus together, or the lack of disagreement. The Greek word is *sumphoneo* (from *sun* = together, and *phone* = sound), and so its literal meaning is to *'sound together'*. It has the same root as our English word 'symphony'.

If we think about a symphony orchestra, it's vital that each member is in tune with the others, and also that each instrument is tuned to perfect pitch. Without that, just one person sounding a discordant note will spoil the whole piece. In the same way, as we pray together, we need to be in tune with one another, but what's even more important, in tune with God and perfectly lined up with the truth in His Word. Otherwise our prayers won't flow with the unity of agreement that Jesus is talking about.

In a symphony orchestra timing is also important. The conductor directs the players, and they need to keep their eyes on him, following his direction for expression and timing. And that's how it should be when we pray together. Each one of us should be looking to God for direction, waiting for His timing to bring our contribution. Sometimes the percussionist, for instance, has to wait patiently for the right moment to bring the clash of cymbals, which might be his only contribution. If done too early or too late, it could ruin the whole piece of music!

When considering what agreement in prayer means, we need to look at the context of this verse. It is sandwiched between Jesus' teaching on what to do when someone sins against us, and His teaching on forgiveness. The 'symphony' of agreement in prayer can only be there if we've first tried to deal with any grievances we may have in a right way, with the aim of restoring relationships, and also if we've forgiven everyone who's sinned against us, from our hearts. Then we'll be able to expect that what we ask for will be done for us by our Father in heaven.

PRAYER: *Father, please forgive me for not always being in tune with You and Your Word, and for holding on to grievances and un-forgiveness against others. Help us, as Your Body, to flow together in agreement in a way that will please You, in Jesus' name, Amen.*

MAY 3 | A LONG JOURNEY OF FAITH

PAUL WATSON

> *Moses returned to the LORD and said, 'O Lord, why have you brought trouble on this people? Is this why you sent me? Ever since I went to Pharaoh to speak in your name, he has brought trouble upon this people, and you have not rescued your people at all.'*
>
> Exodus 5:22–23

God has called upon Moses to go to Pharaoh to ask him to set the Israelites free, but after his visit, Pharaoh makes things worse for the people. Far from letting the people go, they are now in a worse predicament than before! Moses comes before the Lord and cries out the words quoted above.

Moses has begun a long journey of faith! He will begin to learn about God's plans versus his own understanding of how things should work out. He will learn about God's timing which is not his own timing. He will learn about trust. He's beginning to interact with God.

It's interesting that in verse 22 Moses cries out, 'O Lord!' Often in the Old Testament God is referred to as LORD, from the Hebrew expression *Jehovah* – the self-existent one.

Here, however, Moses calls God 'Lord', from the Hebrew *Adonai*, meaning 'the Lord my Lord'. Moses is using a proper name of God, with a very personal meaning. 'O Lord my Lord!' he cries. The foundation of the faith journey ahead is a close relationship with his God. This relationship ensures that despite circumstances, Moses knows the character of God personally, and is able to trust Him, even though God's ways are not his ways.

Our life too is a journey of faith. There are often times when we feel that God has made things worse. We can be tempted to believe that we could have done it better than God has. The essence of faith is to resist this temptation, to wrestle with God by sharing our heart with Him, and ultimately to put our trust in Him. And as Moses learned, God never lets us down.

PRAYER: *Father God, I love You. You are perfect in all Your ways. The truth is that You will not fail me nor forsake me. Please help me to trust in Your unfailing love, in Jesus' name, Amen.*

MAY 4 | VALUED BY GOD

ANDREAS HEFTI

> *And He said to me, my grace is sufficient for you, for my power is made perfect in weakness. Most gladly therefore I will rather glory in my weaknesses, that the power of Christ may overshadow me.*
>
> 2 Corinthians 12:9, The Lutheran Bible

God knows all about our strengths and our gifting, but He also knows all about our weaknesses, our difficulties and our limitations. So often we feel inadequate for the tasks with which we are entrusted or the challenges of life we have to face. We feel so small and often there is that sense of having failed. The enemy loves to whisper these kinds of lies into our ears. I was very much encouraged by a story I was recently told:

In India there once lived a water carrier who carried two big jugs of water on his shoulders along a road. One of these two jugs had a big crack through which the water dripped out along the route between the well and the master's house. Whenever they reached the house, one jug was only half full. The other one, however, could always deliver to its full capacity.

We can imagine how the cracked jug talked to his carrier:

'I feel so bad, ashamed and inadequate!' said the jug.

'Why is that?' the master asked.

'Because, due to my terrible crack, I have only been able to bring half of the water to your house,' the jug replied.

'Don't worry!' the master said. 'Have you seen the beautiful flowers along the way between the well and the house?'

'No,' the jug answered.

So the master finally told the cracked jug: 'I knew exactly about your crack and that you lost a lot of water along the way. So I put flower seeds along your side of the road, knowing that you would water them. For years now I have been able to pick these beautiful flowers to decorate the table in my dining room.'

Do we commit our weak points and our human inadequacy into our Master's hands? In His infinite wisdom He can use them for His glory. Jesus says that without Him we can't do anything, but that with Him all things are possible. In one way or another we are all like cracked pots in our potter's hands. I have found that in the place of my deepest need God has often used me in extraordinary and unexpected ways. In those instances I knew that it was God who did it as there was nothing left of myself to offer.

I have met deeply broken people who have such a strong fragrance of Jesus around them and have often been a source of inspiration, comfort and encouragement to me. In Psalm 31:12 David describes himself as a broken vessel. God promises that He is close to the broken-hearted. A life entirely committed to God will always be a precious vessel and tool in God's hands, reflecting His glory. According to Isaiah 65, God is able to bring forth beauty from ashes, joy from sadness, life from death, freedom from captivity and restoration from failure. The question Jesus is asking us is not 'What can you do for me or what are your talents?' Rather He is asking us, 'Do you love me?' If we are able to answer this question with a 'yes' from the bottom of our hearts then nothing is impossible for Him to do through us. Even if the enemy presses in on our weak areas we don't have to lose heart but can take courage. Don't forget that this side of heaven we are an imperfect and yet precious work in progress and that God can use us any time He wishes. If He is for us, who or what could be against us?

PRAYER: *Dear Heavenly Father, please help me to realise that You are not a performance-oriented God, but a God who is interested in a loving, personal relationship. I am so grateful that You are not limited by my weaknesses, inadequacies or limitations, but can be glorified through them as I trust You. Please help me, Father, to discern the enemy's voice when he tries to put me down and condemn me in my weak areas. Help me to be strong and overcome in You. In the name of your precious Son, Jesus, I pray. Amen.*

May 5 | Blessing and Offence

Margaret Silvester

Blessed is he who takes no offence at me.

Luke 7:23, RSV

Jesus offended many people. He offended both his enemies and his disciples, because He always spoke the truth and was not afraid to confront sin. He says the ones who are blessed are the ones who do not take offence.

To be offended means to be hurt, resentful, annoyed, repelled or made to stumble because of a circumstance. An offended person usually believes they have been treated wrongly, even if they haven't. Taking offence is the cause of the breakdown of countless relationships and it is the opposite of intimacy and fellowship.

To take offence may seem justified. It is rarely seen for the sin that it is. People who give offence do not always do so deliberately whereas taking offence is a deliberate choice. On that basis, I believe we can say that to take offence is usually a greater sin than to give it.

When Jesus said the above words, a vivid picture would come to the minds of His hearers. The verb 'to take offence' had to do with the trapping of birds. It referred to the action that depressed the bait-stick and triggered off the trap and caught the bird. When we live with offence, a part of us is trapped in the past and we are not living in freedom.

Proverbs 18:19 tells us that *'An offended brother is more unyielding than a fortified city'*. Walls around a city were for protection. Offended people are usually inward-focused. They build walls around their hearts to prevent further hurt. These invisible walls intended for protection are keeping other people at a distance and, consequently, God seems far away.

To move from offence into blessing can only happen through forgiveness. Forgiveness from God for being offended and forgiveness to those we perceive have offended us. God desires us to live in close relationship with Him. This is indeed blessing. It is joy and peace.

Prayer: *Heavenly Father, please forgive me for the times when I have taken offence. I ask You to search the motives of my heart today that I might see myself as You see me. I choose to forgive those who have offended me. Please help me to take down the walls I have built around my heart, in Jesus' name, Amen.*

May 6 | In Fear of Making a Mistake

David Cross

> *And so I tell you that people can be forgiven any sin and any evil thing they say; but whoever says evil things against the Holy Spirit will not be forgiven.*
>
> Matthew 12:31, GNB

Many people worry about this verse. It speaks of an unpardonable sin, but for whom? This warning is actually spoken by Jesus in the context of the evil deception and eternal opposition of the demonic realm towards the true work of the Holy Spirit. Jesus seems particularly determined to reassure us of God's persevering heart of forgiveness towards mankind.

I was talking to a young man recently who was troubled by some of the things he was seeing on a Christian TV channel. During prayer ministry, people were sometimes reacting in seemingly uncontrollable ways. The movements were often violent, sustained, haphazard and certainly very undignified for those involved. But everyone present seemed to be seeking even more of them!

The young man decided to talk to a pastor friend, who told him that when encountering spiritual power like this, it was important to 'go with the flow' and not quench what the Holy Spirit wanted to do. 'But what if it's not the Holy Spirit manifesting the spiritual power?' asked the young man. 'Surely God wants us to discern what spirit is at work?' His friend replied that he'd always been concerned not to speak against the Holy Spirit, so he'd much rather not confront such manifestations, but wait and see what happened afterwards with those involved.

The young man went home still troubled and relayed the pastor's comments to his wife. He found her response simple and very wise. She said, 'Our friend is being controlled by fear, and that will never be how Jesus wants our lives to be directed. We need to pray for him to be willing to confront as God gives him discernment.'

The Holy Spirit is certainly not waiting to trap us into eternal damnation if, on occasions, we fail to recognise Him. It's consistent rebellion which separates us from God, not if we make a mistake when we sincerely seek to discern and confront the difference between the true manifestation of God's Spirit and the defiling deception of the enemy.

PRAYER: *Thank You, Lord, that discernment is one of the gifts of the Holy Spirit. Help me to use it to recognise and bless what You are doing, and not be trapped by deceptions from the enemy. In Jesus' name I pray, Amen.*

MAY 7 | ARE YOU NOT WORTH MUCH MORE?

JOAN RONO

> *Therefore I say unto you, Take no thought for your life, what ye shall eat, or what ye shall drink; nor yet for your body, what ye shall put on. Is not the life more than meat, and the body than raiment?*
>
> Matthew 6:25, KJV

As I lay outside in the spring sun, I saw hundreds of little flies flying freely and enjoying the space and warmth. Spring brings everything to life: the birds, the butterflies, nicely trimmed grass, the flowers and trees, all of different colours and designs. As if in obedience to one voice, everything springs into beauty and colour.

This might make you and me wonder about the wisdom and creativity of our Creator, Father God.

Yet as I look into all this beauty, the scripture comes to life in me when Jesus told His followers, *'Are ye not much better than they?'* (Matthew 6:26, KJV). You and I are more important than the birds, the flowers or anything else. We are made in His image and He knows your every single need before you ask Him.

Our Father owns everything. He does not live far away from us but is omnipresent and only a prayer away. He withholds no good thing from those who love Him. The world worries about physical and material needs. We don't need to join in the world's worry and strife, but trust in Him. He will fulfil what we need because He is our Father.

PRAYER: *Father, thank You for creating me and rejoicing over me. Forgive me for worrying about my needs and help me to trust in Your provision. Now I give You all my needs and desires. Thank You, Lord. Amen.*

May 8 | Don't Fret

Angela Weir

> *Do not fret or have any anxiety about anything, but in every circumstance and in everything, by prayer and petition (definite requests), with thanksgiving, continue to make your wants known to God.*
>
> Philippians 4:6, AMP

I can almost hear the sighs! 'It's all right for you, Paul, telling us not to fret or be anxious, but you have no idea what it is like trying to live in the 21st century.' This is true, but we have to remember that Paul was writing this from his prison cell in Rome, chained to a Roman soldier, and never knowing from one day to the next when he might be put to death. Amazingly, the whole letter to the Philippians is full of joy and Paul's positive attitude to life. Despite the fact that he knew he might die at any moment – or perhaps because of that – he was filled with rejoicing and praise for his beloved Saviour and he never allowed worry to come between them.

One of the biggest hindrances to our relationship with God is that we worry about our day-to-day problems – the many different things which crop up at work, or at home, or at church. It is said about some people that they are never happy unless they have something to worry about! But in today's verse, Paul tells the Philippians not to be worried about anything, but to focus on Jesus. I was interested to discover that the Greek word for worry is *merimnao* which comes from another Greek word: *merizo*, meaning 'to divide in parts'. We want to focus on God but are unable to, because all our daily concerns divide our minds and cause us to be distracted.

In Luke's Gospel (10:38–42), we read of Jesus' first visit to the house in Bethany. Martha is *'anxious and distracted by much serving'* and Mary, instead of helping her sister, is sitting quietly at Jesus' feet building her relationship with Him. When Martha protests to Jesus, He tells her she is worried and troubled about many things, but that Mary has got the right idea. I can imagine Martha getting inwardly furious. 'How can He say she is right? Here am I slaving away, trying to prepare a meal for Him and all those others who came with Him. I need help!' But Jesus is saying, 'Focus on Me first, get your priorities right, and then the other things will seem less complicated and less challenging.'

So often we stumble off into a new day without finding time to spend with Jesus and allowing Him to calm our minds. It may mean getting up a little bit earlier, but just being quiet with our Friend, and putting ourselves into His hands, helps to get things into perspective, our priorities sorted, and even a really busy day then seems to run more smoothly.

PRAYER: *Dearest Father, Thank You that You are concerned about even the trivialities of my life, such is Your love for me. Please help me to place the concerns of each day in Your loving hands, knowing that You care about each one of my concerns and that You will guide me through them. Amen.*

MAY 9 | LIVING WITH WEEDS

LINDSEY HANEKOM

The seed that fell among the thorns represents those who hear God's word, but all too quickly the message is crowded out by the worries of this life and the lure of wealth, so no fruit is produced.
Matthew 13:22, NLT

It was a year ago when we planted grass seed over our newly dug garden area to create a dream lawn, suitable for play and pleasure. With diligent care we nurtured the grass, feeding it, watering it, cutting it and removing the weeds that grew alongside the tender grass shoots. This year we are reaping the rewards of the effort taken and we are fulfilling our dreams of a place for us to enjoy.

However, there is a problem – weeds! Having felt as though our efforts of last year should have been enough to handle such things, we were naturally disappointed to find them multiplying. My initial reaction was to dismiss them with the thought, 'Well, they don't look that bad.' I had failed to realise that the real issue was not about looking good. This was about the weeds stealing space, food and water from the grass.

This is how it is for us in our Christian walk. We often start off with an amazing amount of effort being poured into our journey with God. We open ourselves up and start to dig out the weeds of our lives. But as life moves on we often feel that we have 'done all that' and we just want to move into our calling and destiny under God. Yet the reality is that the cares and concerns of the world and the desires of our carnal nature continue to create such 'weeds' in our lives, even as we walk along our Christian journey.

It may seem as though you never reach the end of the weeds, which is just how I feel when I look at my lawn. Maybe there is some truth in that.

None of us are perfect and none of us have dealt with all that has passed that encroaches into our daily lives with God. The truth is the weeds in our lives are robbing us of a deeper relationship with God, where we receive His love, care and provision.

Being of a stronger constitution than grass, the weeds would eventually overtake the grass and my lawn would not be the place of play and pleasure we intended it to be. In our lives, if we disregard the weeds as 'non-obtrusive' or 'not that bad', they will eventually grow into a more dominant force in our lives and we will fail to enter the fullness of the life, destiny and calling God has for each one of us.

Let us all today ask God to show us the weeds of our lives so that we can live in the fullness of all that He has for each one of us. Let us do this, not for our own ends but to enable us to fulfil our ultimate destiny – to be a pleasure to our Holy God.

PRAYER: *Lord, I know that there are weeds in my life. Help me to see what they are and to deal with them accordingly. Lord, I ask this so that I can grow deeper into You and to give You more pleasure as I love and serve You. Amen.*

MAY 10 | SOCCER

CATH TAYLOR

> *The LORD your God is with you, he is mighty to save. He will take great delight in you, he will quiet you with his love, he will rejoice over you with singing.*
>
> Zephaniah 3:17

All three of our boys are avid soccer (football) fans. If they aren't playing it, talking about it, reading about it or watching it I can guarantee it must be because it's bedtime, mealtime or school!

This winter Ben and Isaac are on soccer teams. Isaac's games are pretty tame, but Ben's (at nine) are pretty hard-core serious! As Mum, watching a group of passionate nine-year-old boys tackle each other for the ball each Saturday afternoon, there is now one little routine I have adopted as we pull into the soccer ground car park. I pray!

This week as we skidded in late to the game, again we took that moment to pray for protection and a good time for Ben. As I prayed, I was suddenly overwhelmed with a very real understanding that God actually really cared about this game that Ben was going to play. I sensed that in the same way that Ben was excited to go and play, and we were all excited to go and watch him, the Lord was excited too! This really touched my heart. The God who made all the heavens and the earth was going to delight in watching His creation play something that He'd gifted him to do!

Now, perhaps you all had this revelation long ago, but I was struck at that moment by how easily we box God in. We know He's there for our troubles and our concerns – there to sort out the whole world and keep it in order – but sometimes we fail to remember that He delights in us! We're His creations! He delights in watching us, with all the characteristics and personality that He created for us. He delights watching us walk in the giftings He's given us. He isn't just checking we're getting everything right and being good. He really enjoys us and loves nothing more than spending time with us, because we're His own personal creation.

PRAYER: *Dear Lord, You're holy and powerful, the King of kings and the Lord of lords, but You're also my Father God. Thank You that You love me with an intimacy that only comes from You being my Creator. Help me to receive the truth that You delight in me and that You love nothing more than spending time with me, in Jesus' name, Amen.*

MAY 11 | LIVING BY FAITH

LIZ GRIFFIN

> *More than anything else, however, we want to please him, whether in our home here or there. For all of us must appear before Christ, to be judged by him.*
>
> 2 Corinthians 5:9–10, GNB

My sister and I have not been in touch for a long time and when I asked how she was she said that even though her physical being was gradually decaying, yet her spiritual being was renewed day by day. She knew that was a verse in the Bible but couldn't think where. Later I found it was 2 Corinthians 4:16. But there was a little bit before those words which intrigued me. It said: *'For this reason we never become discouraged'* (GNB). What a statement of faith!

Why did the apostle Paul never become discouraged? If we read what he said in his letter before that, we find the most marvellous passage about how he knew God had given him work to do and had made the light shine in his heart, *'the knowledge of God's glory shining in the face of Christ'* (2 Corinthians 4:6, GNB). Yet Paul was aware that he himself was like a common clay pot with spiritual treasure within. He went on to tell of the tremendous hardships and sufferings he was enduring but knew it was all worth it as more and more people were being reached by God's grace. These people *'will offer to the glory of God more prayers of thanksgiving'* (4:15, GNB).

Paul's life was a matter of faith, not of sight. He looked forward to his home in heaven with the Lord but said, *'More than anything else, however, we want to please him, whether in our home here or there. For all of us must appear before Christ, to be judged by him'* (2 Corinthians 5:9–10, GNB).

I realise that God wants to show me how to live this way, pleasing Him and being aware that I must give an account of what I've done to Jesus. If I knew I only had a short time to live on this earth I would consider very carefully what to put my time and efforts into, not wanting to waste the time. Why don't I live that way all the time? Some things would not be worth bothering about, although people put a high importance and value on those things. Other things would gain tremendous value and would gain eternal rewards in heaven.

PRAYER: *Please help me, Lord, to see what is valuable in Your sight and give me the strength and power to do those things. Help me not to be dragged down, discouraged or diverted by what other people say or want me to do. Help me to keep my eyes fixed on You and to live by faith not sight, in Jesus' name, Amen.*

MAY 12 | THE SCAPEGOAT

ANGELA WEIR

> *And Aaron shall lay both his hands upon the head of the live goat and confess over him all the iniquities of the Israelites and all their transgressions, all their sins; and he shall put them upon the head of the goat [sin-bearer], and send him away into the wilderness by the hand of a man who is timely (ready, fit).*
>
> Leviticus 16:21, AMP

What an amazing prophecy that verse is of all that Jesus would do for us when He came to die on Calvary. In Leviticus we read all the instructions God gave to Moses for the animal sacrifices, which would temporarily cover the sins of the people. The penalty for sin is death, but God allowed innocent animals to be sacrificed instead of guilty human beings. Those sacrifices, however, would never be enough, and would have to be repeated continuously until Jesus Himself came to pay the penalty once for all. How wonderful it is to know that there is now no sin too big to be covered by that sacrifice, which He made for us all on the cross.

There are parts of the Western Church today which want to ignore the cross and concentrate solely on the words of Jesus, believing that the cross is off-putting to people. They believe that if we preach a 'social gospel' it will surely be more attractive to the unsaved, who find it humiliating, exclusive and offensive to hear of their need for a Saviour. But from Genesis 3:15 onwards, the Bible is preparing the way for Jesus to come to rescue us from the death we all deserve because of our sinful nature, and set us free from guilt and shame. This means we can have restored contact with our loving Father in heaven – something impossible for us until we're covered with the righteousness of Jesus.

In Britain we're being encouraged by some of our church leaders to speak out for our Christian beliefs in the '*Not Ashamed*' campaign. Let's hope that we shall indeed proclaim, loud and clear, the wonderful message: Jesus, the sin-bearer, died on the cross, outside the city walls, thus carrying away our sins like the scapegoat. He paid the full price, so that when we come to Him, inviting Him to be our Lord and Saviour, we're forgiven and set free.

PRAYER: *Lord Jesus, Thank You for dying on the cross for me so that I could be forgiven. I recognise my need of You as Saviour. I offer every part of myself to You – my body, soul and spirit. Please fill me with Your Holy Spirit. Thank You, Jesus, Amen.*

MAY 13 | REFLECTIONS

MARGARET SOUTHEY

As water reflects a face, so a man's heart reflects the man.

Proverbs 27:19

Reflections on a still pool of water are a wonder of nature. I never cease to be fascinated by the amount of detail and colour that are reflected. If there's the slightest breeze the image shimmers a little but remains intact.

Scripture, in telling us that '*a man's heart reflects the man*', is saying that our heart reflects who we are. It reflects our inner person. It's from the core of our heart that we live out our life. Our decisions, emotions and ultimately our behaviour originate in our heart. This means that whatever is going on in our heart is in some way evident in our life.

This is a truth that we may not necessarily like. Attitudes, beliefs, resentments, dislikes, anger, fear, arrogance are a few examples of what is lodged in our heart and we don't want people to know about them.

The world we live in is one that promotes deception. This is nothing new. Deception originated at the fall when the serpent deceived Adam and Eve into believing that they wouldn't die if they ate the forbidden fruit. Satan has been leading us on paths of deception ever since.

A common deception that we experience is when something is made to look better than it really is. Think of the images of beautiful women who don't have a flaw in either their looks or their shapes. This isn't reality but the work of an airbrush. What about the picture advertisements for hotel rooms that always look bigger and smarter in print than they are in reality or whose magnificent view can be seen only from one corner of the bathroom window?

When it comes to what's going on in our heart we too can use deception. The person we want to portray is different from the inner reality. We can pretend to be calm when actually we're very angry, to be kind when we're harbouring unkind thoughts, to be forgiving when deep down there's resentment, and to be happy when we're actually sobbing inside.

What we often don't realise is that people can see through the masks that we're hiding behind. They may not see the fine details that are reflected in clear water, but they do see the outline of what's in our hearts. They aren't fooled. But we are!

So what are we to do? We must turn to our loving Father who wants to heal and restore us deep within. We must ask Him to show us what we're trying to hide, whether it's sin or hurt. We must ask Him to help us deal with it so we can be restored and reflect pure hearts. We want to be open, transparent and guileless so others see something of the reflection of Jesus in our lives.

PRAYER: *Father, I want an open heart, a heart that reflects a pure life committed and dedicated to You. Please show me the things that are staining my heart and also my life and help me to deal with them. Thank You that with You all things are possible. Amen.*

May 14 | Go, and Do It

David Silvester

He [Jesus] called His twelve disciples to him and gave them authority to drive out evil spirits and to heal every disease and sickness.

Matthew 10:1

I wonder how many of us really believe that God can use us in the same way He used Jesus' disciples and early church members?

In my late twenties, when I was suffering from a severe bronchial asthma spasm, my wife was told I would not see forty. From the age of twenty-three, this affliction had taken hold of me and was increasing its grip at a rapid pace. It restricted all physical activity, and my presence was announced by a noisy wheezing.

Then, one evening, as we met with a group of friends to look at the Scriptures and investigate the dimension we sensed was missing in our Christian experience, one of them suggested they pray with me about this affliction. They stood around placing their hands on me, and prayed that Jesus would heal me.

From that day onward, the difference has been amazing. During those years of affliction, walking the promenade to the town (two and a half miles each way), going up hills and mountains in the Lake District, playing tennis and riding a bicycle would have been impossible, but now these are regular activities for me. The bronchitis has gone, and almost all trace of asthma. The Lord did a marvellous work of healing as a result of those simple prayers.

When Jesus sent the twelve disciples out, He gave them authority to drive out evil spirits and to heal every disease and sickness (Matthew 10:1). The group who prayed with me all those years ago had been trying to find out why such healings were not being experienced in churches today. I'd asked the question, 'What's happened to the power and authority Jesus invested in those disciples?' I'd read the Gospels and Acts and believed that Jesus' power is just the same today as it was then, so I'd been asking why it wasn't the normal experience in every church.

Since then it has been a privilege and a joy to minister to others in Jesus' name, and watch as He has touched and healed many, whether it's been in spirit, soul or body. If we are truly His disciples, then isn't it reasonable to say that the same power and authority is available for all of us to use as in the early Church?

PRAYER: *Dear Lord God, please forgive me for those times I've failed to recognise the gifts and use the authority given by Jesus to His followers to help the sick and suffering. Give me insight and sensitivity to recognise when You've placed me in situations to be used for Your glory and the blessing of others, in Jesus' name. Amen.*

MAY 15 | ALL OF YOURSELF?

RICHARD FILA

> *'No,' said Peter, 'you shall never wash my feet.' Jesus answered, 'Unless I wash you, you have no part with me.'*
>
> John 13:8

In life we often present the good parts of ourselves to others and keep the less desirable, more ugly bits, to ourselves. It's only natural to want to keep less presentable things hidden from the view of others – for example I wouldn't like everyone to see me first thing in the morning before I've had a chance to shower and sort out my hair!

But it's most important that we don't hide any part of ourselves from Jesus. The minute we start to hide the unpresentable things in our hearts from Him, we enter into unreality. We aren't offering Him our whole selves, but instead we're making a 'soulish' effort to be something other than totally in need of Him.

Jesus wants all of us, not just bits of us. He's passionate about knowing the real you, warts and all. When we reveal our whole heart to Him, and, in utter humility, let Him, the holy and blameless Son of God, even wash our feet, only then do we truly enter into the depth of relationship with Him that He wants so much. We often try and self-remedy our flaws, a bit like Adam and Eve did with fig leaves (Genesis 3:7). But we know from that story that when we acknowledge our nakedness before God He will clothe us in a much better way than we ever could ourselves (Genesis 3:21).

It takes trust on our part to be this vulnerable, and often determination to overcome our desire to try and fix things ourselves. For some this journey can be more troublesome than others. It depends how deeply we have put our trust in ourselves, and it takes time to unravel it all. Our very nature, together with the enemy's strategy of focusing on our weak areas, can sometimes make our old habits come back again. The blessing for us is that God looks at our heart attitude and will walk alongside us on this journey, no matter which point of it we are on, and He never loses His passion or zeal for intimacy with us!

If you haven't already done so, why not make a decision today to give your true self – wholly and unedited – to Jesus. That might take some time to follow through on, but remember where the heart goes, the feet will follow.

PRAYER: *Father God, thank You for the stunning reality that You want to be close and intimate with the real me. I'm sorry for the times when I haven't been completely open with You. I want to give You my whole unedited heart. Please show me how I can do this day by day. Thank You for Your faithfulness to me, in Jesus' name. Amen.*

MAY 16 | FACING TRIALS

JILLY LYON-TAYLOR

> *Consider it pure joy, my brothers, whenever you face trials of many kinds, because you know that the testing of your faith develops perseverance.*
>
> James 1:2–3

When facing hardship and difficulties, we are often far from being able to count it pure joy and are more likely to be struggling through with gritted teeth. However, James is reminding us in this verse that trials are there to test us in order to develop perseverance. It is encouraging to think that God might be testing us, as He would only be testing those He wants to use.

When I was a child we used to go to Scotland on holiday, travelling on the overnight train. The journey was a great excitement to me and I would do my best to stay awake, especially as we crossed the Forth Bridge. The builders of this great feat of engineering would have needed to test the materials being used, to ensure that they would be able to carry the weight of the trains that were to thunder across it and to withstand the pull of the tides and the storms that would batter it. In the same way, God tests us to ensure that we will be able to carry the weight of responsibility that He wants to give us, and to withstand the tides of opinion that will seek to pull us away from our calling and the storms that will batter us.

If you are facing trials and difficulties today, be encouraged that God may be testing you because He wants to use you in a deeper way. Like gold having the dross removed, the times of testing also refine us, so that we become more like Him. Persevere, and count it all joy!

PRAYER: *Help me, Lord, to learn the lessons that trials and testings bring, so that my future life will be stronger and more effective for Your Kingdom as a result. In Jesus' name I pray. Amen.*

MAY 17 | LOVER OF THE TRUTH?

RICHARD HEMERY

> *The coming of the lawless one will be in accordance with the work of Satan displayed in all kinds of counterfeit miracles, signs and wonders, and in every sort of evil that deceives those who are perishing. They perish because they refused to love the truth and so be saved.*
>
> 2 Thessalonians 2:9–10

Many believe the days we are living in today are ever nearing the end times the Bible tells us about. We are warned again and again to expect deceptions within the Church – Scripture tells us even the elect are at risk of being deceived.

I find myself asking, 'What is the difference between a Christian who would be deceived and one who would not? What is it that keeps us from being deceived? What is it that keeps us on the straight and narrow with God?' I have pondered over this question for some time as I personally really don't want to be deceived. My heart yearns for Jesus to welcome me at the end with the words, '*Well done, good and faithful servant*' (Matthew 25:21), as opposed to casting me away with the words, *'I never knew you. Away from me, you evildoer'* (see Matthew 7:23).

Just the other day in my own quiet time with God, 2 Thessalonians 2:10 leapt out at me. You know, one of those moments when it's almost like God comes down with His heavenly highlighter! It says those who are deceived refused to 'love the truth'. I realised this is such a key aspect of being a Christian. We must love the truth – unconditionally – whatever it is – however much we might not like it. For example, that could be accepting personal truth about our own life or accepting what is written in the

Scriptures as it is, and loving God for who He really is, not coming up with an easier God of our own making.

Sometimes truth can be hard to accept and live in. I know in my journey as a Christian I have had to face some things about myself that are really ugly and accept them as part of myself before God. As well, my understanding of God has changed a lot as I have read and come to understand more of the Scriptures. As I think back I know in the past I have definitely believed in a God of my own making – one who fitted my understanding and interpretation of the world around me and my feelings as opposed to the true character of God as portrayed in the Scriptures. Breaking away from lies we've believed about God (or anything else for that matter) is not easy and doesn't happen at the drop of a hat. It takes persistence and determination to know and live in the truth.

So my challenge is: 'Are you a lover of the truth? Are you determined to know the truth about yourself and about God and everything else no matter how difficult that might be?' I can personally testify that no matter what pain that might cause in the short term, the long-term rewards here on earth and eternally with Jesus are worth any cost.

PRAYER: *Father God, thank You for the gift of truth. Thank You that You're faithful and don't abandon me to the deceptions of the enemy, but give me a free-will choice to follow You. Please help me to be a lover of the truth, and give me courage to face the consequences of making that choice I will have to face. I trust You to show me the way through every trap of deception the enemy lays for me. Thank You so much for Your faithfulness to me! May I be a blessing to You today, in Jesus' name, Amen.*

MAY 18 | SAFETY

PATRICIA LAKE

> *The LORD then said to Noah, 'Go into the ark, you and your whole family, because I have found you righteous in this generation.'*
>
> Genesis 7:1

'*Go into the ark, you and your whole family*'; those were God's instructions to Noah in the final days before judgement was poured out on the then known world. Noah was obedient and faithful to God in his generation, first building the ark to God's precise instructions and then warning the people to repent and that the end was near. However, when the time came, only eight were saved!

At the cross our Lord and Saviour Jesus Christ became the new Ark which God Himself prepared for the saving of His people. In His mercy God has always provided a window of opportunity for mankind to escape … giving us 'space to repent'.

The Bible is clear: *'As it was in the days of Noah, so it will be at the coming of the Son of Man'* (Matthew 24:37). In other words life will continue as normal with people going about their everyday business, oblivious of the spiritual danger that they are in, as the mire of corruption sucks them in like quicksand – comparable to that of Noah's day. However, just as stark and clear as the warnings that God has given in the Holy Bible are the signs of our Lord's Second Coming which come through the news channels on our TV screens repeatedly each day.

With earthquakes proliferating in diverse places, universal banking systems tottering, nations in uproar … all are signs that the Age of Grace as we know it is fast coming to a close. It is as though the Lord is standing on the balustrades of heaven and shouting, *'Go into the ark, you and your whole family!'* The Church (universal) seems to be sleepwalking its way through life. The urgency of God's call in these last days is no less forceful than it was in Noah's day. It carries with it an emergency warning of imminent danger … of impending doom.

Are we preparing as Noah did: going about our Heavenly Father's business, praying our families, friends and nations into the safety of the Ark of God's presence in the Lord Jesus Christ? The name of Jesus is the only name under heaven given among men whereby we MUST BE SAVED. *'Salvation is found in no-one else, for there is no other name under heaven given to men by which we must be saved'* (Acts 4:12). Or are we among those with dissenting voices who still think … The Lord delays His coming. There are plenty of things to happen yet! (Matthew 24:48). No doubt there were those who still thought that way right up to the day when God closed the door of the ark – who, alas, then found it was too late. If only they could have turned the clock back sixty seconds … or more!

Jesus painted a verbal picture of what would happen in the last days when at His coming the five wise virgins made sure they were ready, but the five foolish virgins were not (Matthew 25:1–13). What will it take to make people call upon the name of the Lord?

Prayer: *Dear Lord, help us to live holy and consecrated lives and be ready for Your return as You have warned us to be. Help us also to continue to pray earnestly for our loved ones who are still not in the safety of Your protection. Amen.*

May 19 | Peace in the Storm

Julie Smith

You will keep him in perfect peace, whose mind is stayed on You, because he trusts in You.

Isaiah 26:3, NKJV

Whilst visiting our son in Australia last year, my husband and I went on a whale-watching boat trip. As we set off the water was calm, but on leaving the harbour for the open sea, instead of spying whales playfully leaping above the surface, we were confronted by a 6-metre swell of water! Smooth sailing had suddenly become an alarming roller-coaster ride!

The skipper merely commented that the ocean was 'a little choppy today'! It seemed much worse than that to the rest of us landlubber passengers! However, I was reassured by his casualness and not afraid for our safety. What did trouble me though (and most of the rest of the passengers too) was the nausea we were feeling that was getting worse by the minute, and the horrible fear of being seasick!

With my balance upset, I prayed hard and did what someone told me to do: fixed my eyes on the horizon. I kept telling myself that however much we rolled and surged up and down, the horizon never changed. The nausea subsided, and once I discovered this key – to concentrate on what was unchanging, straight and true – my determination to keep doing so never wavered!

At the end of the day, my disappointment at not having seen any whales paled into insignificance compared with the relief at not having been seasick! But as I thought about how determined I had been to focus on the horizon, I realised how much more I needed that kind of persistent dedication to keeping my spiritual eyes fixed on Jesus. For we live in a world that is ever changing, where there are intimidating realities all around us, and where, from time to time, we all encounter the turmoil and confusion of stormy seas in our lives. We can so easily be filled with fear and anxiety, or even hopelessness and despair.

But what a blessing it is when we remember, in the middle of whatever turbulence we are experiencing, to lift our eyes to our Heavenly Father and fix them on Him, who is completely unchanging, who is our Rock, whose love for us is unchanging, who is faithful and right there with us in our particular storms. When we do that, although completely undeserved, by His grace and mercy, He rewards us richly with peace for our distress, safety for our vulnerability, stability and security for our confusion and uncertainty, and hope for our hopelessness.

PRAYER: *Father, I am sorry that I so often focus on the circumstances of my life and forget to lift my eyes to You. Please help me to develop that persistent determination to keep my eyes fixed on You, so that I will always remember in whatever I am going through that You are with me. Thank You that You are the one who never changes in the ever-changing circumstances of life, thank You that Your love for me never changes and thank You that it is in You I can find real peace and security. Amen.*

MAY 20 | CLIMB A TREE!

ANDY TAYLOR

> *Jesus responded, 'Salvation has come to this home today, for this man has shown himself to be a true son of Abraham. For the Son of Man came to seek and save those who are lost.'*
>
> Luke 19:9–10, NLT

If anyone had a dramatic encounter with Jesus in the Gospels it was Zacchaeus. His reputation went before him as someone who gained great wealth at everyone else's expense. One day, however, Jesus passed through his home town of Jericho and to ensure he had a good view of the procession, he climbed a tree so that he could see above the gathering crowds. What happened next was a shock to everyone – especially Zacchaeus.

Jesus stopped in His tracks, looked up into the tree, called Zacchaeus by name and told him to come down quickly because He was going to be a guest in his house for the day. Zacchaeus was amazed and excited and hurried down while everyone else talked about how disgraceful it was that Jesus was mixing with sinners. During this encounter with Jesus, however, Zacchaeus made a dramatic life-change. He committed to give away half of his fortune to the poor and to repay those he'd cheated four times what they had paid. It was definitely a day of surprises!

The sequence of this special day was simply desperation, love and surrender. Firstly, Zacchaeus was desperate to see Jesus – desperate enough to climb a tree. Next, he was confronted with the unconditional love and acceptance of Jesus. The truth was that Zacchaeus was not popular. He was overlooked – not just because of his physical size, but because of who he was. But Jesus picked him out and this had such an impact on him that he surrendered to His Lord.

Money, which used to be his god, had become nothing in comparison to the treasure that he found that day. This is what Jesus is referring to in the verses above – that salvation had come to Zacchaeus that day because of his surrender.

Maybe today you need to 'climb a tree', in desperation, to meet with Jesus. Be sure that He will pick you out and show you unbelievable love and acceptance which will lead you further down the road of full surrender to your Lord.

PRAYER: *Thank You, Lord, that You didn't overlook Zacchaeus because of his past, and that You gave him a new future. Help me, Lord, to be so open to You that when You see me as I am, I will respond like Zacchaeus to Your love, in Jesus' name, Amen.*

MAY 21 | JESUS CHOSE JUDAS

ANGELA WEIR

> *One of those days Jesus went out to a mountainside to pray, and spent the night praying to God. When morning came, he called his disciples to him and chose twelve of them ... and Judas Iscariot, who became a traitor.*
>
> Luke 6:12–13, 16

It always astonishes me that Jesus chose Judas to be one of His disciples. Because He was fully God, He knew all things that were in men's hearts: '*"Yet there are some of you who do not believe." For Jesus had known from the beginning which of them did not believe and who would betray him*' (John 6:64). Even knowing that one day Judas would be the one to betray Him for thirty pieces of silver, Jesus still chose him to be one of the Twelve.

During those three years of Jesus' ministry, Judas was treated exactly the same as the others. He saw all that Jesus did, heard His teaching, and was sent out with the other disciples on their missionary journeys. Like the others he also came back full of excitement.

Had Judas repented for what he did, he could have been forgiven, for the blood that Jesus shed on the cross covers all sin, no matter how big. He might even have been restored to his place among the Twelve. But he never got beyond remorse.

There are times when we feel that we have committed a sin so big that we can never be forgiven and we wonder why Jesus chose us in the first place. We are robbed of our peace and are so ashamed that we find it hard to come to the Lord for forgiveness.

God's love is so amazing that He forgives us the moment we confess our sins to Him and then chooses to forget it (Jeremiah 31:34b) – it's the enemy who loves to keep reminding us. It says in the Bible that we were chosen before the creation of the world (Ephesians 1:4). God still chose us, knowing everything about us!

PRAYER: *Amazing God, thank You for Your wonderful love which never changes, no matter how far I stray from You. I choose to forgive myself for the sins I have committed [name them]. I come before You afresh today, asking that You would forgive and cleanse me, and I offer myself to You again, body, soul and spirit. In Jesus' precious name. Amen.*

MAY 22 | PRAISE THE LORD!

LIZ GRIFFIN

> *Speak to one another with psalms, hymns and spiritual songs. Sing and make music in your heart to the Lord, always giving thanks to God the Father for everything, in the name of our Lord Jesus Christ.*
>
> Ephesians 5:19–20

How are we doing with this instruction from the apostle Paul? He also wrote it in his letter to the Colossians, *'Let the word of Christ dwell in you richly as you teach and admonish one another with all wisdom, and as you sing psalms, hymns and spiritual songs with gratitude in your hearts to God'* (Colossians 3:16).

I like what Charles Haddon Spurgeon, 'the Prince of Preachers', once said in a sermon: *'You must either praise God or be miserable. You have a choice. If you don't go forward, you go backward.'* He took singing very seriously and wrote several hymns himself. His congregations of thousands were led in singing without any musical instruments. He encouraged people to praise the Lord in their shops, kitchens and bedrooms and not wait to come to a church building. If they felt their singing voice was no good, he said they could speak praise. Nobody had an excuse not to praise the Lord.

But God is pleased with our singing, however it might sound to human ears. The birds sing because they can't do anything else. God has programmed it into their existence. But when it comes to human beings there is always a choice.

Little babies respond to singing and enjoy rhythm, melody and words. But sometimes the gift of singing is stifled by mockery or criticism later in life. We can be robbed of the ability to sing by illness. Occasionally I wanted to join in the singing at church but my throat was too sore. It was so frustrating, but what joy when the ability to sing came back to me!

I think Jesus must have enjoyed singing. When He celebrated the Passover meal with His disciples they sang a hymn before going to the Mount of Olives (Mark 14:26).

I don't want to be miserable and I've found the best way to avoid that is to *'Sing and make music in your heart to the Lord, always giving thanks to God the Father'*. But the Lord wants me to do more than that. He wants me to share my joy with others. The apostle Paul says, *'Speak to one another with psalms, hymns and spiritual songs.'*

PRAYER: *Heavenly Father, help us to enjoy the gift of music and song You gave to us. May we encourage ourselves, and others, by using it to praise You. May our voices express true praise and worship to You and bring You pleasure and joy. In Jesus' name, Amen.*

MAY 23 | SACRIFICE OF PRAISE

PAM SMITH

> *Therefore by Him let us continually offer the sacrifice of praise to God, that is, the fruit of our lips, giving thanks to His name.*
>
> Hebrews 13:15, NKJV

It is often a sacrifice on our part when we're burdened or in a very hard place to open our mouths and give praise and glory to God. But Jesus has promised to help us. It's also a sacrifice of praise when, with Jesus, we live our lives according to God's ways rather the ways of this world and we go through persecution because of it.

This is how we begin to rise up in praise. Praise is a powerful, secret weapon that we can keep in our hearts ready to use. This will drive away the powers of darkness and show the world that His praise is glorious. *'Sing out the honor of His name; make His praise glorious'* (Psalm 66:2, NKJV). We can speak to our souls and say, *'Bless the LORD, O my soul, and forget not all His benefits'* (Psalm 103:2, NKJV). God inhabits the praises of His people (see Psalm 22:3), so I believe we can open the way for the Lord to come and lift us up into a higher place. And He will.

But it's not until we've first been down at His feet that we can truly rise up in praise. That often involves our whole being, body, soul and spirit. King David danced before the Lord. Offering up praise in song and with instruments and waving a banner is a meaningful way of honouring the Lord. There are many ways to praise God – together with others and personally on our own. But the one thing to remember is our praise and worship is to be holy, set apart for the Lord.

As we praise the Lord and rejoice in Him and sing to Him, it's good to remember that the Lord rejoices over us with singing (Zephaniah 3:17).

PRAYER: *Dear Lord, we thank You that You have called us into the most high place, which is down at Your feet. This is where we find Your Presence, when we gaze on Your glory and worship You.*

MAY 24 | THE TONGUE HAS THE POWER OF LIFE AND DEATH – PART 1

GRACE MARSHALL

> *The tongue has the power of life and death, and those who love it will eat its fruit.*
>
> Proverbs 18:21

Did you know that you have the power of life and death? Perhaps that comes as a surprise? Today's verse from Proverbs 18 says that you have the power of life and death and so do I. That power is in our words. What we say can have that sort of effect on someone.

Can you remember any words which brought life to you? Perhaps it was when someone told you about the hope of eternal life in Jesus. Perhaps it was an encouraging comment which strengthened you just when you most needed it. Kind words bring life to us when we are anxious or distressed. And prayer is powerful. Can you bring life to someone you know today through your words?

The second part of the proverb says that those who love it (the tongue) will eat its fruit. Perhaps you know someone who loves to talk. It might be you! The issue is not really how much we talk but whether our words are bringing life or death. If we love to build other people up with our words, we will eat the fruit of that one day. The fruit will be life.

On the other hand, if we love to demonstrate our own 'rightness' by explaining to our friends our detailed understanding of exactly how a third party is getting things wrong, we will eat the fruit one day – the fruit of death. Death in relationships and opportunities.

God doesn't have impossible standards for us – He knows we all stumble frequently. I definitely do.

Who will want to share their heart with me if they hear me criticising someone else? Subconsciously my friend will be reluctant to share her really vulnerable places with me if I do that, because I'm demonstrating my ability to pull someone apart rather than build someone up.

James 3:2 is reassuring. It says: *'We all stumble in many ways. If anyone is never at fault in what he says, he is a perfect man, able to keep his whole body in check.'*

God doesn't have impossible standards for us – He knows we all stumble frequently. I definitely do.

What can we do? I read about a lady who went on a fast. It was a fast from saying anything negative. No negative words for a week. She said it was excruciatingly difficult, but so valuable. I wonder if the Lord might be speaking to me? How about you?

PRAYER: *Lord Jesus, thank You for the people in my life. Please forgive me for the many times when I have spoken words that did not bring life. Please help me to build people up with my words today. I really mean it. I would appreciate Your help. Thank You so much for Your love. Amen.*

MAY 25 | GRACE MARSHALL

THE TONGUE HAS THE POWER OF LIFE AND DEATH – PART 2

The tongue has the power of life and death, and those who love it will eat its fruit.

Proverbs 18:21

Continuing the theme of the power of words to bring life or death, today I have another question. Do you remember any words spoken to you which brought death? Death of hope. Death to your spirit.

Perhaps you heard this sort of thing as a child: You are hopeless! No one will want to marry you! Why can't you be like your sister (or brother)? You're stupid. You're no use!

Why not take a moment to ask Jesus to bring to your mind any words that were spoken about you which cut your heart.

When such words come from people we love and trust, it hurts so much more. Also words carry more power when they come from someone in authority – because we are more likely to believe what they say. Have you ever spoken to God about it? Have you ever said, 'I forgive that person'?

Now someone may say: Well, I don't really need to forgive because what they said about me is true. I wonder if you've ever thought of really sitting down and questioning whether some of those words are actually true. True by God's definition of truth.

They might feel true! Feelings aren't always right, however. Does the Bible say, 'If you feel something is true then it is true'? No, I can't think of any verse that says that!

So what is God's definition of truth? John 1:17 says, '*... truth came through Jesus Christ*'. Jesus said, '*I tell you the truth*' at least eighty times. And '*I am the way and the truth and the life.*' So if we want to know the truth, we can look at the Bible and see what Jesus says about us. What does He say about you? You could ask Him to show you.

PRAYER: *Lord Jesus, I was cut inside when that person said those words about me. I think I did believe it. If this was not Your truth about me then I'm asking You to show me. I forgive them for what they said. I ask You to remove any negative spiritual power from those words. Your words are life; Your words are loving and kind. Please speak Your words about me. Thank You. Amen.*

May 26 | An Excellent Spirit for Challenging Days

Pat O'Reilly

There is a man in your kingdom in whom is the Spirit of the Holy God.

Daniel 5:11, NKJV

Recently while listening to the news I was amazed at how many Government leaders were being torn apart by the media for their lifestyles and that jokes and emails were being sent around the world about these people and their behaviour. This was also happening amongst us as God's children. Immediately the Holy Spirit reminded me of the life of Daniel.

Daniel found himself as an exile in a strange land in the palace of a heathen king, yet he served the king with honour, respect and excellence, not because of what the king did or didn't do, but because of who he was – the king. Daniel understood that those who are in authority have been placed there by God for a reason, and a season. Because Daniel had an excellent spirit, in the way that he honoured the king, God's favour was on him. Not only did he become the king's chief advisor but his life made such an impact on the king that the king declared, *'Now I, Nebuchadnezzar, praise and extol and honor the King of Heaven'* (Daniel 4:37, NKJV).

This has had a huge impact on my life, my outlook on the political situation in our country, and the way in which I talk about those in authority, especially in front of my children and friends.

Maybe you find yourself in a country or in a job situation where God is not being honoured and it's really tough. I would encourage you to keep on honouring those in authority and do your work with excellence. In this way you will be a representative of the Kingdom of God and you'll begin to experience God's favour on your life.

Prayer: *Lord, please forgive me if I have been weighed in the balance and found wanting in this area of my life. I pray that when I hear rumours about my leaders I will pray and intercede for them, instead of mocking them, judging or joking about them. I pray that instead I will honour and respect those in authority, in Jesus' name, Amen.*

May 27 | Pressing In

Jim Person

Therefore, since we are surrounded by such a great cloud of witnesses, let us throw off everything that hinders and the sin that so easily entangles, and let us run with perseverance the race marked out for us.

Hebrews 12:1

When I was in high school I was part of the cross-country ski team. Many nights I practised – sometimes with the team, sometimes on my own. Our coach would often stress the *necessary* discipline to 'press in' and attack the many hills laid out on our school's 10 kilometre course. It was necessary to maintain our pace and even to increase it when going up the hills. That way we wouldn't lose our momentum. It was interesting that during the team practice, I was greatly motivated to press on up the hills when I had team mates ahead or especially when they were behind me. But when I was on my own, when no one else was looking, I was tempted to take it easy or even to stop and rest.

I think it's like that as Christians. When we have others around us, also going through the tough situation, we often rise to the occasion and triumph over the obstacle set before us. But what happens when we're on our own, with no one around to examine our efforts? What happens when there's no one to 'see' how fast we're going in the race that's set before all who profess Jesus as their Lord? There are many lonely tracks stretched out on the course for believers. In my youth the efforts I put in when I was alone in the hills on the 10 km course dictated how well I was to do when called upon to carry my team to victory. Great would be the cheers of the spectators on the day of the race as they saw the effort we made as we pressed on up those hills! *How are you doing when the hills of life come upon you in your race?*

I encourage you to maintain your momentum and keep the pace, as you keep the necessary discipline of pressing in to what is set before you. The Lord is our strength in times of trouble. He will strengthen the weary in their hardship and will help you up the hills and through to the other side towards victory, as you lean on Him and trust in Him! Don't let's forget that those who've gone before us are witnesses to our efforts, and they're cheering us *with great exuberant cheers* through the hills of our course, *as we keep pressing in*!

Prayer: *Lord, we need You. Our efforts to run the race sometimes seem so small, and often futile. Give us the strength to endure through to the end, and help us, dear Lord, not to quit even when we're discouraged, but to rise up with new effort as You come and strengthen us in our spirits. Would You come and minister to us, giving us new vision for the course before us, and renewed hope to press in? Thank You, Lord Jesus, for giving us strength to continue to run the race set before us and to live victoriously in this day. Amen.*

May 28 | Know the Good Shepherd

Angela Weir

I am the good shepherd; I know my sheep and my sheep know me.

John 10:14

There is a large field of sheep just outside our sitting room window and we sometimes see them all running together in one direction. This is usually because the farmer has come with some food for them. He whistles and they all come running. They recognise his quad bike too, so that when he rides up, sometimes with his sheepdog sitting precariously on the back of the bike, they know exactly what's happening. However, when I take a walk through the fields they usually run in the opposite direction!

There are often sheep put to graze on areas of open moorland. Generations of the flock will have been on that same patch so they know not to stray too far, but these sheep are often vulnerable to rustling. One or two may be attracted by the call of a false shepherd, the others follow and as a result large flocks can be stolen.

There are many alien voices in our world which, like wolves, are intent on destroying the flock of God. It's easy for us to be distracted by false shepherds and be lured into temptation. Jesus wants His 'sheep' to know Him and recognise His voice. We need to practise listening to that still, small voice that comes to us in our prayer time, through our Bible reading or through pictures and impressions that He gives us, so that we may stay close and not be led astray by the voice of a false shepherd.

Prayer: *Lord Jesus, thank You that You do speak to me. Please help me to hear Your voice clearly and not be distracted by false shepherds, however plausible they may seem. Amen.*

May 29 | David Cross

It's Never Too Late!

But now, look. It has been forty-five years since the LORD said that [word] to Moses. That was when Israel was going through the desert, and the LORD, as he promised, has kept me [Caleb] alive ever since. Look at me! I am eighty-five years old and I'm just as strong today as I was when Moses sent me out. I am still strong enough for war or for anything else.

Joshua 14:10–11, GNB

I was recently asked to speak a word of encouragement to some of the older members of a church fellowship. The pastor was concerned that many seemed apathetically resigned to being replaced by the younger members of the Body of Christ. I thought of Caleb.

He was a very remarkable man, described by God as having *'a different spirit'* from those around him. Only he and Joshua made it into the Promised Land because they refused to be intimidated by the giants opposing the children of Israel. After a wait of forty years Caleb was still ready and willing to fulfil his personal destiny. At eighty-five years of age, he was determined to battle against the giants and claim the inheritance which God had promised to him and his family.

Hopefully most of us who are senior members of the church will not be called into a physical war, but we should be the best-equipped troops for the spiritual battle. Our long walk with Jesus and our experience of the enemy's tactics should make our intercession before God and our confrontation with the powers of darkness highly effective, if we remain faithful followers of the Commander of the Lord's army. Our destiny is fulfilled as much through who we are as through what we do.

Caleb was a man who trusted God more than he feared man. Within a short time he had not only displaced the giants from their high ground, but he had also secured an everlasting inheritance for his family. We may not have quite the physical strength of Caleb but there's still plenty of time to seek God's direction, agree with His battle plan and complete the destiny that He has purposed for us on earth. We each have a responsibility to play our part in establishing a secure spiritual inheritance for those that will come after us. Let's not miss God's best both for ourselves and for them!

Prayer: *Thank You, Lord, that however old (or young) I am, there is always a place for me to serve in the Lord's army! In Jesus' name I pray, Amen.*

May 30 | Memorial Stones

Paul Watson

Joshua set up the twelve stones that had been in the middle of the Jordan at the spot where the priests who had carried the ark of the covenant had stood. And they are there to this day.

Joshua 4:9

I have a small collection of stones which I have collected from various places around the world. You might think that is a rather strange hobby. I don't see it that way. You see, each stone represents something special to me. There is a pebble from the beach in Vanuatu where de Quirios landed over 400 years ago and declared that he had discovered the *'great southland of the Holy Spirit'*. Another stone is from a walking path around a lake near the Ellel Ministries Centre at Pierrepont, in Surrey, UK. Here I had many very special walks whilst attending the NETS school.

There are several stones from our centre in Western Australia, the purchase of which was a large component in growing my ability to trust God. When I look at the stones, they remind me of the wonderful things God has done. I recall His character of grace and love and His ability to do the seemingly impossible. It helps me to keep on trusting Him even in the really tough and scary times. They are memorial stones.

My little quirky hobby has a Biblical precedent. God told Joshua to have twelve men from the tribes of Israel take one stone each from the middle of the Jordan as they crossed, and to place them on the river's edge in a pile. This would be a memorial of the miraculous event that would stand for years to come and would serve as a reminder of God's faithfulness in keeping His covenant promises. The stones would 'speak' of what can be accomplished by those who trust in God.

Maybe you could take a few moments to ponder what 'memorial stones' you might have in your life – the things that remind you of what God has done for you, so that you can give Him thanks and praise. A memorial – something you can look back on in remembrance, and which will encourage you to look ahead, in faith.

Prayer: *Dear Father, as I recall the many wonderful things You have done in my life, these memories serve as testimony of Your love for me and that You are faithful. Please help me to use these memorials as a stimulus to being able to trust You with the future. Amen.*

May 31 | Servants and Sons

Joan Rono

> *Your attitude should be the same as that of Christ Jesus: Who, being in very nature God, did not consider equality with God something to be grasped, but made himself nothing, taking the very nature of a servant, being made in human likeness. And being found in appearance as a man, he humbled himself and became obedient to death – even death on a cross!*
>
> Philippians 2:5–8

In my country, Kenya, it's normal to walk around the streets and hear people arguing about politics, discussing who's going to be elected as the next President, the Prime Minister, a Member of Parliament or some other position of authority. It's the talk of every household. As I look at the disciples of Jesus I see they had the same kind of arguments. Who was to be first? Who would sit on the right and left hand of Jesus in His Kingdom? Their focus was on themselves.

Jesus was never tired of answering their questions concerning this matter. We get His teaching on it in many parables in the Gospels. His entire life was centred on serving us, even to the point of dying for us. He didn't consider Himself great, nor did He want people to know Him as anybody great. He took the very nature of a servant. And He taught His disciples and followers to be servants (Matthew 20:26). We need to grasp that the way to greatness is through being a servant.

Our attitude should be that of Jesus. We should take the very nature of servants. However, not only should we take the nature of servants, but also that of sons.

Jesus was also a Son in every way. He didn't seek to do His own will but that of the Father because He was one with the Father. As a Son, He was obedient to His Father; He trusted His Father even when He was given as a sacrifice for our sins.

A son should trust, obey, and love his father. He should find security in his father, ask for what he needs and learn from him. But unlike a servant, a son can inherit what belongs to his father. That's what we ought to be: servants and sons, having the nature of servants, and also the nature of sons, being obedient, loving and trusting the Father.

PRAYER: *Father, help me to be both a servant and a son as I love and trust You and seek to be obedient to Your will. Amen.*

JUNE 1 |
MARGARET SILVESTER

WHO AM I THAT I SHOULD GO?

Moses thought, 'I will go over and see this strange sight – why the bush does not burn up.' When the LORD saw that he had gone over to look, God called to him from within the bush, 'Moses! Moses!' And Moses said, 'Here I am.'

Exodus 3:3–4

Whilst shepherding his father-in-law's sheep in the desert, Moses met with God. Forty years is a long time to wander in a desert, but for Moses it was preparation time; at the burning bush God called him by name and revealed to him the purpose for which he had been born. He was chosen by God to rescue His people from Egypt and to take them into the Promised Land, because God was 'concerned about their suffering'.

Moses thought God had got the wrong man and at the burning bush, in a conversation with God, he asked a series of questions revealing his deep lack of confidence (Exodus 3:11–4:13). God gave the reassuring answers needed for Moses to step out in faith to fulfil his life's destiny.

The first question says it all. *'Who am I that I should go?'* In his own eyes he was insignificant and he needed God's reassurance, *'I will be with you.'* Moses was concerned that his knowledge of God was so limited he didn't even know His name. *'If they ask me, "What is the name of the God of your fathers?" what shall I tell them?'*

The revelation of God's name, *'I AM WHO I AM'*, addressed Moses' insecurity. God was saying: 'I am now, and always will be what I have always been'. Moses' sense of inferiority arose in his third question, *'What if they do not believe me or listen to me and say, "The LORD did not appear to you"?'* But the miracle of his staff turning into a serpent assured Moses that God's work is a supernatural work done in His power. His next excuse was that he was inarticulate. *'O Lord, I have never been eloquent ... I am slow of speech and tongue.'* In desperation he asked God to send someone else.

Most of us experience desert times. As we look back we can often thank God for those times. They were times when God was preparing us, times of refining and change, and, above all, times when God revealed Himself to us in a new way. It's reassuring to hear Him say, *'See, I am doing a new thing! Now it springs up; do you not perceive it? I am making a way in the desert and streams in the wasteland'* (Isaiah 43:19).

'Moses was very meek' (Numbers 12:3, KJV). A meek person can be described as someone who humbly acknowledges their dependence on the goodness and grace of God. An insignificant person in the world's eyes, whose security is in God, is a person who can be used by God. Such a one may not be very eloquent, but Moses' prayer can be their own: *'Let ... my words descend like dew, like showers on new grass, like abundant rain on tender plants'* (Deuteronomy 32:2). This is a prayer that can't fail to be answered. Have you known desert times when God has spoken to you? Are you presently in a desert time when you long to hear His voice?

PRAYER: *Heavenly Father, thank You that You've promised to make a way in the desert. Help me today to keep my eyes on You and Your faithfulness, rather than on my circumstances. Amen.*

JUNE 2 |
PAUL LAWRENCE

ARE WE ON THE RUN OR DO WE NEED FRESH VISION?

> *There he went into a cave and spent the night. And the word of the LORD came to him: 'What are you doing here, Elijah?'*
>
> 1 Kings 19:9

It's a funny thing that when we go on holiday or even wander around our own town and bump into people we know, we, or they, often ask the question, 'What are you doing here?'

The question was asked twice to one man in the Old Testament. *'And the word of the LORD came to him: "What are you doing here, Elijah?"'* (1 Kings 19:9). *'Then a voice said to him, "What are you doing here, Elijah?"'* (1 Kings 19:13).

This question can be friendly, but, if one were in the wrong place, the question could seem quite hostile. It may be a question we would have liked to ask Jonah when he was running away. *'But Jonah ran away from the LORD and headed for Tarshish. He went down to Joppa, where he found a ship bound for that port. After paying the fare, he went aboard and sailed for Tarshish to flee from the LORD'* (Jonah 1:3).

Sometimes this challenging question is laid down before us by the Lord. Sometimes we are in the right place and the question is not a prompt to make us think that we're in the wrong place but rather a prompt to make us re-evaluate what it is we're doing, and why we are there in the first place. A bit of a shake, rattle and stir question.

However, there are times we know we're in the wrong place and the question is there to stir us up and move us on. There's a fresh realisation that this isn't the right place for us and a fresh stirring to seek God's face and the plans He has for us.

Perhaps there are times when we've responded to the question from the Lord in Isaiah 6:8 asking, *'Whom shall I send? And who will go for us?'* And we've said, *'Here am I. Send me!'* However, we have then sat and sat, knowing God has asked us to move. And so a variant of the same question arises from the Lord: 'What are you still doing here?'

So today let's rise to the challenge and boldly face this question before the Lord and ask, 'What am I doing here?' And maybe, 'From what or from whom am I running?'

PRAYER: *Father, unless You build the foundation I build in vain. I want to be in the right place with You, physically and spiritually. Please show me Your will in my situation today. Will You re-ignite me with Your vision and stir me with Your passion. There is so much more and I want to be part of it with You. Amen.*

JUNE 3 | COMPARING OURSELVES

JIM PERSON

We have different gifts, according to the grace given us.

Romans 12:6a

Recently I spent some time in the woods around our centre in Hungary, talking with God. As I prayed, I sensed the Lord gently correcting me, because I was comparing myself with others. I then realised I was taking for granted what I had been given by the Lord, and in doing so was inadvertently despising my own unique gifting and abilities.

Many of us do the same, yet God has uniquely given each of us abilities and gifting that we alone can excel in. So why do we look at what He's doing in the lives of others and say, 'If I could only be like that' or 'Why can't I be used by the Lord in that way?'

Sadly, it's in our fallen human nature to want to compare ourselves with others, and the fruit of that can be discord, envy, jealousy, and even rage, that can then lead us into disappointment and discouragement.

Moses had a similar problem believing in his own abilities, when God commissioned him to lead the Israelites out of Egypt. He said, *'Who am I, that I should go to Pharaoh and bring the Israelites out of Egypt?'* (Exodus 3:11).

The Lord has made each of us with specific talents and has given us just the right gifting for us to be all He has designed us to become. God does nothing sparingly or inadequately. He lavished His creative genius upon us all! So today let's be encouraged and not regret who we are, but rejoice that He made us to excel and finish the race set before us.

PRAYER: *My Lord and Saviour, help me to not compare myself with others but to rest in the security of Your love. Help me to really see what You have done in my life and begin trusting in Your grace to be my sufficiency. Help me to not compare myself with my neighbour or grumble about my perceived lack of abilities. I want to look to You and see myself as You see me. Help me, Lord, to do this always. Amen.*

JUNE 4 | THE LIGHT OF LIFE

PATRICIA LAKE

> *The true Light which gives light to every man coming into the world.*
>
> John 1:9, NKJV

On a very ordinary day 2,000 years ago the extraordinary happened. The beauty, majesty, and wonder that is the Light of the World burst into the dark world of mankind when our Lord Jesus Christ was born. The Holy Scriptures declare that He is the *'Light which gives light to every man'* (John 1:9). Such was His might and majesty, that even as a baby, He banished forever Satan's plans of locking God's creation into a prison of darkness. Without Jesus we would know nothing but hopelessness and despair.

But God wanted us to know how much He, our Creator, loves us.

He wanted us to know something of His manifest presence and He wanted us to share in all that He has for us – so He came to deliver us from evil and the clutches of sin, translating us into the Kingdom of His dear Son (Colossians 1:13).

In the natural order of creation plants need the light of the sun to prosper – without it they are stunted in growth, remain closed and do not reach their full potential. So, too, we humans need the warmth and light of the sun. It is crucial to our well-being. Oh but how much more we need the light of the *'Son of God'* to enable us to reach our full potential, fulfilling the destiny that God has planned for us.

This Light which lights every man governs our destiny, and guards our footsteps. How wonderfully comforting it is to know that none can pluck us from His hand.

God has also given to us His precious Holy Word, the Bible, to guide us to Himself. Little do we realise it, but every time we read the Bible, we handle, absorb and digest the gold of eternal life entrusted to us by the Lord of Life himself, tasting of the world to come. For, as we believe, it is by those *'great and precious promises'* that we become *'partakers of the divine nature'* (2 Peter 1:4, NKJV).

These same Scriptures also speak of another imminent day when once again the Light of the World will personally burst into the ordinariness of daily life – but this time as King of kings. We know this will happen because Jesus came the first time according to the Scriptures. Winter is almost over and the tyrannical reign of evil is fast drawing to a close, and we eagerly await the Second Coming of Jesus!

In this Advent Season (before His Second Coming), wise men still seek Him. This Light which lights every man governs our destiny, and guards our footsteps. How wonderfully comforting it is to know that none can pluck us from His hand. Never will man be alone or without hope. Maranatha!

Prayer: *Dear Heavenly Father, thank You for shining Your glorious light into our dark lives and for making us Your own. Help us to give You Your rightful place in our lives every day, so that You might find us ready when Jesus comes again, in Jesus' name. Amen.*

June 5 | Skyscrapers

Joan Rono

If any man builds on this foundation using gold, silver, costly stones, wood, hay or straw, his work will be shown for what it is, because the Day will bring it to light. It will be revealed with fire, and the fire will test the quality of each man's work.

1 Corinthians 3:12–13

Skyscrapers have been built over many centuries; in fact I would say that the first one ever built is recorded in the Bible when men built the tower of Babel. I'm not sure how tall it was but it brought a great concern in the heavens. God confused the language of the builders.

It never ceases to amaze me how such tall habitable buildings can remain standing tall and strong in the sky. How can so much weight be balanced?

I spent some time reading more about skyscrapers and realised that tall skyscrapers are so heavy they must be built on a sturdier foundation than would be required for shorter, lighter buildings. A firm foundation has got everything to do with a good tall building or a skyscraper.

Jesus gave a parable about a wise and a foolish builder and the vulnerability that's there when the foundations in our lives are not good. Whatever foundations we build upon will determine what will happen when the storms come.

Not only should our foundations be strong because of the storms and torrents of life but also every man's work will be tested. How are your works? How do you live your life? Are you obedient to God's will? Does your life reflect Jesus' character?

I learned about so many things that can affect the foundations of a building; like trees, the type of soil, proximity of drains, wind speed, building regulations, the height of the building and the ground itself. Think about the things that hinder you from building on a good foundation.

When foundations are built on a rock, the building is firm and strong. It takes a lot of work to dig through the rock but it's worth the work when we go through the test later on.

The foundation we lay in our lives will be tested by fire. Have you laid the foundation on the rock (Jesus) or on wood, hay or straw (the worldly things)?

Prayer: *Lord, there are many foundations that I can build on, but today I choose to make You my foundation, my rock and my strength. Help me to get rid of the things in my life that hinder me from building on You. I choose You as my foundation, in Jesus' name, Amen.*

June 6 | Are You Wearing Old Clothes?

Jill Southern-Jones

> *But you, man of God, flee from all this, and pursue righteousness, godliness, faith, love, endurance and gentleness.*
>
> 1 Timothy 6:11

Holiness is separating ourselves from the world, the flesh and the devil, and putting off *'the old self'* (our old sinful ways), and then putting on *'the new self, created to be like God in true righteousness and holiness'* (Ephesians 4:22–23). It means separating ourselves to the Lord. We must throw out the old dirty carpet tiles before we can lay the new carpet tiles. We have to put something old off before we can put something new on.

The apostle Paul writes to Timothy and tells him to pursue *'righteousness, godliness, faith, love, endurance and gentleness'*. To do this we need to deal with 'unholiness'. When all known 'unholiness' has been washed away we can focus on pursuing holiness. We begin with repentance and cleansing and then we find we have a greater desire to spend time with God and develop a closer intimacy with Him.

In his book *Set Apart: Discovering Personal Victory through Holiness,* Bruce Wilkinson quotes two shocking statistics. The first one is that the average born-again believer prays for less than two minutes a day, not counting prayers at meals or at Christian functions. Secondly, the average born-again believer reads the Bible for less than three minutes a day, discounting corporate Bible readings. Do these statistics surprise or shock you? Or instead do they make you feel uncomfortable because they describe you?

I believe we need to start breaking free from spiritual shallowness and move out in radical, Biblical Christianity. We need to sow the seeds of holiness now if we are to reap a harvest of holiness later on. *'For he chose us in him before the creation of the world to be holy and blameless in his sight'* (Ephesians 1:4). Jesus Christ is going to return for *'a radiant church, without stain or wrinkle or any other blemish, but holy and blameless'* (Ephesians 5:27). Are we preparing ourselves now, to be ready for when He returns?

In order to be holy we have to flee from everything 'unholy' and pursue righteousness as our verse today tells us. This is a person-to-person call placed by God on you and me. He is beckoning us to come out from all ungodliness and all conduct we know is inappropriate and to be separated unto Him, to depart from everything that isn't Him and to devote ourselves fully to Him.

Pursuing righteousness is not optional for us. Our hearts need to discover the incredible power of God which is released when we're obedient to this Scripture verse. We need to flee from all that is ungodly and pursue righteousness. Today is a good day to start.

PRAYER: *Lord Jesus, help me to be obedient to You in this and to get rid of everything that displeases You in my life, and to have a passion for righteousness, godliness, faith, love, endurance and gentleness. Please release the power of the Holy Spirit to enable me to embark on this today, in Jesus' name, Amen.*

JUNE 7 | EXPOSED

LINDSAY O'REILLY

Come, see a man who told me everything I ever did.

John 4:29

What a statement for a woman to make to her whole town – to the people who knew her and her background! But she'd come face to face with Jesus, and that made all the difference. She'd come face to face with true love, not use and abuse; pure love, not lust. His love was forgiving love, unending love, love that covered her and set her free – free to be the person God had originally meant her to be – valuable and precious. Now she was a person of influence – a person who could lift her head high – no longer under a yoke of guilt and shame.

She hadn't experienced that kind of love before. Now all the shame, abuse, guilt and dishonour were gone. She could face the people of the town and be the channel God could use to introduce the whole town to Jesus. She could be the instrument which resulted in Him staying for two more days and many more becoming believers. In our eyes she was the most unlikely candidate, but in God's eyes she was a broken but valuable vessel, now restored and available to be used in His Kingdom for honour and blessing.

God sees our hearts – the mistrust, hurt, and pain – and there's nothing we've done, nothing we've experienced that He doesn't know about. Yet He still loves us. He's approachable. We're always welcome in His presence. Come to Him, and allow Him to bring restoration to your broken heart. Exchange your guilt and shame for His freedom, your sadness for His joy, your death and depression for His new life. Receive acceptance, security, love and peace to replace your rejection, insecurity and fear. God loves you and is completely trustworthy. The safest place to be is – close to His heart.

PRAYER: *Thank You, Lord, that Your love is so amazing. Your love is approachable, no matter what I've done. Today I open my heart to receive that love. I allow You to complete the work You began in my life, so I can be the vessel of honour that you ordained me to be, before the foundation of the world. Amen.*

JUNE 8 |
PAM SMITH

SO RICH IN MERCY

> *But God is so rich in mercy; he loved us so much that even though we were spiritually dead and doomed by our sins, he gave us back our lives again when he raised Christ from the dead – only by his undeserved favour have we ever been saved.*
>
> Ephesians 2:4–5, LB

The other morning I woke up thinking that there are more people that have lived in this world than there are grains of sand on the seashore, so how could God know and love each one? But a father can know and love each one of his children in his family, and God our Heavenly Father knows intimately every one He has made in His image. He showers His love and mercy on all He has created. It's almost too deep to comprehend.

But this one thing I know, that His love and mercy has reached me. I know, not just through faith, but also through the Holy Spirit, whom God has placed deep within me. We may take the step of believing that there is a personal Creator who cares for each child He has made. We may take the step of believing that He has made a way for us to come to Him and be accepted and forgiven through our Saviour, Jesus Christ. We may take the step of receiving His love and mercy, but then, He comes.

He comes to us and makes His presence known in no unsure way, by His Spirit. With a baptism of love, He fills our being with the knowledge of His character, His purity, His kindness, and His love and mercy. And we go on to love Him because He first loved us.

Man has tapped into the riches of this world and yet very often hasn't tapped into the richest and highest treasure there is. It's God's great mercy through Jesus to mankind, through the Holy Spirit.

So yes, our Great God and Father does know each person in this world and can be known to everyone personally through the Lord Jesus Christ. He brings the gentle Spirit within us as the tangible evidence of God's rich love and mercy to those who believe.

PRAYER: *Dear God and Father, thank You that You have revealed to us Your rich mercy. Thank You that You came right down to our level on the earth, through Your Son, our Saviour. Thank You that it is possible to know You through Your Holy Spirit. Praise Your name. Amen.*

June 9 | Do Not Be Anxious

Angela Weir

> *Therefore I tell you, do not worry about your life, what you will eat or drink; or about your body, what you will wear. Is not life more important than food, and the body more important than clothes?*
>
> Matthew 6:25

There have been a number of 'seeds' recently about how fragile our lives are and how important it is to centre ourselves on God. It's a cliché to say that life is full of uncertainties, but like most clichés, it's true.

Jesus taught His disciples not to worry about the future because God has it all in hand. He says to them, and to us, that we should seek first God's Kingdom and His righteousness and as we walk before Him in holiness and righteousness, God will provide for us.

This was shown to a friend of mine one evening when she had almost run out of milk. There was just a little in the bottom of a jug and all the shops were shut, so she couldn't get any more. She was holding a 'Prayer for Israel' meeting at her home that evening and when it was time for coffee, she found that there was more than enough milk to go round and that the jug was still full when she had poured out what they needed. For three days afterwards that jug remained full, supplying all the family's needs!

As human beings we focus so much on our tomorrows when we may not have a tomorrow. As Jesus said: *'Do not worry about tomorrow, for tomorrow will worry about itself. Each day has enough trouble of its own.'* Let's learn to concentrate on today, living life to its fullest, and keeping short accounts with our Father.

PRAYER: *Dear loving Father, thank You that You are the Alpha and Omega and that You know the end from the beginning. Please help me to put my anxieties about tomorrow into Your safe keeping and focus on the blessings You give me each day. Amen.*

JUNE 10 | REST

CATH TAYLOR

> *Then Jesus said, 'Come to me, all of you who are weary and carry heavy burdens, and I will give you rest. Take my yoke upon you. Let me teach you, because I am humble and gentle at heart, and you will find rest for your souls. For my yoke is easy to bear, and the burden I give you is light.'*
>
> Matthew 11:28–30, NLT

I have come to believe that the one thing many of us thirst and hunger for, sometimes beyond anything else, is REST. Not rest like a weekend at the beach or a midday nap, but a deeper rest that speaks peace and calm to the turmoil that can occupy our minds and our hearts. Rest that refreshes us deep on the inside where we are tired to the very core.

So if it is the one thing that we all long for, why do we find it so hard to simply lay down our burdens and run to the Lord? Surely it sounds so easy, and yet the reality is that to surrender goes against our very human nature. If we are not in control, how will we know we are safe?!

Maybe there are many different reasons we struggle to truly surrender, and the weariness is permeating our hearts. Perhaps we don't recognise what the burdens we are carrying actually are. Unforgiveness, worry, guilt, shame, hopelessness, despair, sin, wrong responsibility – these are all things that can weigh down our hearts and rob us of the peace and rest that our Father has for us today. A peace and rest that affirms our Father God has us safe in the palm of His hands, as we allow Him to be in control.

True rest from the Lord is never conditional on our circumstances. As we run to the Lord, it may not automatically erase the struggles that we are going through, or the difficulties we face. It is purely a gift from the Lord as we come to that place of surrender – a deep assurance that no matter what is around us, our Father God is way big enough to carry what is too much for us to bear. What a wonderful relief!

There is a beautiful song called 'Still', written by David Hind, and the words sum it up perfectly:

For every disappointment
For every broken heart
For everyone in darkness – a light.

For every wounded person
For every tired mind
For hopeless situations – a hope.

For everyone who's desperate
For everyone who's lost
For everyone who's fearful – a shelter.

For every painful question
For everyone's regrets
For every cry of 'Why God?' – an answer.

The cross still stands
The cross still towers
His blood still cleanses
Eternally the same.

PRAYER: *Lord Jesus, thank You for Your humble, gentle character that beckons me to come to You and lay down the burdens of my heart. Thank You that when I do, You hold them safe and know exactly why I have carried them for so long. Lord, I am sorry for trying so hard to be strong in my own strength. Please teach me to run only to You that I may experience the relief of Your rest, knowing You hold it all in Your control. Help me, Lord, to remember that for every situation and burden in my life, Your cross and who You are stands eternally the same. I love You, Lord Jesus, Amen.*

June 11 | He has Scattered

Richard Hemery

He has performed mighty deeds with his arm; he has scattered those who are proud in their inmost thoughts.

Luke 1:51

In Luke 1 we read that Mary, pregnant with Jesus, visited her relative Elizabeth. As soon as Elizabeth heard Mary's voice, her own baby (the future John the Baptist) leapt in the womb and she was filled with the Holy Spirit. She exclaims a blessing in a loud voice, to which Mary, also inspired by the Spirit, responds with a declaration sometimes known as *'the Magnificat'* (verses 46–55). Verse 51 reads: *'he has scattered those who are proud in their inmost thoughts'*, which means, literally, those who are proud in the thoughts of their hearts.

Scattering is seen as something God does to those who are proud. Do we have any example of this?

The first generations after the flood, instead of obeying God and filling the earth, stayed together and started building a tower of their own manufacture. God had said that if they remained united, there was little they could not do. God had to divide their language and scatter them around the world. The tower remained unfinished (Genesis 11:1–8). In fact, God considers the proud in heart his enemies.

It's interesting that it's inward pride that Mary spoke of. God sees through our outward show of humility to the pride and self-reliance that lurks within. Too often the outward *'Thy will be done'* contrasts with the inward 'my will be done'. The danger is we trust in our own ability, our own works and righteousness, and our faith is in ourselves and not God. Perhaps this attitude is one root of disunity in our lives. Are our lives 'scattered' and disjointed, full of unfinished towers? Are our churches like that as well, full of ineffective troops?

Being proud is the opposite of Proverbs 3:5–6, *'Trust in the LORD with all your heart and lean not on your own understanding; in all your ways acknowledge him, and he will make your paths straight.'*

Let's ask God to give us humility in the thoughts of our hearts, in that secret place – to trust in Him and not in our own strength – then we won't be scattered but united and effective.

PRAYER: *Lord, please give me an undivided heart. Help me to acknowledge You in all my ways and to be humble in the thoughts of my heart, in the inward place where only You see. I choose not to lean on the bruised reed of my own abilities, but on the strong, comforting staff of God. Please make the twisting paths of my life straight. Amen.*

JUNE 12 | SPENDING TIME WITH JESUS

JIM PERSON

> *Assuredly I say to you, whoever does not receive the kingdom of God as a little child will by no means enter it.*
>
> Mark 10:15, NKJV

One morning a few years back, I began my day with a cup of coffee and breakfast in our flat's small kitchen. While I sipped my coffee and pondered my hectic schedule, my middle daughter entered the kitchen and, opening our pantry door, went in and shut it behind her. Soon, I began to hear her singing songs quietly from within. So I rose and went over and opened the door and asked her what she was doing. She answered, with a grin from ear to ear, 'I'm singing songs to Jesus!' Pleased but slightly taken aback, I affirmed to her that this was OK and closed the door, going back to my thoughts of a busy day. Shortly after that, I noticed that I was hearing no sounds from the pantry. Again I went over and opened the door. There, sitting on a large cooking pot, was my daughter eating pretzels. Asked again what she was doing, she replied, again grinning ear to ear, 'I'm eating pretzels with Jesus!' So I did the only thing I could do … I left her with Jesus.

That day I learned a valuable lesson: I was too busy and I needed a relationship with Jesus like that, where I could fellowship with the Lord in songs and times of refreshment like a little child. How I long to sit at the feet of Jesus and listen to Him, but as an adult my busy life takes me away from those times of refreshment. My friends, we need to be like a child and in total awe and total innocence spend time with Jesus away from the busyness of ministry, the job, housework, or general things that are constantly eating away our days. The busyness of life robs us of hearing the voice of the Lord. Jesus said that His sheep know their Shepherd's voice (John 10:4, 14). When was the last time you went into a closet (or pantry) and spent time with Jesus with the innocent acceptance of a child?

Prayer: *Lord, how often my life carries me away and I find myself collapsing into bed, weary and exhausted from the busyness of my life. Help me, Lord, to make the time to spend some quality hours with you! I want to know You, Lord! I want to know Your voice! Would You take me by the hand today, right now, and lead me into my quiet place? Thank You, Lord. Amen.*

June 13 | New Things Have Come

Liz Griffin

> *Therefore if anyone is in Christ, he is a new creature; the old things passed away; behold, new things have come.*
>
> 2 Corinthians 5:17, NASB

'*Therefore if anyone is in Christ, he is a new creature; the old things passed away; behold, new things have come*' is a verse to memorise, display on the wall, and put into song. In two previous verses the apostle Paul explains how, as believers, we are controlled by the love of Christ since Christ died and rose again on our behalf (2 Corinthians 5:14–15). He then goes on to say something drastic has happened to those who are 'in Christ'. They have become 'new creatures'; old things have gone and new things have come. What are the new things that have come? Paul talks of being reconciled to God, in close relationship to Him through Jesus, having our sins washed away, becoming ambassadors for Jesus and becoming the 'righteousness of God' in Jesus.

We get a new start in life and if you've been aware of your sinful choices before you became a believer, this is a precious truth to hold on to. In the healing ministry we find many who still hold themselves in condemnation and feel ashamed of their past.

I have often explained to people who have broken down and cried about their sins, that the devil wants them to be tormented by the memories of the past. Now we have a new start in life we can make choices from now on that please God and glorify Jesus. We don't have to strive and strive on our own. The Holy Spirit has been sent to help us in our journey of sanctification and healing. In Ellel Ministries we often teach that healing is a process and not an instantaneous thing.

Shortly after this marvellous proclamation the apostle Paul quotes the Old Testament and tells the Corinthian believers, '*Do not be bound together with unbelievers*', that they must '*come out from their midst and be separate*' and '*not touch what is unclean*' (2 Corinthians 6:14, 17, NASB). If they do this

God promises to welcome them and be a Father to them. He continues in this letter to say, *'Therefore, having these promises, beloved, let us cleanse ourselves from all defilement of flesh and spirit, perfecting holiness in the fear of God'* (2 Corinthians 7:1, NASB).

Paul preached the lordship of Jesus – it's the most important issue in our lives. It's thrilling to become a 'new creature' in Jesus but we can't stop there and become complacent. We must go on growing and maturing in our faith, becoming stronger and stronger in the Lord Jesus. If we are willing and obedient to Jesus, submitting to His lordship, He will show us by His Holy Spirit areas of our life that need to be cleansed from all defilement.

PRAYER: *Father God, I want to grow closer and closer to You. Please show me any areas of my life that you want to cleanse. I thank You that You have made me a new creature, that I'm Your child, and that You love me dearly. In Jesus' name I pray, Amen.*

JUNE 14 |
LINDSEY HANEKOM

NICE AND NASTY MEDICINE

My son, do not despise the LORD's discipline and do not resent his rebuke.

Proverbs 3:11

Recently our son went down with a bad cold/flu virus. With a raging fever, runny nose, very sore throat and a loss of appetite, we struggled with a day and night cycle of childhood medicines to try and control the fever. Designed especially for young children, Kyle had no problem taking the medicines; they tasted yummy!

After a week of it only getting worse, a doctor prescribed a course of antibiotics since it was clear that there was something causing such a continuously high fever. That is when the medicine consumption took a turn – this medicine most definitely did not taste yummy. In fact it tasted nasty. No effort had been made to make this particular drug palatable to children.

And so a battle of wills ensued! Each time Kyle even caught a glimpse of the medicine approaching him, he would run. Having eventually cornered and caught him, we would then lovingly but firmly have to restrain him enough to get the medicine in the mouth, but getting him to swallow the medicine was beyond our control.

As I sat frustrated, considering how to win this particular battle with my son, my mind started to wander about how I respond to God's 'medicine'. I am always willing to take the nice ones … the comfort, the care, the protection, and the provision, but when it comes to Him trying to give me a dose of discipline, correction, rebuke or conviction, I'm not always so willing to respond positively.

Without his medicine, Kyle would only have got sicker and it's the same for us. We can enjoy the good medicines and they can help, often dealing with symptoms rather than the cause of the symptoms, but sometimes the only thing that can make us better is the 'nasty' ones. Sometimes it takes a rebuke, clear and unpalatable as it may be, to make us realise that there is a cause to our pain and repentance is the only way we will find healing.

Let's take this scripture to heart, for God only wants the best for us and sometimes that means taking a dose of the 'not so nice' medicine.

PRAYER: *Father God, help me not to despise Your discipline. Help me see that You only bring me discipline when I need it. Thank You for Your comfort, care, protection and provision, but Lord, I need to hear Your voice of rebuke when I am wrong. Amen.*

JUNE 15 | RECEIVING A KINGDOM THAT CANNOT BE SHAKEN

ALISTAIR PETRIE

> *Therefore, since we are receiving a kingdom that cannot be shaken, let us be thankful, and so worship God acceptably with reverence and awe, for our 'God is a consuming fire'.*
>
> Hebrews 12:28–29

In Hebrews 12:26, we are told that God's voice once shook the earth, but that we can expect Him once again to shake both the earth and the heavens. A similar warning is found in Haggai 2:6 in which the heavens, the earth, the sea and the dry land – and even the nations – will be shaken. Why? Because He wants to fill His house with His glory. He wants us to understand what it means to receive a Kingdom that cannot be shaken – no matter what circumstances or challenges or fears or battles we must face. We may not enjoy being shaken in this manner, but God has real purpose in it all – and it is earthed in His amazing love for us.

We are literally being prepared for a life lived with the Lord Himself that will last all eternity. However, we can actually receive the benefits of His Kingdom in our life now! God is training and preparing us in these very challenging and stretching days. In Hebrews 12:10–11, reference is made to our being disciplined by God for the sole reason of sharing in His holiness. But it gets better. This takes place in order that we receive a harvest of righteousness and peace which are the benefits of this training.

No doubt about it, we are living in a very volatile world at this time. Only those who are able to view things from God's perspective will actually understand what is going on – and why. We have all heard the amazing testimonies of the Miracle on the Hudson in which everyone survived a jet airliner making an emergency landing in the Hudson River. Now more recently we are experiencing the aftermath of another commuter airliner that crashed in Buffalo – with no survivors. Does this mean God did not intervene? Is this not shaking and challenging our belief system somewhat? It certainly allows us to see the frailty of life, and challenges us to ensure that our lives are truly hidden in Christ. The vicissitudes of life seem very unsettling these days!

Human structures and systems are being soundly challenged by God. The heavens and the earth are receiving a significant divine wake-up call as God Himself addresses our economics, our politics, our ethics and morals, our ever changing weather conditions – and even our opinion of what He is like! Without God at work in our lives today, there appears to be little hope.

But knowing that He is at work in spite of our weakness and frailty – and at times our ignorance – means He is serving notice that He is at work for those who have eyes to see and ears with which to listen to His counsel. The God we serve both comforts and consoles, but when necessary also roars and shakes the earth, because He is telling us time is short – and He is preparing, for those of us who accept His training and discipline, a Kingdom that can never be shaken.

Prayer: *Lord, You have invited us to share in Your holiness. What an amazing thought! You are training us in order that we receive a harvest of righteousness. You are asking us to strengthen our feeble arms and weak knees and to be healed. Father, You are speaking loud and clear today in both the heavens and the earth and we want to be watching and listening, ready and waiting. Remove from our lives what can be shaken so that we understand what You are doing in the heavens and on the earth – and prepare us for a Kingdom that cannot be shaken – that begins even now, and lasts right on into eternity, in Jesus' name. Amen.*

June 16 | Denise Cross

Are You Comfortable in Your Uncomfortable Place?

And throwing aside his garment, he rose and came to Jesus.
Mark 10:50, NKJV

Blind Bartimaeus was ready for change! He knew he needed healing and understood it couldn't come without something changing. This meant leaving his comfort zone and his 'normal' life as a blind beggar.

It's amazing how many people say they want healing but are resistant to change. They are holding on to being 'comfortable' even in their uncomfortable, unhealed place. Bartimaeus wasn't like this; he was ready to take a risk. The story tells us that Bartimaeus threw aside his garment and started out, presumably groping his way forward, toward Jesus.

That garment represented his old life with its old schedules and daily routines. How vulnerable he must have felt as he moved toward Jesus. His old life and identity were now left behind. There was no cloak to hide behind and no more membership of the beggar community. He was in a new and uncomfortable place, alone, still in the dark, but he was determined to go forward, whatever it took, in order to be healed.

Recently, whilst suffering from sciatica, I was bed-bound for a week and in a great deal of pain, with my leg in spasm. I learned an amazing lesson about how easy it is to stay in one position even if it isn't very comfortable. The reason is that it might be *more* painful to try to move, even if that move could possibly result in an improved situation. Sometimes it seems easier to stay in the uncomfortable place rather than risk more discomfort getting to a better place. *'Better the devil you know'* is the way people sometimes put it, but this attitude wasn't one that Bartimaeus subscribed to.

It was before Jesus spoke personally to him and healed him, that he threw off the old lifestyle. His choice didn't bring instant comfort. Initially he must have felt very vulnerable, but he was ready for change. He wanted to be healed so he could fulfil a 'yet to be discovered' destiny as a useful part of society. He was willing to go for it. Are you?

Prayer: *Jesus, forgive us when we allow ourselves to become comfortable in an uncomfortable place and are unwilling to take the risk to change. Help us to take courage and, like Bartimaeus, walk forward into the fullness of life You can give us. Amen.*

June 17 | From Obscurity to Glory

Patricia Lake

Then the king [David] said, 'Is there not still someone of the house of Saul, to whom I may show the kindness of God?'

2 Samuel 9:3

Life could have been so different for Mephibosheth, King Saul's grandson, if only Saul had been obedient to God. As it was, Mephibosheth's young life did not begin well, being hit by the triple tragedy of the death of his father Jonathan, and of his grandfather Saul, and being dropped by his nurse during their escape to safety, as a result of which Mephibosheth became lame in both feet.

Consequently, the young prince spent many years of his life being totally dependent on the help of others in less than princely circumstances. He could do nothing for himself. But, just when all seemed lost and Mephibosheth had all but given up hope … God intervened and rescued him.

The new king, David, remembered the covenant he had made with Jonathan to show kindness to Jonathan's descendants. Suddenly the king's call came for Mephibosheth, and like a shaft of brilliant light, pierced his darkness. He was plucked from obscurity and hopelessness and seated in the king's house where he ate at the king's table for the rest of his life. What a transformation! The call of the king had made all the difference.

The great news is that the call of the King of kings has done the same for you and me.

Mephibosheth had the choice – he could have politely refused King David's invitation and allowed pride to keep him in poverty and obscurity – but he wasn't about to miss the best offer he'd ever had in life!

Know today who you belong to! The King of kings has prepared the best for you. No matter how bad your start in life, or whatever your circumstances are now, God is calling you by name. Jesus is the lifter of your head and through His sacrificial death on the cross of Calvary, and resurrection power, Jesus has made it possible for you to enjoy ALL the blessings He has in store for you. He loves you with an everlasting love and DELIGHTS in you!

Prayer: *Dear Lord, thank You for calling me by name and coming to my rescue. Thank You for Your favour, love, life and hope, in Jesus' name, Amen.*

June 18 | Restoring Immunity

David Cross

But if any of you lack wisdom, you should pray to God, who will give it to you; because God gives generously and graciously to all.

James 1:5, GNB

As I write this seed, I'm preparing to teach on a course looking at the issue of allergies. So many people these days are seriously affected by seemingly harmless substances such as pollen and food proteins, experiencing a hypersensitive and distressing response from their immune system.

Our amazing immune system was designed by God to protect our bodies against harmful organisms, by detecting any threat and producing defensive antibodies. Throughout the Bible, God makes it clear that His covenant promises with mankind include our protection, both spiritually and physically. So how has this part of His system of protection got out of balance? God has certainly not broken His covenant with mankind but unfortunately we have constantly broken covenant with Him!

The immune system is God's way of ensuring that the countless organisms that exist around us and within us are not able to gain a harmful control over our lives. Before the fall in the Garden of Eden, God gave mankind authority over every other living thing (Psalm 8:6). The problem is that the constant sin in the world has upset God's order, and men and women find themselves increasingly subject to a rule of spiritual darkness and disorder (1 John 5:19).

So what's the answer? This is exactly what we'll be exploring together as we seek the truth of God's Word and compare the history of our own lives with that truth. There's certainly not always an easy answer, but I remember a woman's testimony some months ago describing how a long-standing allergic skin rash disappeared overnight when she brought to God the pain and bitterness of a betrayal that had occurred many years before.

It is never wrong to come to God in order to seek a little more of His wisdom.

Prayer: *Father, I thank You for my precious immune system. Please show me if there is any part of my life that I need to get right with You, in order to help bring this God-given protection back into balance. In Jesus' name I pray, Amen.*

June 19 | Unchanging Love

Angela Weir

Assuredly, I say to you, today you will be with Me in Paradise.
Luke 23:43, NKJV

Many of us find it difficult to allow God to accept us as we are. We believe that we are not good enough to come into His presence and do our very best to make ourselves better. This is often because we have received conditional love from our parents – 'If you are a good boy/girl we will give you a special treat', or words to that effect, or through our lives have discovered that in order to gain rewards we have to strive to be the best. We feel ashamed of our behaviour, our constant struggles with sin and our failure to live up to the high standards we set ourselves, or that we believe God sets for us.

What we fail to understand and believe deep in our hearts is that God's love for us is unconditional. He loves us no matter who we are or what we have done, and nothing we do will make Him love us any more or less than He does already. We may have grieved Him, but it will not alter the fact that He loves us. He cannot change because that is His nature. Yes, He is a Holy God and He hates sin, but He loves the sinner.

When Jesus was hanging on the cross, one of the thieves hanging beside Him recognised Him as the sinless Son of God and asked Jesus to remember him when He went to glory (Luke 23:43). Jesus' reply was: '*Today you will be with Me in Paradise*', not 'You haven't been good enough so you can't come in.' No matter what that man had done during his lifetime, the fact that he recognised Jesus for who He was, was enough. That thief became the first person to be saved through the shed blood of the Saviour!

In the parable that Jesus tells about the labourers in the vineyard who come at different times of the day to work (Matthew 20:1–16), those who began work at the last possible moment received the same payment as those who began early in the day. God is not so worried about what we do for Him as He is about the relationship we have with Him. He loves us with unchangeable and unchanging love and simply longs for us to come to Him exactly as we are – then He can begin making the changes in our lives without our striving to do so ourselves.

Prayer: *Dearest Father, thank You for Your wonderful unchanging love, love which accepts me exactly as I am, not as I want to be. You know how You want me to be. Please help me to allow You to work in me so that I become the person You originally planned. In Jesus' name, I ask it. Amen.*

June 20 | Promises

Jilly Lyon-Taylor

> *Not one of all the good promises the LORD your God gave you has failed. Every promise has been fulfilled; not one has failed.*
>
> Joshua 23:14

I wonder how many times you or I have said we would do something, such as make a phone call, write a letter or invite someone for a meal, and we've failed to do it. It's easy to mean what we say when we make a promise, but not always so easy to remember and stick to it.

Thankfully God's not like that. He's utterly faithful to every one of His promises. Joshua was able to remind the people of that before he died. What about you? Are there promises in your life that you're holding on to, waiting for them to be fulfilled – promises regarding your family, your future, your ministry, your livelihood? You can be completely certain that God won't let you down.

For each of us as believers there are general promises in the Bible regarding our inheritance as children of God, and we're told in 2 Corinthians 1:20 that all of those promises are *'Yes' in Christ*. We therefore need to keep coming back to the cross to appropriate different aspects of what Jesus accomplished for us when He said, *'It is finished'* (John 19:30).

Many of us will also have received personal promises from God – *rhema* words that we are holding on to. He will be utterly faithful to those promises too, but we often need to hold them before Him in prayer, showing Him that we remember and are trusting Him over them. It's a bit like a child who has been promised a treat from his dad and keeps reminding him about it!

What promises are you holding on to today? Why not speak to God about them and show Him that you're continuing to trust Him for them.

Prayer: *Lord God, thank You that You are utterly faithful and that not one of Your promises to me will ever fail. Help me to hold on to You, trusting You for the promises You have given me, in Jesus' name, Amen.*

June 21 | David Cross

Carrying the Character of Jesus

For this is the commandment that the Lord has given us: 'I have made you a light for the Gentiles, so that all the world may be saved.'

Acts 13:47, GNB

This verse is recorded during Paul's first missionary journey at a time when he and Barnabas were finding it difficult to minister to the Jews in Pisidia. They both clearly felt that it was time to reflect again on the direction which God had planned for them. In response to the contention which was growing around their ministry, they spoke out the words of this verse which God had revealed for their lives.

It was significant that the essence of this statement of their destiny was as much about what they were to be as to what they were to do. They were to be a light to the Gentiles. Of course Jesus himself is the perfect Light, but amazingly He calls all His disciples to display something of His character. In fact this call upon our lives is the basis of our true destiny. The activities of our Christian walk are very important but they are nothing compared with the character, or fruit, which we display. Although no one individual can show to the world the fullness of Jesus, the Body of Christ on earth can reveal a great deal of His character, if we let the Holy Spirit change our hearts.

Which of the characteristics of Jesus has He particularly destined you and me to demonstrate today in this needy world? Will we display His truth, His grace, or His mercy? Will we display His faithfulness, His kindness, or His love? Like Paul and Barnabas will we display His light? Hearing God's answer could revolutionise the rest of our lives.

Prayer: *Show me, Lord Jesus, the particular aspects of Your character which You want me to display today, so that I might move more into my destiny. It may mean a change of heart for me, but I want to show the world some more of You today, in Jesus' name, Amen.*

JUNE 22 |
ROGER POOK

PERFECT PEACE NEED NOT BE QUIET!

And the peace of God, which transcends all understanding, will guard your hearts and your minds in Christ Jesus.

Philippians 4:7

How often do you long for a little peace and quiet? This is not just the cry of a harassed parent or an overworked employee; all of us sometimes want to take some time away from what's going on around us. Many years ago there was a film with the title *Stop the World, I Want To Get Off!* I think we can identify with this; if only we could relax for a while in a quiet place.

God's peace is not quite the same as this. God's peace means that everything is in order and is working the way that God designed it to work. First of all, we have peace with God. Romans 5:1 says, *'Therefore, since we have been justified through faith, we have peace with God through our Lord Jesus Christ.'* This is the way that God designed us to live.

Next, this peace extends into every part of our life. It means that my life is in order; I am doing what God designed me to do. *'I am doing the right thing at the right time in the right place!'* Can you say this? If you can, then you know a peace which many people have never experienced.

This perfect peace might not be quiet. In fact, it might be very noisy, very busy and very tiring. But if what we are doing is part of God's perfect will for our life, there will be a knowledge of peace that carries us through what is happening. We know that the rest we need will come when we need it: *'There remains, then, a Sabbath-rest for the people of God'* (Hebrews 4:9).

So the next time the children are screaming, your work is demanding, and your relationships are difficult, ask yourself, *'Am I doing the right thing, at the right time, in the right place?'* If the answer is 'Yes', you already have peace. If the answer is 'No', read Philippians 4:1–9, seek God's will for your life and find God's peace.

PRAYER: *Heavenly Father, I want above all to do Your will, so that I can live in Your peace. Please show me where I am going wrong, so that my life can be brought back into Your order. Amen.*

June 23 | Lindsay O'Reilly

A Sweet Fragrance

Then Mary took about a pint of pure nard, an expensive perfume; she poured it on Jesus' feet and wiped his feet with her hair. And the house was filled with the fragrance of the perfume.

John 12:3

Mary gave – not just any perfume, but an 'expensive perfume' – the best she had as it was worth a whole year's wages. She also didn't just give it to Jesus; she emptied it out on His feet and then wiped His feet with her hair. What she did was no secret – it could be smelt throughout the whole house and the fragrance of what she had done remained with her even after she had left, as it clung to her hair.

As we come and give to Jesus our very best and are not hesitant to be poured out for Him, may it not only be a sweet fragrance to those closest to us – those in the house – but also to those we come in contact with in our daily walk – those at work, the one behind the till in the supermarket, the one in the queue at the bank, the petrol attendant, the child next door, the postman, the bus driver, the train conductor, the garbage collector, the street sweeper, the pastor, the leader, the businessman, the manager, and our employer.

As we sit at Jesus' feet and pour out everything we have, may the fragrance of His presence linger with us and be a constant reminder to us of His closeness – a very present help with those difficult situations that need to be resolved – those decisions that need to be made – those people that need to be faced.

As we come and spend time with Jesus, experiencing His love, forgiveness, acceptance (He accepted what Mary did for Him when others criticised and judged); as we experience His mercy and kindness, may we always be a sweet aroma of His love, care and compassion to those we pour out our lives for, and to those whom our lives touch on a daily basis.

Prayer: *Lord, as I come each day and sit at Your feet, may the sweet aroma of Your presence so permeate my life that others may get hungry to get to know You too. Amen.*

JUNE 24 | GOD HAS A PLAN!

PETER HORROBIN

The day for building your walls will come, the day for extending your boundaries.

Micah 7:11

When the prophet Micah wrote these words, the land and the people were in devastation. God hadn't spared His own beloved people from the consequences of their sins. There was always a day of reckoning. Even today, when we live in days of New Covenant grace, we aren't exempt from the consequences of our own choices. As Paul reminded the Galatians (6:7–9) there is an unchangeable law of sowing and reaping!

But God didn't stop loving His people when they sinned, and, even though they had turned their back upon Him for a season, the consequences of their mistakes eventually had the effect of bringing them back to God in repentance. Repentance is always the beginning of hope and the doorway to God's ongoing plan for His people.

> Going through a tough time? Remember – God is a Redeemer. He can see beyond the mess, He has a plan.

God hasn't changed His character. He still loves His people, even when they make mistakes. And, as in Micah's day, God looks forward in anticipation to a time of rebuilding once more! So if you are looking at a scene of personal devastation, or praying for someone who's going through a tough time, remember, God is a Redeemer. He can see beyond the mess, He has a plan – and, if we put our hand afresh into His, then we will soon be able to see what He can already see, and discover His plans for our lives.

PRAYER: *Thank You, Lord, that You always have a plan for each one of our lives. Help me to see beyond the circumstances and to trust You so that there will be a new day of building walls and extending boundaries in my life, in Jesus' name, Amen.*

JUNE 25 |
DAVID SILVESTER

DISCIPLESHIP – ITS CHALLENGE

Peter asked, 'Lord, why can't I follow you now? I will lay down my life for you.'

John 13:37

For many Christians Peter is the disciple we can most readily identify with, because of the shortcomings he displays.

In this verse I identify with his desire to stick close to Jesus whatever the cost and wish I had Peter's directness and boldness at times, especially when I'm amongst those whose faith and commitment seem to have slipped into the 'easy chair'.

Peter's question, *'Lord, why can't I follow you now?'* was really the desire of his heart at that moment, and I don't doubt that he meant what he said. But what Peter didn't know was that a series of circumstances would soon follow where the real weaknesses within him would be revealed.

When we're faced with totally unexpected situations we discover just how powerless we are.

Probably we all have heart's desires that are genuine like Peter's, but when we're faced with totally unexpected situations we discover just how powerless we are, and like Peter, we fall short.

Jesus knew all about how Peter would fail and deny Him, long before it happened, but that didn't prevent Him calling Peter to follow Him.

Jesus reinstated Peter after the Resurrection, and he became a mighty man of God in the early Church. Tradition has it that Peter was crucified upside down at the end of his ministry. When Jesus calls us to follow Him can we face the challenge of what it could eventually lead to?

PRAYER: *Dear Lord Jesus, thank You for calling me to follow You, and thank You for all the help You've given me over the years as I've endeavoured to fulfil that call. Please help me to be aware of pitfalls, and help me avoid those situations where I could so easily fail You, Amen.*

JUNE 26 | JOY

DENISE CROSS

Looking unto Jesus, the author and finisher of our faith, who for the joy that was set before Him endured the cross, despising the shame, and has sat down at the right hand of the throne of God.

Hebrews 12:2, NKJV

The truth of this verse is astonishing. Jesus endured the cross for us because this work of salvation was to be a joy to Him. It isn't always easy to imagine the final joy when the going gets tough, even when we know the end result will be wonderful. As a mother I can remember my effort as I laboured through the births of our children. But I can also recall, with even more clarity, the delight of holding a newborn baby in my arms when the struggle was over. Jesus held on to the knowledge of the joy that He knew was before Him, even through the agony of the cross.

These days it seems that gratification is required to be instant. The idea of working for an end result, let alone being prepared to suffer for it, is anathema to many people. We live in a *'now'* society. Saving up for the desired purchases over several months seems a poor alternative to buying on the *'plastic'* today. Quick fixes, ready meals, instant coffee – we want it all with a minimum of effort or work.

I have spoken to many people who have never reached their goal because they aren't willing to stick at it when the going gets tough. It might be learning to play a musical instrument, studying for an exam, or getting fit. Maybe it depends how much you really want to reach that goal and what motivates you? If the sense of achievement in reaching the goal is your only motive, it may not be enough if the cost becomes too great. The crucial thing is the strength of your personal motivation and the value you place on achieving the end result. Do you want it enough to do whatever it takes?

This verse could imply that for Jesus the prize of joy, for Himself, was the goal. But His own joy wasn't His motive or His goal. The motive for His endurance was love, His great love for you and me, and His goal was to offer us a potential. That potential is the possibility of a renewed relationship with our Heavenly Father. If we respond to this offer we can develop an everlasting relationship with our Heavenly Father. This brings a wonderful release of joy into our lives but, amazingly, it's this that really brings the *fullness* of joy to Jesus.

'The joy that was set before Him' is the delightful by-product of our entering into salvation through Jesus. What an exciting thought. Today let's increase Jesus' joy, and our own, as we walk more fully in all that Jesus won for us.

PRAYER: *Holy Spirit, strengthen me in my resolve to live life to bring joy to Jesus. Amen.*

JUNE 27 | THEY'RE ALL LOOKING AT ME!

ROGER POOK

> *Do not be afraid; you will not suffer shame. Do not fear disgrace; you will not be humiliated. You will forget the shame of your youth and remember no more the reproach of your widowhood.*
>
> Isaiah 54:4

In a village in rural Russia, about the year 1950, a little girl was sent by her mother to get bread from the shop. It was very early, but many people were waiting in line. The little girl burned with shame. Once again she had been sent out without any money, and would have to ask out loud for bread 'on the slate'. Once again everybody would know that she came from a poor family. The shame of poverty was crushing her human spirit.

Sixty years later, after a life of work, she was still afraid to speak before people or voice an opinion. She was ashamed and afraid to be noticed. But then God reached in, healed her crushed human spirit, washed away her shame and restored her joy and life in abundance.

I have found that many things can crush the human spirit and restrict the flow of life itself – poverty, criticism, rejection, abuse, failure, shame – so that we feel we're not living, only existing. But I have also found that God is able to 'restore the years that the locusts have eaten' (see Joel 2:25) and give us life in abundance.

I want to encourage all those who aren't living but just existing, that there is hope. God can come to the place where your human spirit was crushed, bringing healing and restoring life and hope. Perhaps you would like to invite Him to do that by praying something like this:

PRAYER: *God, I don't know how to pray properly. I'm not even sure if You're there. I feel like a walking shadow, not fully alive. Please heal my crushed human spirit, so that I can live again. I want to rejoin the human race. I want to know what it is to be alive. I want to be able to hold up my head. Please help me. Amen.*

June 28 | Working for God

Lindsey Hanekom

Whatever you do, work at it with all your heart, as working for the Lord, not for human masters.

Colossians 3:23

I was recently preparing for some friends coming round with their children for a morning of coffee and fun. We have these get-togethers most weeks, taking turns in hosting the events and providing the coffee and snacks. However, this week was different for me. I was doing the usual cleaning and vacuuming in preparation when I found my thoughts fixated on what one of my friends would think of my house. This particular friend has an exceptionally clean, well organised and tidy house, even with two young children!

As I was going about my work, I found myself comparing my home to that of my friend and felt the burden of this comparison weighing on me. As I was vacuuming, God spoke so clearly to me: 'Are you doing this for your friend or for Me?'

I was stunned! Two things occurred to me. Firstly, I was challenged in my heart; I was putting man's opinion above God's opinion of me and what I do. My motivation for fulfilling my daily routine of life had changed from honouring God through blessing my family with a clean and tidy home to fearing what man may think of my best but seemingly 'not up to scratch' efforts.

Secondly and most amazingly, God was interested in my cleaning! This is what I do, day in, day out, without even really thinking about it. Life does not get any more routine than the daily chores of housework and yet, Almighty God is interested in every little bit that we do. It's easy to think God is very interested in the work I do for Ellel Ministries – after all, surely that is spiritual work. This scripture reminds us that, in God, there is no 'spiritual' and 'non-spiritual' – only right and wrong motivation of the heart.

Whether I am cleaning, teaching, ministering, playing with my son, responding to emails, cooking or taking a short break; it should all be motivated by my love for God and focused on honouring Him. If I'm seeking to be a true worshipper of God, this is how I do it. It's through doing each and every thing I do, for Him. By comparing myself with others and searching for man's acceptance, I cease to serve God with my whole heart and that's something that grieves me.

PRAYER: *Father God, I confess that I put man's opinion above Yours sometimes. I have believed that some of what I do is unimportant to You and have therefore left You out of areas of my life. Help me today to start doing everything for You so that I can honour You with my whole life. Amen.*

June 29 | My Father's Business

Jill Southern-Jones

Did you not know that I must be about My Father's business?
Luke 2:49, NKJV

God usually requires us to spend years of preparation doing ordinary things and learning to be servant-hearted before He can powerfully use us. When Joseph had his dreams, he was at home with his mum and dad, being brought up by Jacob as a good Hebrew boy. But he, like all of us, had to grow beyond the faith of his parents and get to know God and the ways of God for himself.

Are you still being carried along by your parents' faith rather than hearing or encountering God for yourself? Many people live in a dream but not in their destiny. God has both a dream and a destiny for you. Are you dreaming about building the Kingdom for Jesus in some way and about making disciples, but you're afraid to take the risk and step out to do the things God has prepared for you in advance?

Jesus was thirty years of age when He began His earthly ministry, but at the age of twelve he'd said to His parents, 'Don't you know that I must be about My Father's business?' All those years He knew that He was in preparation for His destiny to be the Saviour of the world.

God cares enough about us to invest in us and to watch over us in the years of preparation. God wants us to listen for His voice and to know His ways; to have the courage and faith to follow Him. Timing is so important – wait patiently for the Lord's time, neither rushing ahead of Him nor lagging behind Him. What Joseph learned about God in those early years proved to be essential when God had raised him to his place of destiny. What does God want you to do with your life? What did God last ask you to do and have you done it?

PRAYER: *Lord, please speak to me about Your destiny and purpose for my life. Help me to learn the lessons and to prepare my heart for obedience. I don't want to live in the dream but not in the destiny. Help me to know Your timing, in Jesus' name. Amen.*

JUNE 30 | IDOLATRY

LIZ GRIFFIN

But their idols are silver and gold, made by the hands of men ...
they have ears, but cannot hear ...

Psalm 115:4, 6

I once sat on a bus in Japan and talked to a young woman about my faith. I explained that I spoke to God in prayer and He answered my prayers, so I knew He was real. She was astonished. 'When we say prayers to idols we don't expect them to answer us,' she said. She understood something for the first time and I did too. Two world cultures were meeting and discovering the differences between them.

When I was six years old my father almost drowned in the sea. I was told by my mother that after hours in a lifebelt in the freezing cold sea, when all hope of survival had gone, he prayed and committed his family into God's hands. It was immediately after that prayer that the lifeboat arrived and came to rescue him. At six years old I learnt that God exists and hears our prayers.

On arrival in Japan it was a shock to see lots of stone idols lined up on the wall of the temple. Each had a red bib tied on and pieces of fruit laid out in front of it. The trees at the Shinto shrine had lots of bits of paper tied on to them. On each paper was a prayer, at least a kind of prayer. Why do the Japanese do things like that? If you ask them they say they don't believe in any kind of God. But I believe the reality is that they fear not doing these traditional ceremonies in case something evil might come upon them.

Missionaries in Japan have the wonderful privilege of telling the Japanese people about the true and living God, who created the universe, and that He's interested in us all as unique human beings. He wants to have a loving relationship with us, through Jesus Christ, His Son.

One Japanese lady told me how she went to England and stayed with a family who took her with them to church. Nothing was really explained to her about God. Yet something stirred within her spirit and after returning to Japan she began seeking after a relationship with God. I wonder if we Christians realise what an awesome privilege it is to know that the God who made the universe wants a relationship with us.

PRAYER: *Dear Heavenly Father, I want to thank You that You have revealed Yourself to me. Thank You that I can come to You as Your child and simply speak to You, knowing You hear and answer me, in Jesus' name. Amen.*

JULY 1 |
OTTO BIXLER

UNDER A REST

Remember the sabbath day, to keep it holy.

Exodus 20:8, NASB

Have you been arrested by God, or are you still rushing about madly trying to get everything done? Some time ago God got my and my wife's attention about taking one day in seven as a rest day – a Sabbath (Exodus 20:8–11). As Sharon and I adjusted our lives to less work time we discovered we could get more done. But then He brought dramatic confirmation to us.

One of our dear friends had been diagnosed with breast cancer and was scheduled for surgery in two days' time when we heard about it. Sharon had just returned from the UK where she had attended a course on Keys to Cancer in which Peter Horrobin had emphasised obedience to the Ten Commandments.

We went to see our friend with the simple plan of praying through the commandments. When we got to the fourth one, taking a Sabbath rest, she struggled incredibly since she had an invalid child and needed to be on duty every day. Finally she succumbed to God, being willing to live differently. A mighty deliverance took place as she put this part of her life in order.

None of the other commandments we prayed through seemed to touch her life as that one had. That was Saturday. On Monday she went to the hospital for the operation that would have removed her breast. But before the operation she asked the doctor to X-ray once more where the tumour had been. It was gone. Just to be sure, they operated and removed some lymph glands which were sent out for biopsy. There was no cancer. The disbelieving doctor sent the sample back a second time with the same results.

So, are you arguing with God about not having enough time? Is that the cancer eating up your life? Hopefully you won't neglect this commandment so that God will restore your life and protect your body. In Psalm 95:10–11 and in Numbers 15:32–39 there is a connection made between those who follow after their own hearts, not knowing God's ways, disobedience, and not entering His rest (see also Hebrews 3:18; 4:11). God is real; His commandments are real. It can be a matter of life and death if they are followed.

PRAYER: *Dear Lord, help me see where I have not entered into Your rest, by making flesh my strength. I have continued to use my time in 'productive' ways when You said that one in seven days is for rest. Please forgive me for transgressing Your commandments. It has seemed that there is not enough week for all the things that I have to do. Help me to step back onto the pathway, Your plan for my life. I will actively make changes to put my life in order, in Jesus' name, Amen.*

JULY 2 |
MARGARET SILVESTER

A SAFE AND SECRET PLACE OF SECURITY

> *He who dwells in the shelter of the Most High will rest in the shadow of the Almighty. I will say of the LORD, 'He is my refuge and my fortress, my God, in whom I trust.'*
>
> Psalm 91:1–2

We set off in sunshine for our mountain walk in the Austrian Alps. After some hours we heard the rumbling of thunder and the whole scene changed. We were high up and fully exposed when the storm clouds broke. There seemed nowhere to shelter from the storm until we stumbled upon a small hut on the side of the mountain. The door was locked, so we huddled into the leeward side of the hut until the storm passed. Strangely enough, we felt safe, sheltered from the storm.

Psalm 91 is probably one of the most loved of the Psalms. We cannot be sure who wrote the psalm, but we can assuredly say it was written by someone who truly knew God and had experienced His faithfulness in the good and bad times of life – in sunshine and in storm.

Our text for today uses the words 'dwelling' and 'resting'. Dwelling speaks to me of a permanent place – a daily life of living permanently near to God and in trusting relationship with Him. Resting speaks to me of a more temporary place – a place of safety and trust when the storm blows and things feel unsafe. It speaks to me of a sense of inner peace whatever life throws at us.

Insecurity is an 'in' word today because we live in an insecure world. However, this psalm assures us that it is possible to feel safe and secure whatever happens. It's a psalm about the protection God has for His people and how we can choose to experience it. He provides shelter, shade, refuge, safety and rescue. His faithfulness surrounds us and He even sends angels to guard us from danger.

All this doesn't happen automatically. When we dwell in *the Most High* – a permanent way of living, not just a 'now and then' experience – we acknowledge our dependence upon Him. Whatever changing scenes of life we face, we dwell secure in the knowledge that He can be trusted and He knows best. We love and respect Him and call upon Him in days of trouble, knowing that He will deliver us. This is true security.

In times of testing we can confuse real security with absence of difficulty and pain. God promises that as we love and trust Him He is with us in sunshine and storm, in good times and hard times. Being in trouble with Him is far better than being in trouble without Him.

PRAYER: *Father, thank You that You never change. Thank You that You're always with us, and in a world of insecurity and unrest we can know Your presence, as we walk with You, in joy or sadness, and in peace or storm. Thank You for giving Jesus who has made known to us Your heart of love. Amen.*

JULY 3 | THE FOLLY OF WORTHLESS IDOLS

PETER HORROBIN

> *Those who cling to worthless idols forfeit the grace that could be theirs. But I, with a song of thanksgiving, will sacrifice to you. What I have vowed I will make good. Salvation comes from the LORD.*
>
> Jonah 2:8–9

Jonah was in the belly of the fish. He lay there with seaweed wrapped round his head, having the ride of his life in an underwater roller-coaster from which there was no escape. It's amazing how being in impossible situations changes the intensity and urgency of your prayer life. Repentance comes easily when the only obvious solution to the problem is imminent death and an earlier than expected appointment with one's Maker!

There was no doubt that Jonah was seeing things from a new perspective – very different from the perspective he had when running away from the appointment with destiny in Nineveh, which God had planned for him. Anything which comes between a servant of God and the God he is serving is an idol.

Jonah did not want to go and preach to such a wicked people. The idol in Jonah's heart was selfishness driven by fear. But it was a worthless idol – and as a result he was now forfeiting all the grace that would have been his if he had obeyed God first time round and gone to Nineveh.

'Oh God – I'm sorry. I'll make good my vow to serve you! Whatever you want, I'll do! Even go to Nineveh, Lord. But God, it's rather difficult just now – I've got a bit of a problem. There doesn't seem any way off this roller-coaster. Is there anything you can do about it?' And with that the Lord commanded the fish to vomit Jonah up onto dry land. Jonah's premature appointment with his Maker had been postponed.

There are so many lessons in this amazing story, but the most important one for today prompts me to ask the question, *'Are you running from any of God's plans and purposes for your life?'* If so may I encourage you to get on your knees before God, deal with any worthless idols that have stood between you and obedience, and look to God for His grace as you ask Him how to put things right between you and Him.

PRAYER: *Thank You, Lord, for this amazing lesson from Your Word. Help me to examine my own heart and see if there are any ways in which I have been running from Your calling upon my life. I want to put things right – please show me how, in Jesus' name, Amen.*

JULY 4 |
CATH TAYLOR

DAILY BREAD

Give us today our daily bread ...

Matthew 6:11

When I was sixteen I worked at a local supermarket/grocery store in the North East of England. Three evenings a week after college I would race in late to start my shift on the checkouts. There was little time between college and work to find time to eat dinner, so guaranteed each day I would stand there wishing I had eaten a bigger lunch! The worst part of being hungry and pushing food along a conveyer belt was having to endure the smell of freshly baking bread wafting from the bakery at the back of the store. It was torture to my hungry stomach, causing my body to protest with angry growls and aches.

I am sure today's verse is familiar to you all. Many times I have asked the Lord to indeed *'give us today our daily bread'*, always in my heart referring to my physical and financial needs. Today, I was reminded that this isn't the only kind of daily bread we need.

John 6:35 says, *'Jesus declared, "I am the bread of life. Whoever comes to me will never go hungry, and whoever believes in me will never be thirsty."'*

Just like my stomach would ache at the smell of the bread, so too our spirits ache for daily time with the Lord. Time where we are real with Him and talk to Him about what is really going on inside. Time where we allow Him to talk to us and speak His truth into our hearts. Time where we read His Word and allow His 'living word' to speak life to us on the inside. It is only here we find the sustenance and provision we need to face life, and to walk in His paths. Only here do we receive the strength that comes from Him and the peace that is a basic desire within us all.

At first, while I stood at the checkout my stomach was often loud and obnoxious in its cries of protest for food. As the time passed, I was still hungry but no longer was my stomach reacting and no longer was I even aware of the needs of my body. Maybe we have become a little like that in our walk with the Lord. We can become a little immune to the hunger for Him, and time in His presence. We draw instead from our own resources and face each day with reserves, or alternative provision that temporarily relieves our hunger. How foolish we can all be, to think we can survive without our daily bread!

PRAYER: *Lord Jesus, thank You that You provide all my needs. Thank You that You alone are the bread of my life. You alone are all that my heart needs each day. I am sorry for the times that I forget to spend time with You, or when the busyness of life pushes You to a lesser priority. Please keep me aware of my need of You, Jesus, and give me a desire and passion to always spend time each day with You. In Jesus' name I pray, Amen.*

JULY 5 | TAKING AWAY TEMPTATION – PART 1

LINDSEY HANEKOM

And lead us not into temptation, but deliver us from the evil one.

Matthew 6:13

I remember as a child thinking my parents could see everything I ever did. If they had their backs turned or even were in another room, they always seemed to know when I was up to no good. Now, as a parent myself, I know how they did it!

It's really quite simple: you just know your own child. For example, I *know* that if I leave the dog's water bowl out then it won't take Kyle long to crawl over and start playing in it. You can't really blame him; he loves water and here it is presented in a shiny bowl, right at his level – pure temptation!

But what's my response as a loving parent? Well, initially it's a firm 'No', but in reality the temptation is just too great sometimes. As a result, when the dog leaves to go to work with Johann in the morning, I tip the water out and put the bowl up out of Kyle's reach. Would I really put temptation in his way just to tell him off? Of course not! In fact, if I leave the bowl out we can waste a lot of precious play time by stopping him doing what he's not supposed to. This is no fun for either of us!

Maybe this is what Jesus was talking about when he taught us to pray, '*Lead us not into temptation.*' He knows us so well that He knows our weaknesses. He knows how we want to react to situations in our lives. He knows what tempts us. He also knows that we need to pray, '*but deliver us from the evil one*'. Temptation is often empowered by the enemy's holds in our lives, maybe through previous sin.

So, let's identify and admit our weaknesses to God. Let's ask Him to remove the strong temptations of our lives so we won't be distracted from the enjoyment and pleasure of doing His will.

PRAYER: *Father God, You know everything about me. You know when I consider doing wrong. I ask that You will help me identify and admit these weaknesses, so You can remove them from the path I walk. In Jesus' name I pray. Amen.*

July 6 | Dealing with Temptation – Part 2

Lindsey Hanekom

No temptation has seized you except what is common to man. And God is faithful; he will not let you be tempted beyond what you can bear. But when you are tempted, he will also provide a way out so that you can stand up under it.

1 Corinthians 10:13

Yesterday we looked at asking God to take *away* temptation. I likened it to removing the tempting dog's bowl from my son's reach. However, there are some things in our lives that tempt us, but they're more difficult to remove. For instance the television, the internet, alcohol, and food are readily available to us.

In our house, Kyle often wants to hold onto the oven door handle when we're in the kitchen. We don't want him doing this as he could easily hurt himself. Clearly, we can't respond in the same way as we do with the dog's bowl. It's impossible to remove the cooker!

So how do we handle this situation? Initially, we see Kyle heading towards the cooker and we give him a gentle warning. If he makes a grab for the handle, we issue a firm verbal reprimand and remove him from the cooking area. But we don't just dump him in a different room, far away from us, rejecting him for disobeying us. We offer a more enjoyable thing to do in the kitchen, where he's still with us. We join in with his play.

In the same way, when you're heading towards falling into temptation, your conscience will sound a warning bell. The enemy wants you to believe that once you start down that road, you will inevitably fall. Then God won't be there for you because it will be your own fault. But that's not true. God's Word says He *will* provide a way out, no matter how far we've walked down the road of temptation.

As soon as you allow God into the situation He's able to rescue you and put you in a place of safety. No matter how far down the road of temptation you may travel, He will always be there, ready with a way out to a much better place, where you can enjoy your relationship with Him – but you must choose to want it!

Prayer: *Father God, You know the areas where I struggle with temptation. I know that they're with me every day. I pray that You will help me. May I remember to ask You to rescue me before I fall. Then I can be in a safe place and enjoy my relationship with You. In Jesus' name I pray. Amen.*

July 7 | Comfort

Patricia Lake

'Comfort, comfort my people,' says your God.

Isaiah 40:1

Israel had been through yet another particularly harrowing time with enemy attacks, when God spoke these deeply compassionate words to her. Today He is still desirous of bringing comfort both to Israel and to each of us.

So – how does God bring comfort to us? Through the presence of His Holy Spirit in and through us, bringing His healing words of consolation and compassion, found in Scripture – gently soothing us in times of grief and pain in life's difficulties. He is the great Comforter. It's at these times when we can feel His reassuringly safe arms around us like a huge blanket or duvet, in which we can find protection, peace and safety. Sometimes He comforts us through others drawing alongside with a comforting arm or a timely word, just being there to help in a time of need. Whichever way He chooses we know that the Prince of Peace is at work because He meets us at our point of need.

Certainly in Israel's case it was to bring relief in their time of affliction, when yet more marauding hoards of invading armies assaulted their borders, stealing all that God had given to them and taking their people into captivity. Jesus also comforted His disciples before He went back to heaven, telling them that He was going to prepare a place for them and that the time would come when they would see Him again.

Scripture tells us that the eyes of the Lord range through the earth (2 Chronicles 16:9) and nothing escapes His gaze. God's wonderfully gentle and loving eyes, and equally wonderfully healing hands, can reach into the depths of our being where nothing and no one else can, anointing and healing our gaping wounds and setting us on the pathway of health and wholeness. Such comfort is reminiscent of the warmth of the sunshine breaking through after the ravages of a storm, reassuring the world that danger is past and there is hope for the future. The sun of righteousness has risen with healing in its wings (see Malachi 4:2). Today He beckons you afresh to come to Him, casting *'all your anxiety on him because he cares for you'* (1 Peter 5:7).

PRAYER: *Thank You, Lord, that You are the God of all comfort and You know all about us. Today we ask You to draw near to all who need Your comfort; may they feel the closeness of your abiding presence, in Jesus' name. Amen.*

JULY 8 | THERE IS A FRIEND

PAM SMITH

There is a friend who sticks closer than a brother.

Proverbs 18:24, LB

If you want a friend – be a friend. Reach out and take that first step. So often lonely people are the ones that draw away from folk and are afraid to be friendly or to reach out. Ask the Lord for the courage.

When I was eleven, on my first day at a new school, a very shy girl came up and asked me if I would be her friend. We have been friends ever since. She decided to choose me as her friend.

Jonathon was a real friend and soul mate to David and believed that David would be king one day even though he, himself, was in line for the throne. He put his own life at risk by protecting David, supporting and helping him. His last words were encouragement to him. *'Don't be afraid', he said, 'My father Saul will not lay a hand on you. You shall be king over Israel, and I will be second to you'* (1 Samuel 23:17). How beautiful was the deep friendship of David and Jonathan in the Lord. Sometimes God gives such friendships to us.

Jesus chose His disciples as His friends, to live and share His ministry with them. How they must have loved being in His presence. *'Jesus said to them, You are My friends if you do whatever I command you. No longer do I call you servants, for a servant does not know what his master is doing, but I have called you friends, for all things that I heard from My Father I have made known to you'* (John 15:14–15, NKJV).

And Jesus is the friend that is closer than a brother to us. He is our Best Friend, Brother, Saviour, Redeemer, Healer, Sustainer and Protector. He is everything to us – and He calls us 'friends'.

What a Friend we have in Jesus,
All our sins and griefs to bear!
What a privilege to carry
Everything to God in prayer …
Can we find a friend so faithful

Who will all our sorrows share?
Jesus knows our every weakness,
Take it to the Lord in prayer.
(Joseph Scriven, 1855)

PRAYER: *Dear Lord, I thank You that You are my Best Friend. May I be that one You call 'friend' too. Keep me faithful and true to Your commands. Help me to reach out to those who so need a friend, in Jesus' name, Amen.*

JULY 9 | CHOSEN

LINDSEY HANEKOM

> *Furthermore, because we are united with Christ, we have received an inheritance from God, for he chose us in advance, and he makes everything work out according to his plan.*
>
> Ephesians 1:11, NLT

My son, Kyle, really blessed me earlier today when we were playing at a local park. All of a sudden he took great interest in the expanse of daisies that covered the grassy play area. Ignoring the usual climbing frames, swings and slides, my not quite two-year-old took it upon himself to go looking for the perfect daisy to give to me. I stood watching him race to and fro amongst the patches of daisies and responded with great joy and pleasure when he finally found one that he thought was suitable and offered it to me. Encouraged by my response, he headed off again, racing around, examining daises. He rejected many before he found another daisy that he considered suitable and offered this one to me as well.

This continued for quite a while and as I watched my son, I was touched by a sense of what Jesus has done for each of us. The Bible says that we were chosen by Him. Just as Kyle turned away from his own pleasure of the park and averted his attention onto blessing me, so did Jesus turn away from His home in heaven to bless us here on earth. Not only that, but He continues to seek out those who catch His attention and brings them back to the Father (through the cross) as an offering of joy and pleasure.

As I considered this, I looked at the collection of daisies I was accumulating, expecting them all to be perfect and carefully chosen because of their beauty or outward appearance. The reality is that many had lost petals, damaged stalks or just looked as though they were dying. I have no idea what Kyle's criteria for a 'suitable' daisy was, just as we cannot understand why we ourselves would be chosen to be an offering of love to the Father.

With such a thought, surely our only response can be one of wonder and praise as we thank Almighty God for choosing you and me, despite our weaknesses and imperfections. May we never lose sight of what God has done for us and how blessed we are to be chosen by Him.

PRAYER: *Thank You, God, that I am chosen by You. Thank You that You respond to me with joy and pleasure. I praise You and give thanks to You for saving me, despite my weaknesses and my imperfections. In Jesus' name I pray, Amen.*

JULY 10 | GIVE THANKS TO THE LORD

GORAN ANDERSSON

> *Praise the LORD! Give thanks to the LORD, for he is good; his love endures for ever.*
>
> Psalm 106:1

Giving thanks to the Lord is far too often just a religious activity that we perform without really giving ourselves to it. It was only after meeting a couple of men who used an entirely different vocabulary and style when 'giving thanks' that my eyes were opened to new ways of expressing thankfulness to the Lord.

Their vocabulary was different because it was so down-to-earth, as far away from any religious jargon as it's possible to be. It was just as if they were saying thank you to a neighbour for helping them when the car had broken down. The Lord was so real to them.

One of them was a worker in a paper mill. His education was very rudimentary, his life had been ravaged by drinking, and it was only as a middle-aged man that he'd found the Lord. His theological understanding was quite limited, but he knew the Lord! God was as real to him as his work mates in the mill, and when he talked to God he used the same language he used to talk to them. He would stand up in church and say, 'Jesus, you did it again! Good work, Jesus! I like that, that's really like you!'

This lifestyle brought him peace and joy, and I'm sure the angels in heaven were really rejoicing every time this man opened his mouth! He certainly knew how to give thanks to the Lord! And he meant every word he said! He recognised what Jesus did in the minute details of life, and said thank you. And the more he thanked the Lord, the more the Lord seemed to do for him. He was so natural, because he'd never learned any other way of doing it. I, and probably many with me who have grown up in church, would struggle to be so natural, because we've learned so many other ways that are more 'churchy'.

Giving thanks to the Lord isn't a religious duty; it's a natural reaction of our heart when we recognise what Jesus is doing. If I have a relationship with Jesus that is marked by distance and ceremony, thanksgiving will never come naturally. If, on the other hand, I'm conscious of His presence with me all the time, at home, at work, in school and anywhere else, thanksgiving will be my natural lifestyle.

When I give thanks it's pleasing to the Lord, but it also does something to me. As I recognise the Lord, and His goodness, and ascribe to Him the honour and the place that really is His, my life comes under His authority and protection. My life comes into the order described in Psalm 91, one of blessing.

Day by day I'm trying to learn the lesson God is teaching me from this brother, and surprisingly I find it harder to be natural with the Lord than to be religious!

PRAYER: *Dear Heavenly Father, may we discover what You are doing for us in our daily walk and learn to thank You more, in a simple, natural way. May our eyes be opened even more to Your blessings great and small, so that our hearts begin to overflow in gratitude to You, in Jesus' name, Amen.*

JULY 11 |
JILLY LYON-TAYLOR

FOCUS ON WHAT YOU CAN'T SEE!

So we fix our eyes not on what is seen, but on what is unseen. For what is seen is temporary, but what is unseen is eternal.

2 Corinthians 4:18

Many of you are facing problems today – concerns over employment, finance and provision; difficulties with family and relationships; issues with inner hurts, pain or depression; struggles with sickness, and physical problems. Often these things loom so large in the forefront of our minds that it's difficult to think of anything else.

But in today's verse the apostle Paul urges us not to focus on what's seen, those difficulties and issues that we're facing today, but to fix our eyes on what's unseen. What's unseen is the utter faithfulness of God as revealed in His Word – that He chose each one of us before He created the world (Ephesians 1:4); that we have been adopted into His family (Ephesians 1:5); that He's our Father (2 Corinthians 6:18); that His love for us is lavish and unfailing (1 John 3:1); that He will never leave us nor forsake us (Hebrews 13:5); that He will always provide for us (Philippians 4:19); that He's our Healer (Isaiah 53:3–5), and that He's the Father of compassion and the God of all comfort (2 Corinthians 1:3).

All of these statements (and many more) are true for every believer in Jesus Christ, but the outworking of them isn't always automatic in our lives. We're told that *'no matter how many promises God has made, they are "Yes" in Christ'* (2 Corinthians 1:20). So we need to keep coming back to the finished work of Jesus on the cross to appropriate God's promises in each area of our lives, and we do that by faith, not by sight (2 Corinthians 5:7).

Whatever difficult circumstances you're facing today, they're temporary compared to the eternal nature of God and His promises to you in Christ. Will you choose today to fix your eyes *'not on what is seen, but on what is unseen'*? The more we can focus on those unseen things, the more they'll become true in our experience.

PRAYER: *Heavenly Father, forgive me for spending so much time focusing on my problems and my pain. I choose today to fix my eyes on the unseen truths contained in Your promises. Thank You that these are eternal, in Jesus' name, Amen.*

JULY 12 | LESSONS FROM THE BBQ

ANDY TAYLOR

> *This is why I remind you to fan into flames the spiritual gift God gave you when I laid my hands on you. For God has not given us a spirit of fear and timidity, but of power, love, and self-discipline.*
>
> 2 Timothy 1:6–7, NLT

Like most people, I love a good barbeque. The smell of the smouldering charcoal and the taste of burnt sausages coated in ketchup are enough to brighten just about any day! I am definitely not a professional though. I don't have a fancy gas grill but I do it the hard way – charcoal bricks and about three boxes of matches! If I do manage to light a coal it then takes huge effort to get the fire going. The best method I've found is to get a plastic tray and to fan furiously until all the charcoal is ablaze. It takes time, effort and sweat to move from the small flame of the match to a charcoal fire which is useful.

In the above scripture we see how Paul was encouraging Timothy to 'fan into flames' the spiritual gift that God had given him. What does that mean?

God had planted in Timothy a spiritual gift – but that was not the end of the story. There was something that Timothy had to do. He had to fan it into flames. In other words he had to stir it up or rekindle the gift. To me, this is done through obedience. At some point, Timothy had to be obedient to the call God had put on his life, and walk in the gifting that he had been given. Through obedience (which can take time and effort) he is effectively fanning his spiritual gift into flames – flames which would be fruitful for the Kingdom of God.

So, what are you doing with the spiritual gifts that God has given you? Are you expecting God to take it from a small flame to a blazing fire or are you beginning to walk in obedience to Him and to exercise your gifting in obedience to Him? Often, fear is what holds us back but verse 7 encourages us that we have not been given a spirit of fear and timidity, but of power, love and self-discipline.

PRAYER: *Thank You, Lord, for the gifts You have given me. Help me to fan into flames the sparks of life, so that all my gifts will be a blessing to You and all whom You have sent me to serve, in Jesus' name, Amen.*

JULY 13 | SEATED WITH CHRIST

JILLY LYON-TAYLOR

> *God raised us up with Christ and seated us with him in the heavenly realms in Christ Jesus.*
>
> Ephesians 2:6

When I travel by air I always ask for a window seat as I love to look out at the landscape below and see the houses, cars and trees seemingly in miniature. Even the mountains appear flat when high above them. That seems to me to be a picture of the perspective on life and its problems that God wants us to have. He has promised that when we are saved we are raised up to be seated with Christ in heavenly realms – *'far above all rule and authority, power and dominion'* (Ephesians 1:21). That means we should be able to look down at obstacles from His perspective, from our position in Him.

I had a revelation of this when one of our sons started at secondary school. He was struggling after the first day, finding everything quite daunting, so after I had left him on the second day I launched into prayer for him as mothers do! I started to pray that he would make a friend, that he wouldn't get lost and that he would manage the work. Then I heard a voice very clearly telling me to 'Stop!' I knew it was the Lord.

He told me to stop praying for the circumstances in my son's life to change and to pray instead that he would be above the circumstances, knowing who he was in Christ. I started to pray in this way and when I met him at the end of the day there was complete transformation. His day had gone well and he was seeing everything from a different perspective.

What about you today? Are you seeing obstacles towering above you, or are you looking down at them from the perspective of *who* and *where* you are in Christ?

PRAYER: *Lord, thank You that You have raised me up with Christ and seated me with Him in heavenly places. Help me to remember this today so that I can see everything from Your perspective, remembering who I am in You, in Jesus' name, Amen.*

JULY 14 | PAYING THE PRICE – BUT WHAT PRICE?

ROGER POOK

> *'For I know the plans I have for you,' declares the LORD, 'plans to prosper you and not to harm you, plans to give you a hope and a future.'*
>
> Jeremiah 29:11

'*Paying the price.*' Oh dear. Is this going to be another of those depressing religious lessons that attempts to spur me on to even greater sacrifice when I've got nothing left to give anyway?

Actually, no. It's a revelation about the price that we really have to pay. It may surprise you. Recently I was praying about how I wanted to move on with God and see Him doing greater and greater things. Quick as a flash, the response came: *'Are you willing to pay the price?'*

This brought me up short. I knew I had to be careful how I replied! We had already given up everything to serve God in Eastern Europe – what more could God want? Homelessness? Hunger? Suffering? Imprisonment? Even death?

Every time I prayed there was the same response – 'Are you willing to pay the price?' I was really afraid to answer. Then I remembered what Jesus said in Luke 14:28: *'If one of you is planning to build a tower, you sit down first and figure out what it will cost, to see if you have enough money to finish the job'* (GNB). So I was bold enough to ask God: 'What exactly is the price that you want me to pay?'

God's answer was amazing! 'The price is all the things that you want to get rid of! Anger, irritation, pride, self-righteousness, fear, anxiety … This is the price that I want you to pay! I'll take all this rubbish off your hands, and in exchange I'll give you everything you ask for.'

Now that's what I call a bargain!

PRAYER: *Heavenly Father, if getting rid of the rubbish is the price for moving on with You, then I accept! I really don't want it, so I give it all to You. I am more than willing to pay this price, and to receive whatever plans You have for me. Thank You so much for this amazing offer, in Jesus' name, Amen.*

JULY 15 | FEARFULLY AND WONDERFULLY MADE

NICKY HEMERY

> *For you created my inmost being; you knit me together in my mother's womb. I praise you because I am fearfully and wonderfully made; your works are wonderful, I know that full well.*
>
> Psalm 139:13–14

A few years ago when on holiday in Spain we discovered a museum for all things miniature. Some items were so tiny you could only appreciate the craftsmanship through a magnifying glass.

I was especially amazed by some grains of rice which had been intricately carved into different shapes. To the naked eye they looked little more than a grain of rice, but when magnified you could see the incredible intricate detail carved into each tiny grain.

Sometimes I wonder what it would be like to look down on planet earth at all the billions of people. So many of us that from a distance we could look like grains of rice or the sand on the seashore. Yet God has created every one of us and intricately knit us together in our mother's womb. Each one of us is different and a work of art in the Craftsman's hand.

And after we are born God's work is not finished. He continues to make us and mould us into unique individuals with a purpose and destiny in life.

We may think we are 'just another person' on this vastly populated planet and 'no one in particular' – but to God, our Heavenly Father, every one of us is unique and special.

Do we feel that way today? Perhaps it is time to ask God to show us who we are and how He sees us under the magnifying glass of His craftsmanship.

PRAYER: *Lord, I praise You because I am fearfully and wonderfully made; Your works are wonderful. Please help me to know that fully in my life and to begin to understand how You see me. Thank You for making me, me. Amen.*

July 16 |
Margaret Southey

Your Word is a Lamp

Your word is a lamp to my feet and a light for my path.

Psalm 119:105

During a recent holiday in the Swiss Alps, we walked a great deal; through forests, by rivers, up hills, into valleys and across fields. Along the route there were regular signposts pointing out the different directions with indications of how long the journey would take. In some places there were also markers showing the degree of difficulty of the walk.

As I walked I set to thinking about life and the numerous crossroads we face. On first reflection I wished our life's path had signposts with indications of direction, time and degree of difficulty. So often life seems anything but clear and the options appear confusing rather than exciting choices. This is especially so when we rely for our choices on our own understanding, knowledge and 'worldly' wisdom.

As I reflected further, however, I realised our life's path really is well signposted after all! God's Word gives us plenty of guidance and direction. In the Ten Commandments alone, there are several signposts. We're instructed not to steal, commit adultery, murder (this can be taken to apply to abortion and euthanasia in our modern society) or worship idols (this could be understood in the wider sense of worshipping money, power, success, or our bodies and our minds).

It's possible to breach all the commandments of God if we rely on our own human understanding, rather than finding out what is acceptable in God's eyes by studying His Word. As a result we fall into crevasses and over cliffs. They may not be physical crevasses or cliffs, but they certainly are mental, emotional and spiritual ones. At Ellel Ministries we regularly have the privilege of ministering to people who have fallen along the way because they didn't heed the signposts, sometimes deliberately and sometimes through ignorance. Whatever the cause, they were injured and often badly so.

Through the redeeming work of Jesus on the cross, they have a way out of the crevasse and up the cliff, but it's frequently a painful and slow climb back. Those we minister to often tell us that they wished they had heeded the signposts in the first place. God's Word is full of guidance to us for our own well-being and protection. It is indeed a lamp to our feet and a light to our path.

PRAYER: *Father, I want to turn to Your Word as a signpost for my life, rather than rely on my own judgement and understanding. Please help me, in Jesus' name, Amen.*

JULY 17 |
ANDY TAYLOR

BE A TAXI DRIVER OF THE WORD!

Your word is a lamp to guide my feet and a light for my path.
Psalms 119:105, NLT

If you were dropped into a major city of the world, chances are you'd have some idea of the major landmarks that you could visit. In Paris you'd know about the Eiffel Tower, in Sydney you'd head for the Opera House, but the one person who really knows about a city is a local taxi driver. These guys are amazing! Not only are they normally highly entertaining in their story-telling and maybe a little over-confident in their ability to dodge pedestrians and cyclists – but they know every detail of the city. If traffic starts to build up or a set of traffic lights break down, they know exactly which detour to take so that you can reach the desired destination. They know the main routes but they also know every side road and short cut.

This is often how it can work for us and the Bible. We know the major landmarks – Psalm 23, John 3:16, the Sermon on the Mount – but we don't know all the amazing 'side roads' of the Word. These are the things that we need in order to navigate through the accidents and road works of life – the fullness of God's Word. The reason a taxi driver knows all the details of his city is simply because he spends all of his time there. Every day he drives around its streets. He didn't know it all when he started out but the more he drove around, the more he knew.

The Bible is effectively a 'city' with endless side streets – so let's commit before God to be taxi drivers of this great 'city'. To spend time in His Word so that we can navigate all that life brings our way and we can know the greatness of our God.

PRAYER: *Thank You, Lord, for the amazing vastness of Your Word which provides us with the ultimate guidance for our lives. Help us to spend so much time in Your Word that we will know how to navigate through all the circumstances life brings our way, in Jesus' name, Amen.*

JULY 18 | TEARS

LIZ GRIFFIN

> *You have kept count of my tossings; put my tears in your bottle. Are they not in your book?*
>
> Psalm 56:8, ESV

When David was seized by the Philistines in Gath he wrote the words of a prayer (Psalm 56). He asks for mercy, he asks for God to deal with his enemies, and he affirms that his trust is in the Lord and that he will not be afraid of mortal men. He mentions his tears and says that God has saved them in a wineskin, or a bottle, and that they are written down in God's book, or scroll. David was saying that God cared about his grief and troubles; that He knew about them intimately and understood.

It appears that there was an ancient custom of the Romans and Greeks for the mourners at a funeral to have someone wipe their tears with a cloth and then squeeze them into a small bottle which would be buried along with the body. It seems a strange custom, but maybe those tears were regarded as proof of how much the dead person was loved.

We know Jesus wept at the tomb of Lazarus, that He was overwhelmed with sorrow in the Garden of Gethsemane and that He wept over Jerusalem. *'And when he drew near and saw the city, he wept over it'* (Luke 19:41). He was crying tears for the sins and suffering of others. The prophets did the same as they delivered God's message of impending judgement and doom. They were reflecting God's heart. God weeps over His people and longs to restore them.

In the healing ministry we see many tears shed and we have boxes of tissues ready. There are tears of deep anguish, pain, disappointment and sorrow as people's dreams for the future are smashed, relationships fall apart and Satan does his worst.

But there are tears that bring healing as the grief of the past is emptied out, creating a space for new life to enter, life from the Holy Spirit of God. And there are tears of relief and joy shed as darkness is dispelled and the light of God's presence appears. We can share in these tears as we hear the testimony of God's people being healed.

But there are tears that bring healing as the grief of the past is emptied out, creating a space for new life to enter, life from the Holy Spirit of God.

David says, *'You have kept count of my tossings; put my tears in your bottle. Are they not in your book?'* How comforting those words are to us as we receive them today in our darkest hour and realise others have gone through deep distress but their trust and faith in God has sustained them. David goes on to say, *'Then my enemies will turn back in the day when I call. This I know, that God is for me'* (Psalm 56:9). God is for us. He's on our side. He understands. He knows how many hairs we have on our head. He keeps account of every tear we shed. His heart is to restore every broken place in our lives.

PRAYER: *Dear Heavenly Father, how encouraged I am to know that You love me so much that You care about every tear I've ever shed. You understand all my pain and sorrow and You want to bring Your comfort and healing to me. Help me to trust You and be confident that you are 'for me', in Jesus' name, Amen.*

July 19 | Joyful Christians

David Silvester

I have told you this so that my joy may be in you and that your joy may be complete.

John 15:11

Jesus has just been speaking to His disciples about being fruitful after His departure. He had spoken about them 'bearing fruit', 'more fruit' and 'much fruit' and He illustrated His talk with examples of a vine and the need for its pruning in order to stimulate fruitfulness. Then He said, *'I have told you this so that my joy may be in you and that your joy may be complete'* (John 15:11).

Sometimes we may find that we're going through a difficult time and we wonder if we'll ever recover and get back to the days when we knew God was working in us and using us in fruitful service.

Once my wife and I were going through a particularly testing time in leadership until God revealed what was going on and gave us the wisdom to deal with the matter following Biblical guidelines. Shortly after that the congregation began to experience an outpouring of blessing, greater than anything they had ever known before. We knew then we had just been through a pruning process. The end result was an experience of joy and rejoicing as we were drawn closer to each other and to the Lord.

Whatever the nature of the 'pruning' it's always for our good. The writer of Hebrews says, *'No discipline seems pleasant at the time, but painful. Later on, however, it produces a harvest of righteousness and peace for those who have been trained by it'* (Hebrews 12:11). Or as Paul could say, *'We also rejoice in our sufferings, because we know that suffering produces perseverance; perseverance, character; and character, hope'* (Romans 5:3).

When God's at work in our lives by His Holy Spirit we know that *'in all things God works for the good of those who love him, who have been called according to his purpose'* (Romans 8:28), even though at times we may be going through a pruning process.

One of the fruits of the Holy Spirit is joy (Galatians 5:22) and joy doesn't depend upon our circumstances. So, if we're going through one of those difficult and testing times, let's rejoice, and not become despondent. Let's look up to Jesus, and rejoice in the fact that God is at work in us in order to deal with the things that are unproductive. He can fill us with joy as we see Him making our life more fruitful for His glory.

Prayer: *Father God, I thank You that You are patiently working in my life in order that I might become fruitful for You. Please help me to look beyond the difficult time and rejoice that You have something better in store for me and I will experience more of You working through me. Amen.*

July 20 | The Will and the Mind

Paul Watson

> *The man who has settled the matter in his own mind, who is under no compulsion but has control over his own will …*
>
> 1 Corinthians 7:37

A very important aspect of our walk with the Lord involves the interaction between our mind and our will. I have been thinking about this quite a lot recently.

It has often been said that the mind is the battleground. It's the place where we wrestle with temptation, and where we reason, plan and strategise in our life. The will, however, has the final say.

The mind is where the old nature stages its comebacks, or suffers its defeats.

The human will is crucial to the godly walk of a disciple of Jesus. The command to *'take every thought captive'* is actually an act of the will.

So, it may be said that the will is the governing aspect of the soul.

If I'm to live a holy life I need to take thoughts captive to Christ and allow my mind to be renewed, which leads to transformation (Romans 12). But my *will* needs help from the Holy Spirit to make right choices.

My will needs help to choose to turn off the television and pray with my family, to act lovingly, to forgive, to think God-honouring thoughts, not to eat junk food and to exercise.

The apostle Paul says in Philippians 2:13, '*… for it is God who works in you to will and to act according to His good purpose.*' It's God's grace that enables us to make right decisions and act in godly ways.

Prayer: *Father, would You please help me to make right, godly choices. Strengthen my will to make decisions that please You, that honour You, and give glory to You, in Jesus' name, Amen.*

July 21 | When it's Hard to Obey

Grace Marshall

Does the LORD delight in burnt offerings and sacrifices as much as in obeying the voice of the LORD? To obey is better than sacrifice.
1 Samuel 15:22

Recently I was having difficulty with a particular matter; there was something I felt the Lord wanted me to do, but I didn't want to do it! Then today's verse came to my mind: '*To obey is better than sacrifice.*'

As I thought about it, I realised that obedience is actually a form of sacrifice. When I choose to obey God in something I don't like, I'm sacrificing what I want to do and choosing to obey God instead.

Sacrifice means giving up something I value. In today's verse, God says that the sacrifice of obedience is what matters most to Him. When we use the word 'sacrifice', we often think of giving up material things or time. But obedience can be bigger than that. I may need to give up a behaviour, an activity or an attitude. It can be easier to sacrifice material goods and more difficult to sacrifice actions and behaviours.

But the value of a sacrifice is measured by how hard it is to make the sacrifice. Think about the poor widow who put two tiny coins into the temple treasury in Mark 12:41–44. Jesus noticed it (how often I'm tempted to think He doesn't notice) and He said she had given more than all the wealthy people who had put in much larger amounts. God weighs a sacrifice according to how much it costs us personally.

This is how He describes our sacrifices: '*They are a fragrant offering, an acceptable sacrifice, pleasing to God*' (Philippians 4:18). Not forgetting that the Lord Jesus is the one we follow: '*Christ loved us and gave himself up for us as a fragrant offering and sacrifice to God*' (Ephesians 5:2).

Sacrifices are hard, and obedience can be the hardest kind of sacrifice, but that also makes it the most fragrant and pleasing to God, who certainly does notice!

Prayer: *Lord Jesus, thank You so much for the huge sacrifice You made for me. I do want to please You. Please help me to obey You, even though it is hard. Thank You. Amen.*

July 22 | It is Going to be OK

Cath Taylor

For God has said, 'I will never fail you. I will never abandon you.' So we can say with confidence, 'The Lord is my helper, so I will have no fear.'

Hebrews 13:5, NLT

As a child, with three brothers to keep up with and being the only girl, I can remember countless times hearing these words from my dad: 'It's OK. I've got you. I won't let you fall.' 'It's OK – you're doing fine. Keep going.'

Whether I was trying to keep up with my older brother climbing huge rocks in the North East of England, being encouraged up mountain slopes or attempting some new playset equipment, I can remember the moment of freezing where my legs no longer thought my attempt at bravery was such a good idea, and behind me, from just behind or below, I would hear my dad with these familiar words.

I look back on those days now as a parent myself, and smile at how often I find myself speaking the same words to my own children. Whatever the new venture or attempt may be in their lives, coming from Mum or Dad, those words, 'It will be OK', speak such confidence and peace deep into their hearts on the inside. Such simple, nondescript words really, and yet they contain so much depth of meaning to us as children. Somewhere inside we know they don't mean, 'Everything is going to be perfect and I promise you won't get hurt' but instead they mean quite simply 'Whatever happens, keep going; it is going to be OK and I will still be here and loving you.'

As adults nothing is more comforting to hear than these simple words from Father God – 'It is going to be OK.' It doesn't necessarily change our situation in the day to day. It doesn't erase the circumstances that have caused us to be worried in the first place. BUT it does something so much more … it brings a deep peace and security to our hearts deep on the inside. It reminds us, just like in today's scripture, that He will never let us down. He will never leave us. We may still have to climb the mountain or scale the rock, but what new courage and energy we can experience to know, no matter what … 'He is my helper and I don't need to be afraid.'

Prayer: *Father God, what a peace it brings my heart to know that You will never leave me, that You will never let me down. Thank You, Lord, that I don't walk through the challenges of life alone, that if I only listen for Your voice I will find You right by my side, speaking Your words of assurance and truth to my heart. In Jesus' name I pray, Amen.*

July 23 | Use Your Mind

Richard Hemery

But we have the mind of Christ.

1 Corinthians 2:16

Sometimes it seems to me that the mind – I'm talking about the reasoning part of our soul which responds directly to our senses, to what we see and hear – is an undervalued part of our beings. Sometimes it is viewed with suspicion, or seen only as an enemy of our spirits, an enemy of faith. The subtle lie is introduced that intellect and faith are incompatible, and especially it seems in today's culture, that science and God are incompatible. We are repeatedly told that our mind is a battleground, and that every sin starts in the mind.

Of course there is the unregenerate, sinful mind of which these things are true. But there is also a renewed mind, and a reason that leads to faith and does not oppose it. God gave you a mind. He gave you a hand, and you use it without thinking. You use your feet without hesitation. So why not your mind?

If sin begins in the mind, how much more powerfully will righteousness begin there if we allow God to renew our minds?

Christ had a mind, an intellect, and I am sure He used it in a godly way that glorified His Father. Indeed, we too can have the mind of Christ (1 Corinthians 2:16).

Moreover there were plenty of people in the Bible who put their minds to good use.

The centurion had heard about Jesus (Matthew 8:6–10). As he considered what Jesus was like, he reasoned that Jesus didn't need to visit his house to heal his servant – Jesus only had to give a command. Jesus was amazed at his faith – and it started in his mind. Abraham too thought it all through. Hebrews 11:19 tells us that before he went to sacrifice Isaac at God's command, he reasoned that God could raise him from the dead. So there is a godly reason that leads to faith, which prompts and strengthens it. Paul had it – consider the godly logic of Romans chapters 1–8, where every new thought is built upon the 'therefore' of a previous set of statements. Faith and intellect can mutually encourage one another. So don't leave your mind at the door of the church – use it to build your faith!

PRAYER: *Lord, please help me to use my God-given intellect in a right way. May my reason produce and encourage faith, as I consider Your way, Amen.*

JULY 24 | HE REALLY KNOWS IT ALL

DENISE CROSS

But the very hairs of your head are all numbered.

Matthew 10:30, NKJV

This verse fascinates me. Could God really be interested in the hairs on my head? I'm reminded of the verse every morning when I brush my hair and a few silver strands float on to my clothes or fall to the ground. Does He really have my hairs numbered? The original Greek word for '*numbered*' is the root from which we get our English word 'arithmetic'. It means '*counted*' but it also has an understanding that each number is important and has its own identity. Numbers require comprehension of what they mean, as anyone who struggled with maths at school will know well.

Like many of the things Jesus said, this statement is a picture parable. A profound truth expressed in just a few words. It's a parable of God's care and attention to *every* detail of our lives. His interests are beyond our comprehension. Whether extremely small or enormously large, nothing is outside His knowledge and understanding.

The prophet Zechariah tells us He '*stretches out the heavens*' (Zechariah 12:1) and the psalmist tells us, '*He counts the number of the stars; He calls them all by name*' (Psalm 147:4). The Hebrew words imply God has enumerated the stars and defined their exact position. He knows about the farthest reaches of the cosmos but He also knows about the smallest microscopic plankton, that we can only see with the help of a microscope. '*Let the waters abound with an abundance of living creatures*' (Genesis 1:20).

You may not be very concerned about how many hairs are on your head but your Heavenly Father is. Every hair matters because it indicates that you matter in every aspect of your life and well-being.

Whether you have a full head of hair or are completely bald, what Father

God wants you to know today is that He cares about you in every detail of your life.

PRAYER: *Father, it's hard to grasp the fact that things about me that I may not think are important, or that I may be unaware of, are still of great interest to You. Thank You for Your attention to the detail of my life which shows Your great love for me. Amen.*

JULY 25 | FROM STORMY TO PEACEFUL IN AN INSTANT!

ANDY TAYLOR

> *Then they were eager to let him in, and immediately the boat arrived at their destination!*
>
> John 6:21, NLT

Imagine the scene: the disciples had just had a busy day with Jesus (feeding 5,000 people!) and were waiting for Him at the shore of the Sea of Galilee. Darkness was falling and there was still no sign of Jesus, so the disciples got into their boat and headed out across the lake towards Capernaum.

Before long a strong wind was blowing and the waters were very rough. It was then that Jesus appeared to His disciples – walking on the water. Their standard response followed – terror! But Jesus called out that it was Him. At hearing this, the disciples were eager to let Him into their boat and immediately they arrived at their destination.

The Greek word used to describe how they 'immediately' arrived at their destination is the same word used to describe the miracles of healing that Jesus did – the man with leprosy in Matthew 8, the woman with the issue of blood in Mark 5, the deaf and dumb man in Mark 7. It was a dramatic change from one moment to the next. In an instant the disciples were taken from a place of darkness, turmoil and storm to their destination – a place where they could secure the boat and find refuge from the storm. This happened the moment they welcomed Jesus into their boat.

You may feel that you are in the middle of a storm. It might feel as though you will never escape it – that all your energy has gone. The truth is that Jesus will come to you and, when the time is right, is able to take you from that place of turmoil and darkness to a place of peace in an instant.

PRAYER: *Thank You, Jesus, that Your presence always transforms every situation.*

Help me to trust You in the storms of life, knowing that You are sufficient for every need, in Jesus' name, Amen.

July 26 | True Royalty!

Patricia Lake

> *But you are a chosen people, a royal priesthood, a holy nation, a people belonging to God, that you may declare the praises of him who called you out of darkness into his wonderful light.*
>
> 1 Peter 2:9

With some excitement and some trepidation, some inquisitive families set out on a quest each week to find out if they are related to royalty. For some the search ends in disappointment as the trail goes cold, as there's no evidence of their connection to a royal person of their choice. For others, their hopes rise as they turn the pages of historic documents to see if they are related to this important person or that titled landowner. If that all-important link proves that they can claim kinship to a royal person, they are overcome with tears of joy. The search can take days, weeks, months, years and even take them across continents.

But what a difference one moment makes when a person decides to become a Christian. There's nothing that can compare with the wonderful experience of those who have knelt in repentance before Christ Jesus, the Son of the Living God, and invited Him into their lives.

My heart surged with joy as I mused on the fact that Jesus has made it possible for any of us to be born into the only royal bloodline that will stand the test of eternity – let alone time! The Scripture declares that God has 'delivered us from the power of darkness and has translated us into the Kingdom of His dear Son' (Colossians 1:13, KJ2000). In an instant we can belong to His generational line! To you and me God has held out the royal sceptre and bids us draw near.

How wonderful it is to know that Almighty God, the King of kings, has actively pursued you and me in order to bestow on us the rights and benefits of royalty. He forgives our sins, heals our sicknesses and clothes us in the garments of praise and the robes of righteousness. He crowns us with loving kindness and tender mercies and satisfies our mouth with good things (Psalm 103). Now that's true royalty!

Would you like to have real royal connections and belong to the most prestigious generational line in history? Here's your opportunity. Don't miss it!

PRAYER: *Thank You, Lord, for the gift of life which comes to all those who know You – a gift which connects me to the King of kings! In Jesus' name I pray, Amen.*

JULY 27 | THE SECOND COMING

DAVID SILVESTER

For the coming of the Lord draweth nigh.

James 5:8, KJV

During the late 1940s to the 1960s it was not uncommon to hear teaching on the Second Coming of Christ. There had been the trauma of the Second World War and a time of rebuilding. Eminent preachers and teachers seemed to be constantly reminding us of the manner of people we Christians should be, so that when the Lord returns, *'we may be confident and unashamed before him at his coming'* (1 John 2:28).

As we have witnessed the rescue mission of the Chilean miners, we rejoiced that not one of them died in that awful pit of darkness and desolation. As each one emerged from the capsule, there was such jubilation.

I am reminded that what Jesus has done for us, and what His Second Coming will do for us, is even more wonderful than the Chilean rescue mission. In time every one of those miners will die, and unless they too have trusted in the saving work of Christ His coming again will not mean the rescue of eternal salvation for them.

There was a sense of urgency in the minds of the preachers years ago as they sensed that events in those days were pointing to the imminence of the Second Coming. It was a very challenging period for many of us as we were encouraged to search our hearts' motives, attitudes and behaviour, in the light of standing before the Lord, when it would be too late to make the necessary confessions, repentance and corrections.

This was where these words of the apostle John struck home for me: *'confident and unashamed before him at his coming'*. Would I stand before the Lord ashamed, with my head hung low because of the consciousness of some unconfessed sin?

During those days we would regularly sing a chorus based upon the words of Psalm 139:23–24:

'Search me, O God, and know my heart today; Try me, O Lord, and know my thoughts I pray: See if there be some wicked way in me, Cleanse me from ev'ry sin and set me free.'

If, today, I were to live my daily life with such a thought uppermost, I wonder what would happen. Would my attitude toward others become different, and would the kind of love Jesus commanded me to display to others be more evident (John 15:12)? What changes would I make if I really thought that Jesus might return today?

PRAYER: *O Lord God, I thank You that You have done everything necessary to save me eternally, and that Jesus is going to come again and bring me before Your holy throne. Please forgive me for those times I have not behaved as You desire, and help me to live in the light of Jesus' return, so that nothing will spoil the joy of that day, and I can stand before You as one who is not ashamed, Amen.*

JULY 28 | STRANGERS IN THE WORLD

JILLY LYON-TAYLOR

> *To God's elect, strangers in the world ... Live your lives as strangers here in reverent fear ... As aliens and strangers in the world ... abstain from sinful desires.*
>
> 1 Peter 1:1, 17; 2:11

In my youth I did a lot of travelling and I always enjoyed going to out-of-the-way places where people from different cultures lived their lives in a very different way from mine. Often when travelling on local public transport in those places I would receive some strange looks, especially from the children, as I looked, and probably behaved, very differently from them.

As citizens of heaven (Philippians 3:20), we as Christians should stand out from those around us and feel just as strange in the world as I did when travelling in places with a different culture, but often we seem to blend in all too easily with the worldly culture around us. Far from it being alien to us, we embrace the world's standards and ways of doing things so that there is little difference evident between us and the people around us. But there should be! God chose us to be holy and blameless in His sight (Ephesians 1:4) and

Peter reminds us in 1 Peter 1:18 that we have been redeemed from the empty way of life handed down to us from our forefathers. We should therefore feel and behave like strangers in the world, but often we are far too friendly with it. James goes as far as saying: *'Anyone who chooses to be a friend of the world becomes an enemy of God'* (James 4:4).

What about you today? Are you choosing to be a friend of the world, or are you going to live your life as a stranger here, redeemed from the empty way of life handed down to you and abstaining from the desires that came with it? The choice is yours!

PRAYER: *Heavenly Father, I am sorry that I have often lived my life as a friend of the world rather than as a stranger here. Help me to hate the things that You hate in the world. Amen.*

JULY 29 | PEACE

JOAN RONO

> *Peace I leave with you; my peace I give you. I do not give to you as the world gives. Do not let your hearts be troubled and do not be afraid.*
>
> John 14:27

During holiday times many seek to go to quiet places hoping to find peace. This is usually somewhere away from their everyday work, home, and family, and sometimes away from all other people. But it's not only people who are looking for peace, but also governments, institutions, communities, and families.

Yet, despite all the efforts of the world there's still no peace. Or maybe I should say the peace the world gives is only temporary. But Jesus said He didn't want to give us the peace that the world gives, but His peace. It's not a temporary peace or a short break from our troubles. It's a deeper peace that's not influenced by our surroundings or circumstances.

Recently during the World Cup, in the big arena amid a lot of noise and cheering, a little bird stood on the goal post for a long time. It looked settled and happy despite all the noise and commotion of the game. Many have had different thoughts about this, but I learnt something very important out of it. It spoke to me of the peace that Jesus gives. It's an inner peace in the middle of the storm. Jesus said, *'I have told you these things, so that in me you may have peace. In this world you will have trouble. But take heart! I have overcome the world'* (John 16:33).

Yes, we shall have troubles in this world, sometimes even big troubles. But in the midst of the trouble we can have peace, and this peace overcomes everything. It transcends even our own understanding. It's peace in the core of our being, in our spirit.

'My peace I give you.' Jesus gives us His peace. In a stormy sea He slept in a boat and the storm grew so violent that His disciples feared they would drown. Where was Jesus? Sleeping! That's the peace He had and that's the peace He gives to us.

PRAYER: *Lord, I give You my fears and anxieties and I open my heart to receive the peace that You give me. Please help me to know the depth of this peace in my life even in the midst of storm and turmoil. Thank You, Lord, Amen.*

JULY 30 | IF YOU'VE LOST YOUR WAY, STAND AT THE CROSSROADS

MARGARET SILVESTER

> *This is what the LORD says, 'Stand at the crossroads and look; ask for the ancient paths, ask where the good way is, and walk in it, and you will find rest for your souls.'*
>
> Jeremiah 6:16

The people to whom Jeremiah wrote had lost their way. There seemed little hope for them because, even though they were lost, they wouldn't ask the way. They preferred to go their own way even though it was leading to disaster.

We live in a world of relativism – if it seems right to you then do it. In other words, there are no absolutes because God is sidelined and His ways of righteousness and justice are obsolete. Consequently, it's easy to lose your way and not even realise that you're lost.

Occasionally when out walking, my husband and I have sensed we were on the wrong path and going in the wrong direction, though we followed the arrow of the signpost. Because someone had twisted the signpost round, we were in fact going the wrong way. The only way to get back onto the right path was to use a map and compass.

From time to time we all stand at crossroads in our lives. These are times when we have either lost our way or need a new direction. To move on we need to find the signpost pointing in the right direction. At such times the Word of God is our only reliable map and the Holy Spirit is the compass pointing in the right direction.

We are told to ask for the ancient paths. These aren't obsolete paths, but paths well-tried, good and right. They're paths that we walk in fellowship with God. It may not always be easy to walk on these paths, but our footsteps are secure because we're not walking alone.

We live in a restless world, but the promise for those who find the good way – God's way – is 'rest for your souls'. This rest is the relief and peace that come from being redirected back to the right path after a time of wandering in the wrong direction.

God's ways and truth are unchangeable. There's no room for compromise. The good way isn't the way that seems good to us. It's the ancient path that Jesus walked when He only did the things the Father told Him.

Do you feel you have lost your way? Maybe you need to go back to the crossroads where you took the wrong turning through making the wrong choice. There, you will find rest for your soul.

PRAYER: *Heavenly Father, I acknowledge that Your thoughts are not always my thoughts, nor are Your ways my ways. Please take me back to the crossroads, if I have made a wrong choice which has led me off the ancient path You have set for me to walk. I desire Your will for my life. Amen.*

JULY 31 | GOD OPPOSES THE PROUD

PAUL WATSON

God opposes the proud but gives grace to the humble.

James 4:6

'*As a speaker in citywide and regional prayer conferences, I am often asked to unmask the "spiritual power" opposing the body of Christ in the conference region,*' says Francis Frangipane. '*City leaders and intercessors have even asked if I knew the "name" of the principal spirit that is resisting the church in their area.*' He goes on to reply, '*Do you want to know the name of the most powerful spirit opposing most Christians? It's Yahweh!*' ('The Land Beneath Our Feet', www.frangipane.org).

When I read this I was stunned. How could that be true? The answer is found in our Bible verse today: '*God opposes the proud.*'

I found a very helpful definition of pride in the New Bible Dictionary – *'Rebellious pride, which refuses to depend on God and be subject to Him, but attributes to self the honour due to Him, figures as the very root and essence of sin.'* In the Bible pride is seen as a good thing in some aspects, for example when the apostle Paul says that he's proud of the spiritual growth of his beloved children in the Lord (see 2 Corinthians 7:4), or when we boast of what God has done (1 Corinthians 1:31).

However, in the majority of references pride (referred to as insolence, arrogance, boastfulness, haughtiness) is regarded as a negative and harmful attribute. In essence it is idolatry! No wonder God opposes it!

Why do I often feel irritable – dare I say angry – when my wife politely suggests I have taken the wrong turn off the motorway? Pride. Or worse, when she suggests we stop and ask someone for directions! Pride. Why do we think that our theology is the best? Pride. What prevents us from fellowshipping with other Christians in our town? Pride. What makes me reluctant to trust God but rather try to make the impossible happen all by myself? Pride.

Why does the Church seem to be losing ground in so many places in the world? Why perhaps do I find the going so tough at times? God opposes the proud.

As Peter writes in 1 Peter 5:6: *'Humble yourselves, therefore, under God's mighty hand, that he may lift you up in due time.'* If I don't humble myself, God will do it for me, and I may not like how He does it!

PRAYER: *Please, Jesus, show me where there is pride in me, and help me to humble myself. Amen.*

AUGUST 1 | PEACE IN THE MIDST OF THE STORM

JILLY LYON-TAYLOR

> *Without warning, a furious storm came up on the lake, so that the waves swept over the boat. But Jesus was sleeping.*
>
> Matthew 8:24

On a visit to Israel, I went to Galilee and saw the remains of a boat that had been unearthed after being buried in the sand on the shore of the lake, probably since around the time of Jesus. It was smaller than I'd imagined, so when I read again the story of the storm on the lake in Matthew chapter 8, I could imagine how the waves would have been sweeping over the side of the boat during a storm. No wonder the disciples were alarmed. But what was Jesus doing in this crisis? He was asleep in the boat. Was this because He didn't care about the disciples and about what happened to them? Not at all. I believe that Jesus was able to sleep in the midst of the storm because He had complete peace. He trusted His Father and the protection He had from Him, and He also knew who He was and the authority He'd been given.

In response to the disciples' cry for help, Jesus said, *'You of little faith, why are you so afraid?'* (Matthew 8:26). The problem was that their fear at that moment was greater than their faith. Fear robs us of the ability to stand in faith in the midst of storms, and it robs us of peace. In the crisis they had lost sight of who Jesus was. They had taken their eyes off Him and all they could see were the effects of the storm and the waves lashing over the side of the boat.

What about you today? I wonder what storms are raging in your life. Be encouraged that as we keep our eyes on Jesus and trust Him with every aspect of our lives, we will know His peace – the same kind of peace that enabled Jesus to sleep in the midst of the storm.

PRAYER: *Lord, forgive me for taking my eyes off You and for focusing on the storms in my life. I know You can calm every storm. I trust You and ask You to give me Your peace now even in the midst of the storm. In Jesus' name I pray, Amen.*

AUGUST 2 | RED AND WHITE BALLS

JOAN RONO

Your word is a lamp to my feet and a light for my path.

Psalm 119:105

On a bright sunny day a few young people and I went out to the Lake District to have some fun. I had no idea that it was the day I would face one of my worst phobias!

We went down to the lake in Windermere, but I was frightened by the idea of going on a boat trip for a whole hour and being away from the safe shores of the lake. I had to face my fear of drowning. With some persuasion from the others I was able to get into the boat, with a flotation jacket of course! I was able to remain calm and I actually enjoyed the whole trip.

I was fascinated by all the safety precautions – wearing the safety jacket, and keeping away from the red and white balls. The red balls were placed near the shores or places where the waters were shallow and the white balls were placed next to the parked boats. We had to avoid them both.

In our lives God has placed boundaries to make sure we're safe and able to enjoy the journey we're in. Some of these boundaries may seem unnecessary because we think we can do it our own way. When you're on a boat you can't see the depth of the water unless it's clear water, so to keep safe we had to avoid those red balls. Though we couldn't see the rocks or shallowness, God can. He sees what's beyond our eyesight and places the boundaries for us to keep us safe. The moment we step out of those boundaries we're risking our lives. We're out of His safe covering.

The boundaries for us are made clear in the Word of God. God instructs us in His Word and we must stay within His purposes and plans for our lives by being obedient to His will.

PRAYER: *Lord, I know You put boundaries in my life for my own safety but I sometimes want to do it my own way instead of Yours. I know I'm not safe when I'm out of Your covering. Please help me to be able to obey Your Word and instructions, and keep me safe in Your cover, in Jesus' name, Amen.*

AUGUST 3 | JESUS BE THE CENTRE

MARGARET SILVESTER

Peter said to Jesus, 'Rabbi, it is good for us to be here. Let us put up three shelters – one for you, one for Moses and one for Elijah.'

Mark 9:5

Jesus chose three disciples to be with Him up the mountain where they witnessed Him being transformed before them alongside the two most revered heroes in Hebrew history – Moses and Elijah.

Peter's immediate response to the vision tells us quite a bit about his perspective on the amazing event. 'It is good for us to be here.' In this short sentence, Peter makes himself and the other two disciples central to an experience to which they are only onlookers. It is not about them – it is about Jesus. The whole event is about Jesus and God's affirmation of His Son and His mission to redeem lost mankind.

Like Peter we too are often egocentric. We approach life from our own perspective instead of from God's perspective. We can be more conscious of ourselves than of Jesus. We may have prayed a prayer making Jesus Lord of our lives many times, but somehow the old self takes over the throne of the heart. We sing songs and call it 'worship', yet some of the songs we sing don't even mention Jesus. They are sometimes songs about ourselves, or songs we sing to ourselves.

Peter's second response to a profound spiritual experience was to say, *'Let us put up three shelters – one for you, one for Moses and one for Elijah.'* He wanted to make a passing experience permanent. He was supposed to be listening to the voice from heaven revealing to them the person of Jesus and telling them to listen to Him. Peter was not supposed to be talking or suggesting; the intention of the transfiguration of Jesus was that he would see Jesus and know the truth about Him.

Like Peter we too can be found talking and suggesting, instead of listening. Like Peter we may have had our mountain experiences and we may want them to be repeated. But they are not meant to be memorials that we long to re-create. They are meant to transform us, to take us deeper into Jesus, so that increasingly He becomes the centre of our lives and the reason that we live.

PRAYER: *Father, please forgive me for the times I have looked at things from my perspective instead of from Your perspective and for the times when I have been centred on myself instead of on Jesus and the purpose for which He came. Thank You that You gave Your Son, and that You have revealed Him to me. Today I choose to make Jesus the centre of my life. Amen.*

AUGUST 4 | BE STILL

IAN COATES

Be still, and know that I am God.

Psalm 46:10

What part has rest to do with our everyday lives? Life seems to be busier and more demanding than ever! What does the Bible say about it? Rest was God's idea as part of creation. Even the seasons have rest! There seem to be strong connections between rest and living in God's Promised Land and receiving His inheritance. *'My Presence will go with you, and I will give you rest'* (Exodus 33:14) and Jesus invites those who are weary to come to Him for rest in Matthew 11:25–30.

What is it that prevents us from resting in the Lord? The old hymn says, *'Perfect submission, all is at rest! I in my Saviour am happy and blest'* (Fanny J.

Crosby, 1873). Here we have the first clue – submission. And, in Isaiah 30:15 which says, *'In repentance and rest is your salvation'*, we have the second. So often it's taught, 'in repentance is your salvation', but actually it's also 'in *rest* is your salvation'. We can strive so much and achieve things, but where is our rest? In Hebrews, chapters 3 and 4, we see that it talks about rest and that those who are disobedient will never enter into rest. Rest is about our obedience to follow Him and do what He wants us to do. It will take some effort (see Hebrews 4:11).

But how do we rest? It's about confidence in Him. We don't have to strive or persuade God with our prayers. It's about being at rest because of who He is! We can relax in Him, because we're confident of who He is! We must go back to what Jesus said in Matthew chapter 6: *'Do not worry.'* Worry is not a place of rest. It's a very different thing to *make every effort to enter His rest*. We enter it because we're confident of who we are and who He is. Therefore we can be confident today. We don't want anything to come between us and God.

Rest was God's idea as part of creation. Even the seasons have rest! There seem to be strong connections between rest and living in God's Promised Land and receiving His inheritance.

We need to check our heart motives. Proverbs 4:23 says, *'Above all else, guard your heart, for it is the wellspring of life.'* The heart is the seat of our spiritual understanding and motivation, and the source of our true spiritual character. It's the root of our doubts and beliefs.

So how do we move into this place of rest? The world's seeking it in more and more leisure time. But it's still not enough! But we can see that recognising the need to SEEK GOD is the key to rest! It's our place of grace and through Jesus we have full access to Him with confidence. This is how we will know HIM and His ways.

PRAYER: *Lord, I can relax in You because I can trust You. I feel confident in You. I want to be rooted and grounded in You and I don't want anything to come between us. Help me to put my trust in You completely and become the person You created me to be, in Jesus' name, Amen.*

August 5 | Waves of Life

Lindsey Hanekom

Mightier than the thunder of the great waters, mightier than the breakers of the sea – the LORD on high is mighty.

Psalm 93:4

We were blessed to spend our holiday this year staying very close to a beach. Every morning we would make the short walk down to the beach to see what the sea had done overnight. We would see if it had washed clean yesterday's footprints, dug a deeper trench for the river to flow along, or brought up any more shells or drift-wood. Each morning the overall landscape looked the same, but always there were some subtle differences.

At the beginning of our stay, the beach was pretty predictable, with a gentle washing in and out of the tide. However, towards the end of our holiday, the wind had picked up dramatically and the tide was at a high point.

The morning after the start of these dramatic tides we took our usual walk to the beach and were amazed at the vastness of the change to the landscape. The small gulley we once walked through to go to the next beach was now a long series of barely passable high rocks – hardly any sand to be seen in it. The river almost looked like part of the sea and there was an amazing amount of debris against the rocky headland, washed up by the ferocious tides.

It led me to thinking of this scripture. Many of us long for God to come in power and perform a mighty and dramatic work in our lives. Yet, the daily washing goes unnoticed. It's worth noting that the sand formation, the rock formation, the river formation … all that makes the beach what it is, is achieved through persistent and frequent tidal forces. The mighty tides that come in power and force merely unearth what has been forged through years of gentle and persistent movement.

Waiting only for the times when God moves powerfully in our lives doesn't change the overall landscape of our lives. It's the gentle, almost imperceptible, daily living of normal life that forges the landscape of our lives. It's our choice how we live that life – with God at the centre or not.

We need to greet each day with a knowledge that God's daily presence in our lives will transform us one day at a time, just as the tide transforms the landscape of a beach. Praise God that His mercies are new every morning

(Lamentations 3:22–23) and that our lives are being forged into something more beautiful each and every day.

PRAYER: *Thank You, God, that You continue to transform me into what You want me to become. Help me not to disregard Your gentle but powerful forging of my life as I walk with You, one day at a time, in Jesus' name, Amen.*

AUGUST 6 | DO WE NEED REPAIRS FOR THE RACE?

DAVID CROSS

> *Run your best in the race of faith, and win eternal life for yourself; for it was to this life that God called you when you firmly professed your faith before many witnesses.*
>
> 1 Timothy 6:12, GNB

I was recently thinking about the international Grand Prix for motor racing. The cars are given so much attention before the big races to bring them into the very best condition for the demanding challenge ahead. Engineers investigate and record every detail of the cars inside and out to see if anything needs adjustment or repair. The investigation is carried out not to criticise the value of the car but simply to best prepare it for the next important race.

We are so much more important than a Formula One car! God wants to bring us into increasing wholeness and freedom for the race He has prepared for us to run. He knows that our spiritual fitness is very important. If we are willing to look with truth at the inside condition of our lives, He is very willing to carry out the necessary repairs. He is ready to convict us but He will never condemn us.

Here is a suggested ten-point personal diagnostic check-up, together with references from the Maker's manual:

1. How is our personal relationship with Jesus today? John 21:15
2. How is our personal relationship with others in the Body of Christ? Mark 11:25
3. Are we willing to let God bring (possibly) big changes to our beliefs and lifestyle? John 15:2
4. Do we truly believe that God loves us and deeply values us? Zephaniah 3:17
5. Are there unresolved issues of guilt or shame in our lives? 1 John 1:9

6. Are there places of wounding that still give significant pain? Matthew 11:28
7. Are there areas in our lives that seem to be more under the control of the enemy, rather than Jesus? John 8:31, 32
8. Do we have teachable hearts? Matthew 11:29
9. Is our following of Jesus active or passive? Matthew 14:29
10. Are we living in reality with ourselves, with God and with others? Luke 22:31

PRAYER: *Heavenly Father, give me the courage to sometimes take a moment to look with reality at the spiritual condition of my life, so that I can allow You to bring more wholeness and freedom for the special destiny of my life. Amen.*

AUGUST 7 | SURELY GOD IS WITH YOU

PAUL WATSON

> *They will bow down before you and plead with you, saying, 'Surely God is with you, and there is no other; there is no other god.'*
>
> Isaiah 45:14b

What an amazing prospect! Someone who doesn't know our Heavenly Father, perhaps even believing in another 'god', comes to me in an attitude of surrendered openness – at the same time both responding and seeking.

Responding – to what they've seen in my life – *'Surely God is with you.'*

Seeking – they want to know my God; for they now see that He is the only God.

Here's the question I asked myself in response to this passage. *'How might someone notice that God is with me?'*

In the context of this chapter of Isaiah, directed towards God's people, we find that the answer lies not in what I can do for Him, but rather it's found in how I respond to Him.

Israel has been unfaithful to God – idols, alliances with the nations, rebelliousness and unrighteous behaviour. God has brought calamity upon them to draw them to repentance, so that He may restore them to Himself. In the response of turning back to Him and trusting the One who loves them, they will see the awesome power of the Lord, the only God, at work in redeeming His beloved.

As I trust Him and live closely with Him, no matter what the circumstances may be at any given moment, the outcome will clearly be on view to others. There will be the fruit of the Spirit sprouting in my life – love, joy, peace, patience, kindness, goodness, gentleness, faithfulness and self-control. *'Ah,'* they will respond, *'we see God is with you – He is the only God.'*

PRAYER: *Father God, thank You that You are always with me. I want others to see that. I want to produce good fruit as I respond to Your love for me. May others see You at work in me so that they may declare that You alone are God and come to acknowledge You as their Lord and God, through Jesus Christ, Amen.*

AUGUST 8 | ENCOURAGEMENT

GORAN ANDERSSON

> *You save the humble, but your eyes are on the haughty to bring them low. You are my lamp, O LORD; the LORD turns my darkness into light. With your help I can advance against a troop; with my God I can scale a wall.*
>
> 2 Samuel 22:28–30

Experience gives authority to a testimony. There's a difference between hearing a teenager speak about God's faithfulness and hearing an old man speak about the same thing. Not that the teenager is saying anything wrong, but the old man is able to talk from a lifetime of experience. When he says that God gives light it's not just because he's heard others say so, but because he's been in the darkness, and seen first-hand how God changes that darkness into light. He's been in the dark tunnel, and knows what it's like when the first light appears in a distance. He's seen that light slowly drive darkness away, and change the whole scene. He knows the thrill of seeing shadows fade away, and dark corners being lit up. His words carry weight, because he's been there!

This is exactly how David describes his life. It's been a life of many ups and downs. His experience disproves the idea that life will always be peaceful, with nothing but success, if you trust God. David had been tested, and tested hard. But all these tests had given him the chance to test God's faithfulness. And David's testimony was that he'd failed many times, but God had never failed him.

The purpose of a testimony is to give courage and strength to others. It's a word from those who've passed through the wilderness – that there's a safe road through. It's an assurance from those who've been in the fiery furnace that someone keeps the heat down. It's telling those who are being tested that there's a way through, and that God's there to save, even if they don't see him. So we do well to remember David's words. We're likely to need them one day.

Are you in need of encouragement? Let me suggest you read the testimony of some characters in the Bible which give us a rich variety of experience: Moses (Deuteronomy 32); Joshua (Joshua 24); Daniel (Daniel 2:20–23); Nebuchadnezzar (Daniel 4:34–37); Habakkuk (Habakkuk 3); and Paul (2 Timothy 4:6–8).

And if you have time for more, there is an abundance of autobiography books written by men and women who have experienced God's faithfulness in adverse circumstances. Their cry to us today is very clear: 'Hang on, it's worthwhile, God is faithful!'

PRAYER: *Dear Heavenly Father, thank You for the encouragement of other Christians who have known Your faithfulness in their lives and the testimonies they have shared. I pray that I may also be able to help others as I also share my experiences of what You have done in my life, in Jesus' name, Amen.*

AUGUST 9 | STAYING PURE

JILL SOUTHERN-JONES

> *And though she spoke to Joseph day after day, he refused to go to bed with her or even to be with her.*
>
> Genesis 39:10

Joseph eventually reached Egypt courtesy of some slave traders, where he was sold into the service of Potiphar's house. God had more important tests in store for Joseph!

Purity is very important to God.

Sometimes impurity doesn't begin in the heart, but begins in the eye. Mrs Potiphar made a pass at Joseph, but Jacob had brought up his sons to follow God and to stay pure. What's more, Joseph also knew he was completely trusted by Potiphar himself, so he refused to go to bed with her or even to be with her.

The Scripture teaches us to *'flee fornication'* (1 Corinthians 6:18, KJV) and this is exactly what Joseph did. However, he thwarted Potiphar's wife by doing so, for she was looking for more. So she falsely accused him of actually doing what in her heart she had really wanted him to do! He ended up being put into prison for something he hadn't done. Could Joseph hang on to the dream God had given him now?

This was clearly an attack from the enemy to rob Joseph of his ultimate destiny. But what the enemy planned for harm, God eventually used for good. This is such an important principle for life that we can learn from the story of Joseph.

Even when it looks totally hopeless, we need to hang on to the dreams and visions God has given us. God was preparing Joseph for his destiny. Romans 5:3–5 says that *'we should rejoice in our sufferings because we know that suffering produces perseverance; perseverance, character; and character, hope'.* And hope produces the appointments of God. Can we pass the tests God will use to prepare us for our calling and destiny? Can we persevere?

PRAYER: *Lord, thank You for choosing me to belong to You. I know that You have a calling and destiny on my life. When I go through the tests please help me to remember that You still love me and You really do want what's best for me. In Jesus' name I pray, Amen.*

AUGUST 10 | TIME TO FORGIVE

PATRICIA LAKE

> *For if ye forgive men their trespasses, your Heavenly Father will also forgive you.*
>
> Matthew 6:14, KJV

Recently I learned of a mother and son who were reunited after fifty years of separation. It was an emotional moment as the two were brought together by an organisation which painstakingly set out to find the lady's eldest son at the request of his brother. He had been adopted as a baby. At the time of the adoption neither she nor her family were in a position to take care of this new life that had come into the world.

Now time was ebbing away and the elderly lady's final desire was to see her long-lost son, to know that he was well, and to ask for his forgiveness. When at last he walked into her hospital room, she threw her arms around him while repeating the words, 'I'm sorry … I'm sorry …' 'It's OK, there's nothing to forgive' came his tender reply as he hugged his terminally ill birth-mother.

In a moment, fifty years of separation melted into emotional reconciliation as the two were reunited – all was forgiven.

In this instance forgiveness seemed easy, but often, forgiveness is a process, especially where the 'wrong' perpetrated has wrought devastation in the life of the victim.

Nevertheless, forgiveness is a HUGE key to healing and freedom, for with it a person is immediately set free from the prison of the past, and can not only begin to enjoy the present, but they can step into the future unshackled by the chains of anger, bitterness and hatred. Also, if we desire our Heavenly Father's forgiveness for our sins (crimes) against Him, then as the Lord's Prayer gently encourages us, we can then ask Him to 'forgive us our trespasses as we forgive those who trespass against us'.

The story of the prodigal son is a well-known and much loved parable in the Bible, but it is also an eternally fresh picture of Father God running towards His much loved creation with open arms, indicating His great open heart of endless love, despite the sins of an errant son.

Not so long ago, I was impacted by Peter Horrobin saying, 'Every day is a new opportunity to forgive.' If you are struggling with this key of forgiveness, try asking God to help you to forgive, as a first step. Today can be the beginning of freedom from the past as you step into your healing and the wonderful future that God has planned for you, for He indeed has *'plans to prosper you and not to harm you'* (Jeremiah 29:11).

PRAYER: *Heavenly Father, help us to forgive while there is still time so that we can enjoy the freedom that You purchased for us on the cross of Calvary, in Jesus' name, Amen.*

AUGUST 11 | ROOTS ARE IMPORTANT

JILL SOUTHERN-JONES

> *Therefore put on the full armour of God, so that when the day of evil comes, you may be able to stand your ground, and after you have done everything, to stand.*
>
> Ephesians 6:13

I am fascinated by trees, especially very tall ones and very old ones. Recently I visited Kew Gardens and traversed their new treetop walkway. It was worth climbing 118 steps to enter a canopy of unique trees and enjoy a spectacular view over Kew. It was, however, down in the tunnel afterwards, where you could see the roots, that I was most impressed. To understand how trees work we needed to go underground and see the strong supporting structure without which there would be no food and water for the tree to grow.

It made me think about bearing fruit for the Kingdom. We need first to be rooted and grounded and firmly established in our personal faith in God so that when the storms come we shall not be shaken. In the storms of 1987 a group of seven oak trees in Kent was reduced to one oak tree, as six of these trees could not withstand the bashing from the weather.

Paul writes, *'and after you have done everything … stand'* (Ephesians 6:13). We will only be able to stand in the coming storm if we have strong and healthy roots underpinning our faith and if we're trusting in God alone. What do your roots look like? Are they being fed on the Word of God, nurtured by the love of God and watered by the one who said, *'Whoever drinks the water that I will give him will never be thirsty again'* (John 4:14, GNB)?

Our roots and foundations are very important. The verse *'Unless the LORD builds the house, its builders labour in vain'* (Psalm 127:1) not only applies to churches and ministries; it also applies to the house of our life. The wise man built his house upon the rock so that when the floods came the house stood firm (Matthew 7:24–27).

Are our roots and foundations today in the rock, which is Jesus?

PRAYER: *Lord Jesus, I know that to face the coming season in my life I need to be rooted and grounded in my faith and be trusting You. I need to be anchored strongly in You so that I can't be shaken. Please help me to grow daily in Your love, Your Word and Your power, in Jesus' name. Amen.*

AUGUST 12 | FOLLOW ME

DAVID SILVESTER

> *And He said to them, 'Follow Me, and I will make you fishers of men.'*
>
> Matthew 4:19, NKJV

Leading a church and discipling new Christians is not dissimilar to my former career of training engineering apprentices to become craftsmen. Those apprentices would be shown and taught the properties of different metals; taught the science and maths necessary for using and machining those materials. They would then go into a workshop to *'have a go'*, use the principles they had been taught, and so produce a designed component.

Jesus had his *'apprentices'* who listened to His teaching, and watched as He healed or delivered the sick and oppressed. Then He sent them into the *'workshop'* of the world, saying, *'As you go, preach, saying, "The Kingdom of heaven is at hand." Heal the sick, cleanse the lepers, raise the dead, cast out demons. Freely you have received, freely give'* (Matthew 10:7–8).

Now having received such a commission from Him, they went and did what they had seen Jesus do. They were excited as they returned, saying, *'Lord, even demons are subject to us in Your name'* (Luke 10:17).

Being a follower (or disciple) of Jesus means that we're given His authority and the power of the Holy Spirit that was at work in Him. We can do the same kind of things He did. We can have power over sin, sickness, disease and death as He did. But in addition to that, if we're willing to learn from His teaching, and obey His instructions, we shall become more like Jesus every day.

PRAYER: *Lord Jesus Christ, thank You that I have not only been called to follow You, but to be empowered by Your Holy Spirit. Please help me to trust and obey what You have shown me in Your Word. Help me to be as effective as those early disciples were, so that others will praise You, in Jesus' name, Amen.*

AUGUST 13 | RUN INTO HIS ARMS

LINDSEY HANEKOM

> *So he got up and went to his father. But while he was still a long way off, his father saw him and was filled with compassion for him; he ran to his son, threw his arms around him and kissed him.*
>
> Luke 15:20

Our son, Kyle, attends a group called *'Messy 2s'* for two hours every Wednesday, where he is left with some brave and capable workers who care for sixteen two-year-olds in a melee of paint, water, sand and other fun things.

Although I enjoy some peace and quiet at home during this time, the biggest joy for me is the special moment when I return to take him home.

At 3pm the children are let out and my view of the room blurs into only one face. My son, running, arms wide-open, straight towards me with a look of pure delight on his face. I bend down and receive him into my open arms as though we have been separated for days, not hours. I lift him up and hug him long and hard as he starts to tell me of all the fun that he has had, including any trouble he may have got into.

As I was waiting this week, I found myself considering how I would feel if Kyle didn't run to me but hid away or held back, reluctant to come and receive my love. As I pondered this, my heart began to ache. What a sadness that would be to me.

We should not let our past mistakes, wrong behaviours or messy lives prevent us from receiving the fullness of God's love. We need to come to Him with an open and honest heart, ready to confess and repent…

It reminded me of this wonderful story of a Father who is awaiting our response to His unconditional love – arms outstretched, ready to receive us. Why then, do so many of us respond to Him with reservations, holding back from receiving the fullness of His love? Is it because of our guilt and shame? Is it because we don't think we have done enough to earn it?

We should not let our past mistakes, wrong behaviours or messy lives prevent us from receiving the fullness of God's love. We need to come to Him with an open and honest heart, ready to confess and repent but doing it from a place of a loving embrace of a Father that has waited ever so patiently for us. Not doing so only hurts the heart of God. Just as my heart ached at the very thought of Kyle not running to me, God's heart aches for each and every one of us who hold back from receiving His love.

If you really want to please God, this is the way to do it. Just run, arms open wide, vulnerable and totally honest, into His loving arms and receive all that He has for you.

PRAYER: *Father God, help me to open my heart completely to You and accept Your love. I'm sorry that I've saddened You by holding back in areas of my life because I thought they were too dirty or messy for You. I want to open my whole heart to You and know Your love in the very depths of my heart. Amen.*

August 14 | Fresh Bread

Pam Smith

But He [Jesus] answered and said, 'It is written, "Man shall not live by bread alone, but by every word that proceeds from the mouth of God." '

Matthew 4:4, NKJV

One of my favourite things is a slice of fresh, homemade bread and butter, especially when I am hungry. In this scripture Jesus is quoting from Deuteronomy 8:3, where God showed the Israelites that although he could satisfy their hunger with manna from heaven, His words were far richer, more satisfying and essential for Life. Jesus is the called the Word of God, and He also said, *'I am the bread of life'* (John 6:35).

How satisfying it is when someone shares a message that comes straight from the heart of God. Our hearts burn within us, just like the two disciples on the road to Emmaus, when they recognised Jesus in the breaking of bread. I always hear God speaking to me when our pastor preaches. You know, in your spirit, that he has been in the presence of God and you are changed by the power of the Word he gives as you receive 'fresh bread' from the Lord.

It can be so easy to give away yesterday's bread but when Jesus is your first love and you have an open, humble and listening heart, you have fresh bread to give away, which feeds and nourishes souls.

Jesus said, *'I am the living bread which came down from heaven. If anyone eats of this bread, he will live forever; and the bread that I shall give is My flesh, which I shall give for the life of the world'* (John 6:51, NKJV). Much of the world is crying out for bread because they are starving, but the whole world needs the *'living bread'* so that they might have eternal life. May we be the ones, not only to feed the hungry but also to share God's Word, His precious Son, the 'Fresh Bread' from heaven, with those who are around us.

Prayer: *Lord, help me to keep close enough to You to be able to share the fresh bread that You give us daily with others, in Jesus' name. Amen.*

August 15 | Boasting

Liz Griffin

Thus says the LORD: 'Let not the wise man boast in his wisdom, let not the mighty man boast in his might, let not the rich man boast in his riches, but let him who boasts boast in this, that he understands and knows me, that I am the LORD who practises steadfast love, justice, and righteousness in the earth. For in these things I delight, declares the LORD.'

Jeremiah 9:23–24, ESV

The prophet Jeremiah is an interesting character because he suffered so much opposition from all the people he preached to with God's message. What kept him going? It must have been that steady assurance of his relationship with God and the knowledge that he was loved.

He must have studied the Word of God and grasped the importance of the wonderful revelation of God's character of love to Moses. Moses was privileged to be the first to fully understand God's heart of steadfast love (*chesed* or 'covenantal faithfulness') and that He was merciful, gracious, and slow to anger (Exodus 34:6–7). God's love also includes perfect justice and righteousness which means evil will be rightfully punished.

Yet even the evil people had a chance with God if they turned to Him and repented of their sins. Jeremiah constantly reminded the people of that (as did the other prophets), even though they all pointed out the exact nature of the people's sins.

The declaration of God's character was continued throughout the Old Testament in Psalms, Nehemiah, Jonah, and Joel. Moses interceded for the people of Israel based upon this understanding in Numbers 14:16–19. But Jonah didn't want to intercede for the wicked people of Nineveh so that they would repent and be forgiven, and he was angry when they did repent as a result of the message he delivered to them from God.

Jeremiah tells us that if we are to be wise we should be proud of one thing only, knowing and understanding God. He warns us to be humble and not boast in our intellect, our power or our money. The apostle Paul was later to preach to the Corinthian church about this and say: *'you are in Christ Jesus, who became to us wisdom from God, righteousness and sanctification and redemption, so that, as it is written, "Let the one who boasts, boast in the Lord"'* (1 Corinthians 1:30–31, ESV).

PRAYER: *Dear Heavenly Father, thank You that we can know You and trust in Your great love, mercy and kindness towards us. Help us to be humble and not boast in worthless things but to be confident and able to boast in knowing You, in Jesus' name, Amen.*

AUGUST 16 | NEVER-CHANGING GOD!

CATH TAYLOR

> *Because of the LORD's great love we are not consumed, for his compassions never fail. They are new every morning; great is your faithfulness.*
>
> Lamentations 3:22–23

I know some people say that being with children makes you feel young, but my children have developed a way of making me feel incredibly old! Whether they are asking me to describe what it was like to watch television in black and white, or quizzing me over how I survived without a Wii and the internet, their bewildered, inconceivable expressions suddenly bring back distinct memories of doing a similar thing to my parents, and coming to the very definite conclusion that they must be really old to have lived without such normalities!

Getting older is a reality of life and we live in a world where constant change is here to stay. Very little in our lives is permanent. Friendships and relationships come and go over the years. Treasures can break and become lost, new inventions replace old ones, photos and memories fade, moods swing … For a human heart there is little in this world to cling and hold secure to that will last our whole lives.

Even as we grow as Christians we change. As we allow the Lord more intimately into our hearts, He changes us. He moulds us and makes us more into His image. He brings His healing, security and worth more and more into our lives and each day, as we draw close to Him, it changes us significantly on the inside.

Living in such an environment of change and growth, no wonder we sometimes judge the Lord by the same standards. Do we forget, perhaps, that He isn't like us and this world in which we live? Although our lives and all around us is temporary and evolving, He is steadfast and remains forever. His character, His heart for you and me, and His faithfulness, kindness, mercy and grace never weaken or waiver. No matter what we do or don't do, He remains the same.

Prayer: *Lord, what a relief it is to my heart to know that no matter what changes there may be in my life, You never change. Your character and Your heart remain the same. Your love for me and acceptance of me is steadfast and remains forever, so my trust in You is safe. Father, teach me more about You and how I may dwell in the security of relationship with You. In Jesus' name I pray, Amen.*

August 17 |
Paul Watson

Walking with Heads Held High

I am the LORD your God, who brought you out of Egypt so that you would no longer be slaves to the Egyptians; I broke the bars of your yoke and enabled you to walk with heads held high.

Leviticus 26:13

I enjoy a variety of sports. Whether it's in rugby, or soccer or cricket, when a commentator notes that the players on one team have dropped their heads, we all know that they are losing.

Just pause for a while and watch people walking along the street. So often it seems that people have their heads down, moving along, lost in their own problems, hurts and difficulties.

Sadly it also appears in the Body of Christ. I recall being involved in the music group in my local church, playing and singing the lively song, 'We are a people of power, we are a people of praise'. But when I looked at the posture of the congregation (singing with shoulders slumped and heads lowered), I thought to myself, 'Really? It doesn't look like it.'

In our ministry centre, we see many Christians coming to us for healing retreats with their heads down – slumped over with fears, emotional pain and the heaviness of bondages to the enemy.

However, we have the great privilege and joy of seeing those same people leave the retreat with new levels of hope, joy and freedom. What effects the change? The answer is actually about Who effects the change. It's through His Son, Jesus Christ, that God the Father brings about the lifting of our heads. It's Jesus who has broken the bars of the yokes of bondage. It's He who has come to bind up the broken-hearted, bring freedom for the captives, and release from darkness for the prisoners. It's Christ Jesus who has destroyed the works of the evil one. As we apply the finished work of Jesus on the cross to our lives, we receive new life, new freedom, and a whole new posture.

We can walk with heads held high!

Prayer: *Father, I thank You for rescuing me from the bars of my yoke – the yoke of sin, the world and the devil. By Your Holy Spirit I pray that You would reveal to me any areas of bondage that are still in my life, and that I might be open to the healing and releasing power of Jesus to receive new levels of freedom, in Jesus' name, Amen.*

August 18 |
David Cross

Out of Line with God

> *He asked me, 'Amos, what do you see?' 'A plumb line,' I answered. Then he said, 'I am using it to show that my people are like a wall that is out of line. I will not change my mind again about punishing them.'*
>
> Amos 7:8, GNB

These are serious words that God is saying to His people through Amos. They are heading for disaster because of their refusal to follow God's instructions for the safety and well-being of their lives. They have decided that they know best!

When a plumb line is held up alongside a wall under construction, there can be no doubt as to whether the wall has been built truly vertical. Walls which are out of line are very vulnerable to collapse. A plumb line lies perfectly vertical because of the physical law of gravity, which requires only that the surveyor hold it up and allow the weight to come to rest.

Whenever God's people are leading lives that are out of line with Him and likely to bring destruction upon themselves, it is very important that someone lifts up the truth of God's Word to allow His spiritual laws to show the straight line. Those that hold up a Biblical plumb line are not themselves the measure of truth, but merely God's surveyors whom He has equipped to show that straight line.

We have a choice to acknowledge or to ignore this line, but it would be foolish to be angry with the surveyor. It is amazing how a bricklayer can convince himself that the wall which he is building is perfectly vertical. It is only when he steps back and views his work alongside the surveyor's plumb line that the truth becomes evident. It can be a shocking moment if a distortion is exposed, but how much better it is to discover the misalignment now rather than at collapse.

In these challenging days of a desperate need for godly discernment, we should be thankful for those whom God gives to us for the purpose of holding up His straight line. They will not be perfect people but we should look for those who demonstrate spiritual maturity in both their words and their behaviour, for we ignore them at our peril.

PRAYER: *Father, help me to be willing to listen to those You use to hold up a plumb line to my life of Your truth. I want my life to be in line with what You say is true. Amen.*

AUGUST 19 | OUR HIGH CALLING

DAVID SILVESTER

> *He called you to this through our gospel, that you might share in the glory of our Lord Jesus Christ. So then, brothers, stand firm and hold to the teachings we passed on to you, whether by word of mouth or by letter.*
>
> 2 Thessalonians 2:14–15

As the apostle Paul looks back, and thanks God for the way he's observed the growth in faith and perseverance of the believers at Thessalonica in the face of persecutions and afflictions, he writes to encourage them further.

He reminds them that God will deal with those who've been oppressing them, and prays for them, that they'll be able to stand firm to the end so that Jesus will be glorified in their lives.

But Paul also reminds them they mustn't let themselves be quickly unsettled or alarmed by the things their opponents say, things that are untrue. They're not to let any strange ideas or spirits they encounter disturb them, but they must steadfastly continue to grow in grace and knowledge of the Lord Jesus Christ.

Whatever the nature of the opposition they encounter, Paul goes on to remind these Christians of their calling by God. It's to share in the glory of our Lord Jesus Christ. Because they know that Jesus is coming again and they'll be gathered to Him, this glory can't be taken away from them by the world.

In recent years Christians worldwide have been made aware that there's a growing opposition toward their God-given principles, and godly heritage. But, like the people Paul was writing to, we also are being encouraged to '*stand firm, and hold to*' those things that have been passed on to us. We're encouraged to look upwards, because the One who has called us to share in His glory will come again to take us to be with Him for eternity.

The writer of Hebrews says: *'Let us fix our eyes on Jesus, the author and perfecter of our faith, who for the joy set before him endured the cross, scorning its shame, and sat down at the right hand of the throne of God'* (Hebrews 12:2).

As we get closer to the return of Jesus and are likely to face difficult times and spiritual opposition, let's follow the words of Jesus: *'Stand up and lift up your heads, because your redemption is drawing near'* (Luke 21:28).

Daniel W. Whittle wrote the hymn which starts:

Jesus is coming! O sing the glad word!
Coming for those He redeemed by His blood.
Coming to reign as the glorified Lord,
Jesus is coming again!

Prayer: *Lord Jesus Christ, thank You for saving me and giving me a hope no one can take from me, that You're coming again. In the meantime, please enable me to keep my eyes fixed on You, keep me faithful to You, and looking forward to Your return so that I shall be unashamed when I meet you, Amen.*

August 20 | Friends of God

Cath Taylor

> *So now we can rejoice in our wonderful new relationship with God – all because of what our Lord Jesus Christ has done for us in making us friends of God.*
>
> Romans 5:11, NLT

I'm not the most technically minded person on the planet! My five-year-old can operate the television remote controls better than I can, and will often be called to come to my rescue. With that in mind, nobody is more surprised than I am that I have become a fan of something so modern and technically advanced as 'Facebook'!

Being overseas from family and friends, I have really enjoyed catching up with everyone's news and photos via Facebook. It has amazed me how easy it is to get back in touch with people you knew years ago in just the click of a button. It also amazes me how easy and effortless it is to collect friends, as my list grows week by week!

As great as it is, we must be so careful with the advancement of technology in social networking, that we don't overstretch the definition of the word 'Friend' in our hearts. When God says that He calls us 'Friend' it means so much more than the quick conversation and 'catch up'. It means a relationship that is deep and intimate – a relationship where we can be ourselves and not be afraid of rejection – a friendship like we will find in no other relationship on this planet. No wife, husband, best mate, mother, father, child or twin can fill that need in our hearts to be loved and accepted like Jesus can!

We don't have to explain ourselves with Jesus. And He never changes His mind. He's not subject to mood swings. He's the same, yesterday, today and forever and His love for us never waivers. His commitment to us never weakens.

All of us can grow in our relationship with the Lord. We can fall deeper in love with Him, and learn more of who He is and His love for us. I want to encourage you today to make Jesus your first love – your best friend. The person to whom you reveal the secrets of your heart and the one in whom you place your ultimate trust.

PRAYER: *Lord Jesus, what a privilege that You would call me Your friend! Lord, I'm sorry if I have looked to others to be the intimate love of my heart. Please show me how to build my relationship with You and to fall deeper in love with You each day of my life, in Jesus' name, Amen.*

AUGUST 21 | YOU ARE CHRIST'S BODY

DAVID CROSS

All of you are Christ's body, and each one is a part of it.

1 Corinthians 12:27, GNB

I've been thinking a lot lately about being part of Christ's Body. I've come to realise in a new way that, as well as having a personal identity, I also have a new corporate identity, along with millions of other followers of Jesus, as the living Body that daily demonstrates the authority, power and character of Christ on earth. Increasingly I'm understanding that we are not *like* a body; we *are* His Body.

This is an awesome thought! Jesus Christ, the One to whom all authority has been given, has chosen to operate, by the Spirit, through me and everyone else who has received Him as Lord of their lives. What a privilege!

What a challenge! What a responsibility to surrender my will to His will each day.

If I can really let Jesus have His way through that bit of His Body which I represent, then a part of His Kingdom truly can come on earth as it is in heaven. Together with all the other parts, working in right order with each other, there should be no limit to what God could do in this desperate world.

No doubt the enemy hates the thought of this Body of Christ exercising rightful and effective authority and power in a world over which Satan has been given rule, through sin. However, if I and all the other parts of the Body let Jesus truly have His way and if we look for the Spirit to distribute the necessary gifting, surely miracles will follow. What an adventure!

PRAYER: *Jesus, You have entrusted to me, and all the other parts of Your Body on earth, the opportunity to let You operate through each one of us in order to establish Your Kingdom. I am ready to do my bit today. Amen.*

AUGUST 22 | THE LORD IS MY SHEPHERD

ANGELA WEIR

The LORD is my shepherd, I shall not be in want.

Psalm 23:1

One of the many wonderful things about living in Cumbria is that over the years I have been able to watch our local farmers at work with their sheep. Sheep haven't changed much over the centuries and I don't suppose shepherding has either in its essentials, despite the mountains of paperwork farmers have to cope with these days!

What I have seen has deepened my understanding of the passages about our Good Shepherd. Our farming friends, without exception, all have enormous hands! Strong and yet capable of handling the newborn lambs with gentleness, they remind me of our Good Shepherd's hands, protecting and guiding us. Whenever I shake one of these hands, my own feels completely enfolded.

Sheep are not particularly intelligent and there is often one which strays beyond the bounds of the field. Last year, one kept crossing the road to go to a patch of very muddy and unattractive grass, and once when someone came walking along with his dogs, the sheep dashed across the road in front of my car. I only just missed it. When I told the farmer he said, 'Ay, there's allus (always) one!' It reminded me that God has given us the safe boundaries of the Ten Commandments, not to be a spoilsport, but to protect us, but the grass often seems to be greener and more tempting on the other side of the road.

PRAYER: *Father God, thank You that you are my Good Shepherd and that You take good care of me. Help me to put my hand in Yours and give me strength not to stray outside the safe boundaries You have given me. Amen.*

AUGUST 23 | I WANNA BE LIKE YOU

LINDSEY HANEKOM

> *But in fact God has arranged the parts in the body, every one of them, just as he wanted them to be. If they were all one part, where would the body be?*
>
> 1 Corinthians 12:18–19

Whilst recently watching the classic film *The Jungle Book* I was struck by the words of a famous song from the film. Many of us will know the song, '*I wanna be like you*', and, if we are really honest, would have probably sung along to it quite happily once or twice! Essentially the song is sung by an ape to a boy who was brought up in the jungle. The chorus says, '*I wanna be like you, I wanna walk like you, talk like you, too.*' Later in the song it becomes clear that the ape wants one thing from the boy – the secret to making fire.

As I listened to the all-too-familiar lyrics (thanks to a devoted fan of the film in the form of my two-year-old son) I found my thoughts drifting to how we can live our lives in this way. We can see other people and yearn to be like them. Yet the question that I found myself pondering was, 'Do I want to be like someone else, or do I want something that person has?' It's easy to get the two mixed up and we can find ourselves wanting to be like others, but only because we want what they have. It may be that we want their gifts and talents, their status, their friendships, their happiness, their authority, their job, their home or anything else!

This scripture reminds us that we shouldn't yearn to be something or someone we aren't because we perceive our status to be insignificant. Each of the parts of the Body has a vital part to play in God's purposes.

If you feel as though you live your life thinking, *'I wanna be like …'* then maybe today is the day to stop. Why not celebrate the role you have to play in the Body of Christ and just enjoy being yourself?

PRAYER: *Lord Jesus, help me to love myself and not live my life trying to be like others because I see them as those who have more than me. Help me to just be the person You made me to be, so that I can fulfil Your divine purposes in my life. Amen.*

AUGUST 24 | I AM WITH YOU

LIZ GRIFFIN

> *Fear not, for I am with you; be not dismayed, for I am your God; I will strengthen you, I will help you, I will uphold you with my righteous right hand.*
>
> Isaiah 41:10, ESV

God speaks to His people, the nation of Israel, through Isaiah the prophet. It is understood that the words of Isaiah chapters 40–55 were specifically addressed to the exiles in Babylon, but they go far beyond that as a message to all God's people for all time to come. God tells them that they were chosen and taken from the ends of the earth as His servant in chapter 41. They are not to be afraid because He will help them and be with them and deal with their enemies. *'I the LORD will answer them; I the God of Israel will not forsake them'* (Isaiah 41:17).

God's character and His heart of tender love, kindness, grace, mercy and compassion are fully revealed in His message. He knows how weak they really are but says, *'I am the one who helps you, declares the LORD; your Redeemer is the Holy One of Israel'* (Isaiah 41:14, ESV).

The words leap out from the page at me: *'Fear not, for I am with you; be not dismayed, for I am your God; I will strengthen you, I will help you, I will uphold you with my righteous right hand'* (Isaiah 41:10, ESV). The battle against surrendering to fear is an ongoing one. I find I have gained the victory in many areas of past fears and I can look back and be so thankful to the Lord. Yet new challenges can result in that sudden return of helplessness, like a child, when things go wrong and I don't understand why. As an adult I'm not in control any more.

God's Word teaches me that my relationship with my Heavenly Father will be different from those of my childhood experiences. There will be no nasty shocks of finding I'm in trouble for something when I didn't know I'd done anything wrong. He is patient and kind. He doesn't make impossible demands. He shows me the best way to go and then helps me to reach the goal.

I can surrender myself to Him and take hold of His hand whenever I feel afraid. I'm not alone. He is with me. The fears can be replaced by security and knowing He is a loving Heavenly 'Dad'. He will never leave me alone. He never rejects me in any way. What a comfort in the midst of turmoil and times of trouble!

Jesus came to show us what our Heavenly Father is like and He often told His disciples not to be afraid. He also promised to give us the peace that passes understanding.

PRAYER: *Dear Heavenly Father, I know I can trust You in all the situations I find myself in. Nothing is too difficult for You. I choose to take Your hand and allow You to uphold me and strengthen me. Thank You that You promise to be with me. Please help me to keep trusting in You, in Jesus' name, Amen.*

AUGUST 25 | ANSWERED PRAYER

GUNVOR REKSTAD

For nothing is impossible with God.

Luke 1:37

John the Baptist was the son of a woman who was unable to conceive. All through her married life Elizabeth, John's mother, had been waiting to become pregnant. The time came when humanly speaking it was impossible. Then God made it possible. *'For nothing is impossible with God,'* as the angel said.

I know a little girl who is now thirteen years old, and she is also a child of parents who were unable to have children. Throughout the years, her mother and father wished and hoped for a child, but each pregnancy ended with miscarriage and tears and sorrow.

Needs and problems were prayed for in our prayer group. One spring a 'moment of truth' dawned on everyone. We suddenly realised that the same prayers were being prayed over and over again: 'Dear God, I need Your help at work. Dear God, my work situation is so insecure. Dear God, my health is so poor. Dear God, You see the cancer. Dear God, You know we want a child.' Everybody wanted gifts from God: help at work, better health, healing, a child.

It dawned on us that we had sought after the gifts more than or even instead of the giver. In the struggles of everyday life our point of focus had shifted. We confessed and repented, asked God for forgiveness and worshipped Him for who He is. Our prayers changed and we now started to listen more. What was on God's heart? Did He have something to say to us? What did God want us to pray about and pray for? And when we listened, God spoke.

And God had heard too. As autumn came, the growing belly was a fact, and during spring she was born, the little girl.

PRAYER: *Lord, I praise You that nothing is impossible for You. You are God of the impossible. We thank You for looking after us in all our impossibilities. Amen.*

AUGUST 26 | WAIT

FIONA HORROBIN

> *On one occasion, while he was eating with them, he gave them this command: 'Do not leave Jerusalem, but wait for the gift my Father promised, which you have heard me speak about.'*
>
> Acts 1:4

Why did Jesus ask the disciples to wait a few days before they would have the comfort of the Holy Spirit after He had returned to His Father? I pondered this question and came to the conclusion that there must be something in the waiting which was important. Why would Jesus not want the disciples to have instant comfort? As I studied the Scriptures regarding the issue of waiting, I found myself unfolding a vital principle for my life and walk with the Lord.

In actual fact, our whole life is about waiting. In the mundane sense, we are waiting for a kettle to boil, for the alarm to go off, for a bus to arrive or the postman to come! Our vocabulary is interspersed with, 'Wait for me', 'Wait a minute', and 'I can't wait!' Time and patience go alongside waiting. In a more serious way we may be waiting for a baby to arrive, a significant event to take place – a birthday, a wedding – or we may be waiting for something to change in our lives.

A small child has to learn to wait. One of the most important lessons in life is the fact that we can't have everything instantly and there is the need to wait. Whilst a young child may become frustrated and have temper tantrums in the waiting, the parent, who holds the wider picture, knows that the waiting is necessary. The meal is being cooked, the outing is being planned and a greater good than that which is instant is being worked out. Certain things have to be done where waiting is necessary and these things take time. There is the need for patience!

Our Labrador dog, Harris (whom we lost at the age of nine, last March), was a very enthusiastic puppy. When the time came for him to take his Bronze puppy-training award, we wondered how he would go on. In fact he passed each part of his test with flying colours – until it came to the time when he had to wait at one end of the room in a sitting position for one whole minute while the trainer held his treat at the other end of the room.

Harris had his eye fixed firmly on the treat and we commanded him to 'wait'. The seconds ticked by – fifty-five, fifty-six, fifty-seven and then … oh dear, Harris just couldn't wait any longer, and right at the last, he flew towards his treat. He missed sitting for that vital full sixty seconds count! Of course, he had his treat but he missed his Bronze reward. The trainer couldn't give him his pass!

On considering this issue of waiting, I began to understand that there is something to be gained in the waiting. Something of great value and effect is being worked out. Indeed waiting and patience hold a reward. Harris did gain his treat, and therefore his instant gratification, but he did miss out on his reward.

We can lose patience, jump too quickly, maybe make a hasty decision and miss out on something the Lord is doing in the crucible of our frustration in waiting. We could be losing heart, believing God is not hearing or answering, or is not concerned with our plight. Yet waiting is working out its own reward and our perseverance is training our character and allowing something to take effect, which is essential for our growth and development.

There's something to be gained by waiting. There's something worth waiting for. Waiting patiently brings a reward. God is at work in the waiting!

PRAYER: *Heavenly Father, please help me to understand the principle of waiting. Whether I'm waiting for a situation to change, someone I know to change, or for myself to change, I want to let this waiting time have its full effect in my life, and not run ahead of You. I don't want to miss out on Your best for me by running ahead of You and not waiting. Teach me patience, perseverance and endurance so I may gain the reward which comes from waiting for You, in Jesus' name, Amen.*

August 27 | Loving One Another

Angela Weir

> *I, therefore, the prisoner of the Lord, beseech you to walk worthy of the calling with which you were called, with all lowliness and gentleness, with longsuffering, bearing with one another in love, endeavoring to keep the unity of the Spirit in the bond of peace ... And be kind to one another, tender-hearted, forgiving one another, even as God in Christ forgave you.*
>
> Ephesians 4:1–3, 32, NKJV

Paul wrote those verses to the Ephesians many years ago but it seems that human nature has changed little and we hurt one another with the same back-biting, criticism and lack of thought for others that he encountered. Sadly, this often seems to be particularly true in Christian circles.

Jesus commanded us to love one another so that by the love we demonstrate, non-believers would recognise that we belong to Him. In other words the love we show for each other, as Christians, should set us apart from the world, make us attractive to be with and draw others to Jesus.

This can be a challenge as we don't always necessarily like those we find ourselves in fellowship with, but we must choose to love them as an act of our will.

One of the ways we can begin to change our attitude is by asking God to show us how He sees those we find it difficult to be with. For in His eyes they are His precious children. When we begin to pray for them God can sow a seed of love for them in our hearts. A group of people working together in an office with a difficult colleague began to pray in just this way and within a fairly short time that colleague had changed and relationships had improved. Perhaps we could be instrumental in praying like this for people in our churches.

Prayer: *Lord, help me to love and pray for those who cause difficulties in my life. I now realise that by loving and praying for them, both circumstances and people can be changed – including me! In Jesus' name I ask it, Amen.*

August 28 | God is Jealous Over You

Jilly Lyon-Taylor

God jealously longs for the spirit that he made to live in us.

James 4:5

There are various translations of this verse in James's letter, but the one which impacted me deeply a while ago was the one which says that God jealously longs for the spirit He put in us.

Have you ever thought of God being jealous over you? For us the word 'jealousy' has connotations of sin and ungodly feelings. However, there is a righteous kind of jealousy. It would be a bit like the feelings my husband might justifiably have if I told him I was going to spend time with another man in preference to him. As I have promised myself to him in the covenant of marriage, he would be rightly jealous of another taking that place. It's a bit like that with God.

> Have you given God cause to be jealous? Is there anything that is drawing you away from Him? He is longing for you to be wholly set apart for Him.

We are spiritual beings, made for relationship with Him, in covenant with Him. When our spirits are drawn into other involvements, which could be idolatry or worship of any kind, or when we look to anyone or anything else to meet our need for love and acceptance, God is rightly jealous. He wants us to be wholly set apart for Him. He tells us this in Exodus 20:3–5 when He commands us to have no other gods before Him and not to make idols for ourselves, '*for I, the LORD your God, am a jealous God*'.

Have you given God cause to be jealous? Is there anything that is drawing you away from Him? He is longing for you to be wholly set apart for Him.

Prayer: *Lord, forgive me for the times when I have looked to people or things to satisfy me, when all I need is in You. Thank You that You love me so much that You're jealous over me. Amen.*

August 29 | Testing Our Sat Nav

Grace Marshall

Dear friends, do not believe every spirit, but test the spirits to see whether they are from God.

1 John 4:1

Have you ever used a Sat Nav (Satellite Navigation System)? I hadn't until earlier this year when a friend brought one for a long journey. It's a small electronic device which helps you to find the right route to an unfamiliar destination. You type in the postcode and other details of the place you want to go. Then as you drive, a voice tells you which turning to take at every conceivable opportunity.

Unfortunately, someone had obviously failed to tell it about a new road off the motorway at one place on our journey. We were puzzled when the voice suddenly said calmly, 'At the next junction, do a U-turn.' That seemed an odd instruction. We knew we were on the right road.

My friend checked the map. Yes, this was the right road, so we ignored the Sat Nav and carried on. Well, it obviously didn't like being ignored, because patiently but firmly it told us again, and again, 'Whenever it is safe to do so, do a U-turn.'

After checking the map again, we decided to ignore the insistent voice and just follow the map. Unfortunately a colleague of ours in another car followed the Sat Nav rather than the map and ended up fifty miles off course before turning round. Later I was told, 'That's nothing. Another person was once taken 300 miles the wrong way by a Sat Nav before turning round!'

It made me think about what the Bible calls 'testing' prophetic words. We should test them against the Bible (our map). The Bible's always right and is always 'up-to-date' spiritually. However, the Bible doesn't give us detailed instruction about everything. That's why we also have the precious gift of the Holy Spirit to speak to us at every turn, often through our conscience, but sometimes in a more direct 'voice', like the Sat Nav.

That little gadget was invaluable when we got to our destination town. It told us details we couldn't find on the map. But it was more prone to error than the map, just as we're always prone to misunderstand the voice of the Holy Spirit. He doesn't get things wrong, but we can 'mis-hear'!

That's why the Bible tells us to always test the spirits, especially when we think it's the Holy Spirit speaking. Test what's being said. (If it's a word from a person, also test the source.) Test it against the 'map' – which is the Bible.

PRAYER: *Father, I thank You for Your Word, the Bible, and that I can test all other words against it. Amen.*

AUGUST 30 | BECOMING HOLY AND WHOLE!

DAVID CROSS

> *May God himself, the God who makes everything holy and whole, make you holy and whole, put you together – spirit, soul, and body – and keep you fit for the coming of our Master, Jesus Christ.*
>
> 1 Thessalonians 5:23, MSG

We believe that God has called Ellel Ministries to welcome people, teach them about the Kingdom of God and bring His healing to those in need (Luke 9:11). It would be hard to find a more succinct description of what God's healing really means, than that which is given above in today's verse.

In just a few words, this scripture, which we so often refer to on our weekend courses and retreats, reminds us of how God made us and how the sin of the world has so defiled and broken human lives. In receiving Jesus, we have been brought back into relationship with the One who made us and He is definitely in the restoration business, not of paintings, but of works of art which He sees as utterly priceless. That's you and me!

Mankind, including each one of us, has many times broken covenant with the Creator of the universe. The result has been that we've been in the hands of a careless ruler who has been more than happy to see us do damage both to ourselves and also to one another. But now we have been redeemed! God has said to the ruler of this world, 'Give them back!'

It is time for each one of us to get repaired and to let God restore His children to a fit state of holiness and wholeness, in order that He and we can enjoy the precious destiny and destination for which He has given so much. Expert restoration is a very costly business.

Jesus will come for His bride, maybe soon, and He is giving us the opportunity now to deal with our damaged lives. He only asks that we might be willing.

PRAYER: *Thank You, Lord, that You alone can truly make us holy and whole. Amen.*

AUGUST 31 | OBEDIENCE

JOAN RONO

> *Whether it is favourable or unfavourable, we will obey the LORD our God, to whom we are sending you, so that it will go well with us, for we will obey the LORD our God.*
>
> Jeremiah 42:6

This was a hard time for the Israelites. The Babylonians had taken some of the Jews into captivity and the remnant that remained sought to enquire of the Lord. They were fearful and wanted to run from the Babylonians into Egypt, because one of the governors had been assassinated by Ishmael. But it was a time to take a risk and they were ready to obey the Lord no matter what He told them to do. Egypt looked like the safest place to run to but the Lord warned them against going to Egypt, because there was calamity ahead.

Sometimes the Lord tells us to do something that looks like a risk to us. Our opinion may seem better than what the Lord might have to say about the next step in our life. This is where we have to make a choice. It's not easy to be obedient in such circumstances. It's a matter of whom we will obey. Who is in control, us or the Lord?

When we know our God, we'll understand that He knows what's best and we can learn to trust His judgements and directions.

Taking risk demands courage and trust. Trust brings about the courage we need to be able to move in obedience to God's will in our lives. We can't fully obey if we can't fully trust!

Let's look at it this way. When babies are learning to take their first steps, Mum is standing in front waiting for them to move towards her. Unless they are able to fully trust that Mum won't let them fall, they are unlikely to move.

In the same way we need to trust in God and move into His will for our lives with child-like trust that He knows the way ahead, all the obstacles, and, most importantly, the joy that comes as the fruit of obedience to Him. *'Trust and obey for there's no other way, to be happy in Jesus, but to trust and obey'* (John H. Sammis, 1887).

Prayer: *Lord, I know that my life is in Your hands and I can trust You in all circumstances, though sometimes I find it difficult to trust. Please help me to trust and obey Your will. Amen.*

September 1 | Tourist or Resident?

Cath Taylor

> *Those who live in the shelter of the Most High will find rest in the shadow of the Almighty.*
>
> Psalm 91:1, NLT

As Brits who have lived in Australia and the USA, we know first-hand the huge difference there is between visiting a country on vacation and actually making a home there. Once the decision to go has been made and the visas are in place, then the worst part of the whole process starts – the packing and the goodbyes! The sorting of junk, the detailed cleaning of the house, the setting-up of new bank accounts and new schools: the list is endless!

If you survive this process, next comes the fun part! You set off with a passion to learn as much as you possibly can about the true identity and character of your new home. You want to know everything you can about this country so that you can establish roots and foundations for yourself and your family. It really is a wonderful experience. It's different from the list of requirements needed for a vacation – where a 'Rough Guide' and directions to the beach will normally be enough.

When you're uprooting your whole life you need more than that. You strive to build bonds and connections with your new home (and its people), and when you do, the bonds remain forever. Without even knowing how or when, it changes you as a person.

As Christians we have already obtained our visa, but we still have to make a choice. Are we going to live permanently in God's shelter and move house, or are we simply going to visit His shelter on vacation, as a refuge during the struggles of life? We all love the sound of '*resting in the shadow of the Almighty*' away from our insecurities, fears and anxieties. But are we willing to do the first part – to decide to '*dwell [or live] in His shelter*'?

If that rest is what we long for so much, then let's sort through our lives, leaving no corner hidden, and bring everything to Him. Let's make relationship with Jesus our permanent residence. If we do this, we will begin a wonderful journey of discovery and true relationship that no tourist can experience, and we will get to know aspects of our Saviour that no temporary traveller would ever discover!

PRAYER: *Lord Jesus, I've been guilty of living as a tourist, visiting Your shelter on vacation, rather than living as a resident child. Lord, I don't want a relationship like that with You any longer. I long to know You intimately and in the way that You intended – to begin a wonderful journey of discovery with You, so that I can finally find the true rest that You offer for my heart. In Jesus' name I pray, Amen.*

SEPTEMBER 2 | THE LOCKED DOOR

PETER HORROBIN

> *Here I am! I stand at the door and knock. If anyone hears my voice and opens the door, I will come in and eat with him, and he with me.*
>
> Revelation 3:20

This is one of the best-known verses in Scripture. Thousands of evangelists have used these words from Jesus' letter to the church at Laodicea to close the deal, as it were, when making an appeal for people to accept Jesus as their Saviour, by opening the door of their heart to Him. Countless millions must have come into the Kingdom of God impacted by the Saviour's words. I thank God for every single one of them.

There is however a big 'but' about how this Scripture is often used! For the message to the church at Laodicea was to believers, not those who were outside the fellowship of the church. This verse was in reality an appeal from Jesus to Christians to give Jesus access to all of their life. The church at Laodicea thought it was rich, but the devastating words spoken to them in verse 17 said that far from being rich (in God's eyes) they were poor, blind and naked!

Sometimes our perception of things is distorted by our own sinfulness, greed, pride and even arrogance, as was the case with the Laodiceans. An important prayer for each of us to pray is: *'Lord, open my eyes – that I may see things as You see them.'* I rejoice that so many people have come into the Kingdom of God challenged by evangelists to open the door of their heart.

But I do wonder what would be the effect on the Church if all believers responded to the Lord by giving Him access to every area of their lives? It's well said that if Jesus is not Lord of all, he is not Lord at all.

I believe miracles would happen in all our churches, and even our nations, if we were to respond enthusiastically to the knocking of the Saviour on the door of His Church, turn the key in the lock and welcome Him in – giving Him His rightful place. What a challenge that is for each of us as we look to Him as the source of life (in all its fullness).

PRAYER: *Thank You, Lord, that You still knock on the door of our hearts, even when we have turned our back on You in the past. I want You to be Lord of my whole life and I invite You to come in and reign in every area of my being, in Jesus' name, Amen.*

SEPTEMBER 3 | MY PRESENCE WILL GO WITH YOU

MARGARET SILVESTER

> *Teach me your ways so I may know you and continue to find favour with you.*
>
> Exodus 33:13

Moses was probably the greatest leader of all time. His task was impossible – leading a nation of people who were unwilling to follow him and preferred to go back to Egypt. After the devastating incident of the golden calf, Moses was told to lead the people on another stage of their journey, with the promise that an angel would go ahead of them.

This wasn't the full assurance Moses asked for. He wanted the presence of the Lord Himself – the friend he had learned to converse with and depend upon (Exodus 33:12–15). The Lord spoke to Moses face to face, as a man speaks with his friend (Exodus 33:11). Moses reminded God of what He had previously said to him: 'I know you by name and you have found favour with me.' Each one of us is intimately known by God. Our names are written on the palm of His hands (Isaiah 49:16) and He cares deeply for us, longing for an ever deepening relationship with us.

Moses had an impossible task ahead, one which could never be accomplished without the known presence of God. His next prayer came from a longing heart: '*Teach me your ways, so I may know you and continue to find favour with you … If your Presence does not go with us, do not send us up from here.*'

The Hebrew word for 'know' is 'yada' – which means 'to know intimately'. Moses realised that he couldn't grow in intimacy with God unless he knew God's ways. But for Moses to journey in the ways of God was to journey with the presence of God. To journey without knowing the presence of God wasn't an option for him.

God's ways are always in keeping with His character. The God who revealed Himself to Moses, and showed him His ways, is the same today. He still reveals Himself, He still speaks, but as with His ancient people, He demands obedience to His words and His ways.

The Bible tells us about God's ways. They are ways of wisdom which are higher than ours. They are perfect, holy, just, loving and right. The way ahead for us may not be easy. We may have to take an unknown path, but we can be assured of God's presence on our journey and we needn't be afraid. Do you have a sense of God's presence with you today? Are there some changes you need to make in your life so that you are living according to God's ways?

PRAYER: *Thank You, Heavenly Father, that Your ways are always best. Help me to choose today to live my life in obedience to You. Amen.*

SEPTEMBER 4 | LED INTO GOD'S PURPOSES

DAVID SILVESTER

But he brought us out from there to bring us in and give us the land that he promised on oath to our forefathers.

Deuteronomy 6:23

These words of Moses to Israel just after he had reminded them of the Lord's commandments spoke with freshness to me as I read them one morning. They reminded me of how God has led and directed my wife and myself into a ministry of healing and deliverance.

From infancy I attended Sunday School and learned about the things Jesus taught and did, and how Jesus sent out His disciples to go and do the same. I longed to have the same experience that those disciples and the early Church had when they saw miracles happen, but I became aware that there was a missing dimension to my Christian life. I wanted to be brought out of that barren place into the place those early Christians had experienced.

My wife and I, along with a group of friends, began to search for what we felt was missing, yet at the time were not fully aware of what that might be. We would meet together each month to pray and search the Scriptures as we tried to understand what it was we were seeking. Then the Lord came to us all in different ways and eventually my wife, our children and myself experienced the Holy Spirit's power coming upon us.

The Lord had been gradually leading us into a new experience of Himself at work in our lives and showing us that we too could experience His power at work to deliver people who were bound and to bring healing to those who were sick. He had truly *'brought us out from there to bring us in'* to a new experience of Himself and His power to work out His purposes, Hallelujah!

Even today, many years later, we regularly thank God for the foundation laid in those early years of Sunday School teaching, and for those godly teachers who taught us so much of His Word. We still pray that the eyes of many more people might be opened to recognise the dimension that is available to us all through the Holy Spirit.

Let us take to heart the words of Jesus who said, *'Ask and it will be given to you, seek and you will find'* (Matthew 7:7) and *'When he, the Spirit of truth, comes, he will guide you into all truth'* (John 16:13). Then let's ask that He might open our eyes and behold the wonderful things God can do when we respond to His leading.

PRAYER: *Father God, thank You for sending Your Holy Spirit to be my Counsellor and Guide. Please forgive me if I have been blind or deaf and have not recognised or listened to Him as He has tried to lead me in Your ways. Please fill me to overflowing with all that You have for me through Your Holy Spirit, I pray, Amen.*

SEPTEMBER 5 | THE WAY INTO THE LORD'S PRESENCE

LIZ GRIFFIN

> *As the musician played his harp, the power of the LORD came on Elisha.*
>
> 2 Kings 3:15, GNB

King Joram of Israel wasn't as bad as his father King Ahab because he did away with the idol to Baal, but he did lead his country into sin. King Mesha took the death of King Ahab as an opportunity to rebel against paying his taxes to Israel. So King Joram sought help from his two allies: King Jehoshaphat of Judah and the king of Edom. They marched for seven days and found themselves in a terrible predicament with no water supply. King Joram obviously had a guilty conscience before God for he assumed that God was punishing him. King Jehoshaphat wasn't giving up that easily, however, and asked for a prophet to come and help them. He wanted to take the problem to God and so the prophet Elisha was found. He was quite confrontational towards King Joram, his king, but he did respect King Jehoshaphat and so agreed to find out God's will.

The interesting thing is what he did next. He asked for a musician. He must have known that was the way to come into God's presence because as soon as the musician played his harp the power of the Lord came on Elisha. He spoke out what God was going to do to save them. God was going to miraculously provide water, but there was something for them to do. They had to dig ditches to receive the water.

He asked for a musician. He must have known that was the way to come into God's presence because as soon as the musician played his harp the power of the Lord came on Elisha.

How do we enter into the Lord's presence? What focuses us on Him and rids us of distractions? When Campbell McAlpine wrote a book called *The Practice of Biblical Meditation* he advised that we sit in a relaxed way with the Lord and either sing a worshipful song, or sit silently in His presence. We are not to let our mind go blank, but to think of Him. Then we are to hear Him speak to us through the Word. Another thing he suggested was that we could memorise Scripture by putting the words to our own music and singing it. Many of the Psalms particularly lend themselves to this.

The apostle Paul says, *'Be filled with the Spirit, speaking to one another in psalms, hymns and spiritual songs, singing and making melody in your heart to the Lord'* (Ephesians 5:18–19, NKJV).

In today's world an excellent way of focusing on the Lord for many of us can be to listen to the Christian digital radio station playing songs of praise and worship. Before you know it you find yourself lifted up into the Lord's presence.

PRAYER: *Dear Father God, please help me to feed my spirit and spend time in Your presence. Let me hear You speaking to me either in that still small voice or through reading Your Word. I don't want to get distracted by all the cares of this world from basking in Your presence and knowing Your love. Amen.*

September 6 | Narrow Minded

Cristy Williams

I will give them singleness of heart and action, so that they will always fear me for their own good and the good of their children after them.

Jeremiah 32:39

I was talking just recently about what church would've looked like in those first few days after Pentecost. Peter has come back in full swing with Jesus' authority to speak truth, thousands of God-fearing Jews are together, and the first Christian revival happens! Jesus' disciples must have been awe-struck!

What was the lead-up to the Holy Spirit's first introduction? Jesus' disciples were together in constant prayer, waiting as Jesus commanded them to. They had 'singleness of heart' in their obedience. You could say the apostles were 'narrow-minded' in the task at hand. They had been given directions from their Lord to stay in Jerusalem for the gift of the Holy Spirit and so 'that was that'. This mismatched group of disciples knew that Whoever this promised Holy Spirit was, He was going to be for their good and for the good of generations to come. We read about the immediate results that came from their obedience, setting the Church in motion in Acts 2.

Later on in Acts we see this narrow-mindedness in Paul. Paul is brought before the Sanhedrin and almost torn apart by the teachers of the law. It's then that the Holy Spirit tells him to go and testify in Rome. Paul is so narrow-minded about this assignment that he appeals to Caesar in his court case, when he could have been freed! Rome was the one thing on his mind.

Our Western culture uses the term 'narrow-minded' as being a negative, self-centred way of thinking. However, in light of the apostles, we need to walk a narrow road both in our thoughts and actions. Being Christ's disciples means living by 'One Way', setting our course to God's spoken destination. Without accurate directions, we'll get lost every time. But with single-hearted determination, we will find life like we've never known.

'Small is the gate and narrow the road that leads to life, and only a few find it' (Matthew 7:13–14).

Prayer: *Father God, thank You for sending Your Holy Spirit to us as our direction-giver. I choose to align my footsteps with Yours and go where You tell me to go. It is my joy to set my course on Your perfect destination for my life. Give me Your mind to stay the course, in Jesus' name. Amen.*

September 7 | Believe and be Baptised

Martin Knapp

I have been crucified with Christ and I no longer live, but Christ lives in me. The life I live in the body, I live by faith in the Son of God, who loved me and gave himself for me.

Galatians 2:20

At Ellel Grange we had the privilege of conducting a baptism in our indoor swimming pool. David Silvester, our team pastor, an ex Baptist pastor, explained the significance and symbolism of full-immersion water baptism. We were all touched as the baptismal candidate gave her personal testimony, answered some basic questions and, on the profession of her faith in Jesus Christ, was submerged in the pool and raised up out of the water. She was, as it were, buried with Christ, and rose to new life in Him as it says in the Bible – *'buried with him in baptism and raised with him through your faith in the power of God, who raised him from the dead'* (Colossians 2:12). We then returned to the Meeting Room to celebrate Communion and a new life in Christ.

The occasion reminded me that for a number of years when I was working in London I used to meet with a friend who was a Messianic Jew. Each time we met for lunch he would challenge me and ask if I had been water baptised, reminding me that it was a command in the Bible. It took me a while to make the decision, but eventually I was baptised in the pool at Ellel Pierrepont in 2000. It was a very special moment for me, but I think the spiritual significance took time to sink in. If I have died with Christ and risen to new life in Him then who I am doesn't really matter any more. The question is: am I living in the resurrection power of Christ?

Some years ago I read the story of a missionary lady in Africa who walked every day along a stretch of road where people were often attacked and robbed, and some had been killed. 'Aren't you afraid?', asked a concerned friend, to which the missionary replied, 'I have only a Bible that someone could steal and I have already "died" so I have nothing to fear as they can do nothing to me.' She had clearly 'died to herself and her own desires' and continued to walk that road unharmed for many years.

Romans 6:4 says, '*We were therefore buried with him through baptism into death in order that, just as Christ was raised from the dead through the glory of the Father, we too may live a new life.*' And the apostle Paul says, '*I have been crucified with Christ and I no longer live, but Christ lives in me. The life I live in the body, I live by faith in the Son of God, who loved me and gave himself for me*' (Galatians 2:20). For me water baptism was an important start to dying to self and living a new life in Jesus.

PRAYER: *Thank You, Lord, for the meaning of water baptism. Thank You that I can surrender my life to You and be reborn into everlasting life in You. May my life be hidden in You, Jesus, that day by day I should grow less and You become more. Help me to walk into the fullness of life that You purchased for me. Amen.*

SEPTEMBER 8 | LIVING WATER AND CRACK-FREE CISTERNS!

PETER HORROBIN

> *My people have committed two sins: They have forsaken me, the spring of living water, and have dug their own cisterns, broken cisterns that cannot hold water.*
>
> Jeremiah 2:13

There were many different things that God's people did when they turned their back on the Living God – the list of sins that would be needed to describe all their ungodly activities would have been very long! But when, through the prophet Jeremiah, God began to speak words of rebuke, He reduced all their sinful behaviour into just two categories.

Firstly, they had deserted the only source of living water and *secondly*, they had tried to generate their own 'water supply' as a substitute for the living water that flows from the heart of God.

In Israel, underground cisterns were vital for the storage of water for use during the dry season. Without a good cistern people would die through lack of water. A cracked cistern was useless. Water would flow into it alright, but the water would all leak away through the cracks, so that when the water was most needed there would be no water there.

God uses this picture to speak to His people about what they had been doing. He uses the need for physical water as a parable of the need for the living spiritual water which sustains God's people through all the ups and downs of life. The first sin of God's people was to decide that they wanted an alternative source of supply, so instead of constantly coming back to the only source of living water, they did what mankind has tried to do throughout history – they built their own cistern, which embraced everything from idolatry to sexual immorality. They finished up believing that good was bad, and bad was good, and going in the opposite direction to the ways of God.

God had provided for them everything that was needful for living in covenant relationship with the God who had created the world and everything in it. But pride in the heart of man will always want to build an alternative way and say it's better than what God provided in the first place. Ultimately this is the foundation for every alternative belief system, false religion or moral order that has ever risen up in the heart of man and been practised on the face of the earth.

It's easy to look at the people of Jeremiah's day and ask, 'How could they?' But all we need to do is look at our own generation and see that 21st century man is no different. Part of the reason why I believe God put the vision for Ellel 365 into my heart was to ensure that within Ellel Ministries there's a constant flow of living water from God's Word and that people are able to know how to build a cistern in their own lives that is sound and without cracks.

PRAYER: *Help me, Lord, to only ever want the living water which flows from Your heart to the heart of man. And give me the determination to rebuild sound and crack-free cisterns in my own life, so that the Water of Life will always be available to me throughout my days – even in seasons of drought, in Jesus' name, Amen.*

SEPTEMBER 9 | CHOOSE LIFE

PAM SMITH

> *I call heaven and earth to witness against you that today I have set before you life or death, blessing or curse. Oh, that you would choose life; that you and your children might live!*
>
> Deuteronomy 30:19, LB

The Lord has given us the wonderful ability to choose. It's called free will. He didn't create us to be puppets. He's set choices before us. We're free to choose, and the Lord longs that we will choose life, for He is life. The only alternative given is to choose death and cursing. I'm sure no one would knowingly choose that, but there's a possibility that, by not making a choice at all, one could find oneself already under that curse. There's no coalition government in the Kingdom of God, and the Lord alone rules. The Bible says, *'And the government will be upon His shoulder'* (Isaiah 9:6, NKJV).

Jesus said, *'I have come that they may have life and that they may have it more abundantly'* (John 10:10, NKJV). God wants us to reach our full potential and to live as the person He created us to be. He has a destiny for each one of us and doesn't want us to miss any part of this. So He wants our bodies to be healthy as our spirit prospers, and He wants us to have good relationships with others and be a blessing to them, as well as to Him.

Choosing life is choosing complete freedom in Christ Jesus, and we have amazing scriptures such as: *'For He made Him who knew no sin to be sin for us, that we might become the righteousness of God in Him'* (2 Corinthians 5:21, NKJV), and *'Christ has redeemed us from the curse of the law, having become a curse for us (for it is written, "Cursed is everyone who hangs on a tree"), that the blessing of Abraham might come upon the Gentiles in Christ Jesus, that we might receive the promise of the Spirit through faith'* (Galatians 3:13–14, NKJV).

Who wouldn't choose Him and live in a Kingdom that God had given His children? As Joshua said to the children of Israel, *'Choose for yourselves this day whom you will serve … But as for me and my house, we will serve the LORD'* (Joshua 24:15, NKJV).

PRAYER: *Dear Lord, thank You for becoming sin for us, that we might choose eternal life. Help us to love and serve You all our days. Amen.*

SEPTEMBER 10 | HE LISTENS

CATH TAYLOR

> *I love the LORD because he hears and answers my prayers. Because he bends down and listens, I will pray as long as I have breath!*
>
> Psalm 116:1–2, NLT

Our house is constantly full of noise. There is always one discussion or another going on. Sometimes happy, sometimes very unhappy! As a mum, you quickly learn the art of multi-tasking! I can now do a myriad of things whilst listening to an eight-year-old's story of his day at school, negotiating exactly whose turn it is on the Play Station, hearing the injustices of a four-year-old having to go to bed earlier than his brother, not to mention fielding requests for antidotes for headaches, leg aches, stomach pains and 'starving' hunger.

All this to say, if there is one thing I am not guilty of as a parent, it would be not hearing the cries of my kids. Having said that, however, there's still a big difference between hearing all these things and really taking the time to listen to each of my children. Nothing can replace the times we sit, one on one, and talk. No distractions for either of us. Looking into their little faces, this is my opportunity to really listen and to perhaps see a bigger picture than the initial stomach pains or the headaches. It's their time to know they have my undivided attention, and maybe with a little probing they can tell me all that is really going on in their lives – the good, the bad and the ugly!

I believe your Father God, the Creator of this whole universe, is quite simply just waiting, ready at any moment to bend down and listen to you, His most precious child!

I love our scripture for today, because it reminds me that God has, to a much greater and perfect degree, that kind of care and longing for relationship with me and you. He doesn't just 'hear us out' but in the midst of all His busyness and all His children, He really listens. It is so easy for us to make our requests to God similar to how I described my children: 'Please can I have this … Please sort this out …' but do you know that God longs to hear more – He wants to listen to your whole heart.

What's important to you, is important to Him. He wants you to trust Him enough to pour it out. I believe your Father God, the Creator of this whole universe, is quite simply just waiting, ready at any moment to bend down and listen to you, His most precious child!

Prayer: *Lord Jesus, thank You that in the midst of the Greatness of who You are and all that You hold in Your hands, You take time to bend down and listen to me. Thank You for loving me that much. Father God, teach me how to make the most of my relationship with You, and to trust You with the depths of my heart. In Jesus' name I pray, Amen.*

September 11 | Carried on Eagle's Wings

Margaret Silvester

Like an eagle that stirs up its nest and hovers over its young, that spreads its wings to catch them and carries them on its pinions, the LORD alone led him; no foreign god was with him.

Deuteronomy 32:11–12

As the plane was beginning to descend I thought I would love to see two things during our August holiday in the Swiss mountains. One was snow and the other was a wonder of nature. I received both of my desires.

For the first two days it rained incessantly, and when we awoke on the third day the mountain range was covered in thick snow – quite a turn in the August weather. The next day we were tramping through the snow high in the mountains when we heard screeching overhead and to our amazement we watched an eagle teaching its young to fly. The two chicks looked so tiny and seemed to be terrified. Repeatedly they came to rest on their mother's wing only to be tossed up into the air to fend for themselves again. The eagle literally hovered over its young, and when distress reached a high pitch, the eagle went alongside, caught the chicks on her wings and soared with them back to the safety of the eerie.

The parent eagle, in teaching her young to fly, protects them and encourages them to imitate her own movements. Despite their protests she is always there to protect and save them from danger. If the young eagles are not pushed out of the eerie they will never learn to fly.

Our text today sets an aspect of God in the image of the eagle teaching its chicks to fly. In order for our character to develop He sometimes asks us to leave our comfort zones and move into unknown, and possibly precarious places, with Him leading us, guiding us, protecting and hovering over us. In unknown experiences we learn to depend more fully upon God, proving in a new way His faithfulness and care for us.

Things happen in our lives that we sometimes do not welcome. It's easy to be like the eaglet, making a fuss and constantly wanting to go back to the safety of the nest. God's desire for all His children is that they grow into Christian maturity. Christian maturity is growing more fully into the likeness of Jesus.

Do you need to be willing to leave your comfort zone and trust God to carry you on eagle's wings as you step out into some unknown purpose that He has planned for you?

PRAYER: *Father, thank You that in faithfulness and love You have plans for me. Thank You for Your trustworthy character. Today I choose to trust You and follow Your ways, so that I can grow in Christian maturity and in the image of Your Son. Amen.*

SEPTEMBER 12 | A RESERVED PLACE

MALCOLM WOOD

... but rejoice that your names are written in heaven.

Luke 10:20

Recently I had to travel on a train from Birmingham to Edinburgh. As so often seems the case these days, the train was extremely busy and vacant seats difficult to find. Passengers desperate for a seat were occupying seats reserved by others and were being asked to move when the person with the reservation arrived at their seat. This happened in my case. When I boarded the train and located my seat, I found it already occupied. A careful look at my ticket and the electronic display above the seat confirmed that indeed it was my seat and reserved all the way to my destination. When asked to do so, the person sitting in my seat moved to find a seat elsewhere.

This incident made me glad that I'd taken the trouble to reserve a seat, that the seat had been reserved for me, and that I was expected on that train! This made me realise afresh how important it is to know that we have a place reserved in heaven and that we're expected!

The ticket price was paid for us by Jesus on the cross at Calvary. The reservation in heaven is assured as soon as we accept what He did there was for us, and start to apply what was made available through Calvary in our own lives.

Once we've taken that step, Jesus assures us that He has personally prepared a place for us in heaven (John 14:2). So we are expected and one day we'll be with Him.

As we ponder these truths, may the hope and the assurance that they give become a source of increasing strength and help in these challenging times. *'Blessed assurance, Jesus is mine, O what a foretaste of glory divine'* (Fanny J. Crosby).

Prayer: *Dear Lord Jesus, thank You for reminding me afresh of the price You paid to ensure that I had a place in heaven, and thank You for preparing that place for me, and that I'm expected there one day. Amen.*

September 13 | Jesus Our Helper

Andreas Hefti

> *He said, 'Throw your net on the right side of the boat and you will find some.' When they did, they were unable to haul the net in because of the large number of fish.*
>
> John 21:6

The disciples had been fishing all night long. Tired, exhausted, frustrated, disappointed and discouraged, and, I guess, with an empty stomach and hungry, they came back to the shore. And there Jesus, whom they didn't recognise at the time, asks them the 'inspiring and encouraging' question: *'Friends, haven't you any fish?'* And He told them to throw out the net once more on the right side. In the end they caught 153 fish; the number of varieties of fish said to be in the Sea of Galilee at that time. After this miracle they finally recognised Jesus and when they came ashore He had already prepared their breakfast.

You remember that Peter had such an experience once before, at the time when Jesus commissioned him in Luke 5:1–11. Peter was an experienced fisherman and yet they hadn't caught a single fish all night. And there came this 'inexperienced stranger' telling them what to do. I believe it was due to the powerful message of Jesus which Peter had just listened to that he was willing to cast the net once more on the right side upon Jesus' word. And then it was Jesus who added the miracle to Peter's obedience.

Sometimes we feel discouraged and weighed down like the disciples when nothing seems to work properly and when the fruit of our labour is missing or doesn't seem to be visible. In such times we can so well identify with the prophet in Isaiah 49:4 who said: *'I have laboured to no purpose; I have spent my strength in vain and for nothing. Yet what is due to me is in the LORD's hand, and my reward is with my God.'*

It is in those times when it looks most bleak that God is just about to come through on our behalf. When we feel most weak and inadequate for the task ahead, He will come through to be our strength and provider, performing miracles way beyond our ability or expectation. What a privilege that we can ask our Heavenly Father for His provision and His perspective on things. And He will provide and answer time and time again, and give us His strategy.

It's not always easy to trust, especially if God seems to ask us to do the impossible. But as we dare to step out and experience His faithfulness our trust will grow step by step. Like the first time when they had fished all night in vain, the disciples dared this time to step out once more upon Jesus' word. They cast the net on the right side, and the rest was Jesus' doing. When they came ashore Jesus ministered His food and love to them. May this be an experience we can have time and time again with our Lord.

Prayer: *Dear Heavenly Father, thank You that You have never ever let me down. Thank You that You always came through on my behalf at the right time and in the right way. I want to trust You for the way ahead and the task You've set before me. Upon Your word I want to move and be obedient in the things You've asked me to do. Thank You that You have provided me with everything I need to walk the walk. When I am at the end of myself You are just about to begin. Amen.*

SEPTEMBER 14 | A DEBT YOU WILL NEVER PAY OFF

MARGARET SILVESTER

> *Let no debt remain outstanding, except the continuing debt to love one another, for whoever loves his fellow-man has fulfilled the law.*
>
> Romans 13:8

The Bible does not encourage debt. However, debt is very prevalent in our world today. Whether we live in the developed or developing world, debt is a major problem. People find it hard to survive and many borrow more money to try to stall existing debt. Of course, this serves only to tighten the debt trap and for many it's impossible to break free from debt.

Immediately before the cross, Jesus gave His disciples a new commandment – to love one another. To love one's fellow believers is the clear evidence of being a disciple of Jesus. It's so important to Jesus that love is predominant amongst His people that He gave the direct command three times in the last week of His life.

Paul told the Roman believers that they should pay off their debts to whoever they owed money and not let debts be outstanding. However, he told them that there was a debt which could never be paid off, and that was the continuing debt to love one another. It was a lifelong debt.

It was an important debt to keep in mind constantly because the Second Coming of Jesus was something the early Christians desired to be ready for. The command to love one another is surely equally as important to us, for the Second Coming of Jesus is so much nearer today.

To be trapped in the love debt is the normal way for any Christian to live. To live with the continuing debt to love one another is to live in obedience to the command of the Lord Jesus. It's the outward expression of our love for Him.

PRAYER: *Lord, please forgive me when I have not loved others as You desire. Thank You for the cross, the ultimate expression of Your unfailing love to me. I ask You to change any heart attitudes in me that block the flow of Your love to others through me. Please help me today to live out the new commandment to love one another. Amen.*

SEPTEMBER 15 | GOD REMEMBERS HIS PROMISE

JILL SOUTHERN-JONES

> *So Pharaoh sent for Joseph, and he was quickly brought from the dungeon ...*
>
> Genesis 41:14

For twelve years Joseph was in prison, from the age of eighteen to the age of thirty. Just when everyone else of his age would probably have been marrying and having children, Joseph was locked away without any knowledge of whether he would ever be released from jail. And all this was for something he hadn't done – he was completely innocent.

But one day Pharaoh had a dream and finally the cupbearer remembered meeting Joseph in prison – the man who had the gift of interpreting dreams. Quickly Joseph was sent for, the dungeon doors opened at last and Joseph was free! Not just free, but as a direct result of interpreting Pharaoh's dreams he was elevated to being Number Two in the whole land of Egypt!

Power comes from God; God never took either His favour or the power to interpret dreams away from Joseph, even in prison. God had promised

Joseph through his dreams what He would do in his life; God hadn't changed His mind. God now used dreams to spring him from jail in the most dramatic of rescue acts!

Romans 11:29 says, '*For God's gifts and his call are irrevocable.*' That means that they are irrevocable. God never changes His mind about you and your call, even when it seems as though everything is against you.

As you serve faithfully and wait on God for your destiny to be fulfilled, don't be surprised if God moves suddenly in your life as well. Whatever God has truly said will be fulfilled. Has God made promises to you? Hold on to those promises today through thick and thin. God hasn't changed His mind. '*Humble yourselves before the Lord, and he will lift you up*' (James 4:10). Can you hang on to what God has promised you even when it looks hopeless?

PRAYER: *Thank You, Lord, that You are utterly trustworthy and I can always depend on You. Help me to hold on to all Your promises to me. Thank You, in Jesus' name, Amen.*

SEPTEMBER 16 | GOING THROUGH SUFFERING

GORAN ANDERSSON

> *Praise be to the God and Father of our Lord Jesus Christ, the Father of compassion and the God of all comfort, who comforts us in all our troubles, so that we can comfort those in any trouble with the comfort we ourselves have received from God.*
>
> 2 Corinthians 1:3–4

It seems that Paul saw himself only able to comfort others by first needing and receiving that comfort himself. And as he couldn't be comforted without first going through real suffering and pain, he saw all suffering coming his way as God's sovereign way of equipping him to serve others. The comfort he gave to new Christians, who were almost overwhelmed by the resistance and hardships they encountered when they began following Christ, was not a cheap thing or words alone. It had been personally tested by Paul, and so he knew it worked.

Theology is good, but it has to work to be of any value. And the only way it can be tested is by people experiencing the reality and then being able to give to others the comfort they themselves have received. That means you can't serve and help people from a lofty position; you have to go down into the depths and walk through them. Then you can tell others there is a way through. You know there is, because you've been there.

This seems to be a principle in the Kingdom of God. Who are usually best equipped to minister to people in need? Those who've walked through the same kind of difficulties. Who are best at convincing those who are tempted that it's possible to overcome? Those who've been through the same experience themselves.

This is why Paul never saw sufferings and imprisonment as a meaningless loss of valuable time and energy. To him it was an investment, a time that would bear fruit, not just in his own life and character, but in the lives of all the people he would minister to.

To become Saviour and Shepherd, Christ had to go through the greatest depths of suffering and death. There was no short cut. *'He had to be made like his brothers in every way, in order that he might become a merciful and faithful high priest in service to God, and that he might make atonement for the sins of the people. Because he himself suffered when he was tempted, he is able to help those who are being tempted'* (Hebrews 2:17–18).

There is a price to being a blessing to others. If we would comfort those in need we must be willing to go through dark valleys – at times so dark that we see no light at all. *'We were under great pressure, far beyond our ability to endure, so that we despaired even of life. Indeed, in our hearts we felt the sentence of death. But this happened that we might not rely on ourselves but on God, who raises the dead'* (2 Corinthians 1:8–9).

God builds firm foundations into His people! And He does it before we understand the meaning of it. That's why it often seems so hard! Can you trust that the 'meaning-less' things you're going through now will eventually enable you to comfort others and be of help to them? When your experiences are transformed into comfort and encouragement for your brother and sister, you'll see it was 'worth the price'!

PRAYER: *Dear Heavenly Father, please help me as I go through times of suffering. Help me to receive the comfort that comes from You and then be able to pass that comfort on to others. Help me to lift others from the darkness into the light, in Jesus' name, Amen.*

SEPTEMBER 17 | WHEN EVERYTHING GOES WRONG

LIZ GRIFFIN

Be merciful to me, O God, be merciful, because I come to you for safety.

Psalm 57:1, GNB

Do you feel as if you're in the midst of a raging storm today? You're powerless to do anything about the circumstances that surround you. In Psalm 57:4, King David said, *'I am surrounded by enemies, who are like lions hungry for human flesh. Their teeth are like spears and arrows; their tongues are like sharp swords'* (GNB).

What kind of storms arise in your life? Did someone say something about you that was completely untrue and before you knew what was happening others were accusing you of all sorts of things? You couldn't straighten out the facts, try as you might. It's painful to feel the rejection and disapproval from others when you haven't done anything wrong. Particularly when you thought they were your friends.

Maybe you tried to help someone with a problem at work. Then all of a sudden you found yourself in trouble for doing the wrong thing. It was politically incorrect. Yet your heart motivation was to do something good.

The Lord is the One who understands it all. He's a God of truth. He's just and fair and must punish wrongdoing, evil and sin. But He doesn't punish us for mistakes and accidents. Our Heavenly Father gives us loving acceptance and we will never hear condemnation from His lips. His approval of our thoughts and actions is more important than approval from anyone else. He is a place of refuge.

'But I will sing about your strength; every morning I will sing aloud of your constant love. You have been a refuge for me, a shelter in my time of trouble' (Psalm 59:16). The Lord is a strong tower which we can run to and be safe. He always has time for us, welcomes us into His presence and He's available 24/7.

PRAYER: *Thank You, Lord, that You never tire of being my security and protection and that in times of storm and testing You are always there to be my comfort and my encouragement. In Jesus' name I pray, Amen.*

September 18 | Pour Out Your Emotions

Roger Pook

O LORD, our Lord, how majestic is your name in all the earth!
You have set your glory above the heavens.

Psalm 8:1

One of God's greatest blessings to mankind is our ability to appreciate the wonder of His creation. It's just so … well, beautiful! Probably most of us have experienced the amazing sensation of gazing into a starry night and just looking at the sky. It drives you to praise and worship quicker than almost anything else.

You can get the same result from seeing a wonderful landscape, a brilliant sunset, or the intricacies of a leaf or small creature through a magnifying glass. Oh God, this is amazing! You made it all so well!

The experience is both spiritual and emotional. It feels so good, and *does* us good, because it's in obedience to God's command to pour our emotions back to our Heavenly Father who gave them in the first place.

If we can get into this habit of expressing our wonder and joy to God, then it becomes much easier to pour out to Him the feelings that are not so pleasant as well. This is part of the same command, and leads to healing.

In Psalm 69, David pours out to God the feelings that are overwhelming him, and goes on to tell God exactly what he thinks about his enemies. To paraphrase verses 22–28: *'I want their food to poison them, I want them to go blind and crippled, I want their family to die out, and I want them to go to hell!'* Now that's honesty for you. That's real emotions. He's not cursing his enemies (the psalm is addressed to God); he's telling God exactly what he thinks!

The wonderful result of this is in verses 30–36, where David is free to sing a beautiful hymn of praise. He's healed!

So how can we praise God in times of trouble? By first pouring out to Him, in all honesty, what we are really feeling. This brings healing, cleansing, and enables the Spirit to flow through us. Try it. It works.

Prayer: *Dear Lord, You already know my innermost feelings; I cannot hide them from You. So help me to be honest with You about how I feel, so that You can heal the pain and show me how to respond in a godly way to those who have hurt me, in Jesus' name, Amen.*

September 19 | Waiting Patiently

Jilly Lyon-Taylor

Wait for the LORD; be strong and take heart and wait for the LORD.

Psalm 27:14

How good are you at waiting? It seems to me that in our society we have become more and more used to instant results – instant coffee, microwave meals, fast travel, and instant credit, and that most of us have lost the art of waiting patiently.

In Exodus chapter 32 we read about the people of Israel who were waiting for Moses to come down from the mountain, where he had gone to meet with God and to receive instructions from Him. He had been gone for forty days and forty nights, and during that time the people became impatient and seemed to forget the amazing miracles that God had worked for them only a short time before in bringing them out of Egypt. In their impatience they demanded that Aaron make them a 'god' to be with them. As they began to worship the golden calf, all restraint went and they began to indulge in all kinds of revelry and debauchery. The consequence of this was death for many of them – all because they couldn't wait.

During the time of waiting, God was giving to Moses very precise instructions about the tabernacle and the pattern for worship and living. This was to be how the people would meet with their God and know His blessing and protection, but by not waiting to receive these instructions they replaced God's plan with their own substitute, and there were dire consequences.

God has a plan for each of our lives. If we fail to wait on Him for specific instructions, and if we substitute our own way of doing things, the consequences can be disastrous. Abraham failed to wait for the fulfilment of God's promise and he put his own solution into effect – resulting in the birth of Ishmael. We are still reaping the consequences of that in our world today!

Are you waiting for the fulfilment of a promise in your life? Don't be tempted to look for the 'quick fix'. Wait patiently for God. Spend time in His presence, listening to Him and receiving His instructions. That's the safest place to be and He will never let you down.

PRAYER: *Father, forgive me for not waiting patiently for You. Please help me to remain in Your presence, listening to You, receiving instruction from You and not acting on my own thoughts and ideas. Amen.*

SEPTEMBER 20 | THE TEMPLE OF THE HOLY SPIRIT

ANGELA WEIR

> *Do you not know that your body is the temple (the very sanctuary) of the Holy Spirit Who lives within you, Whom you have received [as a Gift] from God? You are not your own.*
>
> 1 Corinthians 6:19, AMP

The last few chapters of Exodus give God's detailed instructions to Moses on the making of the artefacts for the tabernacle which the Israelites would build in the wilderness as their place of worship. Everything had to be perfectly constructed and when it was all ready, it was consecrated. At that moment, God came to dwell, or tabernacle, with His people.

Paul tells us that our bodies are now the *'temple of the Holy Spirit'*. We have been *'fearfully and wonderfully made'* (Psalm 139:14), and are cleansed and consecrated by the blood of Jesus to be a holy dwelling place for Him. Our King has come to tabernacle with us and in us. What an amazing privilege!

Jesus tells His disciples to say to those whom they met on their missionary journeys that *'The Kingdom of God has come close to you'* (Luke 10:9, AMP). In a very special way, as we go about our daily lives, we are taking the Kingdom of God with us in our 'temple-bodies' and displaying God to those around us. That's an awesome thought.

In the same way that the Israelites had to make everything perfect for the tabernacle, we need to make ourselves perfect for Him and allow Him to cleanse us to be a fitting place for Him to dwell.

PRAYER: *Father God, I so wish to display Your glory to others through my life. Please cleanse me and make my body a fitting place for You to tabernacle with me that I might be Your light to those around me. In the precious name of Jesus, Amen.*

SEPTEMBER 21 | CHRIST IN US

DAVID SILVESTER

Have this attitude in yourselves which was also in Christ Jesus.
Philippians 2:5, NASB

Paul, writing to the Christian community in Philippi, is urging them to be 'Christ-like' in every way, in body, soul and spirit.

I like the above translation, which can also read, '*Have this attitude among yourselves*'. Paul is trying to emphasise the need for every individual in the Christian community there to develop Christ-likeness.

The Christ-like qualities he is encouraging them to adopt are humility and holiness in every sense of the word, and he gives examples of how Jesus demonstrated this.

Firstly He demonstrated humility and holiness in His human body. Jesus is, and always has been, the Son of the Eternal God, and absolutely equal with the Father and the Holy Spirit. Yet He took on human flesh and became a man among humanity. As a man, He was born as a baby, and was dependent upon His mother to care for and nurture Him. He grew up through childhood and teenage years into adulthood. He then worked as a craftsman until beginning His ministry. In all stages of life He demonstrated those qualities of humility and holiness.

Although we know very little of those years before His ministry, we have the short glimpse of Him as a boy about to become a teenager, when He went with His parents to Jerusalem. His subjection to them demonstrates a humility and holiness we all long to see as our own children are growing up. He knew the principles God had intended for every child in relation to parents.

As He entered His ministry, whether among the crowds of followers, dealing with individuals, or before religious leaders, the two qualities of humility and holiness were always in pre-eminence. Yes, He was prepared to speak the truth, whatever the response to it might be. He never compromised whenever sin needed to be challenged, but His compassion for the sinner was never in question.

We too are challenged to '*Have this attitude in yourselves which was also in Christ Jesus*' (Philippians 2:5, NASB) and to demonstrate the qualities of humility and holiness. It's grievous to God whenever Christians display anything that contradicts these qualities, such as when we display anger, and speak to a brother or sister in Christ with disrespect. We need to be challenged by the Holy Spirit about what effect our attitude is having on the One who suffered all the ignominy and shame of being crucified naked in our place, in order to carry the punishment of a Holy God for our sin.

PRAYER: *Lord Jesus Christ, I'm sorry for those times when I haven't displayed the qualities of humility and holiness, and have grieved You. Please forgive me and put a right spirit in me, I pray. Amen.*

SEPTEMBER 22 | OPTIONAL BUT INVITATIONAL

OTTO BIXLER

> *Call to Me and I will answer you, and I will tell you great and mighty things, which you do not know.*
>
> Jeremiah 33:3, NASB

When we buy a new car we get an owner's manual. The Bible has often been called an owner's manual for life. We might think that if we follow the instructions in the owner's manual we can get God to perform the way we wish. It is quite the other way around. God is our Father by adoption through Christ Jesus (Ephesians 1:5) and as Father, He has behavioural criteria for us. The Bible is a manual for how we should behave if we want our relationship with God to function well. If things aren't as we like them to be in our life, perhaps we've been reading the Bible through a faulty belief system.

For example, Jeremiah 33:3 says, *'Call to Me and I will answer you, and I will tell you great and mighty things, which you do not know.'* Do you see an 'if' written before the word 'call'? It's not there! This is an imperative: a command. It's not an optional extra in your faith walk. It doesn't even say that you are to call out to Him with your problems or wishes. It just says, 'Call to Me.'

Were you thinking that you must only call out to God when you're beyond your abilities and your flesh can't rescue you? How far this is from the truth! He has things that He wants to say to us but often we're not ready to listen. We're so full of the world, our own problems, goals and expectations about life and even about how God should be or how He should treat us. But He's waiting for you to call to Him and say you're ready to listen to Him. Do you love Him? Jesus says that those who love Him obey His commandments.

God wants to talk to you. He waits to share things that are beyond your reach – things that are beyond your intellect, experience, learning or even Scripture reading. There are things that you can't unlock for yourself from the Bible. So, how can you neglect this command and say that you love Him? Do you think that this isn't for you or that He's only there in your time of need – and only if He's not busy solving other problems? Take some time and call unto Him. He's waiting just for you. He wants to talk to you and to bless you.

PRAYER: *Lord, I am calling upon You now. Show me the things You want me to know today. Expand my relationship with You. Forgive me for only calling upon You in times of trouble. I want to talk with You regularly about everything, in Jesus' name, Amen.*

SEPTEMBER 23 | JEALOUSY

GRACE MARSHALL

Let us not become conceited, provoking and envying each other.
Galatians 5:26

I would rather admit to being angry than jealous, would you? It's quite easy to feel jealous, but hard to admit it, because it can feel like an embarrassing fault to have. Perhaps it's easier to call it resentment.

What's at the root of jealousy? I think the basic root is lack. Suppose you are jealous of someone who has a bigger house than you, or a better job or car. You come to Jesus with that pain inside you, confess the jealousy which you feel and ask Him, 'Why do I feel like this?' Perhaps He might show you that you have a deep need to feel that you are someone of value. That's a genuine need, which God Himself longs to meet.

In the same way, perhaps He might show you that your feelings of jealousy over someone else's loving family or happy wedding is rooted in a deep need to feel secure and loved and chosen. We need to acknowledge these longings inside, and that we can't fix them for ourselves. All we can do is come to our loving Father with all our neediness and say 'Help.'

The other root of jealousy can be conceit, as our verse says. If I think that I am better than you, then I may envy you and become harsh in my thoughts or words about you, when I see you being honoured above me. This is sinful and, like all sin, we just have to bring it to the cross for forgiveness and cleansing, which is given freely. Then look for the lack which led to that sin developing. Perhaps it comes from a deep need to find significance, to be somebody. God will show you.

The ultimate truth is this: God Himself loves you. What more can be said about your significance? Or your security and value? Think about it. It says it all, doesn't it?

PRAYER: *Father, I acknowledge that I do feel resentful sometimes, and maybe I should admit that it's jealousy. I'm sorry. Please show me the place of need or emptiness which is at the root of what I'm feeling. I would like to know the depth of love You have for me. Heal me with Your loving acceptance as I open these deep places for Your eyes to see. Through Jesus my Saviour. Amen.*

SEPTEMBER 24 | MAKING A DIFFERENCE

PATRICIA LAKE

> *No-one serving as a soldier gets involved in civilian affairs – he wants to please his commanding officer.*
>
> 2 Timothy 2:4

Recently I watched a TV documentary, enthralled and humbled by the sheer guts and bravery of British NHS volunteer doctors and nurses (members of the Territorial Army) who go each week as Medical Response Teams to war-torn areas of the world. They feel obliged to make a difference, so they leave their families and are commissioned to go on front-line duties to tend to people with horrific injuries. They perform all kinds of operations, ranging from minor surgery to amputations. They don't think of their own rights or comforts, but selflessly think of those who need their help.

Risking all on the front line, they immediately become enemy targets as they enter enemy airspace on their way to their duties. Once there they also discover that life on the front line is full of hidden dangers, for they're not only there as medics. They have to take their turn on front-line duty.

At the request of our Lord and Saviour, Jesus Christ, we are also called and commissioned to leave 'father and mother, brother and sister' to be about our Heavenly Father's business. At the tender age of twelve Jesus was already aware of this when His concerned parents thought they had lost Him in Jerusalem. Like Gideon's men who lapped the water with one hand but were alert with weapons in the other so that they weren't taken by surprise by the enemy, we also find that we need to be on our guard, because we're on the enemy's radar screen.

The above scripture reminds us that as soldiers we are to please our Lord Jesus, our commanding officer, and be focused on the business at hand. We're warned that the enemy is prowling, going about as a roaring lion to devour, but we are not to fear. For dressed in the armour the Lord has given us, and using the weapons of warfare He has provided, while listening to His words directing us, we will prevail. The enemy won't be able to derail us. We're under God's covering and all we have to do is learn to follow His instructions. Let's not be distracted or caught 'off guard' for we will be rewarded if we're courageous and keep going (Revelation 22:12). Although it might not seem like it sometimes, you are making a difference!

PRAYER: *Dear Lord, would You help us to please You by going about our Heavenly Father's business and tending to the needs of the hurting and the broken, whilst being alert to the wiles and tactics of the enemy. Thank You for the victory You've given us in Jesus' name, Amen.*

SEPTEMBER 25 | SECRET AND REVEALED

RICHARD HEMERY

> *The secret things belong to the LORD our God, but those things which are revealed belong to us and to our children forever, that we may do all the words of this law.*
>
> Deuteronomy 29:29, NKJV

This verse speaks of two categories of knowledge: the secret things and the revealed things. The secret things belong to God. The revealed things belong to us, and our children. There are secrets and mysteries that we cannot know now. Proverbs 25:2 says: *'It is the glory of God to conceal a matter; to search out a matter is the glory of kings.'* Yet King David said, *'Such knowledge is too wonderful for me, too lofty for me to attain'* (Psalm 139:6). Jesus displayed the same humility as David in this respect, which it would be good for us to emulate. Jesus said only the Father knew the time when He would return. This is an example of a hidden thing. Jesus didn't know the time, and He was content not to know. He could have asked the Father, but in humility He left that knowledge to Him.

Let's leave the secret things where they belong. The revealed things are all ours – the whole Bible with all its multifaceted wisdom – more than enough for us. But what's the reason for the revelations, given to us and our children? That we may do them, and that we may obey the Word of the Lord. Sometimes we just let God's Word tickle our ears but it doesn't change our hearts. Can we expect more revelation if we don't act on that already given us, and encourage our children to do likewise? In fact, children, and those with child-like hearts, are often better at believing and doing, and God reveals things to them more readily than adults who think they know it all! Jesus once said, *'I praise you, Father, Lord of heaven and earth, because you have hidden these things from the wise and learned, and revealed them to little children'* (Matthew 11:25).

PRAYER: *Dear Lord, we acknowledge that there are secret things too wonderful for us. Thank You for the wealth of revealed things which You've freely given to us and our children. Father, help us to obey them. Amen.*

SEPTEMBER 26 | SEEING THINGS IN THE RIGHT PERSPECTIVE

PAUL WATSON

> *For I envied the arrogant when I saw the prosperity of the wicked.*
>
> Psalm 73:3

The 73rd Psalm has always intrigued me. The writer (Asaph – a worship leader for King David) is very honest as he expresses his feelings. On many occasions I have shared the same thoughts and emotions as this man. I invite you to look at this psalm with me as it is so real and 'earthy' and so – relevant.

The psalm begins with a declaration of truth – *'Surely God is good to Israel, to those who are pure in heart'* (verse 1). Yes, we can easily give mental assent to the truths about God. We have been taught this. However, Asaph then speaks of the reality of his own wavering faith as he looks at those around him who pay no heed to God at all, or perhaps don't even believe in God. He observes that they are rich; they are living life in the fast lane; they seem to have good health and everything is going well for them. The evidence around him makes him ask questions like, 'What's the point of obeying God?' and 'Is it worth the sacrifice of living a holy and righteous life?' To be honest, there are times when I have entertained similar thoughts as those expressed in verse 13: *'Surely in vain have I kept my heart pure; in vain have I washed my hands in innocence.'*

But in verses 16–17 we see a shift in perspective which defines the rest of the psalm: *'When I tried to understand all this, it was oppressive to me till I entered the sanctuary of God; then I understood their final destiny.'* Ah, here is a view from further back. Here is the reality of what comes with knowing God personally: God and man in a loving relationship that continues for eternity. The truth is that we can experience the presence of God and in this we can have assurance that He will never leave us. *'Yet I am always with you; you hold me by my right hand. You guide me with your counsel, and afterwards you will take me into glory'* (verses 23–24). Nothing is better than this!

Those who are apparently living life to the full apart from God will lose it all and be separated from God for ever, unless they turn and believe. We who believe in Christ Jesus have a new perspective on life and eternity. We belong to the Kingdom of our Heavenly Father, and it is better for us to see the world around us from this perspective – a Kingdom perspective.

So Asaph sings in the last verse: *'... it is good to be near God. I have made the Sovereign LORD my refuge; I will tell of all your deeds.'* Now that's living!

PRAYER: *Heavenly Father, I thank You that You are always with me and that You are taking me to glory. Please help me to keep a Kingdom perspective in all things, and not to be led astray by the false allurements of this temporal world, in Jesus' name, Amen.*

September 27 | True Discipleship

PETER HORROBIN

> *To the Jews who had believed in him, Jesus said, 'If you hold to my teaching, you are really my disciples. Then you will know the truth, and the truth will set you free.'*
>
> John 8:31

There's a certain pride in men, and maybe in some women as well, that wants people to believe they can do things, without anyone else telling them how to do it! Commonly, for example, people will set about assembling a piece of equipment without first reading the instructions. Eventually when all their efforts have failed and somehow or other the equipment doesn't look or function like it should, they will dig out the instructions and start again!

Sadly, many believers adopt a similar approach to living the Christian life – they try and work it out for themselves, without reference to the instruction manual. Often, it's only when things seem to be getting really out of order that people begin to think they may have got something wrong. And by the time that happens there could be serious problems in their life.

Many people look to Jesus for the freedom He has promised, thinking that, as believers, such freedom is theirs by right. They can't understand why God isn't answering their prayers! Our scripture for today contains one of the most important keys to the problem. Of course it's true that Jesus wants people to know His freedom and experience His healing. Jesus says as much when He clearly states that *'the truth will set you free'*.

Many people look to Jesus for the freedom He has promised, thinking that, as believers, such freedom is theirs by right. They can't understand why God isn't answering their prayers!

But before that He equally clearly says there's a condition attached to the freedom He promises, and that is *'if you hold to my teaching'*. Or, in other words if you read the instructions and put them into practice in your life! A disciple is not just someone who believes in the truth, but someone who obeys it. And that's the vital point that Jesus is making.

As believers we can expect God to honour the promises in His Word, but only when we fulfil any conditions that are attached to them. In order to fulfil the conditions, we first need to know what they are – or read the instructions! The Bible is God's instruction manual for the human race – if we ignore it our pride will always get us into trouble!

PRAYER: *Thank You, Lord, that You not only want us to know Your freedom, but You loved us enough to teach us what it means to follow and obey You. Forgive me, Lord, for my pride of wanting You to bless me when there are things in my life which are not in line with Your will and purposes, in Jesus' name, Amen.*

September 28 | Surrender

Joan Rono

For we do not have a high priest who is unable to sympathise with our weaknesses, but we have one who has been tempted in every way, just as we are – yet was without sin. Let us then approach the throne of grace with confidence, so that we may receive mercy and find grace to help us in our time of need.

Hebrews 4:15–16

One thing that fascinates me is the courage of those who do sky diving! As I was reading about the different ways that people are trained, I learnt a few lessons. There are those that are beginners and need the help and support of trainers. They depend on those trainers to give them confidence and safety. They don't yet feel confident. They can do it, but with someone near to give them help if they need it. And then there are those that are professional. They can sky dive without any help. They've had enough training and practice and can jump out of the plane and trust the parachute will bring them down safely.

Christians can learn great lessons from the sky divers. Maybe you're a beginner in faith. You hold yourself back, keep things inside, not because you want to, but because you don't know how to surrender. You need someone to come along and give you support so you can feel safe enough to let go! It isn't necessarily the help from people that we need, but the help of the Holy Spirit to bring us into surrender, and to give us the confidence and security we need. We need to invite Him in, and for Him to take His rightful place as a gentle helper. Sky divers who've passed the beginner's course can jump alone, but with a helper nearby, just in case! And that is like the Lord. *'God is our refuge and strength, an ever-present help in trouble'* (Psalm 46:1). I am reminded of the song, 'He's only a prayer away'.

Finally there are those who are experienced and can confidently jump from the aeroplane and enjoy their sky diving! Jesus knows all about us. He knows our weaknesses and He also knows our strengths because He has lived in human form and has undergone the same things we have undergone. In the Bible we're instructed to approach the throne of God with confidence, to receive mercy and grace in times of need. This encourages us to bring our burdens to the Lord and surrender to Him, with the help of the Holy Spirit.

We need to let go and let God. We don't need to be afraid. We can tell the

Lord everything, as we would a trusted friend. He knows all about us and longs for us to come and bring all our burdens to Him.

PRAYER: *Lord, I thank You that You know me and all that I'm carrying on the inside. I pray that, by Your Holy Spirit, You'll help me to surrender it all to You. I lay down everything that I've held on to. Please take control, and give me Your rest and peace. Thank You, Lord, Amen.*

SEPTEMBER 29 | A MISSING KEY?

LINDSEY HANEKOM

> *All Scripture is God-breathed and is useful for teaching, rebuking, correcting and training in righteousness.*
>
> 2 Timothy 3:16

It seems to be one of life's strange phenomena: you find the odd key lying around and you have no idea what lock it is for! It must have a reason for being there; I mean, no one makes a key without a lock for it to work in.

This happened to me a while ago and I was reluctant to throw the seemingly useless key away. So I put it in a safe place in case I ever found a lock without a key. Years down the line I did find the missing lock – it was for my suitcase, which I haven't used the lock on for a long time. Then came into play another of life's phenomena – that mysterious 'safe place' that can never be found again! I hunted high and low, looking in every nook and cranny that I thought likely, possible, unlikely and downright stupid … never to discover the elusive key.

It strikes me that this is how we can be when reading the Bible. We read something, know it is of some significance but can't quite figure out how or why. But this is when we have a choice – do we throw it away from our minds or do we try to store it in a 'safe place' in our hearts in case we discover its significance later in life?

It is very easy to read the Bible and disregard anything that we deem as irrelevant to our lives here and now, but this verse tells us that all Scripture is God-breathed and is useful. As we read the Scriptures, let us not limit our hunger by our human understanding or the immediate application of it.

The truth is, even if we can't seem to find the immediate significance in what we read, it will eventually make sense and may even be important later in our lives. If we know the key is there somewhere, we have a Helper to guide us in our search for it: the Holy Spirit longs to reveal more of the Father through the Word. Let's allow Him to do that so that we can grow and be strong in Him.

PRAYER: *Father God, thank You for Your Word, which is all useful. Help me not to disregard any of what I read but to store it in the depth of my heart. Help me to understand all of Your Word, through the power of Your Holy Spirit, that I may grow strong in You and remain in you forever. Amen.*

SEPTEMBER 30 | SING FOR JOY

PAUL WATSON

Sing and make music in your heart to the Lord.

Ephesians 5:19

On a recent day off, I was on a motorcycle trip to explore some roads in Western Australia, and was enjoying a lunch break at a pie shop. By the tables in the outdoor eating area a man was playing a small harp, and the music was delightful. It really added to the enjoyment of my meal. Later that evening I was particularly thrilled when my daughter began to sing with her little twenty-month-old daughter. They were singing some songs from little Ava's favourite DVD. One song has a line that ends with 'Set them free!', which Ava sings along to in perfect pitch and with a gigantic smile. My heart soars as I hear her sing, 'Set them fwee!' in her cute little voice.

Singing and music are gifts from God that somehow have the ability to touch our human spirit. Music appears throughout the Bible in many contexts – national ceremonies, informal gatherings, to calm an irate king, to lead the army into battle.

Our passage today invites us to sing and make music in our hearts. For many that is a relief – making *'a joyful noise'* (Psalm 100:1, KJV) might better describe the actual sounds that many of us make when we sing! But it's a heart response, not based on virtuosity on a musical instrument or having the voice of an opera singer.

The final part of the verse indicates both the reason for singing and the One whom we are ultimately singing to. The Lord gives us a reason to sing. The Psalms are essentially songs. They contain praise – acknowledging what God is like and what He has done. So, for example, the Psalms invite us to sing of His strength, His great love, and His justice (Psalm 59:16; 89:1; 101:1). Individually, and together, we allow our voices to resonate with our hearts: *'My soul glorifies the Lord and my spirit rejoices in God my Saviour'* (Luke 1:46–47).

Today, let's sing and make music in our hearts to the Lord!

PRAYER: *Father, Your love for me is amazing. You even rejoice over Your people with singing [Zephaniah 3:17]. I want to sing Your praises with all my heart. Amen.*

OCTOBER 1 | OPPORTUNITIES AND CHOICES

PATRICIA LAKE

Yet I have loved Jacob, but Esau I have hated ...

Malachi 1:2–3

There are many opportunities that come to us in life (some of which are life-transforming) which lead us down different roads, according to the decision we make at the time. Of course, most people know when they are choosing between what is good and what is bad, but we sometimes have to weigh between what is good and what is best, so that we are not robbed of God's best.

If we are in the habit of asking the Lord to help us before we decide, we will always choose wisely. The most pivotal opportunity that comes to any of us is the moment when we are faced with choosing Jesus to be our Lord and Saviour, because at that moment we are choosing between life, if we choose Him, and death if we don't.

When Esau chose to despise his birthright, and Jacob chose to take it from him, the course of history was changed for a nation. For when Esau despised his birthright he ultimately despised God, and this cost him dearly, for the birthright was linked to the blessing, which also finally slipped from his grasp. For a plate of lentils, momentarily fulfilling his fleshly desire, Esau exchanged and forfeited God's favour and was not able to reverse the situation even though he sought it *'with a loud and bitter cry'* (Genesis 27:34). Jacob, on the other hand, realised the value of the birthright, and not only grabbed the opportunity to obtain it but, in doing so, subsequently gained the blessing that went with it (although he used deceit to get it). As a consequence in Malachi 1:2–3 we read that the Lord says, *'I have loved Jacob, but Esau I have hated.'* From that time onwards the Lord's favour rested on Jacob for the rest of his life and on his descendants.

We therefore need to give serious thought to the opportunities that come our way in life – some can lead to great gain, others to great losses. Some, as in Esau's case, are irreversible. We need to choose wisely, identifying God's outstretched hand to bless us, while being careful not to take for granted what God has given us. God has entrusted us with the holy riches of heaven, which we need to guard and treat with the utmost respect. Don't let God-given opportunities pass you by!

PRAYER: *Dear Lord, please would You help us to make the right choices in life that are pleasing to You, and help us to have the wisdom to make the most of the opportunities that You give us, in Jesus' name, Amen.*

OCTOBER 2 | REMAINING IN THE PRESENCE OF GOD

JILLY LYON-TAYLOR

> *The LORD would speak to Moses face to face, as one speaks to a friend. Then Moses would return to the camp, but his young aide Joshua son of Nun did not leave the tent.*
>
> Exodus 33:11

The face of Moses was radiant after he had spoken with the Lord (Exodus 34:29) and today's verse speaks further about this special relationship that Moses had with God. God would speak to Moses face to face, as a man speaks with his friend.

Moses would return to the camp after meeting with God, but we're told that Joshua didn't leave the tent. What amazing preparation it was for Joshua, remaining in the presence of the Lord! Later on, Joshua was one of the twelve men sent by Moses to explore the Promised Land (Numbers 13), and while ten of them could only focus on the problems and their own weaknesses, seeing the people there as giants and themselves like grasshoppers, Joshua's response was completely different. Having spent time in the presence of the Lord, he was able to see things from God's perspective and have complete faith that God would do what He promised. God was later able to entrust to him the tremendous responsibility of leading the people into the Promised Land.

Do we remain in the presence of the Lord, or do we pop in and out, hastily asking for help for all that we need? God is longing for us to remain with Him so that He can speak to us face to face. The more we do, the more we will see ourselves as He sees us instead of focusing on our weaknesses and problems, and the more we will see the situations we are up against from His perspective.

Prayer: *Lord, forgive me for the times I have popped quickly in and out of Your presence. I want to learn to remain in Your presence so You can speak to me, and I want to see things as You see them. Please help me to do this, in Jesus' name, Amen.*

October 3 | Unless the Lord Builds the House

Margaret Southey

Unless the LORD builds the house, its builders labour in vain.

Psalm 127:1

When the truth of this scripture dawned on me, I got a shock. It was clear to me that my life could be compared with the house and I could be compared with the labourer. Whatever I did in my life that was not in accordance with God's will for it would be useless. The Oxford dictionary describes 'in vain' as meaning 'to no purpose, with no result, uselessly'.

Understanding this scripture was a turning point in my life because I do not want to spend my life doing things that are to no purpose in God's eyes.

I began examining the motives we have for some of the things that we do. Sometimes it is to please the selfish person within. It may be to please others and gain their favour or acceptance. It could be to build self-esteem by exhibiting our capabilities. We may exhaust our energy serving others, or, perhaps, as a payment to God for some sin or possibly because we see ourselves as indispensable to some people or situations. These are just a few of the motives that spur us on. None of these come from God.

Having spent many years of my life as a doer, I am learning to go slowly before I act, to examine my motives and prayerfully to ask God whether what I am about to do is of Him.

Clearly we are not called to submit every tiny action to God, like, for example, whether we have an apple or an orange for breakfast. God means us to make most routine decisions on our own. There are also times when we submit a decision we have to make to God and He tells us to choose.

What about the times when we have prayed and prayed and still do not know what God is saying? It seems that when we prayerfully and carefully move in the direction that seems right, God redirects us if we are on the wrong track. He honours our having sought his will.

What about the times when we, like the labourer, have acted without God? We have a merciful Father who, when we confess our sins, forgives us and offers us another chance.

PRAYER: *Father, I want to live a life that has a purpose and is fruitful. I can do this only to the extent that I submit to Your will. Help me please, Lord, to seek Your will and way and to be obedient in following it, in Jesus' name, Amen.*

OCTOBER 4 | GOD'S DETAILED PREPARATION

DAVID SILVESTER

> *When you hear them sound a long blast on the trumpets, have the whole army give a loud shout; then the wall of the city will collapse and the army will go up, everyone straight in.*
>
> Joshua 6:5

From Sunday School days, and later, on reading the account of the overthrow of Jericho, my mind pictured the Israelites having to scramble over a huge pile of rubble to enter the city. It had seemed possible that the vibrations of the seven-day stomping of marching troops had so weakened the walls of the city that when the army gave the great shout, those walls simply collapsed in a heap of rubble.

In more recent years, whilst on a guided tour of Israel and being shown where those walls collapsed, that image was transformed. We saw where considerable excavation of a section of the wall had taken place, and a deep trench revealed that the wall had not collapsed as a heap of rubble, but what was exposed was intact: it had simply sunk into the ground! The top of the wall had become level with the ground as it would have been at the time!

God's instruction to Joshua was, '*When you hear [the priests] sound a long blast on the trumpets, have the whole army give a loud shout; then the wall of the city will collapse [i.e. in its place] and the army will go up, everyone straight in.*'

What God had said to Joshua took on a fresh significance as the evidence was there to be examined. This meant that as far as the army was concerned, the defences were down, and they had no difficulty getting in to deal with the city as God had instructed them. It also meant that the house on the wall where Rahab and her family were gathered would be at ground level so the troops could release them without difficulty!

Observing what had been exposed through excavation brought home the truth of how our God carefully puts details in order for His children. This is how He carefully has the details of our lives in order, so long as we are prepared to listen to what He says and obey His instructions.

Joshua and his troops could have gone to endless trouble building siege ramps in order to penetrate the city, and lost many soldiers in the process. But by listening to what God had instructed, and doing what He had said, the whole exercise was made so much easier.

For ourselves, the simple lesson is this: to keep in touch with God so that we hear what He is trying to tell us, then follow those instructions in detail and not do things from our own ideas. It is a matter of putting into practice the words of Proverbs 3:5–6: *'Trust in the LORD with all your heart and lean not on your own understanding; in all your ways acknowledge him, and he will make your paths straight.'*

PRAYER: *Father God, thank You that when I follow the ways of Your instructions, what might appear to be insurmountable obstacles become easy to overcome. Please help me to carefully listen when You instruct me, and then willingly obey You. I ask in Jesus' name. Amen.*

OCTOBER 5 | WALLS AND GATES

DENISE CROSS

Whoever has no rule over his own spirit is like a city broken down, without walls.

Proverbs 25:28, NKJV

In the days when Solomon coined this proverb, cities had protective walls. Everyone understood why. A city needed good walls to keep out the enemy so that the inhabitants could feel safe at night sleeping in their beds! To live in a city without a wall was not secure. A wall-less city was an invitation to anyone who wanted to come in and steal goods, even abusing and violating the citizens who were at their mercy.

Some people seem to have lives that are like a broken-down city.They appear to have no ability to keep out those who would abuse and violate them. They may have had many relationships like that before but they seem unable to recognise the need for a measure of protection for themselves. These wise words from Solomon tell us that it isn't God's intention for anyone to be this vulnerable. It's not wrong to have a wall of protection around our heart but there's something else which is vital to consider.

A city with a good wall can also be a city in trouble. Jerusalem had a good, strong city wall when Zedekiah was the king. The wall was sufficiently strong to protect the people against the enemy forces of Nebuchadnezzar, but there was a problem. The people were locked inside and starving! (2 Kings 25:1–3) The wall was good, but without an ability to open the gates there couldn't be trade to provide the necessary food and supplies. The result was starvation and desperation.

There are people who live their lives behind walls with no gates and people who have no walls. Both are damaging their spirits. No wall leads to possible abuse and no gate leads to probable starvation.

Solomon in his wisdom encourages us to be like a healthy city. Good walls for protection and gates that can be opened to those who are friends bringing the necessary nourishment into our lives. If your walls are broken down perhaps you need to recognise that you're worth protecting. Then you could ask Jesus to help you build a right protection around your human spirit. If your gates are locked shut perhaps you need to ask Jesus to help you to discern who is a trustworthy person to enter the gate to feed your spirit with friendship and love. Challenging, isn't it?

PRAYER: *Lord, I want to have strong walls to protect my life from the inroads of the enemy and to have gates that can be opened to the friends You send. Help me to discern the difference between friend and foe and be strong in You, in Jesus' name, Amen.*

OCTOBER 6 | BROKEN BUT LOVED

PETER HORROBIN

> *The LORD is close to the broken-hearted and saves those who are crushed in spirit.*
>
> Psalm 34:18

I once knew a man who always had eyes for those who were hurting. He would look out for people who were the 'underdogs' of life, people who had little going for them in life and who had few natural advantages. He would come alongside them and make friends.

God had shown him that his mission in life was to be a friend to the people who had no friends, especially young people with their lives before them. The Lord showed him how to be generous to those who had very little of their own resources and to understand that these young people were just as precious to the Lord as the high achievers, who had got it all together and knew where they were going.

God had shown him that his mission in life was to be a friend to the people who had no friends, especially young people with their lives before them.

Many of those young people were rescued from a life of rejection and inner pain, by a man who believed in them and simply loved them into life. Where did he get such love from?

There is only one possible source – the God who inspired the psalmist to write the words of our text was also at the centre of this man's life. Jesus may not at this time be walking this earth physically, but He is in and through the lives of those who truly love Him. For if we really do love the Lord, then we will also really love those who, for whatever reason, are disadvantaged. Annie Flint's poem sums this up so well:

Christ has no hands but our hands to do His work today
He has no feet but our feet to lead men in the way
He has no tongue but our tongue to tell men how He died
He has no help but our help to bring them to His side.

When you read passages in the Word of God about God being close to the broken-hearted you can certainly rejoice. But don't forget that God may be asking you to be God with flesh on and show the world what God is really like!

PRAYER: *Thank You, Lord, that You care about every single human being, and that all are equally precious to You. Forgive me for not being 'God with skin on' for some of the people I've met. Open my eyes to see people with Your eyes and Your understanding and respond to them with Your love, in Jesus' name, Amen.*

October 7 | How to Enter the Kingdom of God

Liz Griffin

I tell you the truth, anyone who will not receive the kingdom of God like a little child will never enter it.

Mark 10:15

Jesus taught His disciples many things and then they wrote them down for all of us. Sometimes they learnt by making mistakes. They thought they knew what was right and wrong, when they told the people off for daring to bring their children to Jesus, so He could touch them. Think how humble they were to let everyone know about their mistakes!

What the disciples wanted to do reminds me of how children were treated in England, in the upper classes, about a hundred years ago. They were to be 'seen and not heard'. The rejection and lack of bonding that those children felt resulted in a lot of heartbreak. Jesus had to correct the disciples and point out that children were welcome in God's Kingdom.

But it's the next thing He said which really impacts me. *'I tell you the truth, anyone who will not receive the kingdom of God like a little child will never enter it'* (Mark 10:15). It's a lesson for all adults. We are to receive the Kingdom of God like a little child. We can only receive it that way.

Children are not, by any means, perfectly holy but they are open spiritually. They can respond to God the Father without barriers of pride, fear and scepticism. They like to have fun and can enter into joy and excitement in a way that adults often miss out on. Spontaneity and disarming honesty are qualities of childhood which seem to be lost during the process of growing up for many people.

As little children we naturally trust and don't question authority figures. For most of us that comes later, but sadly even little children can be abused and learn not to trust. I believe that if we are to enter fully into our Heavenly Father's Kingdom we must decide to completely trust Him. It means believing His promises, that He loves us and that He will never let us down. It means we feel secure in that love.

Prayer: *Dear Heavenly Father, help us to really trust in You as small children trust in their daddy. Help us to enter joyfully into a full relationship with You, in Jesus' name, Amen.*

October 8 | Commanded to Celebrate!

Linda Fode

And you shall eat before the LORD your God, in the place where He chooses to make His name abide, the tithe of your grain and your new wine and your oil, of the firstborn of your herds and your flocks, that you may learn to fear the LORD your God always. But if the journey is too long for you, so that you are not able to carry the tithe, or if the place where the LORD your God chooses to put His name is too far from you, when the LORD your God has blessed you, then you shall exchange it for money, take the money in your hand, and go to the place which the LORD your God chooses. And you shall spend that money for whatever your heart desires: for oxen or sheep, for wine or similar drink, for whatever your heart desires; you shall eat there before the LORD your God, and you shall rejoice, you and your household.

Deuteronomy 14:23–26, NKJV

In Canada, on the second Monday in October, we celebrate a holiday called 'Thanksgiving Day'. Next to Christmas it's the most important holiday of the year. In Western Canada it's the least commercial, most spiritual holiday of the year. The crops are in, the land at rest, colours vivid, yet winter is only weeks away. It's about family; about feasting; about 'remembering'. We often travel long distances to gather for this day. For generations in our family it has truly been a 'holy day'.

Holy days celebrated with family and feasting were so important to the Father that He commanded them in Deuteronomy 12, 14 and 26. For two out of every three years He commanded that the tithe be spent on whatever their hearts desired and be enjoyed with their household.

Why? So we would learn to fear the Lord. This is an awareness of the goodness of God; His longing to bless us; to remember His presence with us and provision for us.

Often we see the commands of God as restrictive; maybe even as principles to avoid punishment or to appease Him. Perhaps we grew up with the rule 'Don't make Dad mad!' and holidays were often times of high stress, fear and tension. We may have transferred that fear to our beliefs about Father God. We miss the joy of relationship with Him and He misses the joy of watching us celebrate life.

Prayer: *Father, for one meal today, may I eat whatever my heart desires; may I eat with a friend, a family member or even a stranger and be thankful for all God provides and blesses me with. With great joy and freedom today, Father, I choose to celebrate and remember with a thankful heart. Amen.*

October 9 | The Choice of Faith

Margaret Silvester

> *By faith Moses, when he had grown up, refused to be known as the son of Pharaoh's daughter. He chose to be ill-treated along with the people of God rather than to enjoy the pleasures of sin for a short time.*
>
> Hebrews 11:24–25

It's tempting to blame the past for what we are today. Moses is a great example of someone who made right choices by faith, despite his past, and was mightily used by God.

He didn't have a brilliant beginning. Pharaoh had ordered the execution of all baby boys and Moses' life was in danger. His parents hid him, but, because they trusted God, they weren't afraid. They took the risk of faith, rather than fear the consequences of their action. Moses experienced trauma in childhood and was brought up in a family and culture other than his own. On more than one occasion he was the victim of circumstances, but he didn't let this keep him from fulfilling the purposes of God in his life. Many people have had troubled beginnings. The lesson we learn from Moses is that it's not so much what happens to us that determines our future, but how we deal with our past.

As an adult, Moses made a life-changing decision. He chose to identify himself with God's people and forfeit his rights as the son of Pharaoh's daughter. This meant hardship and disgrace, danger and discouragement, desert wanderings and despair. But by faith he followed God's call on his life and went God's way. Our choices are determined by faith. The choice of faith might mean sacrifice. It's only by faith that we can choose to go for the things that please God rather than pleasing ourselves. Like Moses we're called to suffer for the purposes of God rather than live for pleasure.

God seems to delight in using weak people. As the greatest leader of all time Moses led God's people out of Egypt across the Red Sea. We're told that when he left Egypt he didn't fear the king's anger. His faith overcame fear. He was looking ahead. His eyes were fixed on the reward to come. His life was rooted in the purposes of the God who had called him and who would be faithful to the end of the journey.

The God of history is our God. The one who worked miracles for Moses is just the same today. He's the God of the impossible and He asks us to trust in Him. He's faithful to His word. His power is immense. However small our faith may be, if it's in Him, it's always sufficient, because God's strength is made perfect in weak people.

PRAYER: *Heavenly Father, thank You that You are unchanging and true. Thank You that You give me the strength to do whatever You ask of me as I trust in You. Thank You that I'm not a victim of my past, but I'm Your child with a purpose in life that no one else can fulfil. Amen.*

OCTOBER 10 | MAGNIFYING THE LORD

JILLY LYON-TAYLOR

> *Oh, magnify the LORD with me, and let us exalt His name together.*
>
> Psalm 34:2, NKJV

Our garden overlooks a small lake and I love to watch the wildlife that is attracted to it. One day I had the joy of seeing a kingfisher flash past and alight on the branch of a weeping willow that overhangs the water. As I watched, I could just see a blurred shape and the brilliant turquoise and orange of its plumage. I quickly went indoors to fetch my binoculars and found then that I could not only see the colours but I could also make out the texture and shape of each individual feather; I could see the pointed beak which is so wonderfully designed for fishing, and I could even see its beady eye watching for movement in the water beneath. The kingfisher hadn't changed, but my view of it had been totally transformed by the magnification of the binoculars.

In the same way, praise and worship transforms our view of God. When the psalmist encourages us to 'magnify the Lord', it is not that we can alter God in any way or make Him greater than He is, but it is our perception of Him that needs to change. Just as my view of the kingfisher was magnified by the binoculars, so praise and worship has the effect of magnifying God in our minds and our understanding. It enables us to know Him better and to see aspects of His splendour and majesty that we were not able to grasp before. It also has the effect of taking our minds off ourselves and focusing on His greatness. As we do this, our own problems pale into insignificance.

PRAYER: *Thank You, Lord, that the closer we get to You, the more we can appreciate the wonder of who You are and Your love for each one of us. Help me to worship You in all things as I take in the wonders of Your creation. In Jesus' name I pray, Amen.*

OCTOBER 11 | ENCOURAGE ONE ANOTHER

ANGELA WEIR

Therefore encourage (admonish, exhort) one another and edify (strengthen and build up) one another, just as you are doing.

1 Thessalonians 5:11, AMP

In his letter to the Thessalonian believers, Paul exhorts them to encourage one another. He understands that we all need words of affirmation, such as 'Well done. You're doing a good job.'

I was on a training course during which the teacher asked each of us to turn to the person next to us and say something to encourage them. The man sitting next to me said something so beautiful that I was almost overwhelmed and didn't know what to say. What he had said truly fed my spirit. When I think about it now it still gives me a warm glow.

But I'm aware that Christians sometimes feel discouraged. They feel that their efforts to help and serve in various ways aren't even being noticed. They don't do what they do just to receive thanks from someone, but they would be mightily strengthened by an encouraging word or a 'thank you'.

Just imagine the difference it would make in our church fellowships if everyone made determined efforts to encourage one other. Perhaps we could send a note to someone, or give them a phone call, or just make a point of saying 'thank you'. By doing so we would help to affirm others and build up their human spirit.

PRAYER: *Heavenly Father, I pray that You will strengthen in me a 'ministry of encouragement' that I may always be ready with the right word or action to build up my fellow Christians. Amen.*

OCTOBER 12 | HIS WAY IS IN THE WHIRLWIND

FIONA HORROBIN

His way is in whirlwind and storm, and the clouds are the dust of his feet … The LORD is good, a stronghold on a day of trouble; he protects those who take refuge in him, even in a rushing flood.

Nahum 1:3b, 7, NRSV

Our temptation, when we experience a storm or a flood in life, is to quake! Life brings with it many such events and as Christians we are not exempt from rough seas. We experience them in our relationships, our health, our workplace, our churches and in our communities, as well as in today's world situation.

God is shaking the nations today. What was once solid and safe ground is increasingly showing the signs of strain and meltdown. Man's ability to fix it is running out and we are left to watch as those who are in power endeavour, in man's way, to steer something which is in God's hands.

What do we do and how do we react when the whirlwind and the storm rises up? The safest place in any storm is in the 'eye' – the place in the centre where peace reigns. This is the place of refuge that the Lord offers to us for protection. He is the 'stronghold on a day of trouble'.

In the midst of all that is going on around us in the world, and all that may be raging around you personally, may we find the place in the centre for our refuge. God's way is in the whirlwind and the storm! He is on the throne. He is in control and, more than this, He is on the move and fulfilling His purposes.

Even in a rushing flood, He protects us and will be our stronghold. His strong arm moves upon us and holds us safe. The challenge for us is not to fight and wriggle but to stay still in this place of trust and safety. It is not a passive place but a place of courage and boldness in the storm, which is victorious over it.

PRAYER: *Lord Jesus, I take up my position with You in the storms of life and in these days of Your shaking. I join with my brothers and sisters in Christ in holding on to You and watching You have Your way in the nations. Amen.*

OCTOBER 13 | MARTIN KNAPP

WHOSE LOAD ARE YOU CARRYING?

Take my yoke upon you and learn from me, for I am gentle and humble in heart, and you will find rest for your souls. For my yoke is easy and my burden is light.

Matthew 11:29–30

While we were in Canada in 2007 I believe the Lord gave me a picture of a 'typical' Canadian pick-up truck. This truck was packed high with boxes with no room for any more. The Lord spoke to the driver and said, 'I want you to pick up a box for me.' The driver remonstrated with the Lord and said, 'Lord, you can see that my truck is already full and there's no room.' The Lord gently replied, 'How many of those boxes have I asked you to carry? If you unload those I have not asked you to carry, you will have plenty of room for the box I want you to pick up.' Are you carrying 'boxes' that the Lord has not asked you to carry?

When we read that Jesus said, *'For my yoke is easy and my burden is light'* (Matthew 11:30), is this what He was talking about? A yoke is easy when it fits the animal for which it was designed well, is comfortable and does not rub or chafe. Jesus can say that His yoke for us is easy because He has made it to fit us.

If you unload those boxes I [Jesus] have not asked you to carry, you will have plenty of room for the box I want you to pick up.

Sometimes we can be burdened with 'boxes' that we have put on ourselves, or that other people have put on us. Jesus has given us His yoke to carry the load that He wants for us, so that we can be walking in what God is calling us to do.

PRAYER: *Lord, help me to lay down anything You are not calling me to do so I can be more available to do what You are calling me to do. Please give me wisdom and discernment to do this, knowing that Your yoke is easy and Your burden light, Amen.*

October 14 | Everything We Need

Jilly Lyon-Taylor

His divine power has given us everything we need for life and godliness through our knowledge of him who called us by his own glory and goodness.

2 Peter 1:3

I remember God highlighting this verse to me years ago when our three children were small and I was busily trying to meet the demands of babies, toddlers and young children, as well as a hard-working husband who was not around to help with bedtimes! What the Lord showed me then was that we already have everything we need in Him, not just for the so-called spiritual aspects of our lives, but also for the nitty-gritty of life, which for me at that stage involved nappies, washing, and housework. God was as much with me in those as He was in the seemingly 'holy' things of life, and in Him I had everything I needed to equip me and enrich me in it all.

> It's not knowledge *about* Him that counts; it's our knowledge *of* Him, through relationship with Him.

His divine power is promised here *'through our knowledge of him'*. It's not knowledge *about* Him that counts; it's our knowledge *of* Him, through relationship with Him. It means knowing Him, communicating with Him, and allowing Him into every aspect of our lives. Then we will have all we need for whatever is going on in our lives, and for godliness through it all.

I wonder what is going on in your life today. Maybe it seems very ordinary and mundane. Maybe there are things you're struggling with – in marriage or family, at work, in relationships, in church or ministry, or in your finances. Be assured that His divine power has given you everything you need. You just need to reach out to Him.

Prayer: *Lord, You know everything about my life and the struggles I'm going through today. Thank You that in You I have everything I need. I'm looking to You today and reaching out for Your divine power to help me now. In Jesus' name I pray, Amen.*

October 15 | God's Remedy for Stress and Burnout

Liz Griffin

Remember the Sabbath day by keeping it holy. Six days you shall labour and do all your work, but the seventh day is a Sabbath to the LORD your God. On it you shall not do any work, neither you, nor your son or daughter, nor your manservant or maidservant, nor your animals, nor the alien within your gates. For in six days the LORD made the heavens and the earth, the sea, and all that is in them, but he rested on the seventh day. Therefore the LORD blessed the Sabbath day and made it holy.

Exodus 20:8

Do you know Christians who suffer from stress and burnout? Maybe you are one. Many have feelings of guilt when they relax; always thinking they haven't done enough for God. I once did a study on God's fourth commandment with some Christian leaders.

Some of them shared that they had a reaction in their mind against the harsh restrictions they had to endure in childhood on Sunday. They believed that now, as mature believers, they were free to do anything they liked on Sunday, because in Jesus we are free from the Law. They went to church in the morning, but the rest of the day was an opportunity to catch up with work and household chores – not very different from the rest of the week – especially in these days of laptops.

When we looked more deeply into God's Word, a very different picture emerged. The Sabbath was God's idea for us – a means of refreshing ourselves, of play and enjoyment. Jesus said, '*The Sabbath was made for man, not man for the Sabbath*' (Mark 2:27). The Sabbath is a day of rest. The Sabbath is God's gracious provision for us.'

The 'one day in seven' pattern was established for the whole of Jewish society including foreigners, slaves and livestock. To this day businesses and shops are shut on the Sabbath day in Israel. The Jewish tradition of Sabbath puts an emphasis on celebration, with beautiful table decorations, candles, special food, and the best tableware. It is a 'holy holiday', and a quality family time.

Dale and Juanita Ryan wrote in *Rooted in God's Love*, 'It will take some creativity and discipline for us to find ways of keeping the Sabbath that work for us. But that's what God wants. God wants the Sabbath to be "for" us.'

Prayer: *Help me, Lord, to use the provision of a Sabbath rest to be restored in You, that I may not be burnt out by ignoring the provision You have made for us, in Jesus' name. Amen.*

October 16 | Fashioning Idols

Paul Watson

> *He feeds on ashes, a deluded heart misleads him; he cannot save himself, or say, 'Is not this thing in my right hand a lie?'*
>
> Isaiah 44:20

It is surprising how easy we find it to fashion for ourselves something that we trust, perhaps subconsciously, to give our lives meaning or purpose. Sadly, in reality, it's a lie. In this passage in chapter 44, Isaiah, as a mouthpiece for God, is referring to a carved idol or 'god' that is constructed from the same log that is also used to make a fire to cook over. He is pointing to the obvious stupidity of worshipping and praying to something that they have made out of a block of wood – the same block that is also used just as fuel to keep a fire going!

But this word applies to anything in our lives that we allow ourselves to 'idolise'. Perhaps subtly we end up elevating something or even someone to a place which effectively sits above our Heavenly Father in our lives. Is my busyness and long hours doing God's work an idol? Does this good work become my defining objective? Maybe it is my family – my role as a father or mother – which gives my life its value and purpose. Perhaps we make an idol of the pursuit of health and fitness – or the gathering of wealth to give us security.

But hope, purpose and security can never be found in the things we construct for ourselves. As declared in Isaiah 44:6, *'This is what the LORD says – Israel's King and Redeemer, the LORD Almighty: I am the first and I am the last; apart from me there is no God.'*

Prayer: *Father God, would You please reveal to me anything in my life which I may have elevated to be like an idol or a 'god'. Help me to remove false idols and live in such a way that You alone are God in my life. Only then will I experience true hope, purpose and security. Amen.*

October 17 | Paper Crowns

Cath Taylor

'Let not a wise man boast of his wisdom, and let not the mighty man boast of his might, let not a rich man boast of his riches; but let him who boasts boast of this, that he understands and knows Me, that I am the LORD who exercises lovingkindness, justice and righteousness on earth; for I delight in these things,' declares the LORD.

Jeremiah 9:23–24, NASB

You may not be shocked to discover that the local Salad & Sushi Bar wouldn't be my kids' favourite place to eat! No, they prefer the more 'royal' option: Burger King! First, there's the complimentary toy which always causes the greatest enthusiasm. Secondly, there's the staple 'kid friendly' menu of chicken nuggets, fries and soda. Lastly, to seal it all off, there's the free cardboard gold crown you can wear as you eat your meal!

My kids love nothing more than wearing their crowns. They take turns issuing decrees and commands, and generally revelling in their newly self-appointed position of splendour as they boss each other around.

On returning home and emptying the car of the empty bags and now-discarded paper crowns, I was reminded of how similar these fake crowns are to the ones we can wear on our own heads as Christians.

How easy it is for us to boast in our own cleverness and works. We can so easily wear crowns (appointed by ourselves) that reflect our service to the Lord, or our faith, or even our humility! Revelling in our own self-appointed splendour, we build ourselves paper thrones on which to sit. Before long we begin to pass cheap judgement and criticism on the lives of the people around us.

I would encourage you today to look at your own heart and ask God to show you any paper crowns you may be wearing. Lay them down at His cross and ask Him to destroy the cheap thrones where you've sat and passed judgement on others.

As we lay down the crowns bought with our own achievements and good deeds, and turn our eyes instead to the One who deserves all glory and praise – only then can we wear the true crown of splendour that He designed. This crown boasts only of who He is!

Prayer: *Lord Jesus, I'm sorry for the pride and arrogance there has been in my heart. Lord, I'm sorry for the cheap judgements I have made about other people, when only You see the true heart of all men. Help me to take my eyes off myself and instead keep them on You. To You be all the glory and all the praise in my life. In Jesus' name I pray, Amen.*

October 18 | Beyond Comprehension!

Peter Horrobin

> *For as high as the heavens are above the earth, so great is his love for those who fear him; as far as the east is from the west, so far has he removed our transgressions from us.*
>
> Psalm 103:11–12

I don't think the psalmist could have had any idea of the significance of what he was writing in these amazing words. All he could see was the stars in the sky, without having any idea how far away they were. More significantly he would have had no understanding of the fact that there's no limit to space beyond the stars. Without realising it he was saying that there's no limit to the love of God!

The north pole and the south pole are specific points on the surface of the earth. The distance between them is measurable. But we don't have an east and a west pole! The distance between east and west is never able to be measured. It's infinite. What an incredible picture of what God, in His love and mercy, has done for us – He has removed our sins an immeasurable and infinite distance from us!

There is no limit to the love of God and no way for forgiven sins ever to catch up with us. God has dealt with them for all of time and all of eternity. I just love the gospel message that is so dramatically illustrated by God's creation.

Next time you look at the stars or fly round the world in a plane – just take a few minutes to marvel at our amazing God. He's out of this world!

Prayer: *Thank You, Lord, for all that You have done for me – for showing me such love and for dealing with my sin so comprehensively. You are amazing! In Jesus' name I pray, Amen.*

October 19 | Unquenchable Thirst

Margaret Silvester

As the deer pants for streams of water, so my soul pants for you, O God. My soul thirsts for God, for the living God. Where can I go and meet with God?

Psalm 42:1–2

The deer's life depended on water, especially when pursued by hunters. In the frantic chase, the desperate deer panted and looked for refreshing water to quench its thirst. In his effort to escape the enemy chasing him, the psalmist felt distant from God. His longing for God's presence was deep. It was a thirst nothing else could satisfy.

The psalmist is in exile. He looks back to better days when he could go to the temple and meet with God, and join in the procession of God's people. In his present circumstances he is unable to seek intimacy with God in the places where he had done so in the past. He is downcast, sad and oppressed by his enemy.

One of Satan's favourite tactics is to oppress God's people and rob them of their joy. He wants to do this so that he can steal from the believer their God-given capacity to be a light shining in a dark world. Oppression and sadness are companions, the opposite of freedom and joy.

The first way of dealing with enemy oppression is to put our hope in God and let Him turn any tendency to give in to despair or defeat into longing for Himself. The second way of dealing with enemy oppression is to rise up, stand against the enemy and, in the name of Jesus, to declare that we refuse to be under his oppression any longer.

The psalmist longed for a familiar place to meet with God. Today, just where you are, He is close beside you, ready to satisfy the deepest longings of your heart.

Prayer: *Thank You, Father, for the way into Your presence through the Lord Jesus. Please increase within me a longing for You, and give me grace to stand today against the oppression of the enemy, in Jesus' name. Amen.*

October 20 | I Wish I'd Taken Notes!

Andy Taylor

But the Counsellor, the Holy Spirit, whom the Father will send in my name, will teach you all things and will remind you of everything I have said to you.

John 14:26

Have you ever had the experience of being alongside someone in a supporting role, but then finding out that the buck now stops with you? That's normally the moment where you wish you'd taken detailed notes on what the other person did.

Imagine how the disciples felt. They had the incredible adventure of walking with Jesus for three years and seeing him perform one amazing miracle after another. Then the bomb drops and they realise that Jesus is going back to heaven, leaving them in charge. Can you imagine the scene of panic as they all look at each other hoping that someone in the group took good notes of all that Jesus said! I imagine all eyes on Doctor Luke.

What comfort Jesus' words must have been in John 14 where it says that the fullness of God would come to them through the Holy Spirit who would not only teach them all things, but would even remind them of everything Jesus had said to them.

It's easy for us to feel jealous of the disciples because they got to live, walk and listen to Jesus for three years but the fact is that the very same Holy Spirit that reminded them of all the things Jesus told them is living within you.

Don't worry about how great your memory is. Don't get stressed if you don't remember every helpful piece of advice or great point from a sermon. Be comforted by the fact that the Holy Spirit of God is living within you and is wanting to converse with you in the same way that Jesus did with His disciples on a day-by-day, minute-by-minute basis.

Prayer: *Thank You, Lord, for the gift of Your Holy Spirit. Help me to trust that He will remind me of the things that are important, as I learn to listen to His voice in my daily walk with You, in Jesus' name, Amen.*

October 21 | The Search for a Painkiller

David Cross

He will wipe away all tears from their eyes. There will be no more death, no more grief or crying or pain. The old things have disappeared.

Revelation 21:4, GNB

I was recently sharing in the teaching of an Ellel Ministries course on the issue of finding freedom from addictions. While preparing for the weekend I sensed the Lord say that mankind has always looked for a painkiller. During the weekend course we were looking at all kinds of wrong dependencies from pornography to heroin. In fact heroin comes from opium, a substance which has probably been used for thousands of years as an analgesic, a painkiller.

Pain is the consequence of a wound in the body. It can come from physical, emotional and spiritual disorder. The main cause of wounding in the life of man is sin, whether done by us or to us. Without God we desperately try to deal with the pain, to kill it or to dull it, by any means at our disposal, including a dependence on substances or behaviours which we believe will help us to cope. More often than not they leave us feeling a little worse than we did at the start, once the immediate effects have worn off. Unfortunately, many of our own coping mechanisms can be costly, sinful and even illegal.

Prescribed medication from the doctor can manage pain for a while, and we thank God for this relief, but there is only one painkiller that gets to the heart of man's problem and brings a permanent, indeed eternal, solution. In the same chapter of Revelation containing today's verse we find one of the names of this powerful painkiller: the Alpha and Omega. Jesus offers a solution available now and effective from start to finish. Submitting our lives to Him and letting Him treat the place of wounding can bring life-changing comfort today, together with the certain promise of a complete remedy when this earth has passed away. What an offer!

Prayer: *Father God, thank You that You see our pain and that You have a perfect solution. Amen.*

October 22 | Challenging Words

David Silvester

The man who says, 'I know him,' but does not do what he commands is a liar, and the truth is not in him.

1 John 2:4

I can say that I'm a Christian, but living the life of a true Christian isn't always so easy. The epistles of John present some of the most challenging and searching statements in the whole of Scripture. In today's verse John is careful to show that receiving God's gift of salvation is one thing, but living out that gift is another. We may know about what God's done for us through the sacrifice of Jesus, but do we know God in the intimate way He desires, the way that will affect our daily living?

As we develop and grow in our faith we're constantly challenged to know what it is God's asking of us. As we spend time reading through the Bible we discover how our lives can become purified. As the psalmist says: *'How can a young man keep his way pure? By living according to your word'* (Psalm 119:9).

Living the life of a Christian is not just a matter of rejoicing in the knowledge of our salvation. It's knowing and doing the kind of things Jesus demonstrated; things like loving our enemy, feeding the hungry, giving to the poor, caring for the stranger, healing the sick and driving out demons. Jesus empowers us to do all these things by His Holy Spirit.

Jesus said, *'Blessed are those who hunger and thirst for righteousness, for they will be filled'* (Matthew 5:6). John Stott explained this means we long for 'a right relationship with God on the one hand and a moral righteousness of character and conduct on the other'. That kind of 'righteousness' will satisfy us completely, and will bear the kind of fruit Jesus is looking for in our lives.

Prayer: *Father God, I thank You for the challenges of Your Word. As I read these challenges, and Your Holy Spirit uses them to disturb me, please help me to respond with the kind of humility and dedication that Jesus demonstrated. In the name of Jesus I pray, Amen.*

October 23 | The Importance of Touch

Jeanne Tate

Filled with compassion, Jesus reached out his hand and touched the man.

Mark 1:41

Jesus touched the man who had leprosy because of His compassion. His loving touch brought physical healing and probably much more than that.

At teachers' training college I learnt about the importance of touch in the development of children. A psychological study was done on a baby who was left in her cot and never touched or nurtured in any way. The effect was devastating! Her development was completely stunted.

I have recently returned to teaching as a substitute teacher and have found a dire need in the children for touch. I have seen my hugs, kind words and smiles change the girls I have taught. I have seen sad, surly teenagers begin to smile and laugh again. Yet I'm told that in some countries teachers are allowed no physical contact with their pupils and are even prosecuted for touching them.

Glynnis Whitwer wrote: *'In this world of virtual relationships, conversations managed via electronic devices and fear of inappropriate touch, I wonder if we are losing our physical connections to each other and yet God designed us to need touch. In fact, it is critical to our health – both emotional and physical. Babies need touch for their brains to develop and children need touch for their emotions to develop. I am challenged to bring healthy touch into my relationships in greater measure. Whether it's a hug, pat on the head, stroke on the arm, or a holy kiss, touch is needed in our society* (online devotion, 'The Touch of Your Hand').

The apostle Peter wrote these instructions a long time ago in the Bible: *'Greet one another with a kiss of love'* (1 Peter 5:14).

Prayer: *Dear Lord, be with each one of us and those with whom we have contact. Let them feel Your wonderful Holy Love flow through us. I pray this in Jesus' name, Amen.*

October 24 | The Shepherd's Crook

Angela Weir

Your rod [to protect] and Your staff [to guide], they comfort me.

Psalm 23:4b, AMP

Shepherds' crooks are not seen so often these days, though one friend always found a place for his on his quad bike in case he needed it to catch one of his sheep. In snowy weather they are used to probe the deep snow drifts as the shepherds search to find buried sheep.

The rod, or crook, was used to part and search the fleece to check for any parasites or damage to the sheep so that 'going under the rod' means it's inspection time. It can be painful sometimes as the Lord searches us and exposes the 'sickness' inside us that doesn't please Him – bad habits and thoughts, for example. We can trust our Good Shepherd even through these difficult times as we know that He's moving in us to make us more like Him.

In the Bayeux Tapestry one of the soldiers is depicted with another giving him a prod in the rear with his staff and this is described as 'being comforted', in other words being given a nudge to spur him into action! Perhaps today there is someone who has felt the call of the Lord but just needs that extra nudge to spur him or her into action.

Prayer: *Heavenly Father, thank You for Your gentle searching and probing. I want to be a clean vessel for You. Please help me to be alert and ready to respond to the promptings You give me. In Jesus' name I ask it, Amen.*

October 25 | My Yoke is Easy

Richard Hemery

For my yoke is easy and my burden is light.

Matthew 11:30

God's first specific command not to do something was not exactly onerous. In Genesis 2:16–17 we read: *'And the LORD God commanded the man, "You are free to eat from any tree in the garden; but you must not eat from the tree of the knowledge of good and evil, for when you eat of it you will surely die."'*

It was not even as tough as fasting. They could eat as much as they wanted from every tree, apart from one.

God is the same today (and yesterday, and tomorrow). He does not burden us with a heavy load. *'For my yoke is easy and my burden is light'* (Matthew 11:30). Rather, we are good at burdening ourselves. We read someone's testimony and imagine we have to measure up to him or her. And we try and put the weight God designed for someone else on our own shoulders. We forget everyone's calling is individual. Peter can't be Paul, nor Paul, Peter. We forget it was a step-by-step process for both Paul and Peter to reach the place in the Kingdom they did.

The yoke that is easy for us, custom-made by an expert carpenter for our shoulders, would cripple someone else, and vice versa. And unless you are one of those rare human beings born with four shoulders, you can only wear one yoke at a time. If you are trying to take up two, your own and someone else's, I suggest you drop the other one! And if your shoulders are chaffed raw from the wrong yoke, swap it for the easy yoke of Jesus.

PRAYER: *Lord, forgive me for burdening myself, or letting someone else give me a heavy yoke. I thank You, Lord, that Your yoke is easy and Your burden is light. I gladly take it up. Please help me to drop the others. Amen.*

OCTOBER 26 | LET GO, AND LET GOD DO IT FOR YOU!

DAVID SILVESTER

Commit your way to the LORD; trust in him, and he will act.

Psalm 37:5, RSV

As Margaret and I have been growing older our children have become concerned that we live too far away from any of them. They have repeatedly encouraged us to make a move before one of us is left on our own.

We have made it a matter of prayer, asking that the Lord would guide us into His will for us. Taking the words of Psalm 37:5, *'Commit your way to the LORD; trust in him, and he will act'*, and putting them into practice has not only brought peace of heart, but we have seen God do things in an exceptional way on our behalf.

As we explored the way ahead in relation to selling our house, the local agent said it could take up to twelve months to find a buyer because of the depression in the current housing sales market. Yet within four days there was the first interested purchaser viewing our property and making an offer. In a matter of three weeks there were four couples vying for it, and the agent had to give them a specific date and time for their final offer in writing to be on his desk!

When we are prepared to commit our way to the Lord, and trust Him in relation to the everyday matters of life, we can step back and let Him act. But how often do we try to do it our way and miss the best? If we really do believe that God loves us and cares for us with an interest in every detail of our lives, why is it that we find it difficult at times to *'be still before the LORD, and wait patiently for him'* (Psalm 37:7, RSV)? Peter exhorts us to *'cast all your anxieties [cares and concerns] on him because he cares for you'* (1 Peter 5:7, RSV). There are enough stressful situations in life to concern us, without us needing to try to carry them alone. God wants us to let Him be the burden bearer and give us peace in such situations.

PRAYER: *O Lord God, thank You that You care so much about the pressures and problems of life that I am concerned with and You want to carry them for me. Please help me to let go, and let You do the carrying. Thank You that there are so many encouragements in Your Word that tell me to do this, and thank You for the peace You give when I let go and hand the situation over to You. Amen.*

OCTOBER 27 | THE MISTS WILL CLEAR

JOHN BERRY

> *Now we see but a poor reflection as in a mirror; then we shall see face to face.*
>
> 1 Corinthians 13:12

John Keats wrote a poem about 'autumn, season of mists and mellow fruitfulness', and recently on a church visit to a 'quintessential English village' I encountered such a time. Driving to the venue in the morning, we encountered thick mist with very low visibility but by mid-morning the sun was shining warmly and the autumn colours of the trees were fully revealed. Of course they had been there all the time; we just couldn't see them!

I was reminded of Paul's comment in 1 Corinthians 13:12, that although now our vision of God is but a poor reflection, eventually we shall have the full revelation of that glory. To use a word common amongst our Young People's Team – that will be *awesome*!

How hard it is for us in this life to keep a clear vision of the Lord! We live more and more by what we experience and can actually see. Yet we are called to walk by faith, not sight. Our problem is keeping the vision of Jesus as we have Him revealed through Scripture despite the mists of everyday life. That Biblical picture is to be enhanced by our experiences of God. The Spirit is here to give life, not to replace the Bible's revelation of God with a series of subjective experiences alone.

How many of us would love to have that face-to-face encounter we see with such Biblical characters as Jacob, Moses, and Paul or hear of from those who have had 'death-back-to-life' experiences! But we may have to wait until eternity.

For now we are to be satisfied with the ongoing relationship we have with the Lord. That relationship comes through our study of the Word, our worship and prayer, our fellowship with other believers and our daily life in the Spirit as we serve Christ and one another. A season of mists maybe, but glory to come. Hallelujah!

PRAYER: *Thank You that one day all the mists will clear and that for now we can trust You, the One who is above all the mists and the darkness of this world's systems. In Jesus' name I pray, Amen.*

OCTOBER 28 | OVERCOMING EVIL WITH GOOD

WENDY WHITTEN

> *Instead, as the scripture says: 'If your enemies are hungry, feed them; if they are thirsty, give them a drink; for by doing this you will make them burn with shame.' Do not let evil defeat you; instead, conquer evil with good.*
>
> Romans 12:20–21, GNB

It seems that every day we read in our newspapers stories of people who have been wronged in some way who are now fighting for justice. The victims of discrimination, those who lose their jobs 'unfairly', are all claiming large sums of money in compensation. When a loved one is injured or dies, they ask, 'Whose fault is it? Who can we sue?' So many people in the world today are looking to blame someone for their problems. 'It's not fair' is the oft-heard cry.

What did Jesus teach us? Fight for what is yours? Take revenge on your enemies? NO – we are encouraged to love our enemies. That means those who hurt us, those who have betrayed us, or treated us unfairly, those who have discriminated against us, those who have let us down, cheated us, taken from us, used us, abused us – we are told not only to forgive them but to actively love them in return! Bless them; give to them.

Our human (sinful) nature is to fight back, retaliate, get our revenge, claim 'our rights', but if we learn to live as Jesus taught us, we will have peace in our hearts.

So, today, perhaps, as we meet young people who swear at us on the street or those who threaten us and cause us fear, as we meet angry colleagues, a critical boss, or difficult family members, let's practise loving them, showing them acceptance and trying to understand them. Let's choose to let go of 'our rights' and allow the love of Jesus to flow through us and disarm our enemies! Let's choose to let Jesus fight our battles for us. Then we will be assured of lasting, eternal victory.

PRAYER: *Dear Lord, You know the difficulties I face today. You know the people who seem to be my enemies. Please help me see them as You do, with Your heart of love. Please give me Your love for them and help me practise that love today, in Jesus' name. Amen.*

OCTOBER 29 | DREAMS AND REALITY

MARGARET SILVESTER

> *When Jacob reached a certain place, he stopped for the night because the sun had set. Taking one of the stones there, he put it under his head and lay down to sleep. He had a dream ...*
>
> Genesis 28:11–12

In the Old Testament God often spoke to people through dreams. Jacob had a dream, which held promises. The first promise was affirmation of a promise given to his grandfather, Abraham, that God would give him land and descendants through whom all the peoples of the earth would be blessed. The second promise was a personal one. Despite the fact that he was running away from home, God promised Jacob that He would be with him, watch over him wherever he journeyed and eventually bring him back to the Promised Land.

When Jacob awoke he knew he had met with God and was filled with awesome fear. On the spot he made a promise to God that he would always give back a tenth of all God gave to him. A principle to live by which assures blessing!

January 19 was the birthday of Dr Martin Luther King. My husband and I were in St Petersburg, Florida where we found ourselves watching countless thousands of black people, who were marching to remember their hero and to proclaim that his dream was also their dream.

Banners displayed three large slogans. The first one read: 'I have a dream.' It was of course the statement their fallen hero made in his famous speech in 1963. The second banner read: 'Keep the dream alive' which was the purpose of the march. The third banner read: 'Fulfil the dream.' The dream cost Martin Luther King his life. He was assassinated in 1968.

The people on the streets of St Petersburg were those who had been set free from the bondage of slavery and inequality as the dream came into reality. They were determined that they would keep the dream alive and they would be the ones actively involved in fulfilling it.

People who have a 'dream' either fulfil their dream and bring it into reality or the vision dies. We might say people with a dream are people with a destiny. They know why they are here – they know God's purpose for their life and they make the choice to fulfil it whatever the cost.

God's purposes are Kingdom purposes. It was for the salvation of the whole world that Jesus died. The desire in His heart is that all peoples should experience the freedom that He alone can give. We are His followers, called to have a dream, to keep the dream alive and to fulfil the dream. By His grace we can do it.

It was for the salvation of the whole world that Jesus died. The desire in His heart is that all peoples should experience the freedom that He alone can give. We are His followers, called to have a dream, to keep the dream alive and to fulfil the dream. By His grace we can do it.

PRAYER: *Heavenly Father, thank You for giving me Jesus, to die for me. By Your grace please enable me to fulfil my God-given destiny and bring glory to You as I live my life day by day. Amen.*

October 30 | The Glory of the Lord

Liz Griffin

When all the children of Israel saw how the fire came down, and the glory of the LORD on the temple, they bowed their faces to the ground on the pavement, and worshiped and praised the LORD, saying: 'For He is good, for His mercy endures forever.'

2 Chronicles 7:3, NKJV

King Solomon spent seven years having a temple built for the purpose of worshipping God. It was to be the place where God was pleased to dwell amongst His people, although Solomon was perfectly well aware that God is so vast and mighty that He would not be confined to any one space such as a building made with human hands. It was a grand and magnificent day when the ark of the covenant of the Lord was brought from the city of David, with all its holy furnishings, to be put in the Most Holy Place within the new temple. Would God really come in a tangible way in this new temple?

King Solomon chose the right time of the year. It was Succoth, the festival of tabernacles or shelters. This was the annual time for the Israelites to remember how God was with them throughout the time they were in the desert for forty years.

King Solomon knew what his responsibility as a leader was. He made sure everyone could see him up on a platform and then he knelt down before the whole assembly of Israel and spread out his hands toward heaven and prayed. We have all the details of his prayer. He prayed on behalf of all the people. '*When Solomon had finished praying, fire came down from heaven and consumed the burnt offering and the sacrifices; and the glory of the LORD filled the temple*' (2 Chronicles 7:1). Everyone fell to the floor in worship. There were no sceptics or unbelievers in the meeting that day.

This was what the temple was for. No wonder Jesus was angry that the temple could be defiled and become a place of trading and not a house of prayer. God comes with His manifest presence when He is welcomed and invited on His terms. It was His idea to come and dwell with His people in the first place. He initiated it.

How much do we long for the manifest presence of God? Are we prepared to find out what God requires of us in preparation?

PRAYER: *Lord, we pray that we will be hungry and thirsty for Your presence in our gatherings. We pray that You will show us how to invite You and make You welcome, in Jesus' name, Amen.*

OCTOBER 31 | FOOD WITHOUT ADDITIVES

DAVID CROSS

> *'I am the bread of life,' Jesus told them. 'Those who come to me will never be hungry; those who believe in me will never be thirsty.'*
>
> John 6:35, GNB

I was recently reading an article by a leading Christian commentator who clearly believes that there's a great spiritual hunger now, right across the nation of Britain. He believes that this hunger's set to increase as financial difficulties and other hardships intensify. However, he cautioned that hungry people will sometimes eat anything that's offered.

Joseph was called to be a distributor of food at a time of severe famine. It's significant that he was a man who, over many years, had learned to listen to the voice of God and follow it. In the New Testament, we find that one day when Jesus was teaching, He specifically instructed His disciples to give out loaves and fishes to a hungry multitude. Today we desperately need those who are ready to distribute good spiritual food, but there's a need for all of us to be careful.

Walking around a supermarket, it's very normal these days to see people studying the food labels to check for unhealthy additives, included to enhance flavour or colour, but not to improve nutritional value. Jesus tells us that the best spiritual food is *Himself*. When we teach or share the truth of God's Word with those who are hungry, we need to be sure that we're distributing the pure *Bread of Life*. Because of our wounded past and sinful nature, it's so easy to let unhelpful additives slip in, additives which reflect more of our character than that of Jesus. We may think that the flavour has been improved, but if the purity has been spoiled then we are putting our hearers at risk.

No one but Jesus speaks perfect truth, but we should encourage one another to *'read the label'* at every Christian meeting to make sure that we're distributing or receiving spiritual food with as few unhealthy additives as possible. Added flavour and colour may make the meeting appear more attractive, but it's only the purity of Jesus that will safely satisfy deep hunger.

Prayer: *Thank You, Lord, that You are the bread of life and that only You can satisfy the deepest longing of my heart. I pray that today You will meet my real spiritual needs as I seek to serve You in the place You have put me, in Jesus' name, Amen.*

November 1 | Jochebed, Moses' Mother

Richard Hemery

By faith Moses, when he had grown up, refused to be known as the son of Pharaoh's daughter.

Hebrews 11:24

This remarkable woman is an encouragement to every parent, when you really unpack what she did – the obvious and the not so obvious.

Let's examine the obvious – the Egyptians had commanded death for Hebrew baby boys. When their son was born Moses' parents saw he was special – so they hid him. Hebrews 11:23 tells us they did this by faith. As well as faith Jochebed had wisdom. When Pharaoh's daughter found baby Moses crying in the basket, and recognised he was a Hebrew baby, Miriam suggested she could fetch a Hebrew nurse for him. Whether this was all part of Jochebed's plan is not stated, but God arranged for her to receive her baby back, and to be paid for it (Exodus 2:1–10).

Jochebed's mothering skills were already apparent, as young Miriam had the confidence to address a princess.

Now comes Jochebed's real achievement, which is not so obvious. She had Moses for an unspecified number of years before he was returned to the princess.

Yet, although he was educated *'in all the wisdom of the Egyptians'* (Acts 7:22), had all the material benefits of Pharaoh's court, spoke Egyptian, dressed Egyptian, was named by the princess, and was totally immersed in that ungodly culture for over thirty years, when we next see him he's seeking out *'his own people'* – the Israelites. This is Jochebed's achievement. In the few short years she had Moses she instilled in him such a godly sense of his identity that nothing he experienced later could erase it. She passed on her own faith to him, so that *'by faith [he] refused to be known as the son of Pharaoh's daughter'* (Hebrews 11:24). For those reading this whose children are still 'Egyptian', notice that it took Moses forty years to get his act together, but he returned to the fold – to rescue his people.

PRAYER: *Lord, may we who have children imitate the faith and godly parenting skill of Jochebed, so that our children may remain true to faith in You, however the world may seek to influence them. Amen.*

NOVEMBER 2 | WILLING TO GET YOUR FEET WET?

ANDY TAYLOR

> *It was the harvest season, and the Jordan was overflowing its banks. But as soon as the feet of the priests who were carrying the Ark touched the water at the river's edge, the water above that point began backing up a great distance away at a town called Adam, which is near Zarethan. And the water below that point flowed on to the Dead Sea until the riverbed was dry. Then all the people crossed over near the town of Jericho.*
>
> Joshua 3:15–16, NLT

This is definitely one of those events that we will want to watch in High Definition replay in heaven! The children of Israel had finally come to the end of their wanderings in the desert and were about to be led by Joshua into the Promised Land. The only snag however was that, in the same way that Moses came to the Red Sea, Joshua had come to the River Jordan. To make matters worse the snow had melted on Mount Hermon and the Jordan had overflowed its banks!

Earlier in the passage God speaks to Joshua and tells him to get the people ready to cross the river – and that's exactly what happens. The people get ready, the priests get ready, everyone moves into position – but nothing happens and the river remains uncrossable.

They could have just waited there for God to build a bridge or to part the water, but God's instructions were clear – the river would stop flowing at the very moment when the priests' feet touched the water. This is yet another example in Scripture of how God wants us to put our faith into action!

It was risky for Joshua. What if He hadn't really heard God's voice? What if it was all just his own idea? It's easy for us because within a few verses we saw what God did. For Joshua it was a different story. He was relying completely on God to do what He said He would do when he put his faith into action and instructed the priests to walk into the water. And as they did so, the river dried up and the people were able to cross over on dry land!

What's your response to God's leading when things seem impossible? Do you want to wait for a bridge to appear or do you take the risk, put your trust in God and get your feet wet? Sometimes that's the only way to walk into the promises of God for your life.

PRAYER: *Help me, Lord, to exercise real faith when You speak into my life, so that I won't miss out on seeing You work a miracle. Give me the courage, Lord, to trust You at all times, in Jesus' name, Amen.*

NOVEMBER 3 | VICTORY IN THE FACE OF DEFEAT

PATRICIA LAKE

He has risen from the dead, and is going ahead of you ...

Matthew 28:7

Just when it seems like all is lost, hope is fading and defeat is looming, God steps in and delivers His masterpiece. Time and again throughout Scripture, God steps in with His great plan of salvation.

The day Jesus died and the day He rose again were days like no other, for during this time He won the ultimate victory and conquered all the powers of hell forever. He defeated, disarmed and made a public spectacle of them. He triumphed over all the forces of evil by the cross. He rescued us.

It was during this most momentous and pivotal of weeks in history that God turned what, to man, looked like utter defeat, into the most glorious victory ever to be witnessed in time and eternity.

Maybe you are facing some great test or trial, the outlook looks bleak, you have been backed into a corner and don't know what to do or where to turn, you seem to be staring defeat in the face. Today, the Lord of Glory wants you to know that He is with you and is able to deliver you. He is mighty to save (Zephaniah 3:17). Call on Him and He will not only defeat your enemies, He will vindicate you. You are His precious child and He will always come to your aid. Jesus is the Victor!

PRAYER: *Heavenly Father, our eyes are on You and we put our trust in You for You are our deliverer. Thank You, Lord, for always hearing our prayer and coming to our rescue, in Jesus' name. Amen.*

November 4 | Jesus – My Expectation is From You Alone!

Herman Redelinghuys

Jesus stood and cried out, saying, 'If anyone thirsts, let him come to Me and drink. He who believes in Me, as the Scripture has said, out of his heart will flow rivers of living water.'

John 7:38, NKJV

In John 7:37 Jesus was addressing a crowd who had spent a week celebrating Succoth, a feast at the turn of the Jewish year. With great expectation people prepared for this time, built booths, drew close to one another, ate and drank and celebrated the redemption from Egypt and God's presence in Israel.

On the last of day of the feast Jesus said (allow me to paraphrase), *'If you are not filled up, still tired, still feeling incomplete and have some things missing, come to Me. Come and drink, come and receive and be filled up!'* He invites the people to receive from Him and receive living water to sustain them through the next year and into eternity!

How do we 'drink' or believe in Him? David knew something about the secret of drinking; in Psalm 62:5 he says, *'My soul, wait silently for God alone, for my expectation is from Him'* (NKJV). David presented the situation to God and waited. His eyes, all of his expectation, confidence and dependency was in God alone to save – a deep trust in God's ability and faithfulness. I believe this was not a one-off activity for David, but a continual standing and turning his expectation towards God. As the year end becomes ever closer, Jesus is inviting us to lay down those things that keep us from resting in Him and to turn our expectation toward Jesus so that He can fill us now with sustenance in our human spirit and be the source of strength on a daily basis throughout the year to come.

Prayer: *Lord, thank You for the promise of living water during this coming year. Like David I bring my situation to You and lay it down at Your feet. Lord Jesus, I wait on You, for my expectation is from You alone, Amen.*

November 5 | Reality Check

Lindsey Hanekom

He called a little child and had him stand among them. And he said: 'I tell you the truth, unless you change and become like little children, you will never enter the kingdom of heaven. Therefore, whoever humbles himself like this child is the greatest in the kingdom of heaven.'

Matthew 18:2–4

It wasn't until after the birth of my baby son that I discovered the hidden depth in these simple words of Jesus – a lesson about the joy of reality.

My four-month-old son, Kyle, cannot hide what he's feeling. He's completely incapable of pretending he's happy when he's not. When he's happy he laughs and gurgles away, merrily playing with his toys. When he's not happy, he cries. There are different types of cry for different reasons, some louder than others!

If Kyle was able to laugh when he was hungry and giggle when he needed comfort we wouldn't be able to care for him so effectively. He would become frustrated at our seeming lack of care and nurture. He would never feel secure. He would never know that we will always take care of his needs.

It makes me think about how we are with God. Are we uninhibited in our relationship with Him, letting Him know our true feelings? Or do we pretend that everything is OK, but then become frustrated with Him because He doesn't bring the care and nurture that we need so badly?

The truth is, my love for my son is unwavering, regardless of whether he cries, laughs or is just peacefully contented. My love doesn't change when he's upset. It simply means that I am able to provide what he needs at that time. In the same way we need to learn to be real with God so that He can provide for us. His love doesn't change according to our mood. But our ability to receive His love does change. It changes according to how vulnerable we are, how humble we are, and how real we allow ourselves to be.

Prayer: *Father God, You're the perfect Father. You're able and willing to give me what I need when I need it. Please help me to be real with You about everything I feel so that You can provide for me when I am in need. I recognise that I sometimes hide my true feelings from You and I ask You to forgive me for that. I choose to trust in Your infinite, unwavering love. Amen.*

November 6 | Time for Pruning!

Wendy Whitten

I am the true vine, and my Father is the gardener. He cuts off every branch in me that bears no fruit, while every branch that does bear fruit he prunes so that it will be even more fruitful.

John 15:1

When did you last get pruned?

Having spent time recently in the garden, harvesting apples, I couldn't help noticing the trees. One tree was very productive this year, bearing many large and beautiful apples. Last year it was a poor crop in comparison, but it underwent a healthy pruning and as a result has been very fruitful this season.

The second tree looks as if it has a good crop but on closer inspection all the apples are small and of poor quality. Why? Well, at the all-important time this spring there was no opportunity to 'thin out' the fruit. If some had been taken out when tiny then the resulting crop would have been of better quality – larger, tastier apples in good condition instead of the many small and damaged ones we have this year.

We have also been cutting back the shrubs, bushes and climbers, getting rid of the dead wood that is crowding out or choking the good branches, identifying those 'out-of-control' stems that are just 'in the way'. We have selected the best and healthiest of branches to remain. Pruning!

So, when were you last pruned?

Let's ask the Master Gardener, our Creator, if there's anything in our lives that may need cutting back. Are there sin issues we need to deal with? Are our attitudes healthy or have we allowed bitterness or negativity to creep in? What about our priorities? Are they God's or ours? Are we really fruitful for His Kingdom? Is there any area where we need to be 'thinned out'?

When did we last lay down our lives before God and surrender everything to Him and say, 'Have Your way'? Are we fruitful or are we just busy? Are we fully grafted into the true vine or are we a wayward off-shoot?

Let's get close to God today, feed on Him, spend time in His presence, 'let our roots go down deep into the soil of His marvellous love' and allow Him to prune us.

Prayer: *Heavenly Father, I desire to lay my life down afresh before You this day – have Your way in my life . Show me what isn't pleasing to You, and draw me close to You today. I give You permission to prune me so that I may be more fruitful for Your Kingdom. I choose to dwell in Your presence and receive Your love, in Jesus' precious name. Amen.*

NOVEMBER 7 | FAITH IS A CHOICE!

ROGER POOK

> *[Jesus] replied, '... I tell you the truth, if you have faith as small as a mustard seed, you can say to this mountain, "Move from here to there" and it will move. Nothing will be impossible for you.'*
>
> Matthew 17:20

How many times has someone told you, 'You need more faith? Or maybe they quote you the words of Jesus that your problems could be solved if you just had *'faith as small as a mustard seed'*. From this we might think that faith is some sort of quality, like courage or mercy, which we have to grow within us until it becomes part of our very nature.

This is all very well until people tell us that we 'don't have enough faith' in our response to a problem – as if more faith meant fewer problems – and then we feel condemned because we are falling short of some unattainable standard of faith.

However, faith is not something that we have to work up inside ourselves by our own effort, maybe by more prayer, more Bible-reading, more church attendance ... In basic terms, faith is a just a choice, a simple decision as to what to do in any given circumstance.

This is the choice: I choose to act AS IF God loves me, AS IF He knows about this problem and AS IF He has the answer.

So, my 'mustard seed' is not a small faith. It is just the time that it takes to make the choice, based on no visible evidence at all (Hebrews 11:1), that I'm going to trust that God knows about my problem and has the answer. Then I'll act on that choice.

PRAYER: *Dear Father, I make this simple choice – I choose to act as if You love me, as if You know about my problems and as if You have the answer. This is my mustard seed, and I offer it to You. Amen.*

November 8 | Mountaintops and Valleys

Goran Andersson

When they came to the crowd, a man approached Jesus, and knelt before him. 'Lord, have mercy on my son,' he said.

Matthew 17:14–15

Christian life is not primarily lived on the mountaintops, but in the valleys. The transfiguration mountain was not to be home to the apostles. They were not to enjoy an undisturbed fellowship with Jesus, Moses and Elijah, but were to mingle with suffering, disturbed and hopeless people, together with Jesus. The contrast between the mountaintop and the valley was enormous.

It's human for us to desire the good days, but it's not right to expect that to mean staying on the mountain forever! The mountain is light, and the valley is darkness; the mountain is revelations and understanding, the valley is challenges and needs. But even so, the very best days may be in the valley, because it's there we see Jesus at work, and the demons must give way. It's in the valley that the needs of the many are being met, and the not-so-fortunate get their touch from Jesus.

The man didn't bring his son up the mountain; Jesus had to go down to him. Had Peter started building shelters on the mountain, the boy wouldn't have received healing. The temptation to seek too much time in the shining light has a price, and that price may have to be paid by someone in the dark valley.

Followers of Jesus, where do you want to spend this day? Yes, this day may be a day on the mountain, but then, where do you want to spend tomorrow? And if you were on the mount with Jesus today, did you gain more understanding of what He can do in the valley?

Peter didn't often speak about that day with Moses and Elijah. He didn't talk about it to let others know that he had been chosen to be there at that historical moment. But the experience on the mount remained with him as a source of assurance that the word of God is true (2 Peter 1:17–18). And it motivated him to let others know who Jesus is. He had understood the message, and was no longer afraid to go into the valleys. The day of Pentecost in Jerusalem may have been another experience like the one on the mountain, but this time Peter didn't express a desire to remain in the upper room. He was ready to take the message to the public places of Jerusalem.

The vision in Simon's house in Joppa was extraordinary, but again, Peter was ready to go into the valley, represented by the Gentile Cornelius's house. It was the people in Cornelius's house that needed Peter's message about Jesus. And if it was in Simon's house that the revelation came, it was in Cornelius's house that the results were seen and God's glory was revealed.

PRAYER: *Dear Heavenly Father, help me not to be afraid of the darkness of the valley! Thank You that it's the place where Your light will be seen, and where my life will be transformed. Help me to trust in You at all times and go without hesitation wherever You lead me, in Jesus' name, Amen.*

NOVEMBER 9 | HEARING GOD'S VOICE

DIANE WATSON

> *The LORD said, 'Go out and stand on the mountain in the presence of the LORD, for the LORD is about to pass by.' Then a great and powerful wind tore the mountains apart and shattered the rocks before the LORD, but the LORD was not in the wind. After the wind there was an earthquake, but the LORD was not in the earthquake. After the earthquake came a fire, but the LORD was not in the fire. And after the fire came a gentle whisper. When Elijah heard it, he pulled his cloak over his face and went out and stood at the mouth of the cave. Then a voice said to him, 'What are you doing here, Elijah?'*
>
> 1 Kings 19:11–13

I remember when I was preparing my very first talk on hearing God's voice and I bought a book all about it. God spoke to me and said, 'You don't need a book to learn about hearing me, just listen!' Over the years, God has spoken to me through various ways, through His Word, directly giving me words through my spirit and through others confirming things to me.

In this day and age there are many things that the enemy uses to compete for our attention and listening skills. It's very hard to find a place free of noise pollution! There are so many other voices we can listen to instead of spending time with God listening to His gentle whisper. A lot of times God has spoken to me in the middle of the night when there's no competing noise and He has my full attention.

If we have trouble hearing God's voice maybe we're not tuned in enough to His channel! Are other voices drowning out God's voice, demanding our attention? If we want to be able to hear God clearly then we must take time to be with Him. As it says in Scripture, do we long for God and seek Him as the deer pants for the water? *'As the deer pants for streams of water, so my soul pants for you, O God. My soul thirsts for God, for the living God. When can I go and meet with God?'* (Psalm 42:1–2).

PRAYER: *Father God, help me to stop and spend time listening to Your gentle whisper. In the busyness of life, help me take time out to stop and give You all my attention. I know, Father, You want to speak to me because I'm Your child and You love me. Help me to earnestly seek Your face, in Jesus' name I pray, Amen.*

NOVEMBER 10 | LIMITS OF PROTECTION

LINDSEY HANEKOM

> *The LORD says, 'I will rescue those who love me. I will protect those who trust in my name.'*
>
> Psalm 91:14, NLT

Our son, Kyle, has reached a new level of freedom in his life. This freedom comes in the form of bright green, frog look-a-like, rubber wellie boots. Previously, in his new shoes, there was a forbidden territory – puddles. Now, with his protective wellies he can just walk right through them; or (as the case often is) he can stop and splash in them.

However, he soon found the limits to his protection. If he sat down (either accidentally or on purpose) he would get a wet bottom. If he wandered into deeper water than the height of his wellies, he would get wet feet. If he took his wellies off, he would get very wet and cold. He had some lessons to learn.

When we consider the protection of God, we must understand that it comes with a limit on it. But this limitation isn't God – it's us. This verse says, *'I will protect those who trust in my name.'* I'm sure we all trust God to a certain point, but can we honestly say we trust Him wholeheartedly – without reservation or hesitation? We don't automatically trust God implicitly just because we're saved. Trust grows as we develop our relationship with Him, just as trust in human relationships grows, over a period of time.

Equally, if we choose to move away from God's protection through disobedience or venturing into areas that are dangerously 'deep waters', then we can find ourselves in trouble and feeling the ill effects of going beyond our protection. As we grow in our relationship with Him, we will find that we can rest in His protection more and more each day. We can enter battles with the enemy in a deeper knowledge and understanding of God and our position in Him, keeping us safe from the enemy's attacks and allowing us to take enemy ground.

Each time Kyle fell down in the cold, wet, muddy puddles, my husband and I rushed to pick him up and comfort him. At the end of the walk we were wet and muddy where we had held our child close to give him comfort – marks of love, despite his falling down. Our Father in Heaven longs to keep us safe. Yet He also knows we need to grow and develop. Whenever we go beyond our limits, the marks are evident on the hands and feet of Jesus Christ, our Saviour who died for each one of us.

PRAYER: *Father God, thank You for being my protection. Thank You that, no matter how often I fall, Jesus bears the marks of my moving away from Your protection and that You can bring me healing and comfort for those times. Amen.*

NOVEMBER 11 | WHEN NOT ENOUGH EQUALS ENOUGH!

ANDY TAYLOR

> *Jesus took the five loaves and two fish, looked up toward heaven, and asked God's blessing on the food. Breaking the loaves into pieces, he kept giving the bread and fish to the disciples to give to the people.*
>
> Luke 9:16, NLT

The amazing story of how Jesus fed 5,000 people with just five loaves of bread and two fish is a personal favourite for many. It's hard for us to truly understand how the disciples must have felt, when they looked out at the huge crowd, with the words of Jesus ringing in their ears, 'You feed them!' From both a physical and practical point of view it was totally impossible – Jesus was well aware of this. He wanted to show the disciples more of who His Father really was.

At the end of their searching for food they were a long, long way short of their target. Yet Jesus was not fazed by this at all. He didn't complain to His Father about their seeming lack of provision, or tell the disciples to go back out and find some more food. He certainly didn't look at the practical, realistic viewpoint and tell the people to go home and find their own food. He looked at the situation from God's point of view, where nothing is impossible, and simply took the loaves and the fish, looked toward heaven and asked God's blessing on what they did have. The rest was up to His Father. It was, without question, a dramatic miracle – and a giant learning curve for the disciples.

Maybe God is challenging you in your life or ministry. Maybe you're being asked to do something 'impossible'. You may not have enough provision. You may be a long, long way short. But, according to this Bible story, that's not the point. Having done your part, take what you do have, look toward heaven and ask God's blessing on it. He's the One who will bring the increase and cause the miracle. Remember, we serve a God who loves to prove that He is who He says He is!

PRAYER: *Thank You, Lord, for Your amazing provision for the people in this story. Help me to be trusting of You, even when things look impossible, in Jesus' name, Amen.*

NOVEMBER 12 | 'BUT … THEY *NEED* ME!'

ROGER POOK

My God will meet all your needs according to his glorious riches in Christ Jesus.

Philippians 4:1

Do you believe this verse for other people – as well as for yourself? Many Christians find that they become committed to more and more activities, and that they become trapped in these activities by an insistent thought: 'If I don't do this, who else will? The people that I am serving in this work need me. If I ever give up, they will suffer. Please God, just give me the strength to keep on going!'

This way of thinking is based on a fallacy – that God will somehow be disappointed in you if you're no longer able to keep up the same hectic pace. There's actually an underlying sinful assumption as well – that God's not able to provide for the needs of those that you serve, if you don't do it.

So, here is the shocking truth: God's more interested in you than in 'your ministry'. What you do is more for your good than for the good of others. God will meet their needs, maybe through you, maybe in another way.

'But God, who will do my present work if I don't? There are people who are counting on me!' God says, 'That's none of your business.' If you have done the work faithfully, and have imparted the same vision to others, then you can move on when God says it's time to do so. God has His own plans anyway, and He loves you too much to let you be burned out.

PRAYER: *Lord, I do believe that You supply all my needs. Now please help me to believe that truth for other people as well. Forgive me for thinking that I'm the answer, because only You are the answer. Thank You for loving me and helping me to grow in faith through the tasks that You give me. Amen.*

NOVEMBER 13 | FOOLISHNESS OR AN ACT OF GRACE?

DAVID SILVESTER

For you know the grace of our Lord Jesus Christ, that though he was rich, yet for your sakes he became poor, so that you through his poverty might become rich.

2 Corinthians 8:9

After many years as an engineering craftsman I moved into lecturing engineering students in a Technical College and one of my duties was to be the chief examiner of an 'O Level' technology paper.

One year a member of the team of assistant examiners came with a group of papers from a school where the candidates had all answered a question in exactly the same way, but the answer was completely wrong! If each candidate was to be given a zero mark for that answer, a number of them would fall below the required total mark for a 'pass'. What were we to do in such a situation?

I telephoned the school in question and spoke to the person who'd taught them. He'd had no practical experience of engineering and had assumed that the details he'd taught were correct. Of course the candidates had naturally believed that what they'd been taught was correct. I referred this teacher to a textbook where the correct information could be found so that his teaching would be accurate in the future.

The Examination Board agreed that the candidates had answered the question as they'd been taught and should be given full marks for the answers they'd given to that particular question. Some people would say that this was foolish, but others would say it was an act of grace.

What God has done for us sinners is similar to what was done for those candidates. He sent His Son Jesus to earth for the purpose of dying in our place, and paying the penalty for our sins. It's an act which might be considered foolishness, but those of us who've received forgiveness and cleansing from sin know it to be an act of grace – God giving us what we don't deserve.

PRAYER: *Thank You, Lord God, for dealing in grace with me. I know that I don't deserve what You've done in giving Jesus to take the punishment for my sin. I'm overawed by Your act of grace. Please help me to demonstrate my gratitude in the way I live my life, and help me to become more like Jesus day by day. Amen.*

NOVEMBER 14 | ARE WE HARD OF HEARING?

DENISE CROSS

> *Of [Christ] we have much to say, and hard to explain, since you have become dull of hearing.*
>
> Hebrews 5:11, NKJV

I suppose subconsciously I realised there might be a problem or I wouldn't have gone to have the test. True, my children had made odd comments about the television volume but it still shocked me when the hearing test proved beyond doubt that there were some ranges of sounds I just couldn't hear. Evidently there was damage that had led to a sort of hearing 'blind-spot'.

I couldn't help wonder if spiritual ears, the ears of the human spirit, could be damaged in the same way and that's why some are 'dull of hearing' as this verse implies. The hearing specialist told me the physical damage was because of excessive noise in the past and that this caused damage because it wasn't what ears were intended for. So what would be the equivalent for the spiritual ears, I wondered?

Jesus says, '*My sheep hear My voice*' (John 10:27, NKJV). He expects us to listen with spiritual ears that are made to listen to the truthful, loving and gentle voice of Jesus. So, if spiritual ears have been subject to spiritual sounds not intended for them, then this may result in 'hearing' damage. So what are these damaging spiritual noises? Perhaps these might include being constantly subjected to a barrage of the enemy's lies or entering into false worship or perhaps harbouring attitudes of hate, judgement or pride. These are the 'sounds' of the enemy's voice, damaging to spiritual ears intended for words of truth and love.

If we have spiritual hearing loss we could be missing something of what Jesus is saying today. We may be thinking we are hearing OK but actually we're missing bits of the message!

Perhaps we should invite the Holy Spirit to come and test our spiritual hearing today and if necessary restore and heal the ears of our hearts so we can hear the full message.

PRAYER: *Jesus, we desire to hear Your voice clearly and fully. Help us to be aware of the possibility that we're suffering from 'dullness of hearing' and allow You to cleanse and restore the ears of our hearts. Amen.*

NOVEMBER 15 | TRUST THE WISE JUDGE

MARGARET SILVESTER

> *When they hurled insults at him, he did not retaliate; when he suffered, he made no threats. Instead, he trusted himself to him who judges justly.*
>
> 1 Peter 2:23

At some time or other we are all falsely accused and suffer at the hands of someone who wrongly judges us. When people speak wrongly of us the human temptation is often to retaliate or defend ourselves. Our attitude can be exactly the opposite to that of the Lord Jesus.

In His darkest hour on the cross, when He was mocked, spat upon and insulted, and where He suffered and died in agony, He didn't retaliate, threaten or judge. He entrusted Himself to the Father who is the true and just Judge.

Jesus warned His disciples of the folly of hypocritically or self-righteously judging others. As human beings it's easy to make a wrong judgement. There's a very narrow line between judging and discerning. Discernment is a gift of the Holy Spirit and should be used wisely.

What a lot of anguish we'd save ourselves if our attitude were the same as that of the One we profess to follow. Like Jesus, we can trust ourselves to the wise Judge. Whatever people may say against us, they can only damage our reputation. But God's more interested in our character than our reputation. Our character is the truth of what we are in the eyes of the One who judges the thoughts and attitudes of the heart.

Prayer: *Heavenly Father, thank You for Jesus, whose attitude was humble and lowly. Forgive me for the times when I've retaliated when others have wrongly judged me, and for the times I have wrongly judged others. Help me to live my life in the light of Your presence, with confidence that You're the One who judges justly. Amen.*

November 16 | Looking for More Power

David Silvester

> *We have this treasure in jars of clay to show that this all-surpassing power is from God and not from us.*
>
> 2 Corinthians 4:7

Some years ago a colleague and I were given the task of examining a small engine and redesigning it. The object of that exercise was to see if it was possible to achieve a greater power output in an engine of the same size.

After studying all the characteristics and applying some basic principles, we then produced detailed drawings, and from them had an engine made and tested. Testing and comparing the performance of both engines, the results were amazing. In the revised engine there was more than a fifty-percent increase of power.

So what was the secret of success? All that had been done was to increase the input and exhaust capacities, and the compression ratio. This allowed more fuel to get into the combustion chamber, greater pressure on combustion, and a more rapid removal of the exhausted fuel. In reality, the power was already there, but needed to be used in a more effective way.

Our Christian lives might be compared with that first engine: needing more of the Holy Spirit to empower us, a more effective use of His power, and also to get rid of anything in our lives that is no longer of any useful purpose in order to make room for the incoming power. This is where Paul's words, '*We have this treasure in jars of clay to show that this all-surpassing power is from God and not from us*', come into effect within us, and we need to let God do that which makes His power most effective.

God has provided the power of His Holy Spirit to be within us to enable us to be effective for Him, and at times He may be showing us that there are things in our lives which hinder us from achieving our potential, and they need throwing out. The similarity may be considered a bit like the difference between the first and the second engine, and the need for a little close examination.

When we first come to Christ receiving His forgiveness, we come with a lot of 'baggage' from our former way of life, and that needs to be dealt with in order for us to achieve what God has planned and desires for us. As more of the hindrances are dealt with and we are 'tuned up', a greater effect of His Holy Spirit's power in us is achieved.

PRAYER: *Dear Lord God, thank You that You see me as I am, and as You examine me closely, You see those things that need to be improved. Search me, O God, try my heart, and reveal to me anything that hinders You fulfilling in me my full potential. Help me to discard those things that are a hindrance to You, and let more of the power of Your Holy Spirit be seen to be at work in me, I pray, in Jesus' name, Amen.*

NOVEMBER 17 | CHECK YOUR SHOES!

CATH TAYLOR

> *You must display a new nature because you are a new person, created in God's likeness – righteous, holy, and true.*
>
> Ephesians 4:24, NLT

Monday to Friday, the number 4100 yellow school bus stops at the end of our drive to pick up our two eldest children, Jake and Ben. The deal is that the kids are supposed to be waiting at the bus stop for the bus to arrive, but I'm sorry to say that it's often not the case. By the skin of their teeth, with lunch boxes and water bottles being thrown after them, they usually scamper up the steps of the bus pleading apologies and vague promises to try harder! Mornings are a little hectic in the Taylor household!

All this to say that the other morning, as the usual rush out of the door was happening, I noticed that my middle son, Ben, was escaping out of the door wearing a pair of trainers that were falling to pieces. This pair, with straps broken and seams swelling, had been replaced with a lovely new pair possibly two months earlier. When Ben arrived home that evening I asked him about it. He explained that he had been wearing the old pair (with velcro straps), because the new pair (with laces) were just so much harder work to put on and keep fastened, and that the old pair were easier for scoring goals!

Ben was doing in a practical sense what we're probably all guilty of doing in a spiritual sense. For all of us, the old pairs of shoes in our closet will be different, but I guarantee we all have them. They're the ugly pair and worn-out pair that sadly fits so well with our flesh!

Maybe they're the familiar shoes of un-forgiveness and bitterness that you slip on without even thinking. Or how about that old comfy pair of anxiety and worry that you lived in for so long, and are moulded to the shape of your heart? Fact is, the new pair that we all desired and asked for takes time to wear in and get used to. It takes practice and sometimes we just don't have the time or want to make the effort.

Make the time today to ask the Lord to show you the patterns in your life that you slip into subconsciously that are not of Him. Ask Him not only to replace your old pair of shoes with a new pair, but also to give you the effort and tenacity to remember to take them out of your closet and put them on!

PRAYER: *Lord Jesus, I recognise my need of You. Led by my flesh, I slip so quickly into old ways, beliefs and patterns. Please, Lord, will You show me how to discard these old familiar shoes and to start to walk in the new, beautiful shoes You have for me to wear. In Jesus' name I pray, Amen.*

NOVEMBER 18 | PREPARATION FOR DESTINY

PATRICIA LAKE

> *So David triumphed over the Philistine with a sling and a stone; without a sword in his hand he struck down the Philistine and killed him.*
>
> 1 Samuel 17:50

God has a purpose and destiny for all of His creation. The problem is, can we endure and be patient enough to withstand His testings, which will ensure that we're ready at the appointed time?

David the shepherd boy knew only that he was visiting his brothers with some food, at his father Jesse's request. But God had a greater purpose in store for this 'one-off' visit to deliver his brothers' lunch! Out came Goliath hurling his insults at the Most High God and Israel's armies – just in time to stir David's righteous indignation. '*Who is this uncircumcised Philistine that he should defy the armies of the living God?*' cried David.

David overcame the first hurdle of his eldest brother's jealousy, but then King Saul dressed David in his own armour. David wasn't used to fighting in someone else's armour. Off it came. While looking after his father's sheep David had killed both a lion and a bear. He was ready to meet Goliath!

Then with staff and sling in hand he chose five smooth stones from the stream and put them in his shepherd's bag. Now these stones must have lain there from time immemorial at the mercy of rushing waters, the scorching heat of the sun and bitter cold night air. But God their Maker had a purpose even for these nondescript stones! Suddenly the day was upon them when they would no longer be trodden underfoot or at the mercy of wind or weather. They were now in the darkness of David's bag.

What next? David's searching fingers selected just the right one as he ran towards Israel's enemy and released it. If that little stone could talk would it have been able to contain its excitement at being chosen? I wonder what it thought at seeing Goliath's forehead coming towards it at an uncomfortably high speed? In a moment of time its destiny was fulfilled! Israel's enemy lay face down on the ground and David finished the job.

Maybe you've felt down-trodden for many a year … overlooked … in the dark … almost forgotten. Don't underestimate God's training school and time schedule. God hasn't forgotten you. In God's agenda nothing is by accident. Be patient. Your time will come and God's purposes will be fulfilled in your life!

PRAYER: *Dear Lord, please help me to understand the delays and testings You allow in my life so that I may fully enter into the destiny You have for me at the appointed time, in Jesus' name, Amen.*

NOVEMBER 19 | YOUR FAITH HAS HEALED YOU. GO IN PEACE.

ANGELA WEIR

He said to her, 'Daughter, your faith has healed you. Go in peace.'

Luke 8:48

Jesus speaks these words to the woman with the issue of blood, a story which touches my heart and which appears in three of the Gospels. I can imagine her, an outcast from society, lonely and frightened, creeping up behind Jesus, praying that at long last her bleeding would stop. Throughout those twelve, long years, everything she touched or sat on or lay down on would have become unclean and she would have known social isolation.

How did she feel as she pushed through the crowd to reach Jesus? How many people had she touched on the way? And here she was, reaching out to touch the 'holy man'! When He stopped and looked round to single her out she must have been terrified, and how embarrassing to have to explain what her complaint was in front of all those people.

Jesus not only confirmed her healing, but with one word He drew her back into society – the word 'daughter.' It's a word of inclusion, saying in effect, 'You're a member of my family, my daughter.' We don't know how old this woman was, but I imagine that she was probably older than Jesus and so for Him to call her His daughter must have been very special and have done much to heal the sense of isolation she had experienced.

Each one of us needs to feel that we belong somewhere. We can feel isolated in our churches, in our workplaces, even in our families sometimes, when no one else shares our faith, and that can be painful. My prayer today is especially for those of you who are feeling alone and isolated, and you can use it to pray for others.

PRAYER: *Dear Father, I pray today that You will be very close to those who feel alone, even within their families. May they know Your lovely presence surrounding them and bringing them comfort. In Jesus' precious name, I ask it, Amen.*

NOVEMBER 20 | OVERCOMING MY FEAR

MARGARET SOUTHEY

> *The Lord is near. Do not be anxious about anything, but in everything, by prayer and petition, with thanksgiving, present your requests to God. And the peace of God, which transcends all understanding, will guard your hearts and your minds in Christ Jesus.*
>
> Philippians 4:5–7

Do you struggle with fear? It's distressing, consumes our emotional energy and distracts us. It can also make us feel that we're not living the victorious life Jesus promises. The fear seems to come unexpectedly through a chance comment made by someone, through something we see or read or through a thought that comes to our mind. Before we realise it, the fear has taken a hold of us.

I was recently in a situation that made me fearful. I was able to recognise it for what it was: an ungodly fear. I determined to deal with it rather than give in to it and become its 'victim'. I read Scriptures. I renounced the fear when it took hold of me and I claimed the victory I had in Christ Jesus. To no avail! I remained fearful. No wonder, because although I was using godly weapons in my battle, I was doing it all in my own strength.

Much to my dismay, I discovered that my strength is actually not very strong. Finally, I did what I should have done in the first place. I went before the Lord. I told Him about my fear, which He knew about anyway. I confessed trying to deal with it in my own strength and asked Him to help me overcome it. It was not long after this that, while reading an article, Philippians 4:5–7 jumped out at me. I knew that it was God speaking to me and that He was giving me the verses He wanted to use in helping me overcome my fear.

I went before the Lord. I told Him about my fear, which He knew about anyway. I confessed trying to deal with it in my own strength and asked Him to help me overcome it.

'The Lord is near.' He felt close, not far away, as sometimes in the past. *'Do not be anxious about anything.'* Because His Spirit was speaking to my spirit, I could receive this instruction. *'In everything, by prayer and petition, with thanksgiving, present your requests to God.'* I presented my prayers to God. I told Him exactly what was on my mind, what I was afraid of and why. I was open with Him and also with myself as I spelled out my story. *'And the peace of God, which transcends all understanding, will guard your hearts and your minds in Christ Jesus.'* This is exactly what happened. His peace came and I was able to rest in it in a way I had not been able to do when I strove in my own strength to muster up His peace rather than ask Him for it. It is now more than six weeks later and I can testify to the fear no longer having a hold over me. So the lesson I learnt, and which I share, is that when I feel fearful again, I will take my fear to the Lord and ask His help in overcoming it.

PRAYER: *Thank You, Father, that, in You, I can overcome my fear. Today I bring You my fear and ask that You will help me deal with it. May my spiritual ears and eyes be open to Your leading and may I be obedient to You. Thank You that in and through You I have the victory over fear, in Jesus' name, Amen.*

NOVEMBER 21 | PROFOUND AND THANKFUL GOSSIP!

PETER HORROBIN

> *Jesus sent him away, saying, 'Return home and tell how much God has done for you.' So the man went away and told all over the town how much Jesus had done for him.*
>
> Luke 8:38–39

A seriously deranged man, who had inhabited the graveyards of Gadara, had been wonderfully healed and delivered by Jesus. This man, who formerly had been a threat to anyone who went near, was now restored and in his right mind. Naturally he wanted to become part of Jesus' travelling party.

But Jesus had a different message for him: Go back home and tell all the people you know how it is that you are now well. Tell them what God's done for you. Let the good news spread. This way many more people will hear and believe the good news.

Jesus said to the man, *'Tell how much God has done for you.'* The man told the people *'how much Jesus had done for him'*. He took out the word 'God' and put 'Jesus' in its place! Without realising what he was doing the former demoniac was making a profound theological statement – he was actually declaring that this man Jesus, who had healed him, must therefore be from God! For his instinctive belief was that only God could have healed him like that. He was speaking the truth – only God had the authority to deal with the highest powers Satan could muster against humanity, and if Jesus had that authority then He could only have got it from God.

A congregation which prays for healing and sees God at work among its people should also be an evangelising church. The world out there needs to know the truth about God, but how will they hear unless God's people speak out into their community what God has done? Fear often keeps people from telling the truth – they're afraid of what people will think.

My guess is that people will be more interested in hearing some outrageously good news than we realise. The Church needs to let the world know that God is alive and well, and Jesus is still healing people today. So if God has done something for you, do what Jesus told the former demoniac. Don't just keep that good news as a closely guarded secret inside a 'holy club' we call 'church'. Get out there and let the world around you know. Do a bit of gossiping of the good news!

PRAYER: *Help me, Lord, to use every opportunity to tell others about what You have done for me. Open my eyes to see the need in others to know the truth about You, in Jesus' name, Amen.*

NOVEMBER 22 | THE WORD OF LIFE

PATRICIA LAKE

> *But the word of the Lord endureth for ever. And this is the word which by the gospel is preached unto you.*
>
> 1 Peter 1:25, KJV

How wonderful and reassuring to know that in an age of shifting sands, crashing financial institutions and a crumbling economic climate, the Word of the Lord, in contrast, is strong, solid, reliable and dependable.

In the book of Samuel, the Scriptures tell us that the word of God was precious in those days, because the sins of Eli's sons, and the consequent sins of the people, threatened to extinguish and annihilate all that was God-fearing in the nation. *'And the child Samuel ministered unto the LORD before Eli. And the word of the LORD was precious in those days; there was no open vision'* (1 Samuel 3:1). *'And ere the lamp of God went out in the temple of the LORD, where the ark of God was, and Samuel was laid down to sleep; that the LORD called Samuel'* (1 Samuel 3:3–4).

God preserved and protected the essence of His truth in the heart of one who was willing to listen to His Word, even though a child, and speak the Word of His truth and subsequently turn the nation of Israel from their waywardness. God always has a remnant.

To the prophet Zechariah, God said, *'But my words and my statutes, which I commanded my servants the prophets, did they not take hold of your fathers?'* (Zechariah 1:6). His Word is for today! It is arresting and transforming; but it also transcends the generations and endures forever. This is why Jesus encourages us to build our house (our lives) on His Word, because the storms of life – not to mention the ravages of sin – would surely take their toll if we built on the wrong foundation.

This Word, which is sharper than any two-edged sword, will correct us when we are wrong; it will stop us in our tracks and will guide our footsteps along the precarious pathway of life with all its pitfalls. And finally, if we heed its instructions and cautions, it will deliver us safely to our destination. It's this Word that still sustains the laws of the universe, so you know you can depend on it!

Today, whatever difficulties, uncertainties or disappointments you are facing, know this: *His Word will be a lamp unto your feet, and a light unto your path* (see Psalm 119:105), because Christ Himself is the Word – the solid rock, reliable and dependable. No sinking sands!

PRAYER: *Thank You, Jesus, for Your Word. Help me to always remember that living according to Your Word is the safest and most dependable way to live, in Jesus' name, Amen.*

NOVEMBER 23 | DAVID SILVESTER

OVERCOMING INSECURITY AND A SENSE OF FAILURE

Go. I am sending you to Pharaoh to bring my people the Israelites out of Egypt.

Exodus 3:10

When it was discovered that Moses had murdered an Egyptian he ran for his life to Midian, a distance of at least 200 miles. Many years later God called to Moses from a burning bush and told him: '*I have indeed seen the misery of my people in Egypt. I have heard them crying out because of their slave drivers, and I am concerned about their suffering. So I have come down to rescue them*' (Exodus 3:7–8).

Having felt for his own people as they were suffering at the hands of the Egyptians, this must have encouraged Moses immensely. But he was completely unprepared for what the Lord said next. He was not prepared when God commissioned him to lead the Israelites out of Egypt.

Moses was to go to Pharaoh and ask him to release the people to go for a three-day journey into the desert to offer sacrifices to the Lord God. Even though God promised to be with him when he did this Moses became panicky, and presented all the reasons why he thought he was unsuitable for the task.

With miraculous signs God tried to convince Moses that He was with him and would help him. Yet Moses still argued that he was unsuited for the task, to the point that God's anger was roused (Exodus 4:14).

Have you ever had the experience when you have felt God speaking to you and showing you a task He wanted you to undertake for Him, but you felt totally unsuitable? When God called me to leave secular employment and train to be a pastor I was convinced He'd got the wrong man, and, like Moses, could give reasons for being unsuitable and even thought of other people who were more gifted for that task. It was only through responding in obedience that I learned how God is able to do what He's planned. He's able to reach and save lost souls, deliver bound people and heal the sick. These were the very things I had read of Jesus and His disciples doing, and questioned why such things were not happening in the churches today.

It's wonderful how God chooses and uses ordinary people like us to do extraordinary things for Him by the power of His Holy Spirit working in and through us. As we consider the way God used Moses, during the next forty years of his life, to bring the children of Israel out of Egypt to the Promised Land, we have an example of how God fulfils His plans. This is possible when those He calls are obedient to His call and His guidance.

As we near the end of the year, may we carefully listen for God, respond willingly in obedience to Him, and look on in amazement as we see Him do extraordinary things through ordinary individuals like us.

PRAYER: *O Lord God, I am sorry, and ask You to forgive me, for those times when I have not listened to You, and let You down by doing things in my own strength. Please help me to listen more attentively to You when You speak, and respond obediently to Your instructions, I pray, in Jesus' name, Amen.*

NOVEMBER 24 | FEEDING ON THE WORD

JILLY LYON-TAYLOR

Listen closely to my words. Do not let them out of your sight, keep them within your heart; for they are life to those who find them and health to a man's whole body.

Proverbs 4:20–22

If we were to take all the advice on nutrition that's offered us by the media, we would be changing our diet all the time! There's so much information about what's good for our health and what foods we should avoid. Some of the advice is sensible, but much of it has the effect of scaremongering and making people become preoccupied with diet.

However, physical food isn't the main source of life and health for us. Jesus reminds us in Matthew 4:4 that *'Man does not live on bread alone, but on every word that comes from the mouth of God.'* God's Word is living and active (Hebrews 4:12), and as we feed on it God's able to impart life to our spirits through His Spirit. He's able to speak to us through the Bible, with words of love, encouragement, guidance, and correction. But these verses from Proverbs tell us that the benefit of God's Word isn't only spiritual. It also brings health to a person's whole body. As we receive His Word into our spirits, life and health flow through into our whole being.

When the people of Israel were wandering in the desert, God instructed them to collect manna for their food (Exodus 16). They were to go out early in the morning each day to gather what they needed. That is an important principle for us. We need to be feeding daily on God's Word, which will nourish and sustain us physically as well as spiritually.

How healthy is your diet?

PRAYER: *Lord, please forgive me for the times I've been preoccupied with physical food and I've neglected to feed on the spiritual food that will nourish me. Please speak to me as I read Your Word, and bring Your life and health to every part of me through it. Amen.*

NOVEMBER 25 | FROM DEATH TO GLORIOUS LIFE!

PETER HORROBIN

> *I tell you the truth, unless a grain of wheat falls into the ground and dies, it remains only a single seed. But if it dies, it produces many seeds. The man who loves his life will lose it, while the man who hates his life in this world will keep it for eternal life.*
>
> John 12:24–25

I can understand why some people have a love-hate relationship with Jesus. They love it when He says things they like and which give them comfort. They love it when Jesus says, *'Come to me, all of you who are weary and burdened'* (Matthew 11:28). They love it when, talking about heaven, Jesus says, *'I am going to prepare a place for you'* (John 14:2). They love it when they realise that because of Jesus, their sins can be forgiven.

But then they hear Jesus telling people to forgive their enemies, to give away what they have to others and then to take up a cross in order to follow

Him! Suddenly, it seems, Jesus is no longer such a welcome friend. His teaching cuts right across the desires of the flesh.

After all, there is only one purpose for a cross – and that's to cause death! Not an attractive proposition at the best of times. And yet, the cross is at the heart of the gospel – for without death, there could be no resurrection and without the resurrection there could be no eternal life.

Our scripture for today illustrates this vital principle. Just as a grain of wheat has to give up its own life before there can be multiplication, it's only as we choose to live for God, instead of ourselves, that we can enjoy amazing Kingdom multiplication. Our life, our time, our money and all our possessions are ultimately a gift from God. How we use them is up to us. But, if we desire our lives to bear much fruit for the Kingdom of God, then first we must choose to die. We must learn to love the things we want to hate! Think about the things Jesus said which, if you are really honest, you don't like. Ask God for His grace and understanding so you can learn to love all that Jesus said.

PRAYER: *Thank You, Jesus, that You were willing to take up Your cross that I might live. Forgive me, Lord, for the times I forget that everything I have belongs to You. I pray now that my whole life may, as good seed, be sown into this world, producing a large harvest for Your Kingdom. Amen.*

NOVEMBER 26 | THIRST

JOAN RONO

> *As the deer pants for the water brooks, so pants my soul for You, O God.*
>
> Psalm 42:1, NKJV

As I watched the *Transformation* videos, I realised why it was that God moved in certain areas where revival was experienced. It was the desire of those who wanted to see change in the lives of people and even whole nations! I believe that this desire is what triggered people to come to a place of repentance and seeking God.

In Africa we have antelopes, which are the same as deer. They run fast in hot and dry grasslands. You can see the way they pant when they need water. The desperation leads them to find streams of water where they quench their thirst.

Unless I thirst I'm not really desperate for a glass of water! The same concept applies to us in our Christian lives. Unless we thirst for the presence of God we can't really get desperate for the outpouring of His Spirit.

Sometimes we get a little complacent and feel self-satisfied. But this isn't what God wants. He wants us to long for Him, to look to Him every day for a new filling, a new revelation and a refreshing of His presence.

Elisha was called to help a widow who was a prophet's wife. After her husband died she was left with a big debt. She had nothing to pay the debt, and her debtors were demanding that she pay with her sons. It was a desperate situation for her. If she gave her sons, she could have been left with nothing. Elisha asked her for empty jars and she had to pour the little oil she had into the jars. The oil only stopped when there were no more jars.

We need to make room in our hearts for God's presence, because we get the same measure we thirst for, or we have made room for. How do we create more room in our hearts? By cleansing ourselves of any unclean thing, and forgiving others who have wronged us. We should keep our hearts clean and clear for Him to move and have a place in us.

We need to make room in our hearts for God's presence, because we get the same measure we thirst for, or we have made room for. How do we create more room in our hearts? By cleansing ourselves of any unclean thing, and forgiving others who have wronged us. We should keep our hearts clean and clear for Him to move and have a place in us.

Also we need to spend time in His presence. I once asked myself: 'What occupies my time?' 'What do I feed myself with?' In our busy technology-oriented society, we might find ourselves stuck in front of the computer screen or the TV, glued to our favourite novel or busy on the phone. There are a lot of things fighting for our attention and time. This can be a great hindrance to spending time in God's presence.

Is your heart panting for the Lord? Is there anything that has stolen the longing to be in His presence? What do you feed on? As you ask yourself these questions, seek to draw near to Him more and more.

Prayer: *Lord, thank You for Your salvation. I acknowledge that I need You every single day and moment of my life. Help me to take out the ungodly things that I have allowed to occupy my heart, and cleanse me. Indwell me with Your Holy Spirit and give me a thirst for You. Thank You for lavishing Your love on me. Amen.*

November 27 | From Darkness to Light

Goran Andersson

And God said: 'Let there be light' and there was light.

Genesis 1:3

We talk about 'from early morning until night', but in the Bible it's usually the other way round. It's from night into day – from darkness to light. Just reflect on it! There's a different feeling about the order it comes in the Bible.

Life isn't just putting together the big things, and once we get those in place everything is OK. No, life is organising a never-ending series of minute details so that everything works well. The more details there are, the more chance there is that something may go wrong, and the more chance we may get discouraged. 'The devil is in the details' is a popular saying.

Even if you don't see the light right now, as clearly as you would like to, God is true to His word, and will lead you into the place of light and clarity!

It's no surprise that in this daily battle to keep all of the small things from going wrong we sometimes get disheartened. We see darkness descend over our day, and we lose the exhilarating anticipation of God's provision and blessing.

This is when we need to receive the message God brings in His Word. In His Kingdom the flow is from darkness to light, not from light to darkness! It's expressed this way in Proverbs 4:18: *'The path of the righteous is like the first gleam of dawn, shining ever brighter till the full light of day'.*

This doesn't mean the righteous will never have any difficulties or never meet with any adverse circumstances. But it does mean that God's will is for darkness to turn into light, and that in everything *'God works for the good of those who love him'* (Romans 8:28). It also means that we can be assured of the direction God leads us. We don't need to fear He will let us down when we have a bad day or when we slip up and make a mistake.

God's will for you is more light! More of His presence, more of His life, and more of His Kingdom. Even if you don't see the light right now, as clearly as you would like to, God is true to His word, and will lead you into the place of light and clarity!

The Bible starts with a creation that rises out of darkness, but it ends with a city where there's so much light that the sun is not needed. If God can do that, surely He can change your darkness into light! Glory be to Him!

PRAYER: *Dear Heavenly Father, I thank You that You bring good out of the difficulties and adverse circumstances I go through. I pray You will shine Your light into all the darkness that surrounds me and bring me into Your presence today, in Jesus' name, Amen.*

NOVEMBER 28 | HEALED AND REIGNING IN LIFE

HERMAN REDELINGHUYS

For if, because of one man's trespass, death reigned through that one man, how much more will those who receive the abundance of grace and the free gift of righteousness reign in life through the one man Jesus Christ.

Romans 5:17, ESV

One evening I heard a high-pitched noise and saw a mosquito circling around me and I thought, 'How can such a tiny, insignificant insect be responsible for such a reign of pain and death throughout the continent of Africa?' The World Health Organization has estimated that every thirty seconds a child dies of malaria in sub-Saharan Africa. As I was staring at this unique little 'flying machine' I was reminded of the scripture in Romans 5:17 which says, *'because of one man's trespass, death reigned'*, and I thought about the devastation throughout the ages caused by one man!

The quest for a cure that will conquer the reign of malaria is still continuing, with millions of dollars spent on this cause every year. The world needs this, but how much more the world needs an eternal cure from all pain and death. The good news is that the cure was achieved through *'the abundance of grace and the free gift of righteousness'* of Jesus Christ. *'Therefore, as one trespass led to condemnation for all men, so one act of righteousness leads to justification and life for all men. For as by the one man's disobedience the many were made sinners, so by the one man's obedience the many will be made righteous'* (Romans 5:18–19). It's through one Man's obedience on the cross that we've received an eternal cure in life!

God didn't just want us to be healed but intended us to *'reign in life through the one man Jesus Christ'*. We were healed to reign! It's this 'reigning' part that I find the most challenging. How do we reign in life? The Bible says we lost life by one man's disobedience and life was restored through Jesus' act of obedience, and if we are in Jesus and obey Him then we can reign in life with Him!

You maybe feel challenged by the situation you're facing right now. It may appear quite overpowering, complicated or just 'a bridge too far'. God encourages you today to take the first small step to obey Him and to keep on taking steps in the direction He's leading you. These small steps of obedience are far from insignificant. They're powerful in Him. As you obey may you grow and discover the joy of being healed to reign in life with Jesus.

PRAYER: *Lord Jesus, thank You so much for Your amazing act of obedience that brought me the 'cure of life'. Lord, I ask You to give me the courage to obey You today, so I may reign in life with You! Amen.*

NOVEMBER 29 | NEW OR MATURE WINE?

DAVID CROSS

> *When the headwaiter tasted the water which had become wine, [he] did not know where it came from (but the servants who had drawn the water knew).*
>
> John 2:9, NASB

In this amazing story, Jesus miraculously created wine at a wedding party. The headwaiter was surprised at the quality. He goes on to say how it's very unusual to keep such good wine until the end of the celebrations. Had the headwaiter analysed the wine he would no doubt have been able to define the variety of grapes. No doubt he could have described the history of the wine going back to a vineyard on some hillside.

Although his expertise and analysis might well have arrived at an indisputable scientific origin for this exceptional wine, he would actually have been totally wrong. The servants who witnessed the miracle were the only ones, besides Jesus, who knew for certain that this apparently mature wine had been created just minutes before.

It's just the same with this extraordinary world around us. Scientific analysis will always discover, and apparently prove, a substantial history going back countless numbers of years. However, if we believe the story of the miracle at the Cana wedding, it's only a very small step to believe in God's creation of this complex world.

When landscape and life came into being, they inevitably came with an apparent history, just like the wine at the wedding feast. By every test available to the headwaiter, the wine had a significant maturity. But really it had only been in physical existence from the moment Jesus miraculously created it. This world appears to have a certain maturity which some say they can prove, but the Bible tells us that it began at a different point in time – the moment of God's creation.

We have the choice to view the origin of this world either like the headwaiter, who depended on his own experience, or like the servants who had the amazing privilege of discovering the supernatural ability of Jesus!

PRAYER: *Thank You, Lord, for creating the amazing world in which we live. Help me to turn my awe to worship as I look at the wonders of Your creation. In Jesus' name, Amen.*

NOVEMBER 30 | THE DESIRE OF MY HEART FOR MY FAMILY

ROGER POOK

> *You have granted him the desire of his heart and have not withheld the request of his lips.*
>
> Psalm 21:2

How often have you heard people praising God because their children and even their grandchildren are believers and are following God's call on their lives? And how often has this brought a deep sadness to you, because your own children have fallen away from the faith that you taught them to the best of your ability?

You probably feel like Job who said, '*My days have passed, my plans are shattered, and so are the desires of my heart*' (Job 17:11). We love our children so much, we believe we've brought them up right, and the thought of them no longer sharing in our salvation is almost too hard to bear.

Of course, we keep on praying for them! Nobody can underestimate the power of prayer: *'The prayer of a righteous man is powerful and effective'* (James 5:16). But as the years pass, a sense of hopelessness threatens to rob us of the faith that we once had. Maybe we are even ashamed of our family, feeling that it's 'a bad witness' that our children have lost their faith. Sometimes, in a private place, our emotions well up and we find ourselves crying out in despair for our lost loved ones – like we have so often before. It really hurts.

We don't know the family details of the apostle Paul, or even if he was ever married, but he had the same desire for his own people: *'Brothers, my heart's desire and prayer to God for the Israelites is that they may be saved'* (Romans 10:1). Two thousand years later, Paul's prayer is being answered more and more as Messianic congregations spring up all over the world and in 'The Land' itself – but we can't wait 2,000 years for our children to be saved!

Never give up! Share your desires with other people so that they can pray with you from time to time. Keep on loving your children and assuring them of your love, even if they seem to be trying to avoid you.

Please believe this: your faith and your prayers are not in vain. God *'shows love to a thousand generations of those who love him and keep his commandments'*, and blessing will always flow from you to your family. God knows the deepest desires and groanings of your heart, and His desire is to grant them. '*Therefore I tell you, whatever you ask for in prayer, believe that you have received it, and it will be yours'* (Mark 11:24).

Never give up! Share your desires with other people so that they can pray with you from time to time. Keep on loving your children and assuring them of your love, even if they seem to be trying to avoid you. Maybe even now the Holy Spirit is bringing a conviction to their hearts and the enemy is trying to stifle it, so don't give up!

PRAYER: *Heavenly Father, I'm so grateful that my children were able to hear Your truth when they were young. I ask You now to speak to them by Your Holy Spirit, break down the barriers that the enemy has built, and call them back to Yourself. Grant me the desire of my heart for my children, because I know that it's also Your desire. I ask this in Jesus' precious name. Amen.*

December 1 | He Shall Cover You

Pam Smith

He shall cover you with His feathers, and under His wings you shall take refuge.

Psalm 91:4, NKJV

Parents instinctively want to cover their children, especially if they have kicked their clothes off or become uncovered in some way. Perhaps, like me, you remember your mum or dad saying when you were little, 'Go up to bed and I'll come and tuck you in.' It was such a comfort to feel the bedclothes being tucked in and be cosy, secure and loved. Most children have duvets now, but they can still be 'tucked in'.

We all like to be covered up. But sometimes we become uncovered, because we've sinned, done something thoughtless, or perhaps it's through being ignorant. The Lord longs to cover us when we become unprotected and vulnerable to danger. The blood of Jesus covers our sin and protects us from the enemy. It's the most powerful covering there is. The power of the precious blood of Jesus comes through everything that was accomplished by Jesus, the Son of God, on the cross of Calvary. It's our shield and refuge.

When we face the darkest evil, the hardest temptation or the fiercest battle, we don't need to be afraid. We can plead for the precious blood of Jesus to cover us. This is the glorious covering that God provides for everyone who believes in Him and receives forgiveness for their sins. So even if you've never had anyone to cover you up or 'tuck you in' until now, there's a Saviour. He loves you so much that He'll enfold you in His love. He'll cover you completely, so that you're wonderfully secure, and forever safe beneath His wings.

God provided a Passover lamb as a blood covering to protect His people Israel when they came out of the land of Egypt: *'Now the blood shall be a sign for you on the houses where you are. And when I see the blood, I will pass over you; and the plague shall not be on you to destroy you when I strike the land of Egypt'* (Exodus 12:13). He was going to provide the future Passover Lamb, Jesus Christ, to be a covering for all His people, and Jesus is described in the book of Revelation as *'the Lamb slain from the foundation of the world'*.

Prayer: *Lord, we worship and praise You for being our covering. We can't cover ourselves, but we know the comfort and freedom we have under Your precious blood. We thank You, Father, in Jesus' name.*

DECEMBER 2 | COME OVER AND HELP US!

PETER HORROBIN

During the night Paul had a vision of a man from Macedonia standing and begging him, 'Come over to Macedonia and help us.'

Acts 16:9

God shows us the way ahead in so many different ways. If there is something happening right before our eyes that needs our help or involvement God doesn't need to give us a vision. We simply need to act responsibly in simple obedience to the love of God, which will always constrain us to do what is right. We don't need instructions to help someone who has fallen, or share our food with someone who is hungry. Those are things we should do without being asked – they are part of the standing orders for the Body of Christ.

But at other times God may want us to do something *'right out of the box'* – something we couldn't possibly have known about in the natural. It's at times like these that God uses different methods to get our attention. Sometimes it's an inner and insistent voice. From being a young child I learnt from my mum and dad how important it was to recognise this inner voice of God. Later in life there were a couple of occasions when God spoke to me like that, and on one of them I was instrumental in saving someone's life.

Then there are those rarer occasions, when God uses more than the 'still small voice' on the inside. He gives a clear vision. This is what happened to Paul when he was in Troas. In his vision a man from Macedonia was calling for help. It was Paul's obedience to this vision that took the gospel into Europe for the first time. The most significant moment in my own pilgrimage was when I was starting to rebuild an old car, but the chassis frame was bent. As I looked at it God spoke to me and said, *'You could repair this broken car, but I can restore broken lives. Which is more important?'* It was that word from the Lord which set me on my life's calling to bring healing and restoration to hurting and broken people.

When God does speak clearly to us, He doesn't override our free will. It is up to us to choose what we do. But when we obey, we will always discover that His way is the path of blessing and fruitfulness.

PRAYER: *Thank You, Lord, that You are a God who speaks – that You are a Father who loves to show Your children the way to go. Help me to be always listening for Your voice and give me the courage to do those things You ask me to do, in Jesus' name, Amen.*

DECEMBER 3 | OBSOLESCENCE

MALCOLM WOOD

> *He who was seated on the throne said, 'I am making everything new!'*
>
> Revelation 21:5

In this 'throwaway age' we perhaps too often hear the words, 'They don't make that model any more' or 'We can no longer obtain parts for that particular model.' No doubt many of us, at some time or another, have had to say goodbye to a piece of equipment or appliance which has served us well for many years and would perhaps continue to do so if someone would take the time and effort to repair it, or if the faulty part worth probably only a few pence was still available.

Isn't it a blessing that God doesn't treat us like that? No matter what may be wrong with us, whether due to our own misuse, or that done to us by others, no one is beyond repair. God has never changed or updated the 'model'! Yes, we are all unique. Each one of us is different, yet made in His likeness. We all too have the same basic needs for love, nurture, companionship and fulfilment, and we all have an inbuilt potential to fulfil the destiny God planned for us even before we were born.

Every part of us, every area of our lives, has a place and purpose in God's blueprint for our life. Our design was not a mistake; nothing is wasted or redundant or obsolete.

If there are areas or parts of our lives in which we feel we aren't functioning as we should be – take it to the 'Manufacturer'! He's the only one who can repair, renew and restore us to the original design He had for us.

So often the enemy would have those of us who are older think that we are 'past our best' or have passed our 'use by date'. If we do start thinking like that we need to take comfort from the words of the apostle Paul who said, '*Therefore we do not lose heart. Though outwardly we are wasting away, yet inwardly we are being renewed day by day*' (2 Corinthians 4:16) and the psalmist when he exclaimed that the Lord '*satisfies your desires with good things so that your youth is renewed like the eagle's*' (Psalm 103:5).

Isn't that what life in the Spirit is all about? Continual renewal!

Prayer: *Dear Lord, thank You for never giving up on us and making us redundant or obsolete. Thank You that You're always willing to remould us and remake us into the people You originally intended us to be. Amen.*

December 4 | Who Has the Better Plan?

Paul Watson

The chief cupbearer, however, did not remember Joseph; he forgot him.

Genesis 40:23

Joseph was an inspiring character. How did he keep a godly attitude when life brought him such a lot of strife, pain, and disappointment? The youngest boy in the family (for a significant period of his life); Dad's favourite; living with the jealousy of the older half-brothers. He had been sold into slavery, but had risen to a place of favour and importance with Potiphar. Then, despite showing remarkable resistance to the seductive advances of his master's wife in a display of uncommon godliness, Joseph was falsely accused and thrown into prison. We don't know how long he was in prison, but again he showed his good character and was entrusted with great responsibility serving under the prison warden. I wonder how he came to terms with his situation. How did he deal with his anger and hurt which would have stemmed from the injustice in his life?

Then, here comes a chance to get out of prison! The cupbearer and the baker have been sentenced to prison for displeasing Pharaoh. Joseph interprets their dreams and while it's not a happy forecast for the baker, the cupbearer is going to be reinstated. I can imagine Joseph thinking, 'OK, here is my chance. If Mr Cupbearer goes back to his job working closely with Pharaoh, perhaps he can put in a good word for me, and I can be released and return home.' So he asks the man to *'mention me to Pharaoh and get me out of this prison'* (Genesis 40:14).

As our verse tells us, Joseph was again disappointed. The cupbearer forgot all about Joseph. In Joseph's position, I would have been tempted to become negative, bitter, and would probably feel angry at all the people who had caused me to be in that situation, and also angry at God. But Joseph was safe in God's will and purposes. God had a much better plan than Joseph had. Joseph's plan was to organise things so he could be released from the prison. God's plan was to rescue His people from starvation. His bigger plan was to rescue the whole world from captivity to sin, the world and the devil.

When things don't work out as I think they ought to, I try to think of this story of Joseph, and I ask my Heavenly Dad to help me to trust that His plan is perfect – far better than mine. How about you?

PRAYER: *Dear Heavenly Dad, please help me to trust that Your plan is the very best, and to be assured that as I trust You I am secure and safe. Amen.*

DECEMBER 5 | TELL OF ALL HIS WONDERFUL ACTS

GORAN ANDERSSON

> *Give thanks to the LORD, call on his name, make known among the nations what he has done. Sing to him, sing praise to him, tell of all his wonderful acts.*
>
> Psalm 105:1–2

There are places in God's Word where His people are called upon to be quiet before Him. The reason given for this is usually that we should reverently consider His greatness, and listen to what He has to say. It's more important to listen to God, than to talk to Him.

But having listened to Him, we are encouraged to talk to each other and to the world around us. *'Speak to one another with psalms, hymns and spiritual songs. Sing and make music in your heart to the Lord'* (Ephesians 5:19). Sometimes we may feel that we've got very little to say, and we're not as skilled as others in saying it. Sure, there are always orators that can form their words beautifully and be eloquent and convincing. But do they really have something to say? There's a difference between just putting words together or saying something important!

So much material is published and so much information is available. Most of it is forgotten in a matter of days or weeks. Can we make our testimony about our God heard under these circumstances? Don't our words just drown in the general cacophony of sounds?

No! Because there's content in those words. They strike a chord in people's hearts, and tell them about hope and truth. There's a market for your testimony about God's faithfulness and mighty deeds! Paul sometimes spoke with fear and trembling, not with powerful words, but the message got through. And it bore fruit. Lives were changed, societies made new and old habits broken. All because of some simple words by a fearful man.

It is the content that counts! So let the nations hear, let people listen! You've got something to tell, something to sing about: the mighty acts of the Lord!

In a big choir it may seem that a single voice isn't very important, but it is, because the mighty sound of the choir is made up of all those single, seemingly unimportant voices. Together they make a whole concert hall vibrate with beautiful sound; together they get the message across to the audience. Very few have a solo part to sing, but the harmony of their voices, the unity in their words, is so powerful. And it is built up from all the many voices!

That's how we can let the nations hear of our God. When all the individual voices, all the different testimonies, all the godly actions, are heard and seen, that's a message which brings good tidings!

PRAYER: *Dear Heavenly Father, I thank You that there is a song I can sing even at my place of work. As I speak words over a cup of tea or coffee, or lend a helping hand to a neighbour, help me to be that one voice in the big choir that speaks to the nations about the greatness of our God so that the earth may hear Your voice, in Jesus' name, Amen.*

DECEMBER 6 | MARKET FORCES

DAVID CROSS

> *Love your enemies and do good to them; lend and expect nothing back. You will then have a great reward, and you will be children of the Most High God. For he is good to the ungrateful and the wicked.*
>
> Luke 6:35, GNB

We're hearing a lot at the moment about the cost and the difficulty of borrowing money. Interest rates are currently falling, but banks are much more wary of lending than they were a year ago. Many businesses are folding up through lack of sufficient cash flow. We are daily becoming very aware of the damaging effects of the credit crunch!

Once again Jesus has already spoken about such issues, with one of His radical statements of how things operate in the Kingdom over which He rules. He says, *'Lend and expect nothing back.'*

Try suggesting that idea to your local bank manager! He will consider you to be a joker or a fool. We live in a world where we're told that *market forces* must inevitably hold sway. This is an interesting expression which implies that there's unseen control operating behind the financial transactions of business. In Matthew 6:24, we find that Jesus calls the ungodly aspect of this controlling power *mammon*. It's actually a spiritual power which feeds on false security and greed. Jesus encourages us not to serve it or be controlled by it, but rather to serve God.

We're in the world and therefore daily affected by its financial systems. We regularly need to participate in financial transactions and these will not necessarily be wrong. Money is not a root of evil but rather it's the *love* of money that's the problem (1 Timothy 6:10). As followers of Jesus, there will be occasions when God gives a clear instruction for us to act in a way which apparently contradicts the world's *market forces*. It may well be a command to give without the expectation of a return. At that moment of hearing God's direction we have the opportunity to show whom we love and whom we serve. What a challenge!

PRAYER: *Father God, help me to live wisely and honestly within the financial systems of this world without being wrongly controlled by them, or letting the love of money direct my life. Help me to hear Your voice at critical times of my own need or the need of others, so that Your Kingdom purposes can be fulfilled. Amen.*

DECEMBER 7 | THEY ARE MY GLORY

PAM SMITH

> *And all of them, since they are mine, belong to you; and you have given them back to me with everything else of yours, and so they are my glory.*
>
> John 17:10, LB

Jesus says, *'and so they are my glory'*. This is what we are – His own special people, His inheritance, His joy. The dictionary says glory is honour, praise, and magnificence. We may desire to bring Him all these things, but sometimes our lives and actions can bring Him the opposite. Sometimes we may bring Him shame.

But here's the wonderful truth. In His grace and mercy He can take away that shame and sin as He forgives us. That's why we should never give up or think that we're not good enough. When we repent of our sins we become 'His glory' and we bring Him joy. I believe this is the joy that was set before Jesus talked about in Hebrews 12:2: *'Looking unto Jesus, the author and finisher of our faith, who for the joy that was set before him endured the cross, despising the shame, and has sat down at the right hand of the throne of God'* (NKJV).

We are God's garden and we are His temple. He lives in us: *'Your own body does not belong to you. For God has bought you with a great price. So use every part of your body to give glory back to God, because he owns it'* (1 Corinthians 6:20, LB).

Those of you who are teachers, coaches, mentors, pastors or helpers will all know the joy when those whose lives you influence do well. This brings a tribute to you. In the same way as parents and grandparents you have pride in your family when they achieve something.

And so we, who belong to the Lord, are His glory. Even when we are weak His power and strength can shine through us and He is the one who gets the glory. His prayer was, and is, that His joy may be fulfilled in us.

PRAYER: *May we see Your glory, Lord, and may we be humbled by Your mercy, in Jesus' name, Amen.*

DECEMBER 8 | THE FORGIVENESS TEST

JILL SOUTHERN-JONES

You intended to harm me, but God intended it for good to accomplish what is now being done, the saving of many lives.

Genesis 50:20

Joseph had undergone many tests and preparations before God allowed him to become the Prime Minister of Egypt. Joseph had now become rich, powerful and famous, but he had to go through another critical test. He had to forgive his brothers for wanting to kill him, for putting him down the pit and then selling him to Ishmaelite traders, who took him down to Egypt to sell him on as a slave.

Now the tables had been turned. Joseph was in charge of food distribution and Joseph's family from back home were hungry. When his brothers came to Egypt for corn, he recognised them. He had the power for taking revenge – but what would he do?

He chose to extend his hand to forgive his brothers. Until he did so there would be a big unhealed area in Joseph that would affect his own destiny. He was able to say to them, 'You intended to harm me but God intended it for good.' Joseph had learnt that God brings good from evil for all those who trust in Him.

He saw the hand of God behind all that had happened and not only reassured his brothers of his forgiveness but also offered to care for them and their families. The dream had been fulfilled; Joseph had walked fully into his destiny of providing for Israel throughout the time of famine. Joseph was now ready to die. He had no doubts that God would keep His promise and one day bring the Israelites back to their homeland.

The secret of that kind of faith is a lifetime of trusting God. Your faith is like a muscle; it grows with exercise. And you can be certain God will always keep His promises to you.

PRAYER: *Lord, help me to exercise faith today as I walk with You. I don't want unforgiveness to stand between me and my destiny in God. Please help me to forgive those who have hurt me. Thank You that nothing is too hard for You, in Jesus' name, Amen.*

DECEMBER 9 | CLEAR DIRECTION TO MOVE ON MOVE ON

DAVID SILVESTER

> *You have stayed long enough at this mountain. Break camp and advance into the hill country ...*
>
> Deuteronomy 1:6–7

On what do we base our decisions to make changes in life? After a period of fruitful ministry, where we saw God do some amazing things in the village church we were pastoring, my wife and I both felt God highlighted Deuteronomy 1:6–7 to us, in our separate quiet times, on the same day.

We had been in a period that could be described as being on a high place where we could look down upon all God had been achieving. When we discussed this with the elders of the church, they prayed, and also recognised that it was God's instructions for us to 'move on', although they wanted us to stay and continue with what God was doing. The clarity of the wording, to '*advance into the hill country*', was for us a clear call to move north and become involved with Ellel Ministries. We had been living in the relatively flat lands of the East Midlands.

In the two churches we had been involved with, God had taken us step by step into a healing and deliverance ministry. Yet when He called us from our secular occupations we only had a scant knowledge and experience of such things. We soon discovered that when God calls He equips, and gives all that we need for the service He has called us to.

In those church situations the challenge of Jesus was uppermost. He had said, '*As you go, preach this message: "The kingdom of heaven is near." Heal the sick, raise the dead, cleanse those who have leprosy, drive out demons*' (Matthew 10:7–8). I was brought up in a Christian home yet I had wondered why these things were not being practised. We soon recognised that when they are, God blesses so many people.

How can we get clear directions for the future, and how does God challenge and direct us? How do we respond when His challenges come? Do we wait for someone to give a word of prophecy, or do we let God speak personally through Scripture? Having witnessed a number of 'false prophecies', I prefer to let God speak directly to me through His Word.

Take time to listen carefully as God speaks through His Word, and look for Him to do His wonders as you respond.

PRAYER: *O Lord God, I only want to do the things You want me to do and go the way You direct. Help me to hear Your voice in my heart and through Your Word, and give me the patience to wait until Your call comes to me clearly and plainly. In Jesus' name I pray, Amen.*

DECEMBER 10 | THE DIVINE EXCHANGE

PAM SMITH

> *For God took the sinless Christ and poured into him our sins. Then, in exchange, he poured God's goodness into us.*
>
> 2 Corinthians 5:21, LB

This is the beginning of his amazing grace towards us and the glorious life He longs to give us in His divine exchange. '*What a difference between man's sin and God's forgiveness! For this one man, Adam, brought death to many through his sin. But this one man, Jesus Christ, brought forgiveness to many through God's mercy. Adam's one sin brought the penalty of death to many, while Christ takes away many sins and gives glorious life instead*' (Romans 5:15–16, LB).

When we become followers of Jesus we can experience some of these divine exchanges. Some of these things take place as we grow in our faith and obedience to His Word.

He takes our burdens and gives us His rest. He takes our despair and gives us certain hope. He takes our weakness and gives us His strength. He gives us beauty instead of ashes and the oil of joy instead of mourning. He exchanges a spirit of heaviness for a garment of praise. He changes our darkness into His brilliant light.

He became poor that we might become rich. He puts our feet on solid rock instead of sinking sand. He exchanges His love for our indifference. He changes our worries for His peace. He takes our brokenness and makes us whole. He changes our sadness into a new song of joy. He exchanges our rags for a robe of righteousness. He changes our insecurity into godly confidence. He changes failed lives into new beginnings. He can make the impossible a possibility.

'No eye has seen, no ear has heard, no mind has conceived what God has prepared for those who love him – but God has revealed it to us by his Spirit' (1 Corinthians 2:9–10). As you search the Scriptures may you discover many more instances of divine exchanges.

PRAYER: *Thank You, Lord, for all Your mercies and the exchanges You are bringing about in the lives of those who follow You. Amen.*

DECEMBER 11 | SLAVE OR SON?

PAUL WATSON

> *But he [the older brother] answered his father, 'Look! All these years I have been slaving for you and never disobeyed your orders. Yet you never gave me even a young goat so I could celebrate with my friends.'*
>
> Luke 15:29

As a father, I have a deep love for my daughter and three sons. Over twenty-seven years of fatherhood, my great delight has been to enjoy relationship with my children. I trust that in that time, despite my obvious failings as a dad, my children will have known that my love and acceptance of them have been freely given, and are not things to be doubted or which have to be earned.

In the parable commonly known as 'the parable of the prodigal son', Jesus quite powerfully presents a picture of His Father – His Abba (Daddy) – to His hearers. It's a stunning image. He's a Father who moves towards His imperfect sons in love and acceptance.

I'm intrigued by the responses of the two sons to the heart of their dad. The younger son has taken the money and run. He has 'blown it' and now seeks to return home after realising that he's doomed if he doesn't. But he believes that by his failings, and his sins, he has forfeited all rights as a son. At best he can only hope to come back as a hired worker – as a *servant* of his father.

How many of us feel that we have 'blown it' by some area of sin in our life? How many of us are dutifully carrying out our tasks as obedient Christians, yet in effect seeing ourselves as slaves? Our Heavenly Dad has so much more for us to enjoy.

The older brother has been working faithfully for his father. He didn't ask for his share of the inheritance. He didn't go and waste it in wild partying. No, he remained at home where, in his own words, he was *'slaving'* for his father all these years.

Here they are – two beloved sons, yet neither one living in the truth of what their status of sonship meant. The younger believed that his status as a son was contingent on him staying perfectly in line. When he moved off line, he believed he had lost his sonship. The elder only saw himself as a slave. Slaves work hard and don't expect privileges. Slaves relate to their masters in subservient obedience – marked by fear of failure and its consequent rejection.

It's quite sad, isn't it? Both sons didn't really know their dad, and both missed out on the fullness of relationship and life that their dad wanted them to enjoy with him.

How many of us feel that we have 'blown it' by some area of sin in our life? How many of us are dutifully carrying out our tasks as obedient Christians, yet in effect seeing ourselves as slaves? Our Heavenly Dad has so much more for us to enjoy. We are sons. Not slaves!

PRAYER: *Heavenly Father, please help me today to know the truth of what it means to be a 'son'. Would You please reveal to me the areas in my life where I am still a slave. I want to be free to enjoy my status as a son [daughter] of the Father, in Jesus' name, Amen.*

December 12 | Taste and See

Anne Lawrence

Therefore, rid yourselves of all malice and all deceit, hypocrisy, envy and slander of every kind. Like newborn babies, crave pure spiritual milk, so that by it you may grow up in your salvation, now that you have tasted that the Lord is good.

1 Peter 2:1–3

As a baby we are helpless and dependent on our parents for food and care. Very early on all we know is what we need for our immediate comfort – things like warmth, safety, love and good milk. If this was provided, then that environment helped us to grow – physically through the food and warmth, and spiritually through the love and care. In this passage, Peter is reminding the believers that as young Christians they, like a baby, craved these things to grow spiritually.

Interestingly he reminds them that they *'tasted that the Lord is good'*. This refers back to Psalm 34:8: *'Taste and see that the LORD is good.'* As a child we taste our mother's milk and it tastes sweet and good. We know that it's good for us. If anyone had given us something that was not good for us, we would have known and probably spat it out. Ugh! Horrible!

As a young Christian, we taste the sweetness of the Lord's presence, love and truth in His Word. This taste gradually becomes familiar and is what brings peace and rest to our spirits and souls.

Peter started by talking about things we should rid ourselves of: malice, deceit, hypocrisy, envy and slander. Having tasted the sweet taste of the Lord, those things – malice, deceit, hypocrisy, envy and slander – should taste bitter and we should want to immediately spit them out. Those things bring unrest and disruption to our spirits and souls. So, let's make the choice to spit them out – to put them off and repent – and to take in the sweetness of the Lord through His love and His Word.

Prayer: *Heavenly Father, thank You for the sweetness of Your presence and Your living Word. I choose to feed on those things as I walk through today. Please help me to recognise things which are not of You and give me the strength to immediately spit them out. Lord, take my hand as I walk into today – feeding on Your goodness. Amen.*

December 13 | Retargeting Our Lives

Otto Bixler

But seek first His kingdom and His righteousness; and these things shall be added to you.

Matthew 6:33, NASB

We are meant to step out of worry, by giving God our issues, concerns and the feelings we have about them. In Philippians 4:6–8 we are given the commandment of God to be anxious for nothing, but through prayer, supplication and thanksgiving to make our requests to God so that the peace that surpasses all our comprehension will come upon us. Neglecting God's commandments keeps God from bathing us in His love and stops His disclosure of Himself to us. If we can't hear Him, how will we know what to do in the face of our problems?

We are to seek first the Kingdom of God. Perhaps this commandment is more difficult since it seems a more supernatural requirement. You may argue that God's Kingdom is invisible, elusive or comes only at the end of the age. So, how can we seek or target God's Kingdom? Or, what in God's Kingdom can we target?

The answer is quite simple. Ephesians 2:10 tells us that we are created for God's good works which He prepared for us to walk through.

As God's sons and daughters, following Jesus, we need to be doing what the Father is doing. Seeking the Kingdom of God is something that we ask of the Father. We need to ask Him to bring into our lives daily the supernatural intervention of His presence. We need Him to open our eyes so that we can see what the Father is doing. Then when we see what He's doing, we need to enter into these good works. He made us for good works. This is one of our purposes!

To be doing His good works is to be on His pathway. If we are on His pathway, operating in His ways and supernatural gifts, then we could expect to be or end up in His Kingdom. His ways, pathways, always lead to Him.

The command is to seek first His Kingdom. What is your priority in life? Is it that, if all your other needs are met, then you have time for God and His Kingdom, or are you willing to step into His works, even before your own perceived needs are met? There is a difference in perception here. You see, He commands us to seek first His Kingdom, and then promises that if we obey that He will take care of all our needs.

PRAYER: *Dear Heavenly Father, please forgive me for neglecting Your commands. I now choose to seek first Your Kingdom. Please break through from heaven into this world. Please do this in my presence in such a way that I may see it and enter into what You are doing. Lord, I am desperate to operate in Your love and power to reach those that You wish to touch: in my workplace, in the stores and shops, in church settings, on the street or wherever You wish. In Jesus' name I pray, Amen.*

DECEMBER 14 | COUNTING THE COST

MARGARET SILVESTER

> *Large crowds were travelling with Jesus, and turning to them he said, 'If anyone comes to me and does not hate his father and mother, his wife and children, his brothers and sisters – yes, even his own life – he cannot be my disciple. And anyone who does not carry his cross and follow me cannot be my disciple.'*
>
> Luke 14:25–27

Sammy, a young asylum seeker from a Muslim nation, shared our family Christmas. His testimony was amazing. Two years ago at the age of seventeen he was truly saved as Jesus revealed Himself to this young man. Two weeks later Sammy was secretly baptised and joined a small group of believers. The young man's family discovered a Bible in his room and threatened to kill him unless he renounced his newly found faith. The only option was to escape for his life and he finally arrived in England. On meeting a group of people of his own nationality, Sammy had a courageous desire to share Jesus with his fellow countrymen here. They tried to murder him and he finished up in hospital needing over 100 stitches.

Sammy is now nineteen. At a preliminary hearing for asylum in this country his lawyer asked him what he would do if he was sent back to his own country. He said he could not keep Jesus a secret in his heart, for if he disowned Jesus, Jesus would disown him. There is no doubt what this testimony would cost Sammy if asylum is not given. In effect he is willing to die rather than deny Jesus.

Jesus is very clear about being a disciple of His in the verses above. The words are radical. Love and hatred are Biblical ways of expressing preference. To 'hate' means to 'love less', not 'dislike'. Crowds followed Jesus but very few of the followers chose discipleship. Jesus said to the crowd following Him, possibly for healing, that it's impossible to be His disciple unless we let Him take first place in our heart.

When referring to the difficulties in life people often mistakenly say, 'It's my cross.' To take up one's cross means something entirely different. It simply means to uncompromisingly obey Jesus Christ as Lord and follow Him whatever it may cost. Discipleship demands readiness to place the claims of Jesus above those of family, friends and self. In some countries the cost is physical death. For most of us in the West it means a daily dying to self and the selfish desires of our old nature.

PRAYER: *Heavenly Father, thank You for all the Lord Jesus did for me when He died and rose again. In response to Your great love help me today to live as a disciple. Help me to choose the way of the cross and live my life in obedience to You whatever that may cost in my circumstances. Help me to own You in a world that has little time for You. Make me Your witness through the power of the Holy Spirit living within me. Amen.*

DECEMBER 15 | SMALL IN SIZE, BIG IN INFLUENCE!

PETER HORROBIN

> *When we put bits into the mouths of horses to make them obey us, we can turn the whole animal. Or take ships as an example. Although they are so large and are driven by strong winds, they are steered by a very small rudder wherever the pilot wants to go.*
>
> James 3:3–4

James uses two powerful illustrations, about a horse and a ship. It's a parable to speak to us about how potentially dangerous a very small member of the body can actually be – the tongue. On the rare occasions that I have ridden a horse I found that I could indeed direct the horse with just a gentle pull on the reins. And on the even rarer occasions when I've visited the bridge of a ship I have been amazed at just how easily someone could turn the wheel, which controlled the rudder, which then changed the direction of a huge vessel.

James tells us that the tongue has the potential to be like a spark starting a forest fire, or to corrupt the way of life of a person so badly that it's like hell fire or full of deadly poison. What a reputation the tongue had in James' estimation. I'm sure we've all been guilty of saying the wrong things on occasions and wishing we could take back the words we have said. But that's one thing we can never do.

Was James over-reacting? For surely the tongue can be a source of great blessing as well? Of course it can, and if I were to stop and think for a moment I could remember many wonderful moments when people spoke things into my life, or teachings that I've heard, or words of encouragement and love from my mum and dad. But I can also think of times when people said very cruel and uncalled-for things and caused much damage and pain.

But let's not blame the tongue for what the mouth speaks. In reality the tongue is a neutral, physical part of the body! All the tongue does is express the thoughts that we have in our mind. The mouth speaks what the heart is full of. So it's what's in the heart that really matters – if we guard the mind from thinking evil thoughts, then the tongue won't speak evil things.

Perhaps we would all do well to speak less and listen more. Then when we do speak, the tongue wouldn't be in danger of letting us down, saying ungodly, untruthful or unkind things. Perhaps we should consciously be praying that the Holy Spirit will fill our mouth with good things, so that the words we speak will always be a blessing and an encouragement to others. We don't want to be guilty of starting fires with wrong words, or of steering the ship of our lives onto 'the rocks' so that our vessel will be wrecked.

The mouth speaks what the heart is full of. So it's what's in the heart that really matters – if we guard the mind from thinking evil thoughts, then the tongue won't speak evil things. Perhaps we would all do well to speak less and listen more.

Prayer: *Thank You, Lord, for the power of speech and for the wonderful way you gave us to be able to communicate with each other. But Lord, I want to confess, there are times when I've said wrong things and hurt people. Please forgive me and freshly anoint me with Your Holy Spirit so that my tongue will always be a blessing and never be a curse on anyone else's life or cause damage to my own, in Jesus' name, Amen.*

December 16 | Transformed by a Touch

Margaret Silvester

While Jesus was in one of the towns, a man came along who was covered with leprosy. When he saw Jesus, he fell with his face to the ground and begged him, 'Lord, if you are willing, you can make me clean.' Jesus reached out his hand and touched the man. 'I am willing,' he said. 'Be clean!' And immediately the leprosy left him.

Luke 5:12–13

Travelling home from Tel Aviv we sat alongside an orthodox Jew with whom we had an engaging conversation regarding faith. It was interesting and friendly as we exchanged beliefs about Jesus. At the end of the journey, the gentleman shook hands with my husband. He asked if he could be excused from shaking hands with me, as it is not permitted for a Jew to touch any other woman but his wife, and a handshake involved touch.

Jesus broke the religious and social rules of His day. He touched the untouchable – sinners, women, outcasts – and in the text for today we see Him touching a leper. A leper was an outcast and the belief of the day was that in order to prevent the disease from spreading, the person suffering had to live apart from society and call out, 'Unclean!' when other people were in the vicinity. This was isolating and humiliating and a deeply wounding experience. When the man met Jesus it's likely that he hadn't been touched for many years. Somehow he'd heard of Jesus who reached out and touched people, healing them on the inside as well as the outside. The leper was wonderfully healed by a touch.

Touch is a basic human need. Probably it's as significant a need as food and shelter. Children who haven't been touched a lot suffer harmful consequences in their developmental process. Touch is one of the five senses. It's essential to the health and well-being of a human's emotional, physical, and spiritual development. Babies who are deprived of touch struggle to survive and struggle with relationships as they grow into adulthood.

A loving touch from someone, motivated by kindness and compassion, can be deeply moving. It says, 'You're worth something, you're valuable, and you belong.' Yes, touch is healing; it's restoring. We all need human touch, but above all we each need to receive the healing touch of Jesus in different areas of our lives.

The Greek word for healing is 'sozo'. It's a little word with a big meaning

– it means 'wholeness'. Wholeness is healing on the inside, as well as on the outside. It's an ongoing journey for the believer in Jesus. The unhealed areas of our lives need to be touched by Jesus as the leper was touched. Our need of a touch from the Lord Jesus might be physical, emotional or spiritual. Like the leper we each need to reach out to Him for His touch, rather than try to fix ourselves.

PRAYER: *Thank You, Father God, that You sent Jesus to die on the cross. Thank You that through His death I can come to Him and receive the fullness of all He did when He died for me. I humbly come to You and ask You to reveal to me the unhealed areas of my life, and give me grace to face whatever is hidden from me but known to You. I bring my prayer in the name of Jesus, Amen.*

DECEMBER 17 | AN INVASION OF LOCUSTS

LIZ GRIFFIN

> *Be glad, O children of Zion, and rejoice in the LORD your God, for he has given the early rain for your vindication; he has poured down for you abundant rain, the early and the latter rain, as before. The threshing floors shall be full of grain; the vats shall overflow with wine and oil. I will restore to you the years that the swarming locust has eaten, the hopper, the destroyer, and the cutter, my great army, which I sent among you. You shall eat in plenty and be satisfied, and praise the name of the LORD your God, who has dealt wondrously with you. And my people shall never again be put to shame.*
>
> Joel 2:23–26, ESV

The devastation that came upon the land of Judah was total and the story of it would be told to future generations (Joel chapter 1). The vines and figs were destroyed. The trees dried up and they lost the pomegranates, apples and dates. There was no wheat or barley; no wine or oil. The people lamented because there was no food. The sacrifices in the temple made by the priests had to stop. The land, the animals and the trees were suffering. There was an invasion of a foreign army, and all this was caused by the people themselves, as they had chosen to go far away from God and even seek other sources of supernatural power to rule their lives.

Joel, God's spokesman, told them to call the whole community together to fast and pray in repentance. The 'Day of the Lord' was so terrible that no one could endure it, but God offered them hope for the future.' "*Yet even now," declares the LORD, "return to me with all your heart, with fasting, with weeping, and with mourning; and rend your hearts and not your garments." Return to the LORD your God, for he is gracious and merciful, slow to anger, and abounding in steadfast love; and he relents over disaster*' (Joel 2:12–13).

Our God is faithful to His covenant of love for His people. His heart is not to see them suffer, but that in their suffering they would turn to Him for mercy and restoration. The beautiful promise of blessings in the future included driving out the invader, restoring the fruitfulness of the land and trees and animals and providing an abundance of food. '*Be glad, O children of Zion, and rejoice in the LORD your God, for he has given the early rain for your vindication; he has poured down for you abundant rain, the early and the latter rain, as before. The threshing floors shall be full of grain; the vats shall overflow with wine and oil. I will restore to you the years that the swarming locust has eaten, the hopper, the destroyer, and the cutter, my great army, which I sent among you. You shall eat in plenty and be satisfied, and praise the name of the LORD your God, who has dealt wondrously with you. And my people shall never again be put to shame*' (Joel 2:23–26).

Joel then heard another exciting promise from God for the future, which was: '*And it shall come to pass afterwards, that I will pour out my Spirit on all flesh; your sons and your daughters shall prophesy, your old men shall dream dreams, and your young men shall see visions. Even on the male and female servants in those days I will pour out my Spirit*' (Joel 2:28–29).

Today many are suffering the consequences in their lives of going far away from God and some have gone looking for other sources of supernatural power. The enemy has ravaged their lives like a swarm of locusts but there is hope for the future in the Lord Jesus. After true repentance and turning back to a relationship with God through Jesus they can have their sins washed away, be set free from the hold of the enemy over them, and enter into a time of restoration, new life, healing and blessing.

PRAYER: *Lord, I pray for all those whose lives are in ruins and who need to hear the message of hope that they can turn back to You. I pray that they will find You restore to them the years the locusts have eaten. May they find courage and determination to trust in You, in Jesus' name, Amen.*

DECEMBER 18 | UNITED WE STAND

DIANE WATSON

How good and pleasant it is when brothers live together in unity … For there the LORD bestows his blessing, even life for evermore.

Psalm 133:1, 3

God's heart for us is that we dwell together in unity of love for one another. Not gossiping or whispering about one another, but speaking the truth in love to build one another up.

It's so easy to let our tongues speak out negative and critical things instead of bringing words of life and encouragement to one another. But don't let's allow the enemy to have a foothold in our 'camp', either at our home, our work, or our churches. Let's keep our hearts clean before the Lord. Let's practise forgiveness daily – sometimes it may be necessary to do it hourly – trusting God and praying for one another. Criticism breeds criticism and this isn't living the 'Kingdom of God' life.

God the Father, Jesus the Son and the Holy Spirit live together in perfect harmony and love. I know that we aren't God; we're sinful and carry hurts and wounds. But to the best we are able, with God's help, let's dwell together in unity and love. As God promises in His Word, He will bestow a blessing!

Living in unity doesn't mean we will always see eye to eye with everyone. God has made us all unique, with our own giftings. So the same task would be done differently by each one of us. We are meant to work through these differences in love, choosing to submit to one another in reverence to Christ. It may seem impossible at times, but if we include Jesus in it, *'all things are possible'* (see Matthew 19:26).

So when we're tempted to complain and to criticise our fellow brother or sister let's remember what the apostle Paul said: *'May the God who gives endurance and encouragement give you a spirit of unity among yourselves as you follow Christ Jesus, so that with one heart and mouth you may glorify the God and Father of our Lord Jesus Christ. Accept one another, then, just as Christ accepted you, in order to bring praise to God'* (Romans 15:5–7).

PRAYER: *Heavenly Father, help me not to criticise or complain against my fellow brothers and sisters. Help me to forgive them for anything they have done against me and help me to encourage and love them as You do. I pray these things through Jesus' name. Amen.*

December 19 | Treasure in Clay Pots

Angela Weir

We possess this precious treasure [the divine Light of the Gospel] in [frail, human] vessels of earth, that the grandeur and exceeding greatness of the power may be shown to be from God and not from ourselves.

2 Corinthians 4:7, AMP

I was listening to a radio play one afternoon recently, telling of the beginning of Jesus' ministry here on earth. What came across to me so vividly in this story, that we all know so well, was how very ordinary Jesus' first disciples were.

This was shown dramatically when Jesus told Peter and Andrew to let down their nets, and having caught nothing throughout a long, hard night's fishing, they hauled in a huge catch. Peter's reaction was one of brokenness and fear as he told Jesus to go away from him, recognising in Jesus a purity and light that showed up all his own sinfulness.

As we look at Peter's life and see the many mistakes he made, we can take comfort from the fact that Jesus still chose him.

So often we feel inadequate and ill-prepared for serving Jesus. We want to give Him our very best but feel failures, as we sin again or make mistakes. As we look at Peter's life and see the many mistakes he made, we can take comfort from the fact that Jesus still chose him – just as He still chooses us – to work with Him for His Kingdom purposes. He really loves us that much!

When we belong to Him we have the treasure of the gospel (good news) within us, frail vessels that we are, which enables us to pick ourselves up, dust ourselves down and, in His strength, start all over again.

Prayer: *Dear Father, I come to You with all my weaknesses and sinfulness to thank You that You will not turn me away no matter how many times I mess things up. Please help me to grow strong in You so that one day You will be able to say, 'Well done, good and faithful servant.' In Jesus' name, Amen.*

December 20 | I Am Sending You

David Silvester

'So now, go. I am sending you to Pharaoh to bring my people the Israelites out of Egypt.' But Moses said to God, 'Who am I, that I should go to Pharaoh and bring the Israelites out of Egypt?' And God said, 'I will be with you.'

Exodus 3:10–12

Moses was an exile in the land of Midian on the eastern side of the Red Sea after fleeing from Egypt where he had been brought up as the son of Pharaoh's daughter. He had to run for his life when he was seen killing an Egyptian who was beating an Israelite, one of Moses' own people. Pharaoh was determined to kill Moses.

Sometimes we might feel like Moses may have done. There's some sin we've committed which makes us feel unfit for God to ever consider using us. This is how the devil will try to condemn us and make us feel totally unworthy and that God can't use us.

When we think that way we need to reflect on the grace of God. People say, 'Grace is when God gives us what we don't deserve.' Paul describes it like this: *'For all have sinned and fall short of the glory of God, and are justified freely by his grace through the redemption that came by Christ Jesus'* (Romans 3:23–24).

Here Paul introduces the marvellous truths of the 'glory' of God's holiness, the 'justification' of us sinners (which means that God sees me 'just as if I'd never sinned') and the 'redemption' price which was paid to release us from the bondage of slavery to Satan.

When we came as a sinner to Jesus, confessing and repenting of our sins, the grace of God came into action. We were forgiven, cleansed and 'justified' before God. The price paid for our redemption came into effect. Hallelujah! It was done for us by God's grace in Jesus. All we had to do was receive the wonderful gift – of forgiveness and salvation.

That's our starting point and now we can move forward. God says to us, *'I am sending you'* and *'I will be with you.'* When God calls, He equips. He enables us to do that which we feel we can't possibly do. As Moses did, we may think there are others who can do things far better. But God's not calling them. He's calling you and me! But with the call He promises to be with us, and to enable us. So let's go with God, and watch Him do extraordinary things through ordinary people like us.

Prayer: *O Lord God, I marvel at Your grace, justification and redemption. Thank You for loving me in such a wonderful way, and for all that You've brought me into through Your Son, Jesus. Here and now I give myself to You. Please make me aware of Your voice when You're calling me. Give me the grace to respond in obedience to You. Please give me the faith that You will do amazing things in the power of the name of Jesus. Amen.*

December 21 | Check Out Your Inheritance

David Cross

> *For you know what was paid to set you free from the worthless manner of life handed down by your ancestors. It was not something that can be destroyed, such as silver or gold; it was the costly sacrifice of Christ, who was like a lamb without defect or flaw.*
>
> 1 Peter 1:18–19, GNB

Everyone likes the idea of a big inheritance. Suddenly finding that we are the principal beneficiary in the will of some distant and forgotten relative is the stuff of dreams. Who knows what treasure might be waiting to be handed down to us at some unexpected moment in the future?

But the Bible reminds us of another sort of inheritance, which could be having a serious consequence in our lives, one that is not necessarily good for us. Many passages of Scripture tell us that there is a spiritual legacy that is handed down from our ancestors and this can have a powerfully negative effect on us if the lives of our forebears were not in line with God.

God's plan for us was to pour spiritual blessing down the family line as our forebears walked in covenant with Him, through their surrender to Jesus Christ. This was intended to give us a sound foundation to our lives from which we could also walk in obedience to the commands of God. Unfortunately, for many of us, that flow of godly inheritance got distorted and defiled by the sinfulness of those that have come before us and also, of course, through our own sin.

But there's good news! Jesus has cleaned up our inheritance, not by some financial deal, but through His being both a sacrifice and a scapegoat on the cross. We can appropriate that cleansing today by acknowledging the sin of our forebears, forgiving them for the effect of the defiled inheritance on our lives and by choosing to receive the new inheritance that has been declared for all those who are part of God's family, through receiving Jesus. This really is worth having!

PRAYER: *Father God, I forgive my forebears for defiling the spiritual inheritance of blessing that You have wanted me to receive. I confess that I have also added my own sinfulness. Thank You that, through Jesus Christ, I can be cleansed from all that has been spiritually harmful to me and I can lay claim to a new family legacy. Amen.*

DECEMBER 22 | MY TONGUE WILL TALK

PAM SMITH

> *My lips will shout for joy, when I sing praises to thee, my soul also which thou hast rescued. And my tongue will talk of thy righteous help all the day long ...*
>
> Psalm 71:23–24, RSV

I was interested in how David continually spoke about the goodness of the Lord in Psalm 71 (RSV). He says: *'My praise is continually of thee'*, *'My mouth is filled'*, *'My mouth will tell'*, *'I will praise'*, *'I still proclaim'*, *'I will sing'*, *'My lips will shout'*, and *'My tongue will talk'*. The psalmist just can't keep quiet about the Lord.

How often do I actually talk about Jesus to those who know Him? I spend a lot of time talking about myself, what I am doing, people's problems, the day's news or a host of trivial things that don't really matter at all. How often do I speak about the Lord, as my best friend, the great things He has done, and how much His love is changing everything? How often do I speak of the great future He's preparing, His answers to prayer and how to share this glorious news with others?

Malachi 3:16 says, *'Those that feared the LORD spoke with one another; the LORD heeded and heard them, and a book of remembrance was written before him'* (RSV).

Let's remember always to talk to each other about Jesus. It glorifies the Lord and encourages the soul. It makes our hearts burn within us when we share about the love He has for us. Even more so when we pray, praise and talk with Him together, for when we do this He promises to be there, right in the midst of us.

PRAYER: *Dear Lord, may we always put You first in our conversation, giving You top priority in our sharing and thinking. May we always be prepared for the opportunities to share the gospel with those that don't know You, in Jesus' name, Amen.*

DECEMBER 23 | GOD'S CRITICS

LINDSEY HANEKOM

> *Do you still want to argue with the Almighty? You are God's critic, but do you have the answers?*
>
> Job 40:2, NLT

We are living in a day and age where God is questioned, ridiculed, minimised and criticised on an open and regular basis. It is easy to judge the people who question God so overtly and seek to diminish Him in any way possible. Yet, on reading the book of Job we see that, as believers, we too can be critical of God and His ways; diminishing Him in our lives and becoming self-focused.

Job was a blameless man who feared God. He had all of his earthly possessions stripped away from him and was left in a bitter and complaining state: *'I must express my anguish. I must complain in my bitterness'* (Job 7:11, NLT); *'I hate my life. I do not want to go on living. Oh, leave me alone for these few remaining days'* (Job 7:16, NLT).

Whilst we can empathise with Job in his state of extreme loss, his reaction to his situation prompted a response from God that was not one of sympathy. God's response is actually quite startling: *'Who is this that questions my wisdom with such ignorant words? Brace yourself, because I have some questions for you, and you must answer them'* (Job 38:2–3, NLT).

The ensuing chapters rank highly in my favourite passages of Scripture where God barrages Job with questions and challenges. After this torrent of confrontation, God simply asks the question, *'Do you still want to argue with the Almighty? You are God's critic, but do you have the answers?'* (Job 40:2, NLT).

How often do we find ourselves complaining and feeling embittered by our situations? We search for a God who will sympathise and pander to our self-pity but God, whilst a caring God, will not allow Himself to be minimised by our selfishness and pride. Job responded to God in repentance and humility having been sucked into the pride of self-focus and self-pity. From there God was able to bring full and abundant restoration.

We must be careful in our pain and anguish not to blame God or criticise Him for His works. He is the Sovereign God whose thoughts and ways are far beyond our understanding. It is not for us to know everything, just to trust Him in all His ways and to seek His face and path for our lives. That is the road to healing and restoration.

PRAYER: *Thank You, God, that you are Sovereign. I come to You in humility and repentance for all the times I have become self-focused and self-pitying. I know that this is pride and destructive to our relationship and to me. Help me to trust You in all things and know You only have what is best for me, even when it is hard. Amen.*

DECEMBER 24 | IMMANUEL – GOD WITH US

MARGARET SILVESTER

> *The virgin will be with child and will give birth to a son, and they will call him Immanuel – which means 'God with us'.*
>
> Matthew 1:23

In the small lounge at Ellel Grange we have a beautiful Christmas decoration. It is very simple, but also profound in the message it speaks. It consists of a row of red candles spread across the width of the mantlepiece with beautifully carved letters spelling Immanuel, spanning the candles. It is a vivid reminder that Jesus, the light of the world, comes into the darkness of our lives to bring newness of life and hope and that His name speaks of His character.

For many people Christmas is a happy time, but for others it can be one of the hardest times of the year. It may remind them of a loved one who has died, or some other sad loss that they have been through which has accentuated their sense of loneliness. But what is the essential message of Christmas? It is that Immanuel has come, and God is with us. Christmas is about undoing loneliness. The message of Christmas is that none of us is alone.

The birth of Jesus is set in history. *'They will call him Immanuel.'* To be called, according to Hebraic understanding, means that the person spoken of will in reality be what he is called and actually fulfil that title. Thus the name Immanuel points to the nature of the One who bears the name. He is God incarnate – God coming into human flesh – and dwells by His Spirit in the hearts of His people.

Jesus Christ – God's Son – God with us. What a comfort, what a joy to know He will never leave His own. He knows the frailty of our humanity, the weakness, the pain and the shame of being human because He became one with us. The wonder of the incarnation is that the baby in Bethlehem grew to be the Man who died on Calvary, taking our punishment, our guilt, and our blame, that His life might be ours.

Reflect today on how God is with you, and let the wonderful word 'Immanuel' come alive in your spirit as you contemplate the true meaning of Christmas.

PRAYER: *Thank You, God, for sending Jesus. Thank You, Jesus, that You came. Holy Spirit, please come and teach me more about that lovely name – Immanuel. Amen.*

DECEMBER 25 | TODAY'S THE DAY

PETER HORROBIN

> *Today in the town of David, a Saviour has been born to you; he is Christ the Lord. This will be a sign to you: You will find a baby wrapped in cloths and lying in a manger.*
>
> Luke 2:11–12

Isaiah had prophesied that when the Messiah came His arm would rule for Him, but that He would also tend His flock like a shepherd. In this prophecy (Isaiah 40:10–11) we see two different aspects of the character of Jesus – Jesus the King who will rule and Jesus the Shepherd who will care for the sheep.

When Jesus was born in Bethlehem, Scripture tells us that there were two sets of unusual visitors – first there were the shepherds, who had both heard the angels telling of the birth of Christ and seen the hosts of angels praising God in thanksgiving. Then there were the kings who brought their rich gifts and bowed before the baby who was also a King, but whose authority far outweighed that of any earthly king. In a remarkable way, these two visits to the baby Jesus reflected the prophecy of Isaiah; both the shepherds and the kings came and acknowledged that they were bowing before a far superior Shepherd and a far greater King.

As we celebrate, with great thanksgiving, the coming of the Messiah, the Saviour of the world, let us never forget that this baby grew to become that great 'Shepherd of the sheep' who cares deeply for every one of His lambs, even you and me. But that He is also reigning as King of kings and that ultimately all authority rests in His hands.

So whatever the situation the world is in, He is ultimately in control. And whatever situation you may be in personally, He is still the Good Shepherd. Try and spend a few minutes this Christmas thinking about your life and choosing to let Him reign in your life as King and bringing to Him, as your Shepherd, all the concerns that are pressing down upon you. He is sufficient for all these things.

PRAYER: *Thank you, Father God, for Jesus, the most amazing Christmas gift anyone could ever receive. Help me to mark this Christmas season with a new understanding of how precious Jesus is. In His name, Amen.*

DECEMBER 26 | HAPPY OR JOYFUL CHRISTMAS?

LINDSEY HANEKOM

> *But the angel said to them, 'Do not be afraid. I bring you good news that will cause great joy for all the people.'*
>
> Luke 2:10

I love Christmas! I love everything about it. I love the decorations, the gifts, the food, the fun, the time with family, the laughter, the cooking. I love it all! For me, Christmas is a precious time of the year. Yet it occurs to me that Christmas is not a happy time for everyone. Many are alone, having to do without necessities (let alone luxuries), missing a loved one for the first time, or not in a place within themselves to celebrate anything. For some, Christmas is a struggle.

I know that my enjoyment is temporal. It doesn't last forever. A time will come when the festivities will come to an end, the decorations will be put away, the food will eventually diminish and we will return home from spending precious time with our families. My happiness will dwindle with the ending of the festivities.

Yet, the *joy* of Christmas is free for us all and is eternal. It's the joy of the knowledge that God Himself entered our world to meet with us and to save us. He came to us as a baby – vulnerable, shamed by the gossip surrounding His very existence, His life under threat from those who feared for their position in life. Our God came down to this and was born into the dirt and squalour of a stable. He wasn't born into a clean, safe environment. His first hours were hours of dirt, mess and fear. He entered our dirty, messy, fearful world to save us from the grip of the enemy. He came because He loves us and wants to draw us back to Himself.

This is the Christmas joy we can all celebrate. This isn't temporal; it's eternal. It will last forever. My prayer this Christmas time is that we all find that joy – a joy that deepens as we look to our Saviour and celebrate all that He has done for us. If you're struggling with Christmas this year, I pray this unfathomable joy will be your strength. For those of us who have much to enjoy, I pray that we won't lose sight of the deep joy that surpasses our understanding.

PRAYER: *What can we say to our Saviour who came to this earth to save us? 'Thank You' does not seem enough but it's all we have. Help us, Lord, to know the joy that is ours for free and is eternal, and help us not to lose sight of this truth as we celebrate Your birth. We especially pray for those who are struggling this Christmas time. May You give each one of us the only gift that matters this year: may Your love penetrate our hearts in a deep and precious way. Amen.*

DECEMBER 27 | EVERY STORY NEEDS A HERO

LINDA FODE

> *When they had gone, an angel of the Lord appeared to Joseph in a dream. 'Get up,' he said, 'take the child and his mother and escape to Egypt. Stay there until I tell you, for Herod is going to search for the child to kill him.' So he got up, took the child and his mother during the night and left for Egypt, where he stayed until the death of Herod. And so was fulfilled what the Lord had said through the prophet: 'Out of Egypt I called my son.'*
>
> Matthew 2:13–15

We love stories about heroes, larger-than-life men or women who do great things against great odds. Hebrews 11 is a chapter that teaches us powerfully about faith and heroes. For thirty-five verses (I like to count things) we read about the big names and the unknown names who were heroes. Then we come to Hebrews 11:36. It begins with: '*Still others*' (NKJV).

Joseph was one of the 'still others'. The wise men who brought amazing gifts had just left to return to their own countries. Tradition and astronomy indicates that these events might have been up to two years after the birth of Jesus. Mary and Joseph had probably settled down in Bethlehem by this time. Maybe Joseph had opened another carpenter shop. They were far away from the wagging tongues and rumours about an illegitimate child.

Then Joseph had another dream. *'Pack up, leave your country, your culture, and go to Egypt,'* said the angel in the dream. What was his response? Instant obedience! I would love to have heard the conversation between Joseph and Mary as they packed up, leaving their home, friends and community once again. Their destination, Egypt, was definitely not on the Jewish favourite places list. And yet off they went.

Joseph is a hero. He operated in faith and obedience. He took leadership and responsibility. This time there was no emotion driving the response to the dream. In fact it was probably more difficult to respond this time because there wasn't an immediate crisis. Heroes are heroes because they act instinctively and quickly out of a heart of trust. They don't debate the issues. They live out of their spirit, not their soul. Like Abraham, they believe God and it is credited to them as righteousness.

Joseph is a hero. Because of his simple faith all of history, all of eternity, was changed forever. The purposes of the Father established before the foundation of the earth are kept in motion by heroes of faith – by ordinary people like you and me.

PRAYER: *Father, thank You that I am one of the 'still others'. Help me to discern Your voice and obey it, in Jesus' name, Amen.*

DECEMBER 28 | CHOSEN TO WAIT!

PETER HORROBIN

Sovereign Lord, as you have promised, now dismiss your servant in peace. For my eyes have seen your salvation, which you prepared in the sight of all people, a light for revelation to the Gentiles and for glory to your people Israel.

Luke 2:29–32

Simeon and Anna were elderly. They had gone to the temple daily all their lives and, other than the daily worship of God, there was only one item on their agenda, to look at all the babies that were being brought to the temple to be presented to the Lord. I can easily imagine them looking intently at every one, asking the same old question of the Lord, day in and day out! *'Is it this one?'*

There had always been an assurance in their heart that they wouldn't die before they saw this special baby being presented. But until that day the answer had always been *'No'*. Today was different. There was a quickening in their spirit, an assurance in their heart and then they found their lips speaking out words that only God could have given them. Their eyes had seen the very salvation of God and they had held this baby from heaven in their arms.

And so they told the world, and all subsequent generations, that the promise of the prophets had been fulfilled. Salvation had come, the Light for the Gentiles, the glory for Israel – people could now look forward to redemption. Simeon and Anna were only asked to do one thing by the Lord – provide prophetic witness to the identity of the child in Joseph and Mary's arms. But every generation of believers since has always remembered what they said and did!

What an encouragement this must be to us – to watch and wait patiently for the fulfilment of the destiny God has for each one of us. He may have many things for us to do or, like Simeon and Anna, there may only be one major responsibility planned for us, but our faithfulness will bring great blessing – even to many generations.

PRAYER: *Thank You for the faithfulness of Simeon and Anna. Help me, Lord, to remain faithful to You in all things as I await the fulfilment of my own destiny in God, in Jesus' name, Amen.*

DECEMBER 29 | BARRIERS TO WORSHIP

ANGELA WEIR

> *[Jesus] replied to him, You shall love the Lord your God with all your heart and with all your soul and with all your mind (intellect).*
>
> Matthew 22:37, AMP

Some of us find it difficult to express love, or indeed any emotion. We know that we should love God but we find worship, and consequently any relationship with Him, extremely hard.

This can be because our emotions are blocked. Perhaps we have been told as children that big boys, or girls, don't cry. Or maybe we have discovered that showing emotion is unsafe, like the five-year-old boy who reacted angrily to his stepfather and was beaten so badly he made a vow never to show anger again. In his case it didn't work and he became a violent and angry man, ending in prison for grievous bodily harm. There he met Christ and through a slow and difficult journey has learnt to express his emotions in a godly way – by forgiving the ones who hurt him and releasing the pain and anger to God.

Sometimes we choose to block our emotions off completely because the pain of what has happened to us is so terrible – all our feelings are stuffed down inside. The effort of holding them down can sometimes cause depression and other similar sicknesses.

But God is a God of love, which is an emotion, and Jesus, who was fully human as well as fully divine, expressed the whole range of emotions from love to grief, anger to joy, and as we are made in His image, He wants us to express the whole range too. Where we have blocked off our emotions we need to ask Him to help us release the pain and anger to Him and know freedom inside.

PRAYER: *Father, I am sorry for the times when I have blocked off my emotions. Please help me to connect my memories with the emotions so that I can deal with them in a godly way and be healed, in Jesus' name, Amen.*

DECEMBER 30 | PEACE

MARGARET SOUTHEY

Peace I leave with you; my peace I give you. I do not give to you as the world gives. Do not let your hearts be troubled and do not be afraid.

John 14:27

Many years ago there was a painting competition with 'peace' as its theme. After the entries had been assessed, three reached the finals.

One picture showed a lush meadow with a willow dangling its branches in a stream. There were a few wispy clouds in the blue sky. It was a picture of calm. The second picture showed a small yacht sailing gently in the breeze on a still sea. There were a few gulls in the sky. Nothing marred the tranquility of the scene.

The prize, however, was not won by either of these but by a very different picture. It showed a stark and steep cliff face lashed by rain and waves from a wild ocean and battered by howling winds under an ominous sky. In the cliff face was a small crevice with a bird's nest. The bird could be seen sitting safely in its nest seemingly watching the formidable storm.

The first two pictures depict peace that the world gives. It is a peace created by calm and tranquil surroundings with no jarring note. The peace of Jesus, however, is a deep security in the midst of a raging storm of life. It is a deep knowing that, however fearful the circumstances, the presence of Jesus is more than enough.

How do we experience this peace? It is not something we can pull out of our pockets when trouble threatens. It is something that grows as our relationship with Jesus deepens. The more we learn to walk with, obey and trust Jesus, the more we will be able to draw on His peace.

December 31 | Do Not Worry

Margaret Silvester

> *Do not worry about your life, what you will eat or drink; or about your body, what you will wear ... Look at the birds of the air; they do not sow or reap or store away in barns, and yet your heavenly Father feeds them. Are you not much more valuable than they?*
>
> Matthew 6:25–26

Recently, walking along a river, surrounded by snow-covered hills, we came across a robin perched on a tree branch, no more than 3 feet from us. It was calm, unafraid, unhurried, unworried and a beautiful sight in a beautiful environment. The words, 'Do not worry, you are of more value than many robins', wouldn't leave me.

People worry about many things. They worry about things that will never happen, things about the past that can't be changed, about criticism from others which is often untrue, about health and about real problems that have to be faced.

So, why do we worry? If the character of the God of the Bible is true, worry is unnecessary. In fact it is interest on a debt you may never incur. Worry stands between you and God. When we worry we're really saying we can't trust God to take care of us in the small and the big issues of life. We don't think He can take care of the practical details of our lives.

Worry often has to do with the future. It says, 'I won't trust where I can't see.' We might call this unbelief. In my experience the cure for unbelief is obedience. Ceasing to worry is about relationship with God, which grows through small steps of obedience, often when we can't see the way ahead.

Jesus never worried. He didn't live to please Himself, but to obey His Father. The Father of Jesus is my Father. He loves me to the extent that my name is written on the palms of His hands (Isaiah 49:16). I can't think of anything He'll ever forget. He'll protect me, lead me and watch over me as I trust in Him.

The big question for you to answer is, 'Why do I worry?' Keep your mind today on the 'much more' of your Heavenly Father. Remember that He *'is able to do immeasurably more than all we ask or imagine'* (Ephesians 3:20). He knows the circumstances of your life. He simply says, 'Don't worry. Trust me.'

An unknown author wrote a simple poem:

Said the robin to the sparrow,
'I should really like to know
Why these anxious human beings
Rush about and hurry so.'

Said the sparrow to the robin,
'Friend, I think that it must be
That they have no Heavenly Father
Such as cares for you and me.'

PRAYER: *Heavenly Father, please forgive my unbelief. Thank You for Your unchanging character and for Your amazing love to me revealed through Jesus. Today I choose to turn my thoughts on You and cease from worrying. Please increase my faith and teach me to trust You more. Amen.*

We hope you enjoyed reading this
Sovereign World book.
For more details of other Sovereign
books and new releases see our website:

www.sovereignworld.com

Find us on Twitter @sovereignworld

Our authors welcome your feedback on their books.
Please send your comments to our offices.
You can request to subscribe to
our email and mailing list online or by writing to:

Sovereign World Ltd, PO Box 784,
Ellel, Lancaster, LA1 9DA, United Kingdom
info@sovereignworld.com

Sovereign World titles are available from
all good Christian bookshops and eBook vendors.

For information about our distributors in the UK,
USA, Canada, South Africa, Australia and Singapore, visit:
www.sovereignworld.com/trade

If you would like to help us send a copy of this book and
many other titles to needy pastors in developing countries,
please write for further information or send your gift to:

Sovereign World Trust, PO Box 777,
Tonbridge, Kent TN11 0ZS
United Kingdom
www.sovereignworldtrust.org.uk

The Sovereign World Trust is a registered charity